Language Contact

To the Salish and Pend d'Oreille
elders of Montana who are working to preserve
and document their beautiful language: Lemlmtš!

Language Contact

SARAH G. THOMASON

EDINBURGH UNIVERSITY PRESS

© Sarah G. Thomason, 2001

Edinburgh University Press Ltd
22 George Square, Edinburgh

Typeset in 10 on 12 pt Times
by Hewer Text Ltd, Edinburgh, and
printed and bound in Great Britain
by MPG Books Ltd, Bodmin

A CIP Record for this book is
available from the British Library

ISBN 0 7486 0719 6 (paperback)

Contents

Preface   ix

1. Introduction   1
   What is language contact?   1
   What about the people in contact situations?   3
   How old is language contact?   6
   Where is language contact?   8
   What happens to languages in contact?   10
   Sources and further reading   13

2. Contact Onsets and Stability   15
   How do languages come into contact?   15
   Stable and unstable contact situations   21
   Sources and further reading   25

3. Multilingualism in Nations and Individuals   27
   Multilingual nations, multilingual people   30
   Attitudes toward multilingualism   32
   One nation, more than one language   36
   Language policies and language planning   38
   A case study: India   42
   Social and political consequences of multilingualism   46
   Multilingualism in individuals:
      learning and using two or more languages   48
   Sources and further reading   55

4. Contact-Induced Language Change: Results   59
   Are some linguistic features unborrowable?   63
   Social predictors of contact-induced change: intensity of contact   66
   Social predictors of contact-induced change:
      imperfect learning vs. its absence   66
   When imperfect learning plays no role in the interference
      process   67
   When imperfect learning plays a role in the interference process   74

Linguistic predictors of contact-induced change   76
Speakers' attitudes: why contact-induced change is unpredictable   77
Effects on the recipient-language structure   85
How can we tell whether contact-induced change has occurred?   91
Sources and further reading   95

5. Linguistic Areas   99
   A definition   99
   Some linguistic areas around the world   104
      The Balkans   105
      The Baltic   110
      The Ethiopian highlands   111
      South Asia   114
      The Sepik River basin, New Guinea   117
      The Pacific Northwest of North America   120
   The complex histories of linguistic areas   125
   Sources and further reading   126

6. Contact-Induced Language Change: Mechanisms   129
   Mechanism 1: Code-switching   131
   Mechanism 2: Code alternation   136
   Mechanism 3: Passive familiarity   139
   Mechanism 4: 'Negotiation'   142
   Mechanism 5: Second-language acquisition strategies   146
   Mechanism 6: Bilingual first language acquisition   148
   Mechanism 7: Deliberate decision   149
   Two final points about mechanisms of interference   152
   Sources and further reading   153

7. Contact Languages I: Pidgins and Creoles   157
   What, when, where?   159
      What?   159
      When and where?   162
   Pidgins and creoles are not maximally simple and not all alike 167
   Pidgin/creole genesis theories:
      where does the grammar come from?   174
         Monogenesis   176
         Abrupt genesis scenarios   177
         Gradual genesis scenarios   183
   Do different genesis routes have different linguistic outcomes? 188
   The rest of the field   189
   Sources and further reading   189

8. Contact Languages II: Other Mixed Languages   196
   What, when, where?   198
   Two routes to bilingual mixed-language genesis   203
   How?   207

The genesis of bilingual mixed languages in
    persistent ethnic groups 207
The abrupt genesis of bilingual mixed languages in
    new ethnic groups 212
Prospects for future study 217
Sources and further reading 218

9. Language Death 222
Defining language death 223
A theoretical framework 225
How do languages die? 226
  Attrition 227
  Grammatical replacement 232
  No loss of structure, not much borrowing 235
Sources and further reading 238

10. Endangered Languages 240
Sources and further reading 245

Appendix 1: A Map of Some Contact Situations Around the World 247

Appendix 2: Official Languages in the World's Nations 250

Glossary 256

References 281

Language index 297

Names index 303

Subject index 306

Preface

This is a personal book: it reflects my own view of the field of language contact. It is not an attempt to provide an exhaustive account of the many different approaches that other scholars have adopted in studying the subject, and it is not a bland survey of all and only those points on which there is general agreement among specialists. (Taking this last approach to textbook writing would have made for a very short book, because controversies are found in every corner of the field of language-contact studies – a typical and probably desirable trait in a lively, fast-developing field.) I have tried to provide suggestions for readings that will enable interested students to explore some of the controversial topics, including of course other people's views. The focus of the book is on linguistic results of contact rather than on the sociolinguistics or psycholinguistics of languages in contact.

Much of the book should be accessible to readers with no training in linguistics, but the book is aimed at readers who have a basic knowledge of linguistics, so that they know what phonemes and morphemes and relative clauses and language families are. A glossary is provided to help readers with little or no background in linguistics to follow the text, and to provide summary information about the locations and genetic affiliations of languages and language families. Inevitably, given the focus on linguistic results, examples must often be discussed in technical terms; to avoid overloading the book with technical discussions, the intricacies of the examples are not described in great detail, but sources are given that will permit interested readers to find more detailed accounts.

Each chapter ends with a list of sources from which information in the chapter is drawn, together with suggestions for further reading on the various topics. Although no specific recommendations for term-paper topics are included, the suggested readings should help students find topics for research projects.

A number of colleagues and students have read all or parts of the book in manuscript. I am especially grateful to those who have provided corrections and comments for improvement: Jacques Arends, Nancy Dorian, Anna Fenyvesi, Anthony Grant, Beatriz Lorente, André Mather, Lesley Milroy,

Becky Moreton, Saskia Moraru-de Ruijter, Christina Paulston, and Mark Sicoli. Some other people have given me specific pieces of information and have checked data and analyses for me; they are mentioned individually in the relevant chapters. I am also very grateful to all the students who have attended various incarnations of my language-contact course – first at the Linguistic Institute at The Ohio State University in 1993, then in a week-long class at the Dutch Graduate School of Linguistics in Amsterdam in 1995, then in three different terms at the University of Pittsburgh, and most recently in a four-week course at the Linguistic Institute at the University of Illinois (1999). All of them have heard me explore the ideas incorporated in this book, and most have seen drafts ranging from a few to most chapters of it; and many of them have asked hard questions or offered useful comments that have led to improvements in the final version. It should (but won't) go without saying that none of these people is responsible for any errors and infelicities that remain.

1 Introduction

What is language contact?

On the Flathead Reservation in northwestern Montana, the remaining fluent speakers of Montana Salish – fewer than sixty tribal members as of 2000, almost all of them elders – speak Salish to each other. But they usually speak English when others are present, whether the others are outsiders or younger tribal members who speak little or no Salish. Describing this as a language-contact situation requires no hard thinking. The same is true of the village of Kupwar in India, where extensive multilingualism has led to convergence among local dialects of two Indic languages (Marathi, Urdu) and one Dravidian language (Kannaḍa); of the Republic of Singapore, an island nation of just 238 square miles which boasts four official languages (Chinese, Malay, English, and Tamil); of the Aleuts who used to live on Bering Island off the east coast of Russia and speak Russian in addition to their native Aleut; and of innumerable other situations around the world. But although recognizing language contact in such obvious cases is easy, defining it precisely is more difficult, for several reasons.

In the simplest definition, language contact is the use of more than one language in the same place at the same time. It isn't hard to imagine a situation in which this definition might be too simple: for instance, if two groups of young travelers are speaking two different languages while cooking their meals in the kitchen of a youth hostel, and if each group speaks only one language, and if there is no verbal interaction between the groups, then this is language contact only in the most trivial sense. The focus in this book will be on nontrivial language contact – that is, on contact situations in which at least some people use more than one language. As we will see, language contact in this substantive sense does not require fluent bilingualism or multilingualism, but some communication between speakers of different languages is necessary. If those two groups of travelers share a kitchen for two or three hours, they will almost surely try to say a few things to each other, and their efforts will be worth the attention of anyone interested in language contact.

Another problem with the simplest definition is deciding what we mean by 'language'. To a nonlinguist this usually presents no difficulty: if you cannot understand someone you are trying to talk to, you will assume that he is speaking a different language. Not always, though. I have observed native speakers of American English having trouble talking to each other, not because of a few unfamiliar words, as when a teenager uses slang while talking to a grandparent, but because they spoke different dialects with significantly different sound patterns. In one case a North Carolinian was able to understand a Bostonian (maybe because John F. Kennedy was President of the United States at the time, so that all Americans had become used to hearing a Boston accent), but the Bostonian was hopelessly lost and frustrated. And yet everyone – laymen and experts alike – would agree that North Carolinians and Bostonians are speaking the same language, even if they do display some striking dialect differences.

The problem here is that the boundary between two dialects of a single language and two different languages is fuzzy. Given enough time and the right social circumstances, dialects will turn into separate languages, and during the transition process there is no sharp dividing line between 'possible to understand' and 'impossible to understand' – it's a matter of types of changes, conversational contexts, attitudes, and other complex linguistic and social factors. The fuzziness of this distinction will not cause serious difficulties for the discussions in this book, because for the most part we will be looking at examples from clear cases of separate languages in contact. But readers should keep in mind that, although most of the analyses below apply equally to dialect contact and language contact, there are also some important differences; several of these will be pointed out in the relevant places.

The simplest definition is implicitly flawed in one other obvious way: speakers of two (or more) languages need not be in the same place for language contact to occur. Consider, for instance, the languages of sacred texts and other writings connected with major world religions. Christianity was responsible for the spread of Latin (and, to a lesser extent, New Testament Greek) to many countries; Pāli, the sacred language of Buddhism, spread with the religion to Thailand, Burma, and other Southeast Asian countries. The Koran (or, more precisely, Qur'ān), the sacred text of Islam, is written in Classical Arabic, but many of the world's Muslims do not speak any form of Arabic. Nevertheless, Classical Arabic is in contact with other languages in many parts of the world through the religion, as is attested by the sizable number of Arabic loanwords in various languages – among them Persian, Turkish, and Malay – that are spoken primarily by Muslims.

Contact without full bilingualism is not confined to religious languages. The most striking example in the modern world is the pervasiveness of English outside the traditionally English-speaking nations. Millions of non-English speakers have come into contact with English through radio, television, Hollywood films, popular music (on CDs and cassettes as well as on the radio and television), and writings of all kinds. Of course some English can be learned through these media, though the knowledge is likely to remain passive unless the listeners have opportunities to practice their speaking or writing skills.

The internet offers more possibilities for active long-distance language learning, and English is the main language on the international internet – so much so that the French government has tried to ban its use in electronic mail (email) communications in France! But learning to write a language does not necessarily lead to an ability to speak it, so depending on how you define 'bilingualism', knowledge that is confined to the written language alone might not qualify. (A functional definition of bilingualism, according to which anyone who uses two languages is a bilingual, would include this case; a definition that insisted on full fluency in all of the traditional four skills – speaking, listening, reading, writing – would not. The functional definition makes more sense: as François Grosjean points out, a person who uses two languages regularly but is not fully fluent in both could hardly be labeled monolingual, but by the second definition of bilingualism, s/he would not qualify as bilingual either.)

What about the people in contact situations?

English and Arabic and the few other languages with worldwide distribution are the exceptions. Language contact most often involves face-to-face interactions among groups of speakers, at least some of whom speak more than one language in a particular geographical locality. Often they are neighbors, as in Switzerland, which is home to four groups whose languages (French, German, Italian, and Romansh) share national-language status. But in the Swiss case bilingualism is asymmetrical: speakers of Italian and Romansh, whose speakers are far outnumbered by the country's French and German speakers, usually speak French and/or German, while French and German speakers are unlikely to speak either Italian or Romansh. Moreover, most or all German speakers also speak French, and in addition they know both the distinctive Swiss German and (at least to some extent) Standard German. It is said to be fairly easy, however, to find monolingual speakers of French in Switzerland.

Neighboring speaker groups may be on friendly terms – sharing resources, engaging in trade, and providing mutual support – as when several small Native American tribes in and near the northwestern corner of the United States state of Montana used to band together in their annual journey eastward to hunt buffalo in the plains. Or they may be hostile to each other, as when those combined tribes were attacked by the nearby Blackfeet, in competition over the buffalo-hunting grounds.

Often individuals from one group join another, through such social practices as exogamy (marrying someone from outside your own ethnic group), slavery, immigration, and adopting captured enemy warriors to fill gaps created when some of your own warriors have been killed in battle. So, for instance, the Dhuwal of northern Australia ban intragroup marriage, which means that every child born to a Dhuwal speaker has one non-Dhuwal-speaking parent. The seasonal contacts in western Montana led to less institutionalized but still common intermarriages among the Montana Salish, Kutenai, Spokane, and Nez Percé tribes, among others. Slavery is unfortunately known from many parts of the world. In the Caribbean and some bordering coastal areas of North, Central, and South America, the enslavement of Africans by Europeans led eventually to the emergence of new mixed languages, called CREOLES; slavery was also practiced before and after European contact in Africa, the Americas, and other places around the world. But not all wars led exclusively to death or enslavement of the losers. The Delawares, who once lived in what is now the northeastern United States, kept their ranks of warriors filled by adopting enemies captured in battle. And especially since Prince Henry the Navigator of Portugal (1394–1460) launched the Age of Exploration, language contact has resulted from the immigration of individuals and families to new territories. Chapter 2 will survey a sampling of these situations in more detail.

Sometimes speakers of two or more languages live together in a single community. In such cases there may be mutual bilingualism or multilingualism, as in the village of Kupwar in Maharashtra, India, where almost all the men speak at least two of the village's four languages (Kannaḍa, Urdu, Marathi, and Telugu). Alternatively, there may be asymmetrical bilingualism. In Ireland, for instance, most or all adults who speak Irish Gaelic also speak English, but not vice versa; the same is true, though not to the same degree, of Spanish and English speakers in a city like Los Angeles – native speakers of Spanish are much more likely to be bilingual than native speakers of English are. And, to take a truly extreme example, all native speakers of Montana Salish also speak English with native-like fluency, but not a single nontribal English speaker can speak Montana Salish fluently. (This does not mean that no one of European origin has ever spoken the language fluently, however. A linguistically gifted mid-nineteenth-century Jesuit missionary from Italy, Father Gregory Mengarini, was said to have become so fluent in Salish that he could pass for a native speaker in the dark, when he could not be seen.) Asymmetrical bilingualism is especially common when, as in these cases, a subordinate bilingual group is shifting to the language of a monolingual dominant group.

Bilingualism may be stable, as (apparently) in Kupwar, where the patterns of multilingualism are of long standing; or transitional, as on the Flathead reservation, where English–Salish bilingualism looks like a stage on the way to English monolingualism. In these and other cases of contact, an important factor in predicting whether a dominant language will sweep the minority languages off the map is whether or not there is institutional support for the nondominant language(s). Irish Gaelic has institutional support, for instance, and so do all four of the national languages of Switzerland – although Romansh, at least, is losing speakers in Switzerland in spite of its status as one of the country's four national languages, a fact that underlines the point that institutional support is not a guarantee of stability. Spanish in the United States has some institutional support (e.g. in the Constitutional Free Speech Amendment and the Bilingual Education Act), but Montana Salish has very little. The languages of Kupwar all have strong support in the patterns of social interaction in the community. The issue of stable vs. unstable contact situations, of language maintenance (in which a group keeps its language in a contact situation) vs. language shift (in which a group shifts from its language to another language) in a contact setting, will be discussed in Chapter 2.

In communities of all sizes, from the tiniest villages to the biggest nations, language contact (which is itself a result of social history) has social consequences. Sometimes these consequences are benign or advantageous. In Paraguay, for instance, the indigenous language Guaraní is spoken alongside Spanish by the majority of the population, and both Guaraní and Spanish are considered national languages. The people of Paraguay are proud of their bilingualism. Spanish is ordinary in Latin America, but Guaraní is their unique possession. (The history of this contact is less benign, however; other indigenous languages of Paraguay vanished because their speakers were pressured by European missionaries to learn Guaraní instead.)

But since homo sapiens is not a peaceable species, it is not surprising that the social effects of language contact are sometimes painful or even lethal. In many such cases the language of a minority culture is used by a dominant culture as a marker of cultural differentness: not only does it provide a means of identifying the people to be discriminated against, but it also offers a target for discrimination. Two or three generations ago, as part of the federal government's policy dictating cultural assimilation, Salish-speaking children in Montana were beaten for speaking their home language instead of English in the boarding schools; and during the apartheid era in South Africa, the use of various indigenous African languages as the medium of instruction in elementary schools for blacks was encouraged in order to prevent most black Africans from acquiring a single shared language and thus to diminish the risk of organized revolution.

Most nations have official languages. On the one hand, citizens who do not know the national language(s) often have trouble getting access to governmental services; on the other hand, citizens who know more than one national (or international) language may have an easier time finding employment than their linguistically less agile compatriots.

In Chapter 3 we'll examine a few of the many ways in which people interact in different kinds of contact situations.

How old is language contact?

Languages have been in contact certainly for thousands of years, and probably since the beginning of humankind – or at least very close to the beginning, as soon as humans spoke more than one language. (Not surprisingly, no date can be given for this starting point: it might have been 100,000 years ago, or 200,000 years ago, or even longer ago. With recent archaeological evidence pushing human habitation of regions like Australia back beyond 50,000 years, the beginning seems increasingly remote.) Even in situations where, at a relatively recent time, people moved into territories that previously lacked a human presence, such as the Americas and Oceania, not all the languages were spoken in isolation: as groups of people spread out into new regions, some of them also maintained contacts with other groups for purposes of trade and finding spouses – as modern groups are known to have done long before coming under the influence of European and Arab explorers and colonizers.

Once we move out of prehistory into history (which begins with the invention of writing in ancient Sumer in the fourth millennium BCE), we find reports of language contacts in historical records of and about all human cultures. The Gilgamesh Cycle, a famous Babylonian epic poem dating from the second millennium BCE, had its origin in an earlier Sumerian epic which spread not only to Babylon (where it was partly translated and partly adapted in the ancient Semitic language Akkadian) but also to other ancient Near Eastern cultures and languages, among them the Hurrians and the Indo-European-speaking Hittites. Other ancient language contacts are attested in bilingual inscriptions that, in the most dramatic cases, helped scholars decipher long-unused writing systems such as cuneiform (wedge-shaped groups of symbols pressed by a stylus into clay tablets). The best-known bilingual inscription is on the Rosetta Stone, which dates from 196 BCE and contains three versions of the same text – Egyptian hieroglyphics, demotic (cursive) Egyptian symbols, and Greek – and which was the key to deciphering the hieroglyphics.

Still other ancient examples are explicit mentions of language contact. So, for instance, Darius the Great (550–486 BCE), who ruled the Persian Empire from 522 to 486 BCE, wrote in his autobiography that, in addition to cuneiform writings in Persian, Elamite, and Akkadian, 'I made inscriptions in other ways, in Aryan, which was not done before.' ('Aryan' would perhaps have been an Indic language. Darius's 'autobiography' was actually written by a ghostwriter, but the comment is still interesting.) Another comment, this one about contact-induced language change, was made by Herodotus (in *The Persian Wars*, fifth century BCE); see the beginning of Chapter 4 for the quotation, which is about the altered version of Scythian spoken by the offspring of Amazons and Scythian men. This may be the first recorded mention of language shift – the shift, by a person or a group, from the native language to a second language – and also of contact as a cause of language change. A close second, or possibly even a tie with Herodotus for first, is in the Old Testament of the Bible, in the book of Nehemiah (13: 23–4): 'In those days also saw I Jews that had married wives of Ashdod, of Ammon, and of Moab: And their children spake half in the speech of Ashdod, and could not speak in the Jews' language, but according to the language of each people.' This passage certainly seems to refer to language change, and it also refers to a process of language shift within the community, provided that one equates the fathers' language with the community's language. (The chronology, relative to Herodotus, is hard to establish. Herodotus lived *ca.* 485–425 BCE. Nehemiah served either King Artaxerxes I of Persia (465–424 BCE) or King Artaxerxes II (404–359 BCE); Biblical scholars believe that certain passages of the book of Nehemiah belong instead to the book of Ezra, and this passage is a good candidate, since chapter 10 of the book of Ezra also concerns the 'strange wives' taken by Jewish men. In any case, these Old Testament books were probably not written earlier than Herodotus.)

More recent examples can easily be found in histories and biographies from all eras. Several of the great medieval Arab geographers comment disparagingly on foreigners' efforts to speak and write Arabic. Examples can be found in Ibn Khaldun (d. 1405), who refers to verses written in 'very bad Arabic' by Berbers who were 'insufficiently instructed'; and in Abu al-Bakrī (*ca.* 1028–94 CE), who cites a traveler's account of the bad Arabic spoken by non-Arabs in a town called Maridi, outside the area where most native speakers of Arabic then lived (it was probably located either in Upper Egypt or in the Saharan Desert in present-day Mauritania). And in Europe near the end of the sixteenth century, when Latin had already lost its position as the main language of international diplomacy in Europe, Queen Elizabeth I of England (1533–1603, reigned 1558–1603) impressed her courtiers, and no doubt her victim as well, with her fluent Latin denunciation of a Polish ambassador who had offended her. This story attests not only to the queen's solid education but also to the then-current status of Latin as a spoken language – spoken, that is, exclusively as a second language, and usually called neo-Latin, for Latin had evolved into the various Romance languages long before 1600.

It is important to keep in mind that written records typically document only societies in which writing is used. The tradition of recording information about unlettered societies, though venerable enough to go back at least as far as Herodotus, is a minor theme in the history of written language. The trickle of information increased in volume when travelers and missionaries followed explorers into the far corners of the world, but it became a flood – relatively speaking – only with the emergence of modern anthropology in the twentieth century. As a result, societies with no written tradition of their own are seen primarily through the eyes of majority cultures, and this circumstance limits our understanding of language contacts among other peoples, especially before the twentieth century. Nevertheless, more than enough information is available to show that extensive and intricate language contacts, with far-reaching social, political, and linguistic effects, are a constant feature of the human condition, not a phenomenon that is limited to large, recent, militarily prominent, and/or technologically advanced societies.

Where is language contact?

Language contact is everywhere: there is no evidence that any languages have developed in total isolation from other languages. Occasionally we see newspaper headlines like 'Ancient Stone Age Tribe Discovered', accompanied by articles claiming that some group has had no contact with other groups (and therefore no contact with other groups' languages). A much-discussed recent case is that of the Tasaday, a small band of people who, when Western journalists and anthropologists were first introduced to them in 1972, were living in a remote Philippine rain forest apparently untouched by modern civilization. The case later became highly controversial, with claims that their lives were primitive opposed by counterclaims that the whole story was a hoax. Certainly 'Stone Age' was an exaggeration, because the band's language is closely related to neighboring Philippine languages, so closely that the language must have diverged from its nearest relatives sometime within the past millennium. But the claim of relatively long isolation from other groups found support in a linguistic analysis carried out by the anthropologist Carol Molony. The language of the Tasaday, she pointed out, has almost no loanwords from Sanskrit, Chinese, Spanish, or English, unlike other Philippine languages; and it has almost no words referring to agriculture, which also suggests lack of contact with the languages of their farmer neighbors over a considerable period of time. To achieve this result in an invented language, a hoaxer would have had to be extremely knowledgeable about modern linguistics, and the prime suspect had no such knowledge. He would also have had to teach a sizable group of people to use his invented language constantly around outsiders, and no one who has visited the Tasaday has reported any lapses in their use of the language they say is their own. But in any case, the language of the Tasaday does have a few words borrowed from other languages, and their isolation (if real) stretches over a period of two hundred years at most.

Other popular candidates for developed-in-isolation status either evaporate on close inspection or remain controversial because of the complexity of their histories. One of the latter type is also one of the most-discussed examples: Icelandic, which is often said to have been isolated from other Germanic Scandinavian languages after the Norse settled Iceland in the ninth century. Aside from the remoteness of the island itself, the argument is based on the fact that the Icelandic literary language appears more archaic than the literary languages of Sweden, Norway, and Denmark, which (so the argument goes) suggests that the absence of contact led to a slower rate of change than in more cosmopolitan languages. But contact between Iceland and mainland Scandinavia was never cut off. Ships traveled back and forth with supplies for the island, and although the degree of isolation was quite sufficient to produce divergence into a distinct Icelandic language, it was not complete. The archaic features of Standard Icelandic are no doubt due in part to the relatively great degree of isolation from other languages, but they are also in part a result of the process by which the language was standardized: the creators of Standard Icelandic deliberately archaized the language's structure, making it look older so as to bring it closer to the language of the Eddas, the celebrated medieval mythological poems of Iceland.

Of course language contacts are more intense in some places at some times than elsewhere and at other times. Speakers of Montana Salish have been under such extreme social and economic pressure to shift to English over the past few generations that their language is seriously endangered; in sharp contrast, a great many English speakers, especially in the United States, see no reason to learn any other language, because they can easily live at home and travel throughout the world using only English. Intense pressure from a dominant group most often leads to bilingualism among subordinate groups who speak other languages, and this asymmetrical bilingualism very often results, sooner or later, in language shift: most Native Americans in the United States, and most immigrant groups as well, have shifted to English. This pattern is repeated in many places throughout the world. The Irish have mostly shifted from Irish Gaelic to English, most Australian Aboriginals have shifted to English, all ethnic Ainus in Japan have shifted from Ainu to Japanese, most Livonians in Latvia have shifted from the Uralic language of their ethnic heritage to the Indo-European language Latvian, most Suba speakers in Kenya have shifted to Luo (the language of the numerically dominant group in their region), and so forth.

Other language contacts are more stable, with both (or all) languages being maintained, at least over the short run. English and Spanish appear to be in a sort of equilibrium in parts of Florida and California, for instance, though this may be only apparent, especially in California. There and in some (most?) other Spanish-speaking communities in the United States, the common three-generation immigrant linguistic pattern holds – immigrants monolingual in the home-country language, their offspring bilingual, and then the third generation monolingual in English – but the number of Spanish speakers remains more or less constant, thanks to the constant influx of new immigrants. The contact between Spanish and Guaraní in Paraguay, where both are official national languages, has been balanced for a very long time. Here too, however, the current situation may in fact be unstable: urbanization and industrialization of the country seem to be causing a swing toward language shift, from Guaraní–Spanish bilingualism to Spanish monolingualism, in spite of the population's continuing loyalty to Guaraní. In many other ex-European colonies, too, the languages of former colonial powers are still used in addition to indigenous languages. Among the best-known examples are English in India, French in Zaire, and English in the Philippines. (The Philippines were under Spanish rule for over three hundred years, but as there were never many Spanish speakers outside urban areas, knowledge of Spanish did not spread far. By contrast, English was widely and successfully promoted by the Americans, who made it the sole medium of instruction in public schools early in the twentieth century.) Long-term contacts without large-scale shift are common in noncolonial situations too: Kupwar is one example, Montana Salish in relation to neighboring Native American languages is another (before they all declined as a result of English-language intrusions), the four national languages of Switzerland have been in place for centuries, and the many languages of northern Australia, Dhuwal and its neighbors, have apparently been in contact for millennia.

The conclusion is clear: language contact is the norm, not the exception. We would have a right to be astonished if we found any language whose speakers had successfully avoided contacts with all other languages for periods longer than one or two hundred years.

What happens to languages in contact?

The various linguistic results of language contact form the core of this book (Chapters 4–9). The general topic can be viewed as a hierarchical set of typologies, starting with a three-way division at the top level into contact-induced language change, extreme language mixture (resulting in pidgins, creoles, and bilingual mixed languages), and language death. Chapter 4 lays out the typologies in detail and, together with Chapter 5, explores the predictors of kinds and degrees of contact-induced change; Chapter 6 examines the mechanisms of contact-induced change. Pidgins and creoles are discussed in Chapter 7, bilingual mixed languages in Chapter 8, and the three main linguistic routes to language death in Chapter 9. Here I will give a preliminary sketch of some of the major topics to be covered later.

The most common result of language contact is change in some or all of the languages: typically, though not always, at least one of the languages will exert at least some influence on at least one of the other languages. And the most common specific type of influence is the borrowing of words. English, for instance, is notorious for having a huge number of loanwords – by some estimates up to 75% of its total vocabulary, mostly taken from French and Latin. A large proportion of these loanwords flooded into the language some time after the Normans conquered England in 1066, bringing their French language along with them. The loanwords do not prove that eleventh-century contact between English and French was more intensive than, say, present-day contact between English and Montana Salish in Montana, because speakers of some languages borrow more words than speakers of others, even where levels of bilingualism are more or less equivalent.

Certainly thousands of loanwords cannot get into a language without contact, so the vocabulary of English provides incontrovertible evidence of former close contact with French. But the implications of loanword evidence are asymmetrical: the presence of numerous loanwords is a sure sign of contact with the donor language, but the absence of numerous loanwords does not necessarily point to lack of contact. Montana Salish, for example, has borrowed some words from English, but not very many; instead, when speakers want to refer in Salish to items borrowed from Anglo culture, they tend to construct new words out of Salish components. So, to take just one of many examples, the Montana Salish word *p'ip'úyšn* 'automobile' literally means 'wrinkled feet' (or, more precisely, 'it has wrinkled feet'), a name derived from the appearance of the tire tracks. In fact, this aspect of Montana Salish speakers' linguistic behavior may be an areal feature characteristic of the Northwest region of the United States and Canada; the Sahaptian language Nez Percé of Oregon, Idaho, and Washington also has few loanwords, and many years ago the great linguist Edward Sapir commented that Athabaskan languages tend not to borrow words from European languages.

It is not just words that get borrowed: all aspects of language structure are subject to transfer from one language to another, given the right mix of social and linguistic circumstances. Asia Minor Greek, to take just one example, has a great many borrowings from Turkish at all levels of its structure. In the most dazzling cases, mixed languages have apparently been created by bilinguals as a symbol of their emerging ethnic identity. Two examples are Michif (spoken in North Dakota and a few other places in the western United States and Canada), which combines French noun phrases with verb phrases from the Algonquian language Cree, and Mednyj Aleut (formerly spoken on one of Russia's Commander Islands), which is basically Aleut but with numerous Russian loanwords and a massive replacement of Aleut verb endings with Russian verb morphology.

Of course most cases of one-way or mutual influence on languages in contact situations are more prosaic, but in these too it is easy to find transfer in all areas of language structure – phonology (sound systems), morphology (word structure), syntax (sentence structure), and lexical semantics. Latvian, for instance, has been influenced by Livonian in both phonology and morphology: its complex accent system was replaced by fixed stress on the first syllable in the word, and one dialect has lost masculine vs. feminine vs. neuter gender distinctions, which are lacking in Livonian and other Uralic languages. Another Uralic language, Finnish, has switched from typically Uralic Subject–Object–Verb (SOV) word order to a Subject–Verb–Object (SVO) pattern, under the influence of neighboring Indo-European languages. Examples like these can be multiplied endlessly; and when human creativity comes into play, there are no discernible linguistic limits to the possibilities for transferring any linguistic feature from one language to another.

In some new contact situations the groups in contact do not learn each other's languages, either because they do not want to or because they lack sufficient opportunity to do so, or both. In such a situation a contact language may emerge, a pidgin (if it arises as a strictly secondary language, used for limited purposes) or a creole (if it arises in the first instance as the main language of a community). The vocabulary of the new language will usually, though not always, be derived primarily from the language of one prominent group in the contact situation – a European language, in the classic trade pidgins that sprang up on coasts visited by European explorers several centuries ago, and also in the pidgins and creoles that arose through the trans-Atlantic slave trade. By contrast, the grammars of pidgins and creoles that arise in multilingual contexts are not derived from the grammar of any single language, but appear instead to be a combination of features shared by the languages in contact and features that are universally preferred, perhaps because they are relatively easy to learn.

What else happens to languages in contact? As we have already seen, one common outcome is the disappearance of one of the languages. In all but a few tragic cases this happens when all its speakers shift to another language; the other possibility is that the language disappears because all its speakers die, when they are massacred by (say) hostile invaders or when they succumb to natural disasters or to foreign diseases imported by less directly lethal intruders. Depending on how rapidly a process of group shift is completed, and on less tangible factors such as speaker attitudes, the language that is being shifted away from may or may not undergo the type of overall change that has come to be known as attrition – the loss of vocabulary and simplification of structure without any compensating additions in the form of borrowings or newly created structure. Many immigrant languages in the United States, for instance American Hungarian, are undergoing attrition as their speaker groups shrink; but in Montana Salish, as in many other Native American languages, the drastic reduction in number of speakers has not been accompanied by any grammatical simplification (though there is vocabulary loss because most present-day tribal elders can no longer remember the Salish names of certain formerly important plants and other aspects of traditional culture). The third linguistic route to language death, a very rare one as far as we know, occurs when the speakers of a threatened language stubbornly resist total cultural and linguistic assimilation – but, under very strong linguistic (and other cultural) pressure from a dominant group, they replace more and more of their original language's structure until at last it retains only some vocabulary and a few structural remnants of their precontact language. This is in fact another way in which extreme language mixture occurs, as we will see in Chapter 8.

We will look more closely at all these linguistic results of language contact in Chapters 4–9. The book concludes with a brief survey of language endangerment, a topic which is of great concern to modern linguists, many of whom are watching with dismay as the languages they study and admire vanish forever.

Sources and further reading

The classic general study in this field is Uriel Weinreich's *Languages in Contact* (first published in 1953, reprinted in 1968). More recent general works are John Edwards, *Multilingualism* (1994), and several books on the closely related topic of bilingualism, especially François Grosjean's 1982 book *Life with Two Languages: An Introduction to Bilingualism* and Suzanne Romaine's *Bilingualism* (2nd edition, 1995). A major recent encyclopedic treatment of the subject, edited by Hans Goebl, Peter H. Nelde, Zdeněk Starý, and Wolfgang Wölck, is *Kontaktlinguistik / Contact Linguistics / Linguistique de contact: Ein internationales Handbuch zeitgenössischer Forschung / An International Handbook of Contemporary Research / Manuel international des recherches contemporaines* (Berlin: Walter de Gruyter, 1997).

Case studies of especially interesting contact situations can be found in many books and in linguistics and anthropology journals; examples are found in this book's list of references. David Crystal's wonderful book *The Cambridge Encyclopedia of Language* has a fine discussion of the problem of deciding what a language is (pp. 284–5). For a systematic discussion of interactions among dialects of the same language, see Peter Trudgill's book *Dialects in Contact* (1986). The linguistic sections of the book you are reading, especially in Chapters 4, 7, and 8, follow to a large extent (though not completely) the framework presented in Sarah Thomason and Terrence Kaufman, *Language Contact, Creolization, and Genetic Linguistics* (1988).

François Grosjean discusses definitions of bilingualism in *Life with Two Languages: An Introduction to Bilingualism*, especially pp. 230–6; his comment about the nonnecessity of full fluency for bilingualism is on p. 232. I am grateful to Charlotte Schaengold (personal communication, 1999) for comments on the probable levels of German and French bilingualism in Switzerland. See Jeffrey Heath, *Linguistic Diffusion in Arnhem Land* (1978), for discussion of exogamy among the Dhuwal and other circumstances of intimate language contact. John J. Gumperz and Robert Wilson, in their 1971 article 'Convergence and creolization: a case from the Indo-Aryan/ Dravidian border', discuss the case of Kupwar in India. The Sumerian example comes from Samuel Noah Kramer's fascinating book *History Begins at Sumer: Thirty-Nine Firsts in Man's Recorded History* (1981). The example from Darius the Great's autobiography is from Olmstead 1948 (*History of the Persian Empire*, p. 116), and the Arabic examples are from Ibn Khaldun and Abu al-Bakrī, respectively; see Thomason and Elgibali 1986 and Owens 1997 for discussion of al-Bakrī's comments. For a summary of the Tasaday controversy, see the 1997 commentary on Lawrence A. Reid's website, and for more detailed analyses see *The Tasaday Controversy*, ed. Thomas N. Headland (1991). Guaraní/Spanish bilingualism in Paraguay is the topic of Joan Rubin's 1968 book *National Bilingualism in Paraguay*, and current trends are discussed in a 1996 article by Yolanda Russinovich Solé, 'Language, affect and nationalism in Paraguay'.

For a case study on the shift from the Bantu language Suba to the Nilotic language Luo, see Franz Rottland and Duncan Okoth Okombo, 'Language shift among the Suba of Kenya' (1992, in Matthias Brenzinger, ed., *Language Death: Factual and Theoretical Explorations with Special Reference to East Africa*); this book also has several other interesting East African case studies. Edward Sapir's comment on Athabaskan nonborrowing is in his book *Language* (1921). I am grateful to Beatriz Lorente for providing information about contacts with English and Spanish in the Philippines. The most impressive study of Turkish influence on Asia Minor Greek is R. M. Dawkins' admirable book *Modern Greek in Asia Minor* (1916). See Sarah Thomason, ed., *Contact Languages: A Wider Perspective* (1997) for case studies on Michif (by Peter Bakker and Robert Papen), and Mednyj Aleut (by Sarah Thomason), as well as studies of eight other contact languages.

Bernard Comrie, in *The Languages of the Soviet Union* (1981), discusses Liv(onian) influence on Latvian. Anna Fenyvesi, in 'Language Contact and Language Death in an Immigrant Language: The Case of Hungarian' (1995), analyzes changes in a dying variety of American Hungarian. For a general book with valuable case studies on language death, see Nancy Dorian, ed., *Investigating Obsolescence: Studies in Language Contraction and Death* (1989). The book edited by Dell Hymes, *Pidginization and Creolization of Languages* (1971), is still an excellent source on pidgins and creoles; there are also good recent books, most notably John Holm's two-volume work *Pidgins and Creoles* (1988 and 1989) and Jacques Arends, Pieter Muysken, and Norval Smith, eds., *Pidgins and Creoles: An Introduction* (1995).

2 Contact Onsets and Stability

The purpose of this chapter is to set the stage for the discussions in the rest of the book by trying to answer two crucial historical questions about language contact situations – how they come about in the first place, and how long they last. Neither question can be answered definitively, because of huge gaps in the historical record for most contact situations and because the future of current contact situations can rarely be predicted with any degree of confidence. Still, even partial answers to these questions, together with some examples, will be useful for orientation.

How do languages come into contact?

The short answer to this question is that we usually have no idea how particular contact situations arose in the distant past. In some cases, though, we do know the nature and date of first contact, and in others we can at least make educated guesses. From known cases we can extrapolate to draw some generalizations about how languages come into contact. Let us look first at some examples, starting with South Africa.

The original inhabitants of what is now the Republic of South Africa, as far as we know, were speakers of Khoisan languages; they were there long before European explorers and traders came in ships, and also long before Bantu speakers moved south into South Africa with their cattle herds. Bantus arrived in the northern part of the region in about 1000 CE or earlier, and Portuguese explorers landed at the Cape of Good Hope in the late fifteenth century. Europeans and the Khoisan groups encountered each other as soon as the Europeans arrived; the Dutch found Khoisan speakers to be skilled interpreters, and employed them for this purpose and also, later, as nannies for their children. And the Bantus must also have met Khoisan speakers soon after moving into South Africa, given the significant influence that Khoisan languages have exerted on several South African Bantu languages – for instance Zulu, which acquired its distinctive click sounds from Khoisan. But Europeans and Bantus did not come into contact (and conflict) until after 1775, when Dutch farmers spreading eastward met Bantu herders spreading westward.

Most other known dates of first contact are also associated with European exploration and colonization. The armies of Alexander the Great (356–323 BCE) brought Greek into contact with Indic languages in the Punjab; the first known significant contacts between European languages and indigenous North American languages took place about 1000 CE, after Vikings landed in L'Anse aux Meadows, in northern Newfoundland; the Spanish conquistador Francisco Pizarro met and conquered the Quechua-speaking Incas in present-day Peru in the first half of the sixteenth century; Captain Cook was the first European to encounter several Pacific islands, and their languages, in his voyage of 1772–5; and so forth.

When the date of contact is not known, we have to make an educated guess about it. But estimating the onset of contact is tricky. The imperial court of China was Manchu-speaking during the long rule of the Qing dynasty (1644–1911 CE), so we know that the Tungusic language Manchu was in contact with Chinese throughout that period. But although that particular contact situation is bounded by those dates, there were certainly also earlier contacts between Manchu speakers and Chinese speakers. Speakers of Indic languages are thought to have arrived in the northwestern corner of the Indian subcontinent by around 1500 BCE, and the region was already inhabited, but it is not clear what languages they would have encountered there at the time – surely Dravidian languages (which now occupy all of southern India and a few scattered speech islands in the north as well), but also Burushaski (a genetic isolate, i.e. not known to be related to any other languages, which is now confined to a remote mountainous region of Pakistan), and perhaps other languages as well.

Many other contact situations are either too old or located in places without recorded history (i.e. most of the world), or both, so that we have no direct evidence to indicate how or when they arose. Archaeological evidence is sometimes useful for unraveling the contact histories. But there may be no ancient archaeological sites, and even where the sites exist, we cannot be certain about what language(s) the people spoke unless they made durable goods like pots and wrote on them – which few people did, and those only in a very few parts of the world. Of course we can often draw inferences about who arrived when, speaking which languages; but not always.

One example is the dense cluster of languages in the Pacific Northwest of the United States and neighboring British Columbia, which have been in close contact with each other for a very long time. Three language families are primarily or entirely located in this region: Salishan, Wakashan, and Chimakuan. To these may be added the isolate Kutenai, whose speakers live near and among Salishan speakers in the eastern part of Salishan territory. Despite vigorous efforts to connect these four families historically with each other and with other indigenous North American language families, they cannot be (or at least have not been) shown to be related. Nor can they be shown to have migrated to their present neighboring locations from elsewhere. This does not mean, of course, that this contact situation had no beginning; it means only that we cannot trace its origin or development. Similar examples can be found in many other parts of the world, notably New Guinea, many of whose eight hundred or so languages fall into small groups that are not demonstrably related to each other or to any other languages. Language contact in New Guinea is so pervasive that Arthur Capell once commented that while adjoining languages in the island's central highlands have their own separate vocabularies, their grammatical features 'recur with almost monotonous regularity from language to language'.

This brief survey shows that in many places where languages are in contact we do not know and cannot find out how the situation came about. But in other cases we do know, and there is no reason to postulate totally different kinds of sources for any of the contacts whose historical origins cannot be established. The rest of this section will focus on the ways in which groups of people, and therefore languages, come into contact, based on known cases and inferred for undocumented cases.

First, two groups might move into previously unoccupied territory and meet there. In such a case neither group is indigenous, so neither has encroached on the other's established territory. Cases of this type are rare or nonexistent in the modern world, where all habitable land tends to be inhabited by someone; but they must have been fairly common in the remote past, as humankind spread around the globe. Antarctica may offer trivial examples, as it has no permanent human population and scientists from different nations come into contact in their encampments there. Some islands were uninhabited in historical times, for instance Mauritius and the Seychelles in the Indian Ocean, until Europeans and their slaves arrived: the beginning of permanent settlement on Mauritius dates from 1721, and on the Seychelles from the 1760s. The meeting of Dutch farmers and Bantu cattle herders in the interior of South Africa would be a good example if it were not for the prior presence of Khoisan speakers – who, however, did not appreciably influence the course of Dutch–Bantu interaction, in part because so many Khoisan speakers died rapidly from smallpox and other European diseases.

A much more common origin of language contact, in the recent past and probably in the distant past as well, is the movement of one group into another group's territory. The movement may be peaceful or otherwise, but the result is all too often a takeover of previously occupied territory. Some Native American tribes welcomed the first Europeans who settled on the east coast of what is now the United States, and the Europeans at first treated the indigenous peoples with a measure of respect. There was plenty of land for all, and ownership of particular pieces of land was not an indigenous concept. This soon changed: the Europeans wanted to own the land, and once they arrived in sufficient numbers to impose their will they did so, with disastrous results for the indigenes. Even then not all the contacts were hostile, of course; there were also active trade relations and Christian missions, not to mention intermarriage. But overall the history of European trade and colonization is one of subjugation of indigenous peoples to militarily powerful invaders. Often there are waves of immigrants, with newcomers taking over territory from older immigrants. This is what happened in New Zealand: it was uninhabited until speakers of Maori – a language belonging to the Polynesian branch of the Austronesian family – settled there before 1000 CE, and then European explorers arrived in the seventeenth century. Today English is the dominant language in New Zealand, though Maori is still spoken and is maintaining a significant presence in the country, thanks to vigorous preservation efforts.

Similarly, Dutch and Bantu speakers moved in on Khoisan territory, Indic speakers took over someone else's land (though it is not clear just whose), and speakers of Austronesian languages settled in areas of coastal New Guinea that had previously been occupied by speakers of non-Austronesian languages. In North America, Spanish speakers displaced Native Americans in California and the Southwest, and then English speakers moved in to take over land and power from Spanish speakers in those parts of what is now the United States.

The British Isles offer a prime example of language contacts arising through successive immigrations, in this instance mostly military invasions and conquests. The first people to live there that we know of were pre-Celtic, but we do not know what language(s) they spoke: they left no written records of any kind. The next wave of immigrants were Celtic speakers, who were dominant in the islands by the third century BCE and whose languages displaced those of the earlier inhabitants. They were followed by Roman occupiers (43 CE to the early fifth century, but only in England and Wales), and then various groups of (pre-)English speakers, such as the Angles, the Saxons, and the Jutes (fifth to sixth centuries). There were just two successful later invasions of England. First, Vikings invaded the island during the eighth and ninth centuries, bringing their Norse language with them, and many of them settled in northern and eastern parts of England. Then, in 1066, French-speaking Normans (descendants in part of Norse-speaking invaders of what is now Normandy) conquered England. Of all these invaders, only the Celtic and English speakers succeeded in maintaining their own languages in their new homeland, and of these English clearly dominates: for centuries now the Celtic languages of the British Isles – Irish Gaelic, Scottish Gaelic, Welsh, and the now-extinct Cornish and Manx – have been losing ground to English. (It should be noted, however, that all these Celtic languages, including Cornish and Manx, have been the subject of revitalization programs in recent years.)

A related route to language contact is the immigration of small groups or scattered individual speakers who join the preexisting population rather than conquering them or otherwise taking over their territory. Many immigrant groups in the United States fall into this general category, among them the famous Pennsylvania Dutch – actually speakers of German, not Dutch – in the east. Other older groups of American immigrants who kept their own languages in their new homeland, for some time at least, were Germans in the Midwest, Swedes in Wisconsin, Norwegians and Finns in Minnesota, Poles, Italians, and Hungarians in Pittsburgh's steel factories, and Japanese in Hawaii and California. Recent immigrant groups come mostly from Latin America (speaking Spanish) and from Asia (speaking Vietnamese, Hmong, Thai, Khmer, Chinese, Korean, and other languages). In recent decades Britain has seen many immigrants arrive from former British colonies in South Asia (India, Pakistan), Africa, the West Indies, and elsewhere. A number of countries in northern Europe, among them Germany and Sweden, have welcomed people from southern Europe and Turkey who come – in principle temporarily, but in fact often permanently – to work in factories; some of these groups now form sizable linguistic minorities in northern European countries. (The popular term for these groups is 'guestworker', as in German *Gastarbeiter*; but the term is now falling out of use, since its suggestion of temporary residence is inaccurate in so many cases.) Some immigrant groups, in Europe, the United States, and elsewhere, migrate as refugees rather than primarily as workers; their integration, or lack of it, into the host country's society parallels that of the workers.

The practice of importing a labor force – a specialized type of immigration – has given rise to complex contact situations elsewhere in the world as well. The large South Asian population of South Africa, for instance, had its origin in the importation of workers for the sugar-cane industry during the nineteenth century; this system made Tamil (among other languages of India) a significant minority language in the country. Indians also emigrated in sizable numbers to other parts of colonial Africa, Southeast Asia, Oceania, and the Caribbean. Language contacts on some Pacific plantations were initiated when laborers were brought in, sometimes by force, from various Pacific islands. Africans from many linguistic backgrounds gathered to work the copper mines of the former Belgian Congo and the diamond mines of South Africa, and they accompanied European traders and colonial authorities on journeys from a colonial center to administrative outposts.

The most notorious case of imported labor is of course the Atlantic slave trade, which brought as many as ten million enslaved Africans to the New World to work the plantations. But although the Europeans may have practiced slavery on the largest scale, they were by no means the only people to bring slaves into their communities: earlier, the ancient Egyptians used slave labor to build their pyramids (though we do not know what the linguistic consequences were, if any); early Arab explorers were often also slave traders, and Arabic slavery continued into the twentieth century and indeed still continues in a few places. In the Americas some Native tribes enslaved members of other tribes, and slavery was also an institution in many

African nations, especially before the colonial period. The importation of slaves motivates the distinction that sociolinguists make between voluntary and involuntary migration, a difference that of course affects the workers' attitudes toward the host country and therefore, very often, the linguistic results of the contact.

A different way of initiating contact is to meet in No Man's Land – that is, to come together for specific purposes on neutral ground. A particular region in the southern Great Plains of the present-day United States used to attract many Native American tribes who met at the same time each year to gather an edible root that grew plentifully there. Another American example is the Jesuit Mission at St. Ignatius, Montana, which was founded in the mid-nineteenth century: on the advice of local Natives, the mission was built in a neutral location that belonged to no tribe but served several Native American tribes as a gathering place for trade and for gambling games. During the Age of Exploration, in many coastal regions around the world, towns sprang up along the European trade routes when indigenous peoples gathered there to meet with the European traders. On the southern coast of China, for instance, Europeans were permitted to land in just two locations, Canton and Macau, to trade with local people; Europeans were forbidden to travel outside narrowly prescribed areas.

Still another source of language contact is the type of close cultural connection that sometimes develops among long-time neighbors. In such cases we are not looking at initial contacts, because those must date to the period in which the groups became neighbors, but new types of contact can develop at any time between neighboring groups. Language contact was one result of the annual merger (for defensive purposes) of several small mountain tribes of the northwestern United States when they moved to the plains to hunt buffalo; it was a result of intermarriage among Australian Aborigines who practiced institutionalized exogamy; it is a very common result of trade between neighboring groups; and so on. On a less organized scale, language contacts among individuals result from scattered instances of intermarriage – like those between Vietnamese women and American soldiers during the Vietnam War, or those between students who meet through travel or study abroad – and other individual actions, such as the recent wave of adoptions of Rumanian and Russian toddlers by American couples or the temporary residence of a young adult in a foreign household as an exchange student or a domestic servant.

Finally, language contact can come about solely through education, or what might be called 'learnèd contacts'. Latin was the language of international diplomacy in Europe throughout the Middle Ages and the Renaissance and thus at least up to 1600, centuries after it had ceased to be learned by any children as a first language; the descendants of the Romans were by then learning French or Spanish or Italian or Portuguese or some other Romance language as a first language, and of course a great many European diplomats spoke non-Romance languages like English, German, Dutch, Polish, and Hungarian. Latin therefore had to be learned as a second language by an educated person. It persisted in some European countries even after its general use had declined; in Hungary, for instance, it was only in 1784 that the Habsburg Emperor Joseph II of the Austro-Hungarian empire issued a decree that replaced Latin with German as the official administrative language of Hungary.

In the modern world English is by far the most widespread lingua franca (language of wider communication). All over the world people must learn English if they wish to study advanced physics, understand the dialogue in ubiquitous American films, fly airplanes to international destinations (English is the international language of air-traffic controllers), and do business with Americans and most other foreigners. English is also the lingua franca for international communication via the vast and ever-expanding internet. Many of the people who use English for all these purposes have no opportunity (and often no desire) to practice by talking to native speakers of English.

Other instances of learnèd contacts can also be found, for instance Standard German in Switzerland, where speakers of the distinctive Swiss German dialect learn Standard German in school, or Putonghua (the 'common language') in China, which is based on Mandarin Chinese and is studied in school by native speakers of other Chinese languages (so-called Chinese 'dialects') as well as non-Chinese minority languages. Similarly, Muslims all over the world learn at least a little Classical Arabic for religious purposes, even if they never meet a native speaker of any modern dialect of Arabic, and the same phenomenon can be observed in other religious contexts as well – not just familiar ones like Catholics' exposure to Latin in the Mass (until Latin was replaced by English and other vernacular languages after the Second Vatican Council in the 1960s), but also cases like the Arabic-speaking Christian community of Copts in Egypt, who still use the long-extinct Egyptian language in their religious ceremonies.

Stable and unstable contact situations

As noted in Chapter 1, some contact situations are stable and quasi-permanent, others are unstable and short-lived, and still others fall between these two extremes. Predicting the future of a contact situation can sometimes be done with confidence, but usually only when change is already under way – that is, in unstable situations. Any contact setting, even if it has been more or less static for many generations, is subject to change at any time, for social reasons that may or may not be predictable. The point that needs to be underlined here is that social factors are the only ones that need to be considered in assessing stability: linguistic factors (such as overall structural similarity of the languages in contact) seem to be totally irrelevant.

Sociolinguists have found that some very general triggers for language shift – and thus for the most common mechanism through which previously stable contact situations dissolve into monolingualism – can be identified. Processes of urbanization and industrialization, for example, will often tip the balance against a minority language. And conversely, factors that promote stability of a minority language have been identified, most obviously numbers of speakers and institutional support. In recent research a great deal of emphasis has been placed on the concept of ethnicity and its implications for language maintenance and shift: relevant issues here are language as a symbol of ethnicity and language loyalty. Ultimately, this concept has to do with people's attitudes toward the languages they speak; and, as we will see repeatedly in this book, the most salient thing about people's attitudes is that they cannot be predicted with absolute confidence. Some robust correlations can be found between certain factors and certain attitudes, and between particular attitudes and particular types of linguistic behavior, but efforts to establish exceptionless correlations, much less causal relationships, have been frustrated by the complexity of human linguistic behavior.

More specific factors that can speed up or slow down the process of language shift have also been identified in certain cases. In Australia, for instance, the number of speakers in a particular neighborhood or region is important for maintaining an immigrant group's language; but in addition, the immigrant groups most likely to keep their ethnic-heritage languages are the newcomers for whom language is a vital part of the culture, connected intimately with such other aspects of the culture as religion, and whose offspring marry within the group. A similar pattern is found elsewhere too. Here is one example. In the United States city of Pittsburgh, Pennsylvania, Italian-Americans shift to English over three generations in the classic pattern mentioned in Chapter 1; but Greek-Americans maintain their language over four generations. The difference in the two groups' maintenance-to-shift history is explained by social differences in their respective situations: the Italian-Americans attended Catholic churches with members of other ethnic groups, with whom they intermarried, and they spoke nonstandard Italian dialects with no connection to, or support from, Standard Italian. By contrast, the Greek-Americans worshiped in ethnically homogeneous Greek Orthodox churches, married within the group – often in arranged marriages to monolingual partners who immigrated directly from Greece for the purpose – and were taught Standard Greek through the churches. As these examples suggest, and as we saw in Chapter 1, the most intense contact situations often, though not always, end sooner or later in language shift by a numerically and/or socioeconomically subordinate group to a dominant group's language.

It is also possible to find culture-specific factors that affect the likelihood or speed of shift. A particularly striking example is found in southern Africa, where in some cultures the status of women is codified in the grammatical structures of the language. The Thonga-speaking minority in northern Zululand is under socioeconomic pressure to shift to the dominant Zulu language, because Zulu speakers control access to goods and services. But Thonga women, especially the older women, resist this shift, because women have a higher status in Thonga than in Zulu culture, and the difference in status is reflected in the languages.

However, most research on sociolinguistic aspects of language maintenance and language shift has focused on socioeconomic and political relations between dominant and subordinate groups. In efforts to predict which circumstances lead to language shift, for instance, one can set out four possible positions for a group in a contact situation: (1) indigenous superordinate, (2) migrant superordinate, (3) indigenous subordinate, and (4) migrant subordinate. Stanley Lieberson and his colleagues have made several predictions about the fate of these groups' languages: group (1) will never shift to the subordinate language, while group (2) might do so, as for instance Norman French speakers in England did about 200 years after the Norman Conquest of 1066. Group (4) will usually shift rapidly to the dominant group's language; group (3) will also shift, but not as quickly. This picture may be too bleak for groups (3) and (4), because even today not all contact situations involve an asymmetrical dominant–subordinate intergroup relationship with pressure toward shift. Still, as we will see in Chapter 10, the pressure to shift to a dominant group's language is responsible for the horrifying rate of language extinction in today's world.

In any case, a contact situation that has persisted without dramatic change for more than three or four generations and that shows no sign of incipient change may reasonably be considered stable, in that it is likely to remain unless and until social change triggers dissolution of the contact. During the rule of the Qing dynasty in China, institutionalized contact between the Manchu spoken at court and the Chinese spoken by most of the emperor's subjects lasted almost three hundred years (1644–1911 CE), a very stable situation by most standards. The French that was introduced into the royal court and other public arenas in England by the Norman conquerors lasted as a major language of public life for about two hundred years. More permanent contact situations can be found: systematic exogamy as practiced by groups like the Dhuwal of Australia produces multilingual children and then adults, and continues to do so as long as exogamy is dictated by the group's norms and the intergroup marriages unite people who speak different languages. (The latter condition does not always hold, of course: the Navajos of the southwestern United States practice a form of exogamy, but the intragroup marriage ban merely forbids marrying within clans, and all the clans speak Navajo.) Stability can also be found in long-term trade relationships, both those in which many groups gather at a central trading location and those in which neighboring groups maintain their own languages but meet regularly for trade.

Areas where lingua francas are in regular use are multilingual more or less by definition: if everyone spoke the same language, there would be no need for a lingua franca. Not surprisingly, these contact situations also vary in stability. Among the world's many lingua francas are, or were, Greek in the ancient Near East and elsewhere around the Mediterranean; Latin in Europe until about 1600 (later in parts of eastern Europe) and French thereafter until it was replaced as a lingua franca by English; Swahili and Hausa in eastern and western sub-Saharan Africa, respectively, for centuries each; the pidgin Chinook Jargon in the northwestern United States and neighboring parts of Canada, for about a hundred years between the mid-nineteenth and the mid-twentieth century; first Spanish (1565–1898) and then English in the Philippines; Putonghua Chinese in China, continuing Mandarin as a lingua franca, thus with a span of centuries; and Russian in northeastern Eurasia, for at least a hundred and fifty years. And, as noted above, English has no serious competitor for the position of the major international lingua franca of the modern world. All these languages had, or have had, reasonably long histories as lingua francas, ranging from about a hundred years (Chinook Jargon) to several centuries (e.g. Latin). English achieved its worldwide lingua-franca status only in the twentieth century, but its status as a major lingua franca originated with the British colonial empire, which spanned a period of several hundred years. And although Putonghua is a new variety of Chinese, or at least a newly standardized variety, it has close linguistic and political links to Mandarin Chinese, which has long served as the lingua franca of China.

Like other contact situations, those involving lingua francas dissolve when social circumstances change, but the status of a lingua franca depends most obviously on history's ups and downs: if the people who hold political and/or economic power lose their power, their language is also likely to lose its status as a lingua franca. It has been many centuries since Greek was used widely for international communication, and some decades since English replaced French as the major lingua franca in Europe (and elsewhere). Chinook Jargon also gave way to English, and English is used more than Spanish for intergroup communication in the Philippines nowadays. By contrast, Putonghua is spreading, not receding, as a tool of cultural unification in China; and the position of Russian in Siberia (which belongs to Russia) is as strong as ever, though its position in the now-independent Baltic nations, and in some other ex-Soviet republics as well, is severely threatened.

The current and growing status of English as a necessary part of higher education throughout the world ensures that English will be in contact with most of the world's languages for the foreseeable future. This could change if social conditions change to reduce drastically the influence of English-speaking countries on the world scene, but for the time being, at least, English is spreading not only in public domains but also in private lives around the world. A striking example from the state of Assam in northeastern India is found in some academic families in Shillong. One mother, for instance, reports that she speaks seven languages: she is most fluent in English, the language she uses at work, and in Manipuri (the main lingua franca of the province she grew up in) and the Assamese-lexicon pidgin language Nagamese. She is also fluent, though less so, in Tangkul, which is her mother tongue; and in addition she speaks some Hindi and Mizo, and to a lesser extent Khesa, her husband's language. (These languages belong to two entirely different language families: English and Hindi are Indo-European languages, while Tangkul, Manipuri, Mizo, and Khesa belong to the Sino-Tibetan family. Nagamese, as a pidgin, does not belong to any language family; its lexical-base language Assamese, like Hindi, is a member of the Indic branch of Indo-European.) Of all these languages, she has chosen English as the language to teach her two-year-old son. The reason is rooted in her culture. She and her husband both belong to patrilineal tribes, which means that their son belongs to his father's tribe. She and her husband therefore feel that he should learn his father's language first. But since she does not know Khesa well enough to use it exclusively with her son, and since her husband's family would not find use of her own mother tongue an acceptable substitute, using English instead offers a way out of the dilemma, as English is culturally neutral in this setting.

Long-term peaceful relations between neighbors produce the most stable contact situations, and these can be found on a small scale all over the world. The least stable are probably those that arise through invasion and conquest accompanied by large-scale immigration: in such situations the languages of peoples overwhelmed by force and numbers are all too likely to vanish when their speakers either die (as a result of mass murder or devastating imported diseases) or shift from their own language to that of the invaders. Most of the Native languages of the United States have suffered, or will soon suffer, this fate; many or most of the Aboriginal languages of Australia have already been completely replaced by English or by an English-based creole language. In both countries the entire process of language loss will have taken several hundred years, but the end was in sight almost from the beginning, as more and more immigrants moved into the Natives' territory, killed, displaced, and surrounded the previous inhabitants, and then conquered the survivors linguistically as well.

Sources and further reading

Arthur Capell's remark about grammatical similarities in languages of the central highlands of New Guinea was cited by Stefan Wurm (1956: 451). A readable discussion of the early linguistic history of South Africa can be found in Valkhoff 1966, but this is just one item in the extensive literature on the long and complex history of languages and language contacts in what is now South Africa. Three other examples are L. W. Lanham's 1978 article 'An outline history of the languages of South Africa', Douglas Young's 1988 article 'Bilingualism and bilingual education in a divided South Africa' (both published before the change of government and the end of apartheid in South Africa), and Bonny Norton Peirce and Stanley G. M. Ridge's 1997 article 'Multilingualism in southern Africa', which brings the story up to date by including information about South African languages since the end of apartheid. (Peirce & Ridge also discuss multilingualism in other countries of southern Africa, but much more information is available about South Africa.) For the history of language in the British Isles, see (among many other sources) Kenneth Jackson's 1953 book *Language and History in Early Britain*. Miklós Kontra, in his article on Hungary in a 1997 handbook *Kontaktlinguistik / Contact Linguistics / Linguistique de contact*, discusses the linguistic history of Hungary. Revitalization efforts devoted to Manx are described briefly in a chapter of George Broderick's 1999 book *Language Death in the Isle of Man* (I'm very grateful to Nancy Dorian for telling me about this book).

There are numerous detailed studies of language maintenance and especially language shift. Three of the most widely cited of these are Gal 1979, Dorian 1981, and Hill and Hill 1986. The last two of these three books focus on language death, with extensive discussion of the sociolinguistics of language shift in the particular situations. Michael Clyne has written extensively about language contact issues in Australia, especially among immigrant populations; his analysis of language maintenance and shift is from Clyne 1997. The contrast in language shift behavior between Greek-Americans and Italian-Americans in Pennsylvania is from Paulston 1993. The southern African example of women resisting language shift because they are reluctant to submit to the lower status that is grammaticalized in the dominant language is from Peirce and Ridge 1997, citing 1992 research by Robert K. Herbert (and, as background, Kunene and Mulder 1992, for a discussion of gender and language change in Swati). The predictions about language maintenance and shift are from Stanley Lieberson, G. Dalto, and M. E. Johnson's 1975 article 'The course of mother tongue diversity in nations', as cited in Christina Bratt Paulston's 1994 book *Linguistic Minorities in Multilingual Settings*. I'm grateful to Jacques Arends for the estimate of ten million African slaves imported to the New World. The discussion of the Indian mother who is teaching her son English is from Anne Hvenekilde's 1997 paper 'Kinship systems, language choice and the construction of identity among academics in Shillong, North East India', which was presented at the First International Symposium on Bilingualism in Vigo, Spain.

3 Multilingualism in Nations and Individuals

Kulĭko jezĭkou člòvīg znâ,
talĭko člòvīg vạḷâ.

> ('However many languages a person knows, that's
> how much a person is worth' – Croatian folk saying)

'A high school teacher in the provincial capital of Surin in northeast Thailand speaks the Northern Khmer language of the area to her neighbors and in many other informal situations around town. She learned it by living and working in the city for several years. On the other hand, she speaks Lao with her husband, a government official, because that is his mother tongue. She learned it (and met him) when she was in training as a teacher in the Lao-speaking area of the northeast. She teaches in Standard Thai, which she herself learned in school. She talks to her children in Lao or Northern Khmer or Standard Thai, as seems appropriate at the time. When she returns to her home village, an hour's ride by bus to the east of Surin, she speaks Kuy, her own native language, the language of her parents, the language in which she grew up.' (*Linguistic Diversity and National Unity: Language Ecology in Thailand*, by William Smalley, 1994, p. 1)

'One female B-Mlabri speaker impressed me particularly when, within one hour of smalltalk, she switched between four different languages depending on the addressee: (1) Mlabri (spoken to her father), (2) Tin Mal (spoken to her husband, who was born a Tin), (3) Hmong (spoken to Hmong villagers entering the hut), and (4) Northern Thai, the lingua franca of the whole area (spoken in a subsequent conversation involving both her father and some Hmong people).' (*Minor Mlabri: A Hunter-Gatherer Language of Northern Indochina*, by Jørgen Rischel, 1995, pp. 54–5; northern Thailand)

'Throughout this period [1750–1858] most of the communication between Whites and Indians was in the trade language known as

Chinook Jargon . . . As befitted their position as traders, Wasco, Wishram, and Cascade Indians often spoke more than one dialect [= language] of Chinookan and one or more of Sahaptin . . . By 1812, at least one [Wishram] man knew some English, and the number increased slowly during the period . . . The multilingualism . . . continued during [1858–1920] . . . A few Wascos and Wishrams learned even more distant languages, such as Nez Perce, which were useful for visiting and trading. There was prestige attached to knowing languages and perhaps aesthetic satisfaction; while serving as an army scout, one Wasco learned a certain amount of Delaware from a fellow scout. While this was not a "practical" accomplishment, it provided a basis for pride and prestige.' (*Perspectives in American Indian Culture Change*, by Edward Spicer, 1961, pp. 370, 396; United States, Pacific Northwest)

'IT'S THE TALK OF NUEVA YORK: THE HYBRID CALLED SPANGLISH – Nely Galan, guest host for a day, and the television actress Liz Torres . . . slip into the language that comes most naturally to both of them . . . Ms. Galan, born in Cuba and reared in New Jersey, and Ms. Torres, Puerto Rican and raised in Hell's Kitchen in Manhattan, were speaking the hybrid lingo known as Spanglish – the language of choice for a growing number of Hispanic Americans who view the hyphen in their heritage as a metaphor for two coexisting worlds.' (*The New York Times*, 25 March 1997)

'BILINGUAL PARENTS DISMAYED BY ENGLISH'S PULL ON CHILDREN – In Marcel A. Apple's bedroom, the book "The Three Little Pigs" rests on a shelf next to 'Mi primer libro de palabras en Español' ('My first book of Spanish Words'). The 3-year-old can sing along to both a Sesame Street song and "La Bamba" . . . But when Marcel tired of pounding on a piano one recent afternoon and sat on the lap of his Nicaraguan nanny, it was English that he spoke . . . "I try to put him in an environment where there's as much Spanish spoken as possible but it never seems to be enough," says Marcel's mother . . . "He knows he can speak in English and people could understand him." . . . what new immigrant families across the nation are learning, as their predecessors did before them, is that the power of American culture, and particularly, the lure of television, is so strong that it is a challenge to raise a child who can speak a foreign language fluently. Parents send their children to foreign countries for summer vacations, hire bilingual nannies and read bedtime stories in a cacophony of tongues, all in an effort to pass on the family's language, give the children a linguistic advantage for the future or simply enrich them culturally. Still, the languages, the parents say, often lose out to television, schools and peer pressure.' (*The New York Times*, 31 August 1996)

'LANGUAGE GAP PLAYS ROLE IN HUNDREDS OF AIR DEATHS – By treaty, controllers and pilots in international aviation are all supposed to speak English, but hundreds of passengers and crew members have died in crashes that were caused at least in part by language problems . . . the language problem can be horrifyingly stark, as in the crash of a China Northern jet on Nov. 13, 1993, on approach to Urumqi, in China's far west. The plane . . . had a ground-proximity warning system, which can sense when an approach is too steep and give an aural warning of "Pull up! Pull up!" The plane descended too steeply, but the crew did not notice because of fog. The cockpit voice recorder showed that 10 seconds before impact, the ground-proximity warning system gave its alarm – in English. Just before impact, one crew member said to the other, in Chinese, "What does 'pull up' mean?" (*The New York Times*, 9 December 1996)

'AN ISLAND AFLAME: TAMIL SEPARATISTS, BACKED BY INDIANS, TEAR-ING SRI LANKA APART – [T]he Sinhalese majority and Tamil separatists, backed by 50 million Tamils in south India, are fighting again . . . Origins of Tamil–Sinhalese friction are ancient, but they also have lived in harmony for centuries, even intermarried. Tamils are considered . . . more successful and prosperous . . . than the Sinhalese. But the contemporary troubles started in 1956 after the government declared a "Sinhalese-only" policy that made Sinhalese the only official language of government business . . . Resentment from Tamil-speakers and ethnic turmoil turned into waves of riots, culminating in an independence movement several years ago.' (*Pittsburgh Post-Gazette*, 23 April 1987)

'ALBANIA BILINGUAL RULE – Hundreds of ethnic Albanians clashed with police during a protest against a new rule requiring bilingual education, and nine officers were injured, the official Tanjug [Yugo-slavia] news agency reported yesterday . . . the predominately young demonstrators in Kumanovo, about 260 miles south of Belgrade, were demanding that local schools form separate classes taught exclusively in the Albanian language.' (*Pittsburgh Post-Gazette*, 30 August 1988)

'TURKEY: TEACHERS' UNION OFFICER TO BE JAILED FOR 8 YEARS, BARRED FOR LIFE FROM TEACHING – Suleyman Yasar, a 37-year-old primary school teacher, is now serving an eight-year sentence . . . Amnesty International believes he was imprisoned for his nonviolent union activities. Yasar had been vice president of the Turkish teachers' association Tob-Der . . . The charges include founding and leading an association that promotes domination of one social class, propagandizing for separatism and communism, and breaching laws on organizational activity. The separatism charge stems from the teacher association's recognition of the Kurdish ethnic minority. The association supported the right of Kurds to be educated in their own language. Turkish authorities have banned use of the Kurdish language.' (*Amnesty Action*, the Amnesty International newspaper, April 1984)

'BREAKING THROUGH THE LANGUAGE BARRIER – At the height of the Vietnam war, an American television newsman visited a South Vietnamese village and interviewed its residents. After initial questions, the newsman, through his South Vietnamese interpreter, asked: "Do they have any faith in their present government?" The interpreter translated into Vietnamese: "Was the crop good? Count up to 12." While one villager counted to 12, another said: "The crop was good. We live happily." The interpreter translated into English: "We are confused. We do not understand." Millions of Americans who saw the entire interview on a network news program were completely unaware of the interpreter's fraudulent translation . . . A copy of [this interview] was obtained by the United States Government, which uses it to demonstrate the crucial importance of language training . . . Linguistic barriers and failure of the State Department's bureaucracy to quickly respond to them are now viewed as principal reasons for many American miscalculations in the war.' (*The Bangkok Post*, 20 April 1973)

As these varied quotations suggest, the extraordinarily complex social and political ramifications of language contacts can reach into all areas of human society and human life. They can also be the subject of a long book, but not this book: by an admittedly arbitrary choice, my focus is instead on the linguistic results of language contact and the processes through which they come about. In this chapter, therefore, my goal will be to offer a few glimpses of the richness and diversity of this topic, rather than to cover the ground comprehensively. After a preliminary glance at multilingualism around the world, we will consider in turn the widely varying attitudes toward multilingualism; the status and problems of multilingualism in nations; national language policies and language planning; a more detailed description of one multilingual nation, India; some social and political consequences of multilingualism; and multilingualism in individuals.

Multilingual nations, multilingual people

The quotations above, though they reflect different viewpoints, are not truly representative of worldwide products of language contact – mainly because most are from newspaper articles. Newspaper articles normally represent only the kinds of stories that become news, and most news is bad rather than good. But the vast majority of language contacts are not newsworthy; they are ordinary parts of everyday lives all over the world, as with the Thai schoolteacher in the second example, the Mlabri speaker in the third, the Chinookan multilinguals in the fourth, and the Hispanic American television personalities in the fifth. How many everyday lives? That question cannot be answered definitively: François Grosjean, a specialist in bilingualism, reported in 1982 that 'no really precise statistics exist concerning the number and distribution of speakers of two or more languages', and the situation does not seem to have changed appreciably since then. We do know, however, that bilingualism is much more widespread than monolingual citizens of countries traditionally dominated by English (the United States, the United Kingdom, Canada, Australia, and New Zealand) tend to believe. The idea that monolingualism is the human norm is a myth.

If we hopscotch across continents and national boundaries, we can find any number of places where many or most people are bilingual. In North America, speakers of Spanglish (see the 1997 newspaper excerpt at the beginning of this chapter) speak both Spanish and English, and all speakers of Montana Salish and most other Native American languages in the United States are fully bilingual in English. (In Canada there are more monolingual speakers of Native languages.) In MesoAmerica there are many monolingual Indians, especially in regions far from highways and cities, but there are also a great many who are bilingual in Spanish; the same is true of South America, where many Indians speak Spanish – or, in Brazil, Portuguese – as well as a tribal language. Moreover, Natives throughout the Americas often speak more than one Indian language; many Montana Salish speakers, for instance, speak Kutenai or Coeur d'Alene or another nearby Native language in addition to Montana Salish and English. Some countries in the Americas also have sizable immigrant populations who have (so far) maintained their ethnic-heritage language; the United States is prominent among these, with bilingual communities of German speakers, Chinese speakers, and others. A number of creole languages are also spoken in the New World, and their speakers are often bilingual: Gullah speakers in the southeastern United States also speak English, some Haitian Creole speakers in Haiti also speak French, most Jamaican Creole speakers in Jamaica also speak some English, and so forth. In Suriname in South America, some speakers of the English-vocabulary creole Ndyuka also speak a pidgin language based on Ndyuka and the Indian language Trio.

Moving to Europe, if we visit the Netherlands – to give just one example – it will be difficult to find a monolingual Dutch speaker under the age of 50 in the larger cities; in fact, it is difficult to find an urban Dutch speaker who does not also speak English. Bretons who speak Breton are almost sure to speak French as well, Basques tend to speak both Basque and Spanish or

French (depending on whether they live on the Spanish or the French side of the border), speakers of Catalan are likely to be fluent in Spanish, most Welsh and Irish Gaelic speakers also speak English, Polish speakers often know some German too, and so forth.

In Africa, educated people in former English colonies speak English as well as one or more African languages, educated people in former French colonies speak French as well as their native languages, a great many Africans speak at least one indigenous lingua franca (e.g. Swahili, or Hausa, or Kitúba) in addition to a local language, and there are also many Africans who speak more than one local language.

Multilingualism in Asia was exemplified at the beginning of this chapter by a schoolteacher in Thailand. It may be easy to find people who are comparably multilingual in India and a number of other Asian countries. Many elderly Vietnamese speakers in Vietnam speak French because of the earlier French occupation of their country, and many younger Vietnamese speakers speak English as a result of contact with American troops during the Vietnam War. The tiny nation of Singapore has four official languages – Malay (which is also a national language) and three immigrant languages, Chinese, Tamil, and English – and most of its citizens know more than one of the official languages. Members of minority linguistic groups in China are likely to know some variety of Chinese as well as their heritage language, and all Chinese citizens with any education will have been exposed to the common language, Putonghua Chinese. In northern Asia, many speakers of minority languages in Asian parts of Russia speak Russian as well as their native languages.

Australian Aborigines speak English and/or an English-vocabulary creole in addition to their native languages; many immigrant groups from Europe and Asia have preserved their ethnic languages in Australia in addition to learning English; and in the more traditional Aboriginal groups in the northern part of the country there is institutionalized multilingualism among the different linguistic groups.

One might expect that remote Pacific islands would have a homogeneous population and a single indigenous language. And so they do, many of them; but they were also colonized by Europeans, so many Tahitians speak French as well as Tahitian, many Samoans speak English as well as Samoan, and so forth.

Attitudes toward multilingualism

Is it good to be multilingual? The answer depends on who is answering the question, and when, and under what circumstances.

People view multilingualism in different and often conflicting ways: it is a mark of high education and great prestige, it is a social or even a psychological handicap, it is a political liability, it is a necessity for daily living, it is an unremarkable fact of life, it is a vital part of a person's ethnic identity. Which of these perceptions is valid? All of them, of course, except for the one about the psychological handicap. In part this is because people's views on language, as on other social issues, are likely to be emotional responses rather than objective conclusions based on solid evidence. On such issues most people seem to subscribe, consciously or subconsciously, to the 'my-mind-is-made-up-don't-confuse-me-with-facts' school of thought. This is not to say that all these views are subjective; in particular, for many people around the world knowing more than one language is a requisite for daily living. Otherwise, too, the distribution of the various attitudes depends on the particular culture and regional setting. Still, two or more of these attitudes can coexist in the same people. In the United States, for instance, knowing more than one language is often considered a sign of intelligence, diligence, and a privileged education – but only if the possessor of this skill is a native speaker of English. Some of the same people who admire an English speaker for knowing other languages are conspicuously unimpressed by reciprocal skills in a nonnative speaker of English, on the apparent assumption that speaking English is just normal. (This is the same attitude reflected in the old story – apocryphal, one hopes – about the rural American preacher who said, 'If English was good enough for Jesus, it's good enough for you!')

Here are some illustrations of different attitudes toward multilingualism. First, take the view that multilingualism is a highly valued skill that confers prestige on the multilingual person. The Croatian folk saying and the comments about multilingualism among Pacific Northwest Native Americans that are quoted at the beginning of this chapter are just two of many possible examples; here is another typical instance. In Native communities around Prince George, British Columbia, it is considered highly prestigious to know several languages, so people are proud of knowing several 'dialects' (actually separate languages, as they are not all mutually intelligible) of the Athabaskan language Carrier and one or more of the neighboring Athabaskan languages as well, for instance Babine. The linguist William Poser, when collecting data from a Carrier elder in 1998, was given both a Carrier translation and a Babine translation for each item; his consultant commented that Poser really should know both Carrier and Babine in order to be properly educated.

This picture of multilingualism contrasts sharply with the most extreme view on the other side – that multilingualism is a psychological handicap. The old notion that growing up bilingual damages a child is no longer considered viable by psychologists, but it persists in nonscholarly circles, as Annick De Houwer notes in an important article on the methodology of studying bilingual first-language acquisition:

> The regrettable impact of . . . the large-scale methodological errors in studies of the purported inferior intellectual capacities of bilingual

children and adults . . . [is] still with us, and it takes many years and a
great deal of outreach effort to set the record straight. In the meantime,
many parents, educators, medical doctors, and speech clinicians everywhere in the industrialized world continue to believe that young
children cannot successfully learn two languages, and that a bilingual
upbringing is in some way harmful to them.

Although the notion that bilingualism is psychologically harmful is scien-
tifically unjustified, many people, including some scholars, still argue that
multilingualism is a social handicap. One consequence of the 'melting pot'
tradition in the United States is a widespread belief that immigrants must
abandon their ethnic-heritage languages promptly and shift to English in
order to become true Americans. This belief is held by many recent immigrants as well as by the offspring and descendants of immigrants, and it is
also aimed at nonimmigrant nonnative English speakers, Native Americans
as well as (in particular) French and Creole speakers in Louisiana and
Spanish speakers in the Southwest. Sometimes the belief has been elevated to
public policy. Early in the twentieth century, for instance, a government
policy of assimilating Native Americans to Anglo culture included vigorous –
and largely successful – efforts to force them to abandon their native
languages in favor of English; and the modern 'Official English' movement
in the United States has led to the adoption of English as the official language
in over twenty states, an approach usually accompanied by efforts to
eliminate bilingual education programs so as to encourage monolingualism
in English.

   In this domain, and often elsewhere as well, the issue of multilingualism as
a social problem overlaps with the view of multilingualism as a political
liability. This view is pervasive; it can be seen in the scholarly literature as
well as in the world at large. In fact, it is quite startling to see how many
scholars refer to bilingualism/multilingualism as a problem, as a phenomenon that is linked to conflict. William F. Mackey, for instance, commented
in 1967 that 'bilingualism . . . is a problem which affects the majority of the
world's population'. Louis-Jean Calvet published a book in French in 1987,
and in English translation in 1998, entitled *Language Wars and Linguistic
Politics*, in which he argues that conflict is inherent in all multilingual
settings. And Peter Nelde, a prominent specialist in contact linguistics,
suggests in a 1992 article that we should 'assume that conflict represents
a counterpart to language contact, and is interdependently connected with
it', and a glance at his bibliography shows that this view is not idiosyncratic:
there are book titles like *Sprachen im Konflikt* ['Languages in conflict'] and
Spracherwerb, Sprachkontakt, Sprachkonflikt ['Language acquisition, language contact, language conflict'], several articles with similar titles are cited,
and Nelde himself wrote an article entitled 'Sprachkontakt als Kulturkonflikt' ['Language contact as culture conflict'] and edited a book called

Languages in Contact and in Conflict. It is not hard to find a reason for this emphasis on language contact as language conflict: these authors focus on multilingualism in modern nation-states, in which problems of overt or covert suppression of minority languages are all too common. The image of multilingualism as a political problem appears in related contexts too, in locutions like Nelde's reference to bearing 'the burden of bilingualism' and titles like that of a recent influential book by Carol Myers-Scotton, *Duelling Languages: Grammatical Structure in Codeswitching.* But bilingualism and multilingualism are by no means always associated with language conflicts, even in modern nation-states: in many societies there are cultural values favoring multilingualism, such as the Carriers' pride in their command of several languages and the elite bilingualism found in the regular use of French by upper-class Russians in the nineteenth century. And in smaller societies, as no doubt in the past more generally, multilingualism is much less likely to be a source or symptom of conflict than an integral part of a culture, an ordinary way of interacting with neighbors and often kinfolk. (Of course the authors who write about contact as conflict would not disagree with the claim that some language contacts lack any conflict component; their emphasis on conflict is determined by their focus on particular sorts of contact situations.)

The view of multilingualism as a political problem is of course not confined to the scholarly literature; both dominant-language speakers and linguistic minorities commonly share the scholars' opinion. In one study, for example, Nelde asked eight hundred minority-language speakers in one city for their views on language conflict, and two of their most frequent responses were 'belief in the superiority of the dominant standard language' and 'more possibilities of social advance with the dominant language'. And recently Nelde described a particularly interesting 1997 language survey conducted in southeastern Belgium in the town of Arlon, where both French and German are spoken. Two mid-twentieth-century census reports for this village contrast dramatically on the language question: in the 1930 census, 97 per cent of the population reported German as their main language, and only 3 per cent reported French; but in the 1947 census, taken shortly after World War II (during which Belgium suffered under German occupiers), the figures were exactly reversed – 97 per cent reported French as their main language, 3 per cent reported German. This striking reversal is apparently due primarily to changed attitudes rather than to changed demographics, a point that is underlined by the 1997 study. Two interviewers canvassed one street, one taking the left side and the other taking the right side. The right-side interviewer wore a suit and tie and spoke in French, asking the householders, 'Of course you speak French here?' The left-side interviewer dressed casually in blue jeans, spoke to the householders in German as well as French, and asked questions about aspects of German culture. The results of the survey showed – but of course only apparently, an artifact of the different interviewing strategies – that the right-side residents spoke French, while the left-side residents spoke mainly German.

The remaining three attitudes mentioned at the beginning of this section – multilingualism as a requisite for daily life, as an unremarkable fact of life, and as a vital part of a person's ethnic identity – can be illustrated by overlapping examples, since they often go together. One example that has already been mentioned is the Dhuwal child who grows up bilingual; the example of the multilingual Thai schoolteacher is relevant for the first two of these attitudes . But needing a second language for daily living may be, and very often is, an unwelcome burden, as in the case of minority-language speakers studied by Nelde and other scholars who investigate language conflict. It is easier, therefore, to find examples for the necessity attitude that do not include the other two views than vice versa.

Varying community attitudes toward the importance of language as a marker of ethnic identity are easy to find. One especially sharp contrast stands out in two book reviews in the same issue of the journal *Anthropological Linguistics*: the endangered Tibeto-Burman language Chantyal is being abandoned by its speakers because 'their language is not seen as a key feature of their Chantyal identity', while extensive multilingualism and language maintenance are the norm in the Vaupès River basin in Colombia and Brazil because 'the rules governing marriage and residence in communities throughout the area are determined by language, which . . . functions as a "symbol of social identity"'.

One nation, more than one language

Obviously no nation is monolingual in the sense that all its citizens speak one and only one language, and probably no nation is monolingual in the less trivial sense that everyone who lives there speaks the same language natively. Most, perhaps all, of the many nations that have only a single official language also have minority languages within their boundaries – Australia (English), Brazil (Portuguese), Cambodia (Khmer), Ethiopia (Amharic), Guinea (French), Hungary (Hungarian), Iran (Farsi [Persian]), and Sudan (Arabic), to name just a few. A possible exception to this generalization is Iceland, which has a remarkably homogeneous population and just one national language, Icelandic. But contrast the Icelandic case with Australia, which is not particularly unusual in its level of multilingualism. Here many of the two hundred and fifty or so Aboriginal languages still survive, though the country's stock of indigenous languages declined drastically in the twentieth century both in numbers of languages and in numbers of speakers. And besides the indigenous languages there are two other kinds of minority languages in Australia: a few English-lexicon creoles and a much larger number of languages spoken by immigrants from Europe and Asia, among them French, German, Italian, Greek, Ukrainian, Polish, Hungarian, Portuguese, Russian, Turkish, Arabic, and Chinese. Most members of the minority groups speak English as well as the language of their ethnic heritage.

Then there are the many countries with more than one official language, and the even larger number of countries with one official national language but also official regional languages and/or quasi-official national languages. Ex-colonies very often retain the language of their former colonial rulers as an official language, sometimes (but not always) in conjunction with an indigenous language. In Africa, for instance, there are both countries with side-by-side official languages – as in Botswana (English and Setswana), Malawi (English and Chichewa), and Tanzania (English and Swahili) – and countries with one official language beside very important but unofficial national African languages: Central African Republic (French, with Sango widely spoken), Mozambique (Portuguese, with Swahili widely spoken), Nigeria (English, with Nigerian Pidgin English, Hausa, Yoruba, and Igbo also in wide use), and Sierra Leone (English, with Krio widely spoken). It should be emphasized that the single official language in the latter group of countries is likely to be spoken only by a rather small minority of the population, even when, as in Central African Republic and Sierra Leone, another language that is more widely known could have been used. An example: in Zimbabwe, the official language is English, which is spoken by the country's 250,000 whites; but the major Bantu language, Shona, has about four million speakers, and Ndebele, the second most widely spoken Bantu language, has about a million (these figures are from *ca.* 1985). This points to a salient fact about the selection of a national language: the choice does not always fall on the language with the most speakers.

Significantly, several of the official and unofficial national African languages are lingua francas with extended usage among nonnative speakers. Swahili is the most important non-European lingua franca in Africa: Arab traders spread it many centuries ago westward from its original homeland on the coast of what is now eastern Tanzania, and it is now spoken by millions of people in Kenya, Mozambique, Tanzania, Uganda, and elsewhere. Hausa, the native language of a numerous people of northern Nigeria and nearby regions, and Sango, a pidgin based on African languages, are important lingua francas in their respective areas; the Bantu-based creole Kitúba is the most widely used language of Congo, and the English-lexicon creole Krio is an important language in Sierra Leone.

What does it mean for a country to have an official language, or more than one? The answer to this question varies from country to country, of course, but it is safe to assume that an official language is of more social and political significance than, for instance, a national bird (like the bald eagle of the United States). (Before going further with the topic of official languages, I should mention that the information in this section – which is, to the best of my knowledge, true as of the time of writing, in mid-1999 – is all too likely to be out of date by the time people are reading this book: official languages, and even countries, come and go with considerable frequency.) An official language must be a written language, for one thing, because it must be usable for running the government and at least parts of the educational system. In countries that have chosen previously unwritten languages as (one of) their official language(s), efforts have had to be made to develop writing systems for those languages. Nowadays most languages that become official will already be written at least to a limited extent, but they need to be further developed before they can be used effectively for national administrative and educational purposes. Sometimes the official language coexists with one or more designated 'national languages', which are typically not widely used for writing but which are spoken by a high percentage of the population. Countries with both official and national languages are especially common in Africa, for instance in Senegal, where French is the only official language but Wolof is used as a lingua franca throughout the country and is spoken by most of the population; Botswana, where English is official but Setswana is the national language, spoken by almost the entire population; and the Central African Republic, where French is official but Sango, the lingua franca of most of the country, is the national language.

In a new and (relatively speaking) linguistically homogeneous nation, the official language can help to establish a national identity; or an official language may serve – inadvertently or otherwise – to favor one of a country's ethnic groups over all the others; or an indigenous official language may signal a nation's definitive emergence from under the shadow of a former colonial power; or an official language may be chosen because it is a major world language that will help the country's citizens play a role (especially an economic role) on the international stage. And sometimes the diverse potential functions of an official language come into conflict. In a new nation that is linguistically heterogeneous, the problems involved in selecting and establishing a single national language can be daunting.

Language policies and language planning

The process of selecting a single national language, or multiple national languages, and developing the chosen language(s) for designated administrative and educational uses is the province of language policy-makers and language planners. As noted above, a newly official language, if it was not previously used for administrative or educational purposes, must be developed before it can be used effectively. In practice, this means – among other things – first devising or choosing a writing system, if the language was completely unwritten; selecting or codifying a standard variety that will be used in official documents and teaching materials; writing and printing documents and educational materials, including grammar books and readers; promoting and supporting the use of the language for all desired purposes, a process that is likely to involve training civil servants and teachers to switch from languages that were previously used for these purposes; and, very often, coining and publicizing new words for things that people had previously not talked about in the relevant language(s).

Language policies, either covert or overt, set the development process in motion. They also affect the status, and thus potentially the use for official and unofficial purposes, of both dominant and minority languages. A government's choice to forbid, permit, encourage, or require bilingual education is one important factor in minority-language maintenance, for instance. We saw one effect of educational policy in Chapter 1, in the example of Native American children being punished in boarding schools for speaking their own languages; this was one result of the United States government's effort to force Native Americans to assimilate to the dominant culture.

Restrictive pro-English policies have not always been implemented so severely in the United States, however. In a 1998 case study, Susannah Davis found that the state of Nebraska has not made strenuous efforts to implement its long-standing language law. Nebraska has had an 'official English' law since 1920, when Article I, Section 27 of the Nebraska Constitution was adopted with the following wording: 'The English language is hereby declared to be the official language of this state, and all official proceedings, records and publications shall be in such language, and the common school branches shall be taught in said language in public, private, denominational and parochial schools.' This law was inspired by anti-German sentiment, which in turn was mainly due to the status of Germans as the nation's enemy in World War I (1914–18); by 1889 Nebraska had a large bilingual German-American population, and between then and 1920 German was the medium of instruction and/or an academic subject in many public and religious schools. But the state has not tried to enforce the 1920 law in recent years, and in fact the law has not been tested in the courts. The state Personnel Department has no language policy because 'it hasn't come up', the written driver's license examination may be taken in Spanish or Vietnamese (German is no longer the state's most important minority language), Spanish-speaking staff are available to help clients of the state's Department of Health and Human Services, the state's Department of Education has no ban on bilingual education (though there are no state-sponsored bilingual education programs), and state courts must provide interpreters when a judge approves a request to appoint one. Nebraska's 'official English' law has apparently had little lasting effect on the use of languages other than English for official purposes. In other words, making policy is one thing; implementing it is something else entirely.

Language policies vary widely from country to country, of course, and within the same country from one era to the next. In the former Soviet Union, for example, language policy changed dramatically as time went on. Lenin, the head of state from the beginning of the Soviet Union in 1917 until his death in 1924, believed that Russian should not be favored or promoted at the expense of other languages of the U.S.S.R., and he guaranteed equality for all of the country's many languages. (More than a hundred different languages are spoken in the former U.S.S.R.) One result of this policy was a major government effort to produce writing systems for previously unwritten languages and to introduce many more languages into the schools. Some years after Stalin became the head of the Soviet government, however, the policy shifted to a pro-Russian stance, and speakers of minority languages were required to learn Russian. To make it easier for them to learn Russian, which is written in the Cyrillic alphabet, new Cyrillic alphabets were devised to replace the Latin-based writing systems that had been developed for minority languages under Lenin and during Stalin's early years in power (Stalin ruled from 1928 until his death in 1953). After Khrushchev took power in 1958, Russian was promoted even more vigorously, both as the major language of education and as the lingua franca for the entire country.

Other countries have consistently egalitarian language policies, at least as far as non-Native languages are concerned. Finland is one example, with both Finnish and Swedish enjoying official status (though its official status is not preventing Swedish from losing speakers), but the minority Sámi language has not been so favored; Canada is another, with both French and English official (but again, French is disadvantaged, given the vast number of English speakers in North America, and Native languages do not have the same official status as English and French). Post-apartheid South Africa, with its eleven official languages, accords each of them (and other languages too) equal rights, this policy is in sharp contrast with South Africa under apartheid, when there were just two official languages, Afrikaans and English, and a restrictive language policy specifying which languages would be used in educational settings for the different legally specified racial groups.

Not surprisingly, the problems faced by those in charge of developing new national languages also vary from country to country. One interesting example is the Republic of Namibia, home to numerous African languages. For many years the country was administered by South Africa, and its official languages were English and Afrikaans; after independence, however, English was chosen as the only official language – in spite of the fact that very few Namibians spoke it (perhaps 5 per cent of the population). Still, Namibia is concerned to develop national languages, i.e. African languages, for educational purposes. Accordingly, in 1995 a workshop was held at the National Institute for Educational Development for the purpose of exploring these issues. In his opening statement at the workshop, Mr. John Mutorwa, the Minister of Educational Development, declared that 'Language policy formulation in a multilingual society, like ours, is quite a difficult task. I would venture to add that such a task becomes even more difficult when it comes to the actual practical implementation of a language policy.' Mr. Mutorwa could have been speaking for language policy-makers and language planners around the world. The workshop's proceedings, entitled

African Languages in Basic Education, were published in 1997. The publishers' advertising blurb sums up the goals of the government and the workshop participants:

> Before independence 'mother-tongue instruction' in Namibia was used to limit access to jobs and responsibilities in society. It was also accompanied by poorly designed curricula and learning materials. Now the prospects for the development of democracy in Namibia depend to a large extent on whether it is possible to revalue national languages as a means to empower people and to stimulate and create a literate environment in these African languages. Formal as well as non-formal education can make an important contribution in achieving this objective. The papers which are published in this volume . . . reflect the current situation and strike a balance between what has been achieved and, more importantly, what must be done to upgrade the national languages in education and beyond.

Language planning efforts and difficulties are by no means confined to newly independent nations. The phenomenon of the language academy is widespread. The world's most famous language academy is surely the Académie française of France. Founded in 1635, the Académie's role is to approve new words in the language, decide which linguistic structures are part of the standard grammar, and fix the language's orthography. Primarily, the Académie française tries to preserve French in what they view as its pristine form – hence their strenuous efforts to keep out, or evict, anglicisms that have crept into the language. Some other language academies devote their efforts to creation rather than to preservation. Israel, for instance, has a language academy whose purpose is to devise Hebrew words for modern technical domains and thus to make loanwords (especially from English) unnecessary. Some years ago, for instance, the focus was on words for the field of photography: the academy produced a list of suitable words and distributed it to photography shops and professional photographers in order to encourage specialists to use the new words. Similarly, in Turkey the Turkish Language Association was founded in 1932 for the purpose of replacing Arabic and Persian words with 'pure' Turkish words (which were invented, based on Turkish roots). A few years earlier, in 1928, an alphabet reform replaced the Arabic alphabet that had been used for Turkish with a Latin-based alphabet.

A final example of language policies and their implementation is from the New World, beginning as early 1526, even before the establishment of the Académie française: Charles V of Spain decreed in 1526 that the Crown's intention of civilizing Native groups and converting them to Christianity must be explained to all the Native groups in Mexico in their own languages; in the sixteenth and seventeenth centuries, Catholic priests were obliged to learn Nahuatl. As it turned out, this was just the first step in a long and ever-changing series of language policies for Mexico (New Spain). In 1529 a specifically educational dimension was added to the policy when a few schools were established, both elementary and higher schools, for the religious instruction of elite Native boys, who were taught Latin (among other things). In 1542, Charles V assigned the Castilianization and conversion of the Natives to the friars, who began to learn the Native languages for this purpose. Still later, in 1550, Charles V decided to speed up the process by decreeing that the Natives must learn Spanish in order to better understand Catholicism; he also funded the new bilingual education program by providing salaries for Native teachers of Spanish. But progress continued to be slow, and in 1570 Philip II, who had succeeded Charles V on the throne, established Nahuatl as the official language of the Indians of New Spain – in the belief that Natives of all linguistic backgrounds would learn Nahuatl more easily than Spanish. This policy was again reversed in 1634, when Philip IV argued that Natives should learn Spanish so that they could be controlled more easily. Several policy shifts later, and some years after independence from Spain was achieved (in 1821), Mexico's Academy of Language was established in 1835, for the purpose of preserving the purity of Spanish by keeping out all influences from indigenous languages. Policies continued to fluctuate. Since 1970, however, Mexican states have had three choices: (1) they can use Native languages throughout elementary school; (2) they can use Native languages for instruction, introducing Spanish as soon as possible; or (3) they can use Spanish only, so that Native children are immersed in Spanish as soon as they come to school.

A case study: India

One particularly complex case of national multilingualism, with prominent and difficult issues of language policy arising after independence, is India. Because India was united under British rule in the nineteenth century, a merging of separate states which had their own languages and traditions, English was the first language of national administration of India as a whole. In the independence movement of the mid-twentieth century, Mahatma Gandhi (though a native speaker of Gujarati himself) argued strongly for an indigenous national language, specifically Hindi, which had a strategic location (the capital city, New Delhi, is in Hindi-speaking territory) and more speakers than of the country's other hundred to two hundred languages. Gandhi's opposition to English was blunt: 'The only use you can make of English,' he said, 'is to forget it as quickly as you can.' Accordingly, after independence was granted in 1947, the new Constitution of India named Hindi, written in the devanāgarī writing system, as the country's official national language, though this designation was approved only by a one-vote margin and remained highly controversial. Moreover, it was already apparent when the Constitution was drafted that it would be impossible to replace English with Hindi overnight: even aside from the fact that most Indians did not know any Hindi at all, it would inevitably take much time and an immense amount of work to prepare documents, train teachers, and do all the other things required to implement the transition. (For instance, soon after independence the Government of India established a Board of Scientific and Technical Terminology to devise Hindi terminology in these domains, and in 1948 the linguist Baburam Saksena was appointed by the President of the Constituent Assembly of India to recommend a system of shorthand for Hindi and a keyboard for devanāgarī typewriters.) So the Constitution also named English as a temporary official national language, with a time limit – by 1965 English was supposed to have been replaced completely by Hindi.

But 1965 came and went, and English remained a vital part of the Indian environment. It still remains. According to the Official Languages Act of 1963, even after Hindi officially replaced English, English would continue to be 'the subsidiary official language' for as long as necessary. Part of the reason is that English is, and has been for decades, the world's major international lingua franca, so that educated Indians still have a strong motivation for learning English. The country's system of higher education, especially in the sciences, relies on English. Another part of the reason is that a great many Indians, especially Dravidian speakers in the south, strenuously resisted the idea of replacing English with Hindi. With the passing decades the image of English has changed, though not for everyone everywhere, from that of a conqueror's language to that of a regionally neutral language, one whose use prevents any single indigenous language from gaining prestige and privileging its speakers at the expense of other languages and their speakers. Many Tamils, for instance, viewed Hindi as inferior to their own language in culture and history (Tamil has a written tradition dating back to around the time of the birth of Jesus, much older than Hindi as a written language), and resented the notion that their language should be considered subordinate to Hindi. Indians must still learn Hindi if they wish to work for the national government, but they are much less likely to need it if they live in a state that has a different official regional language – and there are numerous such states.

Fifteen Indian languages in all enjoy official status. Fourteen of these – all but Sindhi – were designated in 1951 by the Constitution as 'the languages of India'; at that time they were spoken together by ninety-one per cent of the country's population. Forty-seven other languages and dialects were listed then as having 100,000 or more speakers each, seven hundred and twenty languages and dialects were listed as spoken by fewer people each, and another sixty-three languages were designated as non-Indian, i.e. nonindigenous – including English, which was and is spoken throughout the country by the elite class. Here is the list of the fifteen 'languages of India', with numbers of speakers according to the 1981 Census of India and the name(s) of the state(s), if any, where each language is the officially designated regional language: Hindi (264,189,057, in Uttar Pradesh, Rajasthan, Himachal Pradesh, Madhya Pradesh, and Bihar); Urdu (35,323,282, official in Jammu and Kashmir – in spite of the fact that the vast majority of Urdu speakers are elsewhere and are vastly outnumbered by Kashmiri speakers in the state), a language that is so similar to Hindi that they would be considered dialects of the same language if it were not for the fact that Urdu is spoken by Muslims and written with an Arabic script, while Hindi is spoken by Hindus and written in the devanāgarī script; Bengali (51,503,085, in West Bengal); Gujarati (33,189,039, in Gujarat); Marathi (49,624,847, in Maharashtra); Oriya (22,881,053, in Orissa); Punjabi (18,588,400, in Punjab); Kashmiri (3,174,684); Assamese (only 70,525 in the 1981 Census because no census was conducted in Assam, where Assamese is official, but 8,958,977 in the 1971 Census); Telugu (54,226,227, in Andhra Pradesh); Sindhi (1,946,278); Tamil (44,730,389, in Tamil Nadu); Kannaḍa (26,887,837, in Karnataka); Malayalam (25,952,966, in Kerala); and Sanskrit (2,946), which owes its prestigious position to the fact that it is the sacred language of Hinduism, the religion of the great majority of the country's population. Southern India, in particular, is solidly Dravidian-speaking, and Hindi has made few inroads there; the four official Dravidian languages – Telugu, Tamil, Kannaḍa, and Malayalam – are spoken in states clustered tightly in the south. (Most languages in the north of India belong to the Indic subbranch of the Indo-European language family, but there are numerous other languages there as well: Munda languages, Sino-Tibetan languages, Burushaski, and several Dravidian languages.) In fact, India has seen its share of violent death resulting from language-inspired riots, including 1966 riots in the Punjab over Hindus' objections to making Punjabi the state's official language.

In spite of the usefulness of English, its continuing status as a (or the) major lingua franca in India is a cause of controversy. A newspaper article from early 1998, entitled 'Nehru spoke it, but it's still foreign', discussed the importance of the language question during the then-ongoing national election campaign (*The New York Times*, 28 January 1998). The article began by posing a multiple-choice question: 'In India, the English language is (a) one of the few things that bind the nation together and connect it to the wider world, or (b) an oppressive legacy of colonialism that robs people of their native heritage and identity.' One official of the ruling coalition said on the campaign trail that he 'will not rest until English is driven out of the country' and declared that 'We've had enough of leaders who ask for votes in their mother tongues but spend their parliamentary tenures speaking in English.' A critic of this view argued that English is 'the most potent weapon of India's growing middle class to meet their rising expectations', but he added that '[t]he English-speaking elite are an incredibly selfish lot, aggrandizing their power at the cost of their poor brethren, which is why millions of deprived persons despise the use of English'.

India also serves as a good illustration of the degree of multilingualism that is often found in linguistically diverse environments. Like the Thai school-teacher whose linguistic dexterity was profiled at the beginning of this chapter, an educated Indian may need to learn several different languages. If her (let us assume that our educated Indian is a woman) native language is not one that is used in the schools, she will learn a more prominent regional language in her early schooling. If that is not the official language of the state she lives in, she will learn the official state language in later schooling; then, at university, she will learn English. If in addition she decides to become a government worker in New Delhi, and if Hindi is not the official regional language of her state, she must learn Hindi, which, by law, she will in any case have studied during her schooling.

Even Indians with relatively little formal education may be highly skilled multilinguals. In one of the most famous case studies in the vast language-contact literature, John J. Gumperz and Robert Wilson describe the linguistic situation in the village of Kupwar. Kupwar is located in central India, in the state of Maharashtra (whose official state language is the Indic language Marathi) very near the border of the state of Karnataka (formerly Mysore), whose official state language is the Dravidian language Kannaḍa. The village boasts four different languages and five distinct ethnic groups, and each group has its own place in the local society: the Kannaḍa-speaking Jains, the largest ethnic group in the village, are landowners, while a distinct group of Kannaḍa speakers, the Lingayats, are mostly craftsmen; the Urdu-speaking Muslims are landowners; the Marathi-speaking Untouchables are landless laborers; and the Telugu speakers are rope-makers.

The different groups in the community interact with one another every day, alternating among the different languages, and the level of multi-lingualism in the local variants of the four languages is high: Gumperz and Wilson report that almost all local men are either bilingual or multi-lingual. (They do not comment on the level of bilingualism among women. This could be because, as male outsiders, they were unable to interview women; or it could be because women were less likely to enter the workforce and more likely to remain at home in their own neighborhoods, among members of their own ethnic groups, and thus less likely to be bilingual.) Village residents hear (and perhaps speak) a less local variety of Marathi in the bazaars of the district capital and elsewhere. In addition, some, most, or all members of all four languages are exposed to Standard Marathi, the official language of Maharashtra, and some (especially the Muslims) have also learned literary Urdu. Those with sufficient formal schooling will also have studied Hindi, and some may have studied English as well. The intimacy of intergroup contacts in Kupwar is indicated by the fact that the local dialects of the four languages – two Indic languages (Marathi, Urdu) and two Dravidian languages (Kannaḍa, Telugu) – have undergone so much struc-tural convergence that, according to Gumperz and Wilson, translating a sentence word by word from any one of the languages yields a perfectly good sentence in each of the other languages. Structural changes of this sort can arise only where there is extensive multilingualism.

What are the implications of this picture for a national linguistic policy in India? There is no easy answer to this question, but two things are obvious. First, multilingualism is a fact of Indian life, not something that is imposed from above. It is true that studying Hindi is legally required of all non-Hindi-speaking schoolchildren (and conversely, Hindi-speaking children must study one of India's other official languages in school), but for many Indians, learning a new language is by no means exclusively a schoolroom activity. And second, the fact that there are several hundred indigenous Indian languages, at least sixteen of them with over a million speakers each, means that any effort to promote one of them at the expense of all the others is unlikely to be successful.

Social and political consequences of multilingualism

In many societies multilingualism is taken for granted, because it is hard to function in the culture without knowing two or more languages. The Thai schoolteacher mentioned above, the Dhuwal boy in Australia who must know his mother's clan's language as well as his father's clan's language, the educated citizen of India – all of them, and millions of others around the world, have to become bilingual or multilingual. Here is one more illustration, a kind and degree of multilingualism that was rather common among educated Jewish citizens of many European nations during the middle decades of the twentieth century. One Jewish youngster born in Latvia had, in effect, four native languages: Yiddish, Latvian, Russian, and German. He went to a German-medium school until 1933, when he was ten. In that year Latvia passed harsh racial laws which (among other things) prevented Jews from attending German or Russian schools. They were allowed to attend only Latvian schools or Jewish schools. This boy's parents, like many others, sent their son to a Hebrew-language school, thus adding a fifth language to his repertoire. One of his cousins, meanwhile, had hoped to enter medical school; the racial laws made that an impossible goal in Latvia, so she made arrangements to attend the famous medical school in Bologna, Italy, instead. She knew no Italian. But she had studied Latin, the parent language of Italian, and also French, which is closely related to Italian; on the train to Italy she read an Italian textbook – and then, shortly after arriving in Italy, began her studies in Italian. What is perhaps most noteworthy about this story is that her family and friends did not consider her to have done anything unusual in learning a new language so fast that she could undertake a rigorous course of study, more or less immediately, in which the new language was the medium of instruction.

But sometimes the coexistence of two or more languages in a single nation causes problems that range from moderate to serious. Several of the newspaper excerpts at the beginning of this chapter point to the most newsworthy consequence of national multilingualism: armed conflict. Riots triggered by language (Sinhalese vs. Tamil) in Sri Lanka, riots in Yugoslavia some time ago over Albanian vs. the official language Serbo-Croatian – such examples can easily be multiplied. For instance, the notorious 1976 anti-apartheid riots in Soweto, a township outside Johannesburg, South Africa, were triggered by a government decision to enforce the law requiring the use of Afrikaans as a medium of instruction in some schools. Of course in these cases language is not the sole cause of the conflict, or even perhaps a major cause; the root causes are to be found in social tensions arising from interethnic rivalries, especially one group's belief (justified or unjustified) that another group is getting more than its fair share of the nation's goods and services. But language serves as a powerful symbol for discontented groups.

Language serves a similar purpose in nonviolent responses to ethnic rivalries too, though these responses are less likely to be noticed by the press. In 1967, for instance, a group of Croatian cultural leaders demanded that the Yugoslav government – this was long before Croatia split off as an independent country – recognize Croatian as a separate language rather than a component of the official standard Serbo-Croatian language; their action was understood by the government (probably correctly) as a preliminary attack on the unity of the country, and the supporters of the official language split were dealt with firmly, though not fatally.

Canada provides another example, in the uneasy relations between the province of Quebec (where French is the official provincial language) and the rest of the country. In 1972 the Canadian Prime Minister, Pierre Trudeau, urged that traditionally English-speaking civil servants become bilingual in French, because French Canadians wanted the government to offer its services in French as well as in English – and because bilingualism was necessary to hold Canada together. His efforts were largely successful at the national level, but they did not head off discontent in Quebec. The province passed various laws promoting French, including a law requiring immigrants from non-English-speaking countries to send their children to French-language schools rather than English-language schools. This angered many immigrants, who preferred to have their children learn English because English is the dominant language in North America. The tension between Quebec and the rest of Canada has escalated since the 1970s, with language differences as the most prominent symbol of the tension, and it is still unclear what the eventual outcome will be.

Such examples may suggest that language contact invariably leads to political discontent and strife, but as we have already seen, this is not true. Where there are already ethnic tensions, the symbolic force of separate languages can certainly increase the tension; and this can happen even when, as in the case of Serbian and Croatian, the two 'languages' are mutually intelligible – that is, from a strictly linguistic (as opposed to a political) viewpoint, dialects of the same language. But language can unify as well as divide peoples, as can be seen in examples like Thailand, which, in spite of the presence within its boundaries of eighty languages, has long been unified linguistically with a strong focus on Standard Thai.

Moreover, several striking cases show that new contact languages can be created in order to serve as a symbol of a new group's identity. The best-known example is Michif, which is still spoken on at least one Native American reservation, the Turtle Mountain Reservation of North Dakota, and also by a scattering of people in several western Canadian provinces and neighboring northern tier states of the United States. The Métis, a mixed-blood population with (largely) French-speaking fathers and (largely) Cree-speaking mothers, arose as a new ethnic group during the middle decades of the eighteenth century, in the Red River valley of Manitoba. Some Métis speak a language called Michif, whose structure and lexicon are divided between French and Cree: the noun phrases are almost entirely French, but the verb phrases and sentence structure are Cree. Although the precise time and place of origin are not documented for Michif, it seems clear that the language arose to serve the new identity of the Métis people. (See Chapter 8 for a more detailed description of the history and structure of Michif, and for discussion of comparable cases elsewhere in the world.)

These few comments have barely scratched the surface of this vast and intricate topic; but for this book, except as the issues arise in other contexts below and in later chapters, this sketchy coverage will have to suffice.

Multilingualism in individuals: learning and using two or more languages

In principle a nation could be bilingual or multilingual even if it were populated entirely by monolinguals. The chances of finding an actual nation with such an extreme gap between the country's overall linguistic makeup and its citizens' linguistic skills are vanishingly small, but the fact that it is conceivable in principle underlines the difference between multilingualism at the national level and multilingualism at the individual level. And in fact there are countries where official multilingualism coexists with largely monolingual territorial divisions: Switzerland, as noted earlier, is such an example, at least for many of its German- and French-speaking citizens (though of course there are also many Swiss citizens who are bilingual or multilingual). Once we switch our attention to multilingual individuals rather than multilingual nations, however, we are dealing with different sorts of issues.

First, why does a person in a particular culture become bilingual or multilingual? The reasons are as varied as cultures, and some have already been touched on. Some are social, when group norms require or at least favor bilingualism, so that prestige or full membership in the group or simply the need to communicate provides the motivation for language learning. In what is perhaps the simplest case, if two people marry but share no common language, at least one of them will have to learn a second language in order to be able to talk to her (or his, but usually her) spouse; war brides brought to the United States by soldiers returning from Germany and Japan after World War II or from Vietnam after the Vietnam War found themselves in this position. But foreign travel is not the only setting where this motive arises: in Papua New Guinea, for instance, one of the reasons for the spread of the lingua franca Tok Pisin was marriages between people who spoke different local languages and needed Tok Pisin as a family language.

Some reasons are political, as when South African black citizens during the apartheid era had to learn some Afrikaans because the Afrikaans-speaking policemen insisted on being addressed in their own language. In Russia, citizens must use Russian if they have dealings with the national government. Here too, as with language attitudes, social and political reasons overlap, and both also overlap with economic reasons for bilingualism. But the overlap is not complete: one major economic reason for bilingualism in the modern world is the need to know English in order to carry out most large-scale international business. This is true not only for people at the top of the business hierarchy, but also for lower-paid employees of international companies, such as secretaries, for whom bilingualism or even multilingualism is likely to be a job qualification.

Finally, some reasons for language learning are religious. In order to participate fully in religious activities, Muslims need some knowledge of Arabic, Jews need some knowledge of Hebrew, Egyptian Coptic Christians need some knowledge of Coptic, Orthodox Slavic Christians need some knowledge of Church Slavic, Roman Catholics used to need some knowledge of Latin, and so forth. But religious motives do not necessarily produce active bilinguals, and the kinds of knowledge required for religious participation do not always qualify under the definition of a bilingual as someone who uses two languages regularly.

A second issue concerns the age of the language learner. Learning two languages from birth, or bilingual first-language acquisition, is a different process from sequential bilingualism in which a person grows up monolingual and only then learns another language. These two processes have been studied in two largely separate and independent research traditions, bilingual first-language acquisition and second-language acquisition; the first tradition is connected both to contact linguistics and to research into monolingual first-language acquisition, while the second tradition is closely allied to the field of applied linguistics, in particular language teaching in schools.

One crucial question in the study of bilingual first-language acquisition has to do with the nature of the learning environment. The two most important features of the learning environment are (of course) the language(s) used by the child in interactions with caregivers at home and with others outside the home. A common home-language pattern, especially when the two parents speak different languages natively, is the 'one person, one language' system, where in principle the child converses with each parent exclusively in his or her own language. (In practice, there is very often some slippage; for instance, if one parent's language is also that of the surrounding community, the other parent is likely to use that language with the child sometimes.) Of course this pattern can be extended if there are other languages in the child's environment. For instance, a two-year-old child in Szeged, Hungary, speaks English with his American father, Hungarian with his Hungarian mother, and Russian with his mother's parents, whose home language is Russian. Another common pattern is the use of one language at home, where both parents speak it to each other and to the child, but that of the surrounding community in an outside environment (e.g. nursery school) in which the child hears and speaks a different language. In this case, as with the 'one person, one language' system, the child's languages are environment-specific: each language is appropriate only in certain environments. A third common pattern is mixed usage, where one or both parents, and maybe parts of the community too, are bilingual and use both languages in talking to the child. And then there are the various permutations of these patterns, depending on whether one or both parents are bilingual, on the level and distribution of bilingualism in the community, and so forth.

An obvious question that arises here is whether these different bilingual learning environments correlate with differences in the children's linguistic behavior. There is some evidence that they do, notably in Elizabeth Lanza's study of two children growing up bilingual in Norwegian and English. Siri's parents used the 'one person, one language' strategy, while Tomas's parents (especially his mother) spoke to their son in both languages, with code-switching. Lanza found language mixing in both children's speech, but the patterns differed, leading her to conclude that the differences resulted from the parents' different interaction strategies.

A second crucial question about bilingual first-language acquisition has to do with the representation of the two languages in the child's brain: does the child mix the two languages in a single mental representation during the early stages of acquisition, or does the child keep the two languages separate from the beginning? The one-system hypothesis has been advocated by a number of prominent scholars, on the basis of evidence that children produce mixed utterances – lexical mixing, but also morphological and syntactic mixing. The mixing in turn has often been taken as evidence that the child is unaware that there are two different languages in the environment. As Werner Leopold, author of the first great work on bilingual first-language acquisition, put it, 'infants exposed to two languages from the beginning do not learn bilingually at first, but weld the double presentation into one unified speech system'. More recent research, however, has shown that bilingual children are aware of their two different languages at a very early age, and that much of their language mixing can be attributed to social causes, just as some parents (for instance Tomas's mother) engage in code-switching. Lanza found, for instance, that Siri was aware that she was learning two different languages at least by the time she was two years and three months old. Moreover, there is an increasing body of structural evidence to support the claim that bilingual children's two first languages develop separately. In analyzing word order in very young bilingual children's German and French, for instance, Annick De Houwer and Jürgen Meisel found patterns for each language that were essentially identical to those of monolingual child learners of German and French, respectively.

There are of course other important questions that scholars who study bilingual first-language acquisition are trying to answer, and the research approaches vary widely. Understandably, most scholars would agree that different perspectives must be combined in order to approach complete answers to any of these questions – in particular developmental psycholinguistics for understanding the learning process itself, sociolinguistics for understanding the context of learning, and linguistic theory and typology for understanding the linguistic structures used by the learners.

These same perspectives inform research in second-language acquisition, specifically acquisition by adult learners. The actual dividing line between bilingual first-language acquisition and second-language acquisition is a matter of some dispute, centering around the critical period hypothesis. The critical period hypothesis holds that starting at about twelve years of age – that is, around the age of puberty – a child must approach a second language in a way that is qualitatively different from the approach to language learning taken by a younger child. The claim is that younger children learn a second language as if it were a first language, even if they were not exposed to it from birth, while a post-puberty learner approaches a new language basically in the same way as an adult. The hypothesis is controversial, but one point at least seems clear: young children's language learning strategies differ significantly from adults' language learning strategies.

What accounts for this difference? Answers to this question vary. One claim is that adults have more trouble learning a second language because they are so used to their first language that they cannot easily unlearn long-established habits. Another claim is that adults have more trouble learning a second language because after the critical period has passed they have less (or, in some versions, no) access to Universal Grammar, a theoretical complex of structures that is believed by many linguists to underlie all human language; the idea here is that Universal Grammar is the engine that drives language acquisition, with language-specific input channeling the learner into particular choices within the Universal Grammar framework. Without the help of Universal Grammar, language learning is difficult and likely to be incomplete. These two answers are not necessarily mutually exclusive, of course; both could affect the course of second-language acquisition.

Another issue that interests specialists in second-language acquisition is the relative importance of transfer from the learner's first language. That is, to what extent do learners carry over structures from their first language into their version of the second language? The claim that transfer is an important factor in second-language (L2) acquisition is at the foundation of the approach to language teaching known as contrastive analysis, which predicts that universally marked structures in a target language (TL, that is, the L2) will be acquired last by learners who do not have those structures in their native language (L1). (Determining which structures are universally marked is unfortunately a nontrivial problem, but in general, marked features are harder to learn than unmarked features – so that marked features tend to be less common in languages of the world and learned late by children acquiring their first language.) An opposing approach, called error analysis, rests on the finding that learners from a variety of language backgrounds go through similar stages in learning the same TL, making the same mistakes, so that there must be universals of L2 acquisition that determine the stages and the errors. Proponents of error analysis argue that contrastive analysis therefore rests on a false premise, since it predicts that learners with different L1s should make different mistakes. Some scholars have claimed a connection between the results of error analysis and Universal Grammar. This controversy is now several decades old and has largely faded from view, but the issues themselves are still current in second-language acquisition research. Probably most specialists would now agree that transfer does occur and that there are universals of second-language acquisition, perhaps connected with Universal Grammar; the influence of these different factors in specific learning situations, however, is still poorly understood. It should be added that there is also some evidence that transfer occurs in bilingual first-language acquisition.

Other questions that arise in studies of second-language acquisition concern the causes and results of individual differences in language-learning aptitude and the differences in processes and results between tutored and untutored L2 acquisition (aside from the obvious difference that untutored L2 acquisition is less likely to focus on the standard dialect of a TL). Second-language acquisition specialists might also be interested in trying to answer the question of why it is easier for an adult to learn (say) a fifth language than a second language: that is, there is at least anecdotal evidence that experience in L2 acquisition carries over from one language-learning situation to the next – in other words, that language learning is a general skill that adults can acquire and exploit in approaching a new language.

Turning from issues in the acquisition of two (or more) languages to the topic of bilinguals' use of their languages, we again find a variety of approaches. In one major line of research, psycholinguists have considered the problem of how two languages are stored and accessed in a bilingual's brain. François Grosjean and Carlos Soares, for instance, argue that bilinguals' 'knowledge of two languages makes up an integrated whole that cannot easily be decomposed into two separate parts', and therefore that, in bilingual language processing, 'one language is rarely totally deactivated' when the bilingual speaks or listens to the other language, 'even in completely monolingual situations'.

Another line of research focuses on the neurolinguistic problem of language disorders: what happens to the languages of a bilingual aphasic? A particularly interesting finding is that speakers' emotional ties to one of their languages may promote early recovery of that particular language, as opposed to their other language(s), after a stroke or brain injury. In one famous case, a Swiss German who spoke Swiss German, Standard German, and French recovered his French first after a stroke, although he had spent only six of his forty-four years speaking French regularly, nineteen years before suffering his stroke, and although his wife knew no French. The apparent reason for this odd recovery pattern was that he remembered his years in France as the best years of his life.

Bilinguals' opinions about their languages affect other areas of bilingual language usage too, of course. The bilingual child, for instance, makes decisions about what language to use when: it is by no means true that parents' language decisions and practice will always determine how the child will use her or his two languages. Parents often complain that their bilingual children suddenly refuse to speak one of their two languages, usually when the disfavored language is not the community's language. There are also anecdotes about the final stage in language death being precipitated by the decision of bilingual youngsters. This is reported for minority languages in the United States as different as Chinook in the Pacific Northwest and Swedish in areas of the northern Midwest populated by Swedish immigrants. In both cases, it is said, the elders in the community laughed at the children for making mistakes in the community's ethnic-heritage language; unwilling to undergo continual teasing, the children simply switched completely and permanently to English.

A major topic of research on bilingual language usage is the mixing of languages, especially in code-switching, the use of different languages in the same discourse. One widespread belief, no longer widely held by scholars but still popular among laymen, is the view that competent bilinguals never mix their languages. On this view, code-switching is bad, because it signals insufficient command of one or both of a bilingual's languages. In his classic book on language contact, Uriel Weinreich expressed the opinion that 'the ideal bilingual switches from one language to the other according to appropriate changes in the speech situation but not in an unchanged speech situation and certainly not within a single sentence'. But the enormous increase in code-switching research in recent years has shown without a doubt that bilingual speakers talking to other bilingual speakers may exploit the resources of both of their shared languages for a variety of purposes – and in those contexts, code-switching is a sign of bilingual competence, not incompetence. The quotation about Spanglish at the beginning of this chapter illustrates both the appeal of code-switching and the layman's view that the result is an unstructured mishmash, a 'hybrid lingo' in the reporter's words.

In an exhaustive analysis of Puerto Rican children's bilingual usage in New York City, Ana Celia Zentella shows conclusively that these children's speech – and, by implication, other mixed Spanish–English speech – is far from structureless. On the contrary, it is highly structured. And in sharp contrast to Weinreich's view of the ideal bilingual, Zentella argues that 'where there is intense and prolonged contact . . . it is precisely the ability to switch languages in the same sentence and situation that characterizes the most effective bilinguals . . . [A]lmost all [code-switchers in the community she studied] honor the complex rules of when and where to link the two grammars, and some of them speak "Spanglish" proudly.'

Other specialists too have found that code-switching is one type of conversational strategy used by bilinguals. A similar conclusion, from a very different perspective, is offered in various places in the literature of anthropological linguistics, in studies of multilingual language usage in Native American tribes and other small-society settings. To give just one of many examples, the Coeur d'Alenes of Idaho, who speak a Salishan language, use other languages for comic effect in telling myths. The Meadowlark character is a Spokane, for instance, and Turtle also speaks Spokane, a distinct but closely related Salishan language. (This usage may shed indirect light on the story of Andreas Kemke, a Swede, who proposed several centuries ago that, in the Garden of Eden, God spoke Swedish, Adam spoke Danish, and the serpent spoke French.) The Coeur d'Alenes apparently used their multilingual skills for practical purposes as well: according to an early report, 'a Coeur d'Alene chief, whose band was outnumbered by the Nez Perce in a hostile encounter, stood in front of the Nez Perce at night and, unseen because of darkness, "spoke loudly to them in their own language" to go home because all the major bands of the Coeur d'Alene tribe were there and the Nez Perce had little chance of winning. The Nez Perce believed this and went home without fighting.'

As with the preceding sections, this brief survey has hardly scratched the surface of an extraordinarily complex set of issues and the research addressing them. Again, however, the goal of this section, and of this entire chapter, has been to provide the background that is necessary to understand the specifically linguistic processes and results of language contact. Meanwhile, readers interested in pursuing some of the topics touched on here can find relevant sources below to use as a starting point for further study.

Sources and further reading

See Appendix 2 for a list of the world's nations and their official languages. Thomason 1988 provides a continent-by-continent survey of some of the world's major languages and language families (together with a now out-dated list of the world's nations and their official languages). A good starting point for the study of national multilingualism is the 1976 book *Language and Politics*, edited by William and Jean O'Barr. R. B. Le Page's 1964 book *The National Language Question: Linguistic Problems of Newly Independent States* provides useful insights into this difficult topic.

The quotation about multilingualism in the Pacific Northwest at the beginning of the chapter (from Edward Spicer's 1961 book) was brought to my attention by David Robertson, moderator of the CHINOOK list (an electronic discussion list devoted to the pidgin Chinook Jargon), who posted it on the list.

The 1982 Grosjean quotation is from p. 2 of his book *Life with Two Languages*. I am grateful to William Poser for the report about multi-lingualism among the Carriers of Canada, and also for the report about multilingual Jewish Latvians. Annick De Houwer's observation about the continuing effects of now-discredited research on bilinguals' deficits is from her 1998 article 'By way of introduction: methods in studies of bilingual first language acquisition'; a major source on the problems with early studies that claimed to show psychological problems resulting from a bilingual upbring-ing is Kenji Hakuta's 1986 book *Mirror of Language: The Debate on Bilingualism*.

The quotation about bilingualism as a problem is from William F. Mackey's 1967 book *Bilingualism as a World Problem / Le bilinguisme, phénomène mondial* – a title that suggests that his view of bilingualism may actually not be conflict-oriented, because the French word *phénomène* is simply 'phenomenon' in English, and therefore does not necessarily indicate something negative. Peter Nelde's 1992 article with the references to lan-guage conflict, the burden of bilingualism, and minority-language speakers' responses to questions about language conflict is entitled 'Multilingualism and contact linguistics'; his report of the left-side–right-side contrast in speakers' answers to language questions is from his article 'Identity among bilinguals: an ecolinguistic approach' (2000). Other sources that emphasize, at least in their titles, the conflict aspects of language contact are G. Kremnitz's *Sprachen im Konflikt* ['Languages in conflict] (1979), the volume *Spracherwerb, Sprachkontakt, Sprachkonflikt* ['Language acquisition, lan-guage contact, language conflict'] edited by Els Oksaar (1984), P. Nelde's 'Sprachkontakt als Kulturkonflikt' ['Language contact as culture conflict'] (1984), *Languages in Contact and in Conflict*, edited by Nelde (1980), and Carol Myers-Scotton's *Duelling Languages: Grammatical Structure in Co-deswitching* (1993).

The *Anthropological Linguistics* book reviews cited in this chapter are from the fall 1999 issue of the journal: p. 388 of David Bradley's review of Noonan *et al.*, *Chantyal Dictionary and Texts* (1999), and p. 398 of Michael K. Foster's review of Silver & Miller, *American Indian Languages: Cultural and Social Contexts* (1997; the quotation is from p. 210). The fate of Chantyal is also discussed in Noonan's 1995 article 'The fall and rise and fall of the Chantyal language'; multilingualism in the Vaupes region is the topic of such articles as Arthur P. Sorensen's 'Multilingualism in the Northwest Amazon' (1967; see also Sorensen 1985), Jean Jackson's 'Language identity of the Colombian Vaupès Indians (1974; see also Jackson 1983), and Barbara F. Grimes's 'Language attitudes: identity, distinctiveness, survival in the Vaupes' (1985).

The description of Nebraska's official English law and its nonimplementation is from Susannah Davis's 1998 paper 'Legal regulation of language contact in Nebraska'. Language policies in the former Soviet Union are described in E. Glyn Lewis's 1972 book *Multilingualism in the Soviet Union* and a 1982 book edited by Isabelle Kreindler, *The Changing Status of Russian in the Soviet Union*. Information about Namibia language policies and language planning comes from a 1995 posting on the LINGUIST electronic list by August Cluver and from the advertisement for Karsten Legère, ed., *African Languages in Basic Education*, distributed by the book's publisher, Gamsberg Macmillan Publishers, Ltd., Windhoek, Namibia. The French language academy is discussed in Harold Schiffman's 1996 book *Linguistic Culture and Language Policy*, as cited by Carol Pfaff (1998), who also provides a description of Turkish language reform. The chronology of language policies in Mexico comes from Mark Sicoli's 'Overview of the history of language issues and policy in Mexico' (1998); Sicoli cites Heath 1972 and Justeson & Broadwell 1996 as his sources for this information. The Gandhi quotation comes from Ishwaran 1969 (p. 143), and the 1981 statistics on national languages of India are from Krishna 1991 (p. 244). The *New York Times* article 'Nehru spoke it, but it's still foreign' (January 28, 1998) was written by Stephen Kinzer. Other good sources on multilingualism in India are Apte 1976 and Friedrich 1962.

The anecdote about the rural preacher who claimed English as Jesus's language occurs in various versions, as befits a modern urban legend; one version is reported by H. L. Mencken. Information about speaker numbers for languages of India are from Krishna 1991 (except for Assamese). For more information on the Kupwar languages, see John J. Gumperz and Robert Wilson's 1971 article 'Convergence and creolization: a case from the Indo-Aryan/Dravidian border'. The discussions of Thailand and its languages come from Smalley 1994, *Linguistic Diversity and National Unity: Language Ecology in Thailand* – a book that is as enjoyable to read as it is informative.

Bilingualism/multilingualism in individuals is the focus of a large and increasing amount of research. Besides books like Vildomec 1971, Grosjean 1982, and Romaine 1995, there are journals such as the new entries *International Journal of Bilingualism: Cross-Disciplinary, Cross-Linguistic Studies of Language Behavior* (first issue, 1997) and *Bilingualism: Language and Cognition* (first issue, 1998), and there are innumerable articles and book chapters.

For definitions of bilingualism, see the first section of Chapter 1 and the source cited there, Grosjean 1982 (pp. 230–6). The patterns of language usage in the bilingual child's learning environment are based on Romaine's list of types of bilingual acquisition in chapter 5 of her 1995 book. I am grateful to Anna Fenyvesi for the description of the linguistic behavior of the trilingual two-year-old in Szeged, Hungary. Elizabeth Lanza's 1977 book on Siri and Tomas is entitled *Language Mixing in Infant Bilingualism*. Lanza also provides a good review of the one-system hypothesis (see especially pp. 4–5 and chapter 2); the quotation from Werner Leopold (1954: 24) is cited from p. 19 of her book. Leopold's classic four-volume work on his daughter's bilingual acquisition of English and German, *Speech Development of a Bilingual Child: A Linguist's Record* (1939–49), is based on the very detailed journal records he kept of his daughter's speech. The research on word order in bilingual first-language acquisition was reported in a 1996 paper by De Houwer and Meisel; see also (for instance) De Houwer 1994 and the 1994 volume edited by Meisel.

A good source on the topic of language transfer in second-language acquisition is Terence Odlin's 1989 book *Language Transfer: Crosslinguistic Influence in Language Learning*, and the question of transfer in first-language acquisition is the subject of a keynote article and seven peer commentaries in a recent issue of the journal *Bilingualism: Language and Cognition* (vol. 1, no. 3, December 1998; see the reference to Müller 1998 in the bibliography). In fact, Daan Hermans *et al.*, in a 1998 article, concluded that L2 learners cannot prevent interference from their L1, at least in the early stages of lexical access (word search) in the L2.

Grosjean and Soares's comment about integration and activation of two languages in a bilingual's brain is from their 1986 article 'Processing mixed language: some preliminary findings'; the quotation is from p. 179. Grosjean 1982 (pp. 228–9) recounts the story of the Swiss German aphasic who recovered his French before either Swiss German or Standard German after a stroke.

The quotation from Uriel Weinreich is from p. 73 of his 1953 (1968) book *Languages in Contact*. Ana Celia Zentella's 1997 book is *Growing Up Bilingual: Puerto Rican Children in New York*; the quotation about the code-switching by the best bilinguals is on p. 270. Another study of the uses and structure of code-switching is by Moffatt and Milroy, who report their findings in a 1992 article entitled 'Panjabi/English language alternation in the early school years'. The report about multilingual usage in Coeur d'Alene myths is from Gladys Reichard's works (1933: 545, 1947: 206–7), and the story about the bilingual Coeur d'Alene chief who fooled the Nez Percé is from a study by James Teit that was published in 1930. Both stories are cited in Haruo Aoki's 1975 article 'The East Plateau linguistic diffusion area'.

4 Contact-Induced Language Change: Results

'Asia Minor Greek is a language in which "the body has remained Greek, but the soul has become Turkish".' (R. M. Dawkins, *Modern Greek in Asia Minor*, 1916, p. 198)

'The Sauromatae speak the language of Scythia, but have never talked it correctly, because the Amazons learned it imperfectly at the first.' (Herodotus, *The Persian Wars*, fifth century BCE, book IV, ch. 117)

Trying to sort out the linguistic results of language contact plunges us immediately into a region of enormous complexity. In this chapter we'll follow some of the threads to see what kinds of generalizations can be drawn about contact-induced language change. But a warning is needed at the outset: all these generalizations come with an 'all things being equal' hedge, and of course the trouble is that all things are never quite equal. Even so, there are patterns to be discovered, and the goal is to describe and explain as many patterns as possible.

Giving a realistic view of the range and variety of linguistic phenomena in this domain will require the use of a good deal of technical terminology. Specific examples involving particular structural features are necessary, and technical terms provide precise and economical detail that lengthy paraphrases cannot match. The glossary will help to clarify the meanings of most such technical terms, and in any case the crucial information does not lie in the specifics of the structures themselves, but rather in the fact that there are so many different kinds of structural interference features and that these features range over all components of linguistic structure (phonology, morphology, syntax, etc.). I would urge readers to consult the glossary freely and to read less to confront the detail than to note the structural component involved, and to appreciate the diversity of phenomena met with under conditions of language contact.

Since this is the first of the six chapters that focus on the linguistic aspects of language contact, it will be useful to begin with an outline of the whole area. As mentioned in Chapter 1, this outline can be viewed as a hierarchy of typologies, with a three-way split at the top level into contact-induced language change, extreme language mixture, and language death. But here too a caveat is in order: typologies look neat but cover up an enormous amount of variation in scope and detail. It is useful to have a typology to use as a framework, because it helps to organize one's thinking on a topic. Still, anyone who investigates a case of language contact in depth will soon discover that no list of categories can possibly cover all the necessary complexity adequately. The typology given here (and the other deceptively tidy categories elsewhere in this book) should be viewed as very rough approximations, or abstractions, of a very messy reality.

LANGUAGE CONTACT TYPOLOGIES: LINGUISTIC RESULTS AND PROCESSES
1. *Contact-induced language change*
    A typology of predictors of kinds and degrees of change
        Social factors
            Intensity of contact
            Presence vs. absence of imperfect learning
            Speakers' attitudes
        Linguistic factors
            Universal markedness
            Degree to which features are integrated into the linguistic system
            Typological distance between source and recipient languages
    A typology of effects on the recipient-language structure
        Loss of features
        Addition of features
        Replacement of features
    A typology of mechanisms of contact-induced change
        Code-switching
        Code alternation
        Passive familiarity
        'Negotiation'
        Second-language acquisition strategies
        First-language acquisition effects
        Deliberate decision
2. *Extreme language mixture: a typology of contact languages*
    Pidgins
    Creoles
    Bilingual mixed languages
3. *A typology of routes to language death*
    Attrition, the loss of linguistic material
    Grammatical replacement
    No loss of structure, not much borrowing

Not all parts of the outline are relevant to this chapter, which focuses on the 'what and when' of contact-induced change. The two sections to be covered here, both under the general heading of contact-induced language change, are the predictors of kinds and degrees of change and the effects on the recipient-language structure. This chapter focuses on the simpler cases, primarily changes that occur in two-language contact situations; in Chapter 5 we will examine situations involving more than two languages in long-term contact. Chapter 6 concerns the 'how' of contact-induced change, the mechanisms of change – the third major subheading under contact-induced change. Contact situations that give rise to mixed languages (i.e. contact languages) will be covered in Chapters 7 and 8, and the routes to language death in Chapter 9.

In addition to the first two major subsections of the outline, this chapter will address two other topics. The first section below surveys some proposals for constraints on contact-induced change, or INTERFERENCE, concluding with the claim that none of them is supported by the available evidence. And the chapter closes with a discussion of how to prove that contact-induced change has occurred – that is, how to show that a particular feature or set of features is present in a particular language because of language contact.

The organization of this chapter does not follow the outline precisely, because the section on speakers' attitudes comes at the end of the typology of predictors rather than in the middle, as the last item under social predictors and before the section on linguistic predictors. The reason for this placement is that speakers' attitudes are the wild card in this domain: they can and sometimes do cause violations of most of the generally valid predictions about contact-induced change. So after examining the social and linguistic factors that help us predict contact-induced change, we must reverse direction and consider why, in spite of the fact that robust generalizations can be drawn on the basis of these factors, contact-induced change remains essentially unpredictable.

The point about unpredictability must be emphasized at the outset. We will see in this chapter that predicting when significant contact-induced change can occur and what kinds will occur is a matter of probabilities, not possibilities. In fact, the only prediction we can make with absolute confidence is completely trivial and therefore uninteresting: contact-induced language change cannot occur unless there is language contact. Even this prediction needs to be phrased carefully; for instance, contact need not involve face-to-face interactions among speakers, as noted in Chapter 1. But once the crucial notions are explained, the prediction is valid. For more interesting predictions, though, we have to rely on probabilistic generalizations.

One question needs to be answered before we start a systematic discussion of types: What is contact-induced language change? That is, what kinds of linguistic changes count as contact-induced? The definition I prefer is broad:

any linguistic change that would have been less likely to occur outside a particular contact situation is due at least in part to language contact. This definition includes two major categories of change. First, and most prominently, there are direct importations from a source language – morpheme alone, or morpheme and structure together, or structure alone – with or without structural modification of the source-language features in the process. These changes are the focus of this chapter.

Second, there are indirect effects of language contact which in turn fall into two major categories. One comprises attrition processes that sometimes take place in dying languages. These are changes which would have been less likely to happen if it were not for the contact situation that is causing speakers to shift away from the dying language, but which are not themselves a result of direct or indirect influence from the dominant language; they do not make the receiving language more similar to the source language, and they are therefore not interference features. They will be discussed in some detail in Chapter 9.

In the other category are later changes triggered by an earlier direct importation. Although the later changes are actually motivated by internal pressures within the language, they would have been less likely to happen if the initial contact-induced change had not happened. In other words, there is a snowball effect: the initial change, an interference feature adopted from some other language, triggers another change, which in turn triggers a third change, and so on. Only the first change is an interference feature, but all the changes are contact-induced. A very common type of example is found in the syntax of subordination – that is, in the expression of structures that correspond to English subordinate clauses like *when we were Elvis fans* or *because you did not go to that movie*, which in English begin with a subordinate conjunction (*when, because*). For instance, Siberian Yupik Eskimo borrowed several conjunctions from Chukchi. The borrowing of conjunctions and other function words is very common, and the conjunctions themselves did not disrupt the syntax of Siberian Yupik clause-combining. But later, in a change triggered by the initial borrowing, Yupik replaced its inherited nonfinite subordinate constructions with constructions consisting of conjunction + finite clause – that is, with constructions similar to the English type and very different from the inherited type. Analogous series of changes can be found in other languages, for instance in Brahui (a Dravidian language) under the influence of the Iranian language Baluchi, and in Azeri (a Turkic language), also under Iranian influence.

The final hedge in the definition of contact-induced change – 'at least in part' – is needed because of the possibility, and in many cases the actuality, of multiple causation. Many linguistic changes have two or more causes, both external and internal ones; it often happens that one of the several causes of a linguistic change arises out of a particular contact situation. Here is an example involving three unrelated neighboring languages of the Sepik River basin in northern Papua New Guinea. The three languages, Yimas, Alamblak, and Enga, share a feature that is otherwise rare in non-Austronesian languages of New Guinea: a palatal series of consonants. This series is old in Enga but innovative in both Yimas and Alamblak, and since the three languages form a Sprachbund (see Chapter 5 for details on this linguistic area), it looks like a good candidate for an interference feature from Enga in the other two languages. However, it arose in each of them through a sound change from an apical consonant (such as /t/) + /i/ or /y/, a very common type of internal phonetically motivated change; so multiple causation looks like the best historical explanation for the emergence of the palatals in Yimas and Alamblak.

Are some linguistic features unborrowable?

What can be adopted by one language from another? The short answer is, anything. Various claims can be found in the literature to the effect that this or that kind of feature is unborrowable, but counterexamples can be found (and have been found) to all of the claims that have been made to date. This does not necessarily mean that no universally valid constraints will ever be proposed; but, for reasons to be discussed later in this chapter, I think it is unlikely that any substantive linguistic constraints will turn out to be valid.

In this section we'll consider a few typical claims that have been made about unborrowable features, to set the stage for the detailed discussions of types of contact-induced change in the following sections.

One recurring proposal is that grammatical interference is confined to features that fit well typologically with the structure of the receiving language. The great French linguist Antoine Meillet, for instance, held this view, and it is still fairly popular even today. A related proposal was made by such prominent linguists as Edward Sapir and Roman Jakobson, who argued that (in Jakobson's words) 'a language accepts foreign structural elements only when they correspond to its own tendencies of development'. This view too has been taken by some modern linguists to be valid. The difference between Meillet's prediction and the one made by Sapir and Jakobson is that Meillet's proposed restriction is narrower. For him, the typological fit must be current. But for Sapir and Jakobson the typological fit can be in the future – they focus on potential changes in the receiving language, not on the state of the language before the change.

In any case, there are clear counterexamples to both claims. Not surprisingly, Meillet's proposal is easier to counterexemplify, because all we need is a contact-influenced innovation that departs from the receiving language's current typological state. One example is the partial replacement of the inherited Greek FLEXIONAL noun morphology in some dialects of Asia Minor Greek by AGGLUTINATIVE noun morphology on a Turkish model: instead of typical Greek suffixes that express both case and number, these dialects have developed separate suffixes, the first indicating plural number and the second indicating case. So, for instance, in the Ferték dialect we find the following partial paradigm for the word for 'wife': nominative singular *néka* 'wife', genitive singular *nékayu* 'of a wife', nominative plural *nékes* 'wives', and genitive plural *nékezyu* 'of wives' (the alternation between [s] and [z] in the plural suffix depends on whether the suffix is word-final or word-medial, and is a phonological feature borrowed from Turkish). The interesting form here is *nékezyu*, which contains both the suffix *-ez*, with a meaning shift from 'nominative plural' to just 'plural', and the suffix *-yu*, with a meaning shift from 'genitive singular' to just 'genitive'.

This is also surely a reasonable counterexample to the type of proposal made by Sapir and Jakobson, but notice that proponents of their view could argue that, even though Greek had no such agglutinative paradigms before Turkish influence set in, it nevertheless had a (latent) tendency to develop them. It is hard to argue against such an approach, since it could in principle be used to discard every structural contact-induced change that does not include actual transferred morphemes: proving the absence of a latent tendency is difficult, to put it mildly. But if there are no Greek dialects outside the realm of Turkish influence that have ever displayed a tendency to develop such formations, it is reasonable to argue that the development of agglutination is evidence against the latent-tendency claim.

Counterexamples can also be found in the phonology, the area that Sapir and Jakobson themselves focused on in making the claims. So, for instance, some southern Bantu languages in Africa, notably Zulu, have acquired click phonemes from neighboring Khoisan languages that (as far as we can tell) have always had them; and clicks are so rare among the world's languages that we can say with confidence that no languages outside the Khoisan group have an inherent tendency to develop them. Similar examples are quite easy to find in numerous contact situations around the world.

Probably the most frequently proposed constraint on interference is an implicational hierarchy: words first, grammar later (if at all). This hierarchy is valid in all known cases where the people responsible for the innovations are fluent in the receiving language (but see the section on predictability, below, for potential exceptions). Nevertheless, it is not what we expect, or find, in cases where the people responsible for the innovations are second-language learners of the receiving language: in these cases, as we will see in later sections, the first and most significant interference features are structural, not lexical. So, for instance, Indic languages acquired a number of structural interference features from Dravidian languages in ancient times, but Dravidian loanwords in Indic are notoriously sparse or nonexistent.

Another common proposed constraint is that contact-induced change always makes the receiving system 'more natural' – that is, less MARKED overall. The general idea is that contact-induced change leads to simplification, not complication. There are many examples that support this view, but here too there are also many examples that go against it. Counterexamples range from the borrowing of marked features (such as the clicks in southern Bantu) to the addition of new inflectional morphological categories through interference, such as the innovative distinction between inclusive and exclusive 'we' that arose in some Indic languages through Dravidian interference.

Interestingly, the opposite claim has also been made – namely, that interference always complicates the system, making it 'less natural'. (The reason 'natural' needs to be in quotation marks here is that it is a very slippery notion indeed. The usual equation is that unmarked features are more natural and marked features are less natural, but this equation is clearly too simplistic. The problem of 'naturalness' will not be explored in this book, but I'll continue using quotation marks as a warning to the reader not to assume that it is a well-grounded notion in the linguistic literature.) All the examples that support the claim that interference leads to simplification are of course counterexamples to the opposite claim. So, for instance, marked structures are often eliminated by language contact, as in the loss of glottalized stops in the Tanzanian language Ma'a as a result of Bantu influence (the relevant Bantu languages lack glottalized stops) or the near-total loss of the dual-number category in some Semitic languages of Ethiopia as a result of Cushitic influence.

Finally, a number of more specific constraints on contact-induced change have been proposed. To give just one example, a popular view rules out the adoption of an entire inflectional paradigm, or indeed any morphological interference except for superficial features. Here too there are counterexamples. Some dialects of Asia Minor Greek have added Turkish inflectional suffixes to Greek verbs, and in Mednyj Aleut the entire finite-verb inflectional system has been acquired from Russian.

The situation is similar with other claims about unborrowable linguistic features: counterexamples can be found (and have been found) to all the proposals that have been made to date. Admittedly, some valid linguistic constraints might be found in the future. But at present it makes sense to say that the burden of proof is on those who propose new constraints; no constraint should be accepted as valid without very strong supporting evidence. The proposed supporting evidence has to be considered carefully, too: often a scholar will claim a constraint against a particular type of interference on the basis of a single case study in which that type of interference does not happen. But the nonoccurrence of the relevant type of interference in one case is not useful as evidence; as the old saying goes, you cannot prove that a platypus does not lay eggs by producing a videotape of a platypus not laying eggs. We will return to this issue below, in the section on the unpredictability of contact-induced change, where we will look at some of the reasons for the failure of most constraints on interference.

Social predictors of contact-induced change: intensity of contact

The first social predictor is intensity of contact: the more intense the contact is, the more kinds of interference are possible. Unfortunately, intensity is hard to define. In general, though, it has to do with the amount of cultural pressure exerted by one group of speakers on another, and some relevant social factors can be identified to help clarify this notion. First, the duration of the contact period is important: in borrowing situations (see below for the distinction between borrowing and shift-induced interference), the longer two languages are in contact, the more time there is for speakers of one or both groups to become bilingual, thus setting the stage for extensive structural interference. Second, numbers count: if one of two groups in contact is much larger than the other, the smaller group's language is more likely to acquire features from the larger group's language than if the two groups are roughly equal in size. In part this is due to the fact that a larger culture is likely to be a dominant culture, which points to the third and most important intensity factor: the more socioeconomic dominance one of the groups exerts, the more likely it is that the subordinate group will adopt features from the dominant group's language. The social reasons are complex, but one obvious point is that members of the subordinate group are likely to become bilingual and, again, this makes extensive interference possible.

More detailed predictions based on intensity of contact depend on the specifics of the next social predictor: absence vs. presence of imperfect learning by at least one of the groups in a contact situation. A more detailed discussion of intensity effects will therefore be postponed until after we have examined this dichotomy.

Social predictors of contact-induced change: *imperfect learning vs. its absence*

A major sociolinguistic distinction separates changes that occur when imperfect second-language learning plays no role in the process from those that occur when imperfect learning is a significant factor in determining the linguistic outcome of contact. The dichotomy is illustrated by the two situations referred to in the quotations at the beginning of this chapter.

The distinctive Asia Minor Greek dialects emerged through contact with Turkish, primarily through borrowing of Turkish features into Greek; that is, most of the people who introduced Turkish interference features into Greek were native speakers of Greek. Since Greek was their native language, and since they had to be bilingual in Turkish at least to the extent of understanding the Turkish features they were borrowing, this is a case in which imperfect learning played no significant role in the interference process. However – and this is typical of language contact, where things are so often more complicated than they appear at first glance – this scenario may be oversimplified. It is entirely possible that native speakers of Turkish who had learned some Greek as a second language also helped bring some of the Turkish features into Asia Minor Greek. But since we know that a great many of the Greeks in Turkey were fluent in Turkish as well as in Greek, and that Turkish was the dominant group's language, it is safe to assume that borrowing by L1 Greek speakers was the primary route by which Turkish features entered the Greek dialects of Asia Minor.

In the second example, in sharp contrast, Herodotus describes the language spoken by the Sauromatae, the descendants of the (possibly legendary) Amazon women and the Scythian men they selected to father their children. The language of the Sauromatae was derived from, though not identical to, the Scythian language. The differences between the two languages (or dialects) resulted from changes that came about because the Amazons (if any) learned Scythian imperfectly and transmitted their second-language variety of Scythian to their children.

A pair of languages in contact may exhibit paired results, one set of linguistic effects that reflects imperfect learning and one set of effects that does not. At least one community of bilingual speakers of Yiddish and English in the United States provides a neatly symmetrical example. These speakers borrowed features from English, their second language, into Yiddish, their first language; and at the same time they introduced Yiddish features into their imperfectly learned variety of English. Of course this situation will have no impact on either language as a whole, because this particular group of bilinguals is hardly numerous enough to affect either Yiddish or English permanently. And in fact the markedly L2 English variety is confined to a single generation of Yiddish-speaking immigrants to the United States: according to J. R. Rayfield, who studied this bilingual group, their children used some Yiddish words and phrases and had a bit of Yiddish intonation, and the grandchildren spoke ordinary American English. (In other words, the community exemplifies the typical three-generation shift pattern for immigrant communities in the United States and other large-immigration countries; see Chapter 2).

But two-way results of contact can also leave permanent effects in both languages. To take a very common but relatively minor example, American English has borrowed a few words from Native American languages (e.g. *wigwam*, *tipi*, and *potlatch*), while imperfect L2 learning of English has produced a number of American English varieties influenced by native languages, especially in such features as intonation.

The next two sections survey these two socially determined types of interference in more detail.

When imperfect learning plays no role in the interference process

When most scholars talk about borrowing, what they mainly have in mind is interference of this type – that is, the kind of interference that occurs when the process does not involve any effects of imperfect learning. In this book the term 'borrowing' will be used only for this kind of interference, to distinguish it from interference that comes about as a result of imperfect learning. Most commonly, borrowed items are introduced into a language by native speakers of that language, but of course this is not the only possibility: the crucial point is that, in borrowing, the interference features are introduced into the receiving language by people who speak it fluently.

The borrowers do not have to be native speakers. If your native language is English and you also speak Japanese fluently, you could introduce English elements into your version of Japanese as borrowings – not because you failed to master some bit of Japanese grammar, but simply because you wanted to use a particularly convenient English word or phrase or syntactic construction while speaking Japanese. Such introductions could be ephemeral, or they could be permanent parts of your Japanese speech. You might not want to call the temporary English imports borrowings, but certainly the permanent ones would be, regardless of whether or not any other speakers of Japanese imitated your Japanese usage. And the only difference between the temporary and the permanent importations is social, not strictly linguistic: once a feature occurs in someone's version of Japanese, even just once, it can and will turn into a borrowing if it becomes frequent and if it is also used by other speakers. (See Chapter 6 for further discussion of mechanisms and processes of interference.)

A small personal example will show that this possibility is not just hypothetical. When I lived in Germany many years ago, I learned to speak German well enough to pass as a native speaker (or, rather, I could fool some native speakers all of the time and most native speakers some of the time). But I found that I could amuse my German friends by switching to an exaggerated American accent in speaking German; they found the word *Banane* 'banana' especially hilarious with flat nasal American *a*s, as in an exaggerated version of my native pronunciation of the English word *banana*. And then they started to imitate my super-Americanized pronunciation of the German word, so that this quasi-American vowel was introduced, in *Banane* only, into their native German. (The word itself is not originally native either to English or to German; it is ultimately a borrowing into both languages from some West African language, probably via Portuguese or Spanish.) Of course this is a trivial instance, since the new vowel occurs in just the one word and is, or was, used only by a handful of speakers. Still, the innovation constitutes a minor change in the phonological structure of these speakers' German, and it was introduced deliberately by a fluent nonnative speaker of German.

As argued above, the failure of all the linguistic constraints on interference that have been proposed so far leads to the conclusion that anything is possible in this domain. Possibilities and probabilities are different questions, however, and a number of scholars have proposed BORROWING SCALES to predict which types of borrowed elements that can be expected to appear in increasingly intense contact situations. The scale given below is fairly typical, though somewhat more detailed than most other borrowing scales in the literature. It is important to keep in mind that this scale applies only to borrowing in the sense used in this book, not to interference in which imperfect learning is a major factor; as we'll see in the next section, the probabilities are quite different, in fact almost the opposite, for these two types of interference.

The most basic prediction is this: vocabulary is borrowed before structure. Using intensity of contact as our measuring stick, we find that only non-BASIC VOCABULARY gets borrowed under conditions of casual contact; as the intensity increases, the kinds of borrowed features increase according to relative ease of borrowing from a linguistic perspective, until finally all aspects of a language's structure are susceptible to borrowing.

Intensity of contact, as noted earlier, is a vague concept, and it cannot be made much more precise because it interacts with speakers' attitudes as well as with more easily specified factors, such as the level of fluency of the borrowers and the proportion of borrowing-language speakers who are fully bilingual in the source language. You need not be at all fluent in a language in order to borrow a few of its words; but since you cannot borrow what you do not know, control of the source language's structure is certainly needed before structural features can be borrowed. This is the reason for the split between lexical and structural borrowing: according to the prediction, we expect to find lexicon borrowed without structure, but not vice versa. At the higher levels of intensity, however, predictions are much harder to make, because speakers' attitudes toward borrowing come into play more significantly than in casual contact situations. And, as we will see later in this chapter, the 'words first' prediction does not actually hold in all borrowing situations, because in some cultures the borrowing of words from other languages is considered inappropriate, though structural features may be adopted (perhaps unconsciously).

The other major determinant in the borrowing scale is linguistic rather than social: less tightly structured features are easier to borrow than features that fit into tightly integrated closed structures. So nonbasic vocabulary items are the easiest to borrow, since in most languages a new noun (for instance), or even a verb, can be inserted readily into existing constructions. Relatively superficial phonological features (such as stress placement) and syntactic features (such as word order) are the next easiest things to borrow. At the opposite end of the scale, inflectional morphology is hardest to borrow, because its component parts fit into a whole that is (relatively) small, self-contained, and highly organized.

BORROWING SCALE

1. Casual contact (borrowers need not be fluent in the source language, and/ or few bilinguals among borrowing-language speakers): only nonbasic vocabulary borrowed.

   Lexicon Only content words – most often nouns, but also verbs, adjectives, and adverbs.

   Structure None.

2. Slightly more intense contact (borrowers must be reasonably fluent bilinguals, but they are probably a minority among borrowing-language speakers): function words and slight structural borrowing.

   Lexicon Function words (e.g. conjunctions and adverbial particles like 'then') as well as content words; still nonbasic vocabulary.

   Structure Only minor structural borrowing at this stage, with no introduction of features that would alter the types of structures found in the borrowing language. Phonological features such as new phonemes realized by new phones, but in loanwords only; syntactic features such as new functions or functional restrictions for previously existing syntactic structures, or increased usage of previously rare word orders.

3. More intense contact (more bilinguals, attitudes and other social factors favoring borrowing): basic as well as nonbasic vocabulary borrowed, moderate structural borrowing.

   Lexicon More function words borrowed; basic vocabulary – the kinds of words that tend to be present in all languages – may also be borrowed at this stage, including such closed-class items as pronouns and low numerals as well as nouns and verbs and adjectives; derivational affixes may be borrowed too (e.g. *-able/ible*, which originally entered English on French loanwords and then spread from there to native English vocabulary).

   Structure More significant structural features are borrowed, though usually without resulting major typological change in the borrowing language. In phonology, the phonetic realizations of native phonemes, loss of some native phonemes not present in the source language, addition of new phonemes even in native vocabulary, prosodic features such as stress placement, loss or addition of syllable structure constraints (e.g. a bar against closed syllables), and morphophonemic rules (e.g. devoicing of word-final obstruents). In syntax, such features as word order (e.g. SVO beginning to replace SOV or vice versa) and the syntax of coordination and subordination (e.g. increasing or decreasing use of participial constructions instead of constructions that employ conjunctions). In morphology, borrowed inflectional affixes and categories may be added to native words, especially if they fit well typologically with previously existing patterns.

4. Intense contact (very extensive bilingualism among borrowing-language speakers, social factors strongly favoring borrowing): continuing heavy

lexical borrowing in all sections of the lexicon, heavy structural borrowing.

Lexicon Heavy borrowing.

Structure Anything goes, including structural borrowing that results in major typological changes in the borrowing language. In phonology, loss or addition of entire phonetic and/or phonological categories in native words and of all kinds of morphophonemic rules. In syntax, sweeping changes in such features as word order, relative clauses, negation, coordination, subordination, comparison, and quantification. In morphology, typologically disruptive changes such as the replacement of flexional by agglutinative morphology or vice versa, the addition or loss of morphological categories that do not match in source and borrowing languages, and the wholesale loss or addition of agreement patterns.

At the risk of being tiresomely repetitive, I must reemphasize the warning that any borrowing scale is a matter of probabilities, not possibilities. The predictions it makes can be violated, in principle and sometimes in fact. But since these predictions are robust – that is, they are valid in the great majority of cases that have been described in the literature – any violation should provide interesting insights into social and, to a lesser extent, linguistic determinants of contact-induced change.

Probably the largest class of exceptions will be found in contact situations involving two typologically similar languages. The reason is clear, and revealing. As we noted above, a major reason some structural features are easier to borrow than others has to do with relative degrees of integration into organized grammatical subsystems. But this in turn is based on the fact that it is easier to introduce borrowings into typologically congruent structures than into typologically divergent structures (so that greater intensity of contact is needed for the borrowing of structure into typologically different languages). It is not surprising, then, that closely matching types of structures make borrowing possible at lower levels of contact intensity, even if the structures themselves are highly organized. That is, the TYPOLOGICAL DISTANCE between two languages in contact is an important factor in any prediction of types of borrowing: languages that are typologically very different are likely to follow the borrowing scale closely, while languages that are typologically very similar are likely not to do so in all respects.

In the rest of this section we shall look briefly at a few typical examples of borrowing in increasingly intense contact situations, as outlined in the borrowing scale, moving from level to level in increasing order of intensity of contact.

In the least intense contact situations we find only lexical borrowing, and at that usually only nonbasic words rather than basic items like 'mother', 'hand', 'run', 'sleep', 'float', 'sit', 'one', 'five', 'sun', 'water', and 'I'. Here it should be noted that the distinction between basic and nonbasic vocabulary is a rough practical distinction, not a well-supported theoretical notion. Several decades ago the American linguist Morris Swadesh devised two lists of basic vocabulary items – one with two hundred words, the other consisting primarily of a hundred-word subset distilled from the longer list – for use in his search for distant relationships among languages. His goal was to include only words that are unlikely to be borrowed because they can be expected to be present already in every language, so that no language will 'need' new words for the relevant concepts. There was, and is, no theoretical foundation for this notion of universal-and-thus-hard-to-borrow basic vocabulary, and in fact all the words in Swadesh's lists can be and have been borrowed. Still, the lists are useful, because in most cases these items are at least less likely to be borrowed than more culture-specific vocabulary: there are many more languages with borrowed words for 'telephone' than languages with borrowed words for 'walk' or 'mother'. And this leads to a prediction that can be stated with unusual confidence (unusual, that is, for a prediction about language change): if, in a given contact situation, numerous basic vocabulary items have been borrowed, even more nonbasic items will have been borrowed as well.

Lexical borrowing can be found even in the total absence of bilingualism of any kind. One noteworthy example is the word *taboo*, which was introduced into English by the famous navigator and explorer Captain James Cook in 1777: Cook learned it in Tonga – it would not have been difficult for him and his men to understand its meaning with the help of gestures, in spite of their ignorance of the Tongan language – and it entered the English language by way of Cook's narrative of his voyage of discovery.

Modern contacts between English and French, at least in the United Kingdom, the United States, and France, also fall into this most-casual-contact category – certainly for English borrowing from French, and almost certainly for the reverse direction too, in spite of the French government's distress over the flood of English loanwords invading the French language. There are no governmental efforts in English-speaking countries to bar French loanwords, but in this direction the traffic is a trickle rather than a flood, and it is confined to such nonbasic vocabulary items as *chaise longue*, *hors d'oeuvre*, and *bonbon*. Most English speakers adapt the pronunciation of such loanwords to native English sounds, for instance using the English *r* sound rather than the quite different French *r* and replacing French nasal vowel phonemes in words like *longue* and *bonbon* with English sequences of vowel + nasal consonant. This kind of phonological adaptation is typical in more casual contact situations, but it is not predictable under more intense contact conditions.

Other cases of nonbasic vocabulary borrowing in casual contact situations are easy to find. In the Native American language Southwestern Pomo (now called Kashaya) of northern California, for example, some loanwords from

Russian have been identified, apparently dating from the thirty-year period (1811–40) when Russians occupied territory in the vicinity. The borrowings are words for 'cat', 'spoon', 'sack', 'wheat', 'wild mustard', 'milk', 'coffee', 'tea', 'dishes', 'apple', 'socks', and 'letter/book' – that is, mostly words for items that were introduced to Pomo speakers by the Russians. Another example can be found in early borrowings into Siberian Yupik Eskimo from Russian, dating from the period before the Soviet era when few Yupik speakers spoke Russian fluently. As in English and Southwestern Pomo, these Russian loanwords mainly denote cultural items such as 'tea', 'tobacco', and 'saucer, and they are phonologically nativized (and therefore sometimes so different from Russian pronunciation as to be unrecognizable); compare, for instance, Russian *čaj* and Yupik *saja* 'tea'.

Not surprisingly, some contacts that start out as casual become more intense as time goes on. So, for instance, bilingualism in Russian increased greatly among Siberian Yupik Eskimo speakers during the Soviet period, with a concomitant increase in types of interference – including, among other things, a decrease in phonological adaptation of loanwords, so that new sounds and sound sequences (especially consonant clusters) entered Yupik via Russian loanwords. To give just one example, the later Yupik form of the borrowed word for 'tea' is *čaj*, which is more or less identical to the Russian pronunciation of the word.

Other typical examples of borrowing in not-entirely-casual contact situations are found in the influence of Arabic on the languages of various peoples for whom Classical Arabic is the sacred language of their Moslem religion. In the most formal Turkish, for instance, several Arabic phonemes are (or were) used in Arabic loanwords, and the Arabic coordinating conjunction *wa* 'and', a function word, is used in construction types that are rare elsewhere in Turkish. Similarly, the sacred language of the Hindu religion, Sanskrit, has influenced some literary Dravidian languages in various phonological and syntactic ways. For instance, aspirated stops, which are foreign to Dravidian, are used in Sanskrit loanwords, not only in words where Sanskrit itself has aspirated stops but even in some loanwords that have unaspirated stops in Sanskrit itself; and syntactic features such as non-Dravidian relative clause and passive constructions have also been borrowed from Sanskrit. This structural interference occurs in addition to extensive lexical borrowing that includes function words such as conjunctions, and also derivational suffixes and even a few derivational prefixes – a notable departure from normal Dravidian word structure, which is exclusively suffixing. The Turkish case is likely an example of level 2 borrowing, though it is hard to be sure without more information about the range of structural borrowings; the Dravidian case fits into level 3 borrowing.

At level three in the borrowing scale, we find cases like the borrowing from Caucasian languages, notably Georgian, into the Iranian language Ossetic: lexical borrowing is heavy, glottalized stops that originally entered the language on loanwords have spread to native vocabulary, new cases have been added to the inherited Indo-European case system, expression of case and number distinctions is agglutinative (like Georgian, unlike Indo-European), and word order features are more typically SOV, with more postpositions, than in other Iranian languages of the region.

Level four borrowing transforms the receiving language more dramatically. Asia Minor Greek, as we saw above, has borrowed a great many features from Turkish. There is heavy lexical borrowing, both in content words (including many verbs, which seem to be borrowed as often as nouns) and in function words (including conjunctions and various grammatical particles, e.g. postpositions and an interrogative particle). Some Greek phonemes that Turkish lacks, such as interdental fricatives, are replaced by stops in these dialects of Greek, and phonological and morphophonemic rules have been borrowed (e.g. a vowel harmony rule, in the most-affected dialects). In the dialect of Ulaghatsh, the inherited flexional noun morphology has been replaced by a totally agglutinating noun morphology, a major typological change. The syntax, too, has been extensively remodeled typologically so that it matches Turkish in many respects: the article is usually omitted, Turkish verbal categories have been introduced, grammatical gender has been almost abandoned, and relative clauses partly follow a Turkish pattern.

When imperfect learning plays a role in the interference process

Most of the situations in which imperfect learning is a route to interference involve shift by one speaker group to another group's language. Of course many cases of group language shift result in perfect acquisition of the target language (TL), in the sense that members of the shifting group speak the same variety of the language as original TL group members. But in other cases, for various social reasons, the shift results in changes in the TL. It is important to keep in mind that imperfect learning in this context does not mean inability to learn, or even lack of sufficient access to the TL to permit full learning: learners must surely decide sometimes, consciously or unconsciously, to use features that are not used by native speakers of the TL. Another point that must be made emphatically is that this type of interference can occur without language shift. In India, for instance, there is a variety of English known as 'Indian English' that has numerous interference features of this type from indigenous languages of India; Indian English is spoken by many educated Indians who speak other languages natively, so although it is a variety that is characteristic of one country, it is not, strictly speaking, a variety formed under shift conditions. The references in this section, and throughout this book, to language shift and shift-induced interference therefore carry an implicit warning label: the linguistic predictions are the same for all instances of imperfect group learning of a TL, regardless of whether or not actual shift has occurred. One other terminological point should be mentioned here: the most common term in the literature for shift-induced interference is SUBSTRATUM INTERFERENCE, so called because often a shifting population is sociopolitically subordinate to the people whose language they are shifting to. I avoid using substratum as a general label because imperfect learning has similar structural effects regardless of the sociopolitical relations of the speaker groups; however, the term is appropriate and will be used in discussions of clearly hierarchical societies (such as the plantations on which creoles arose among slaves; see Chapter 7).

The process through which interference features are introduced by a group of learners into a second language – a target language – has two or three components, depending on whether or not the learners are integrated linguistically into the target-language speech community or not. First, learners carry over some features of their native language into their version of the TL, which can be called TL_2. Second, they may fail (or refuse) to learn some TL features, especially marked features, and these learners' errors also form part of the TL_2. If the shifting group is not integrated into the original TL speech community, so that (as in the case of Indian English) its members remain as a separate ethnic or even national group, then the TL_2 becomes fixed as the group's final version of the TL. But if the shifting group is integrated into the original TL-speaking community, so that TL_1 speakers form one speech community with TL_2 speakers, the linguistic result will be an amalgam of the two, a TL_3, because TL_1 speakers will borrow only some of the features of the shifting group's TL_2. In other words, TL_2 speakers and TL_1 speakers will 'negotiate' a shared version of the TL and that will become the entire community's language. (See Chapter 6 for a discussion of this type of 'negotiation'; the quotation marks are meant to warn the reader that no claim is being made about its being a conscious, deliberate process. The process is also called 'accommodation'.)

The crucial prediction about shift-induced interference is that, unlike borrowing, it does not start with the lexicon. Instead, it starts with phonology and syntax; the TL_2 may include lexical interference as well as structural interference, but structural interference will dominate. A possible exception to this generalization might occur if the shifting group is a superstrate, a socioeconomically dominant group, rather than a substrate. The case of Norman French speakers shifting to English in England is the most famous example: hundreds and later thousands of loanwords poured into English as an indirect result of the Norman Conquest, and in fact the structural interference from French in English was much more modest. But that picture is complicated by the fact that English speakers were probably borrowing words from French speakers during the process of shift – that is, both borrowing and shift-induced interference were likely to have been occurring at the same time.

Since in most group shift situations it is not the dominant group that shifts, however, most cases of shift-induced interference support the basic prediction. In fact, it is fairly easy to find examples of mutual interference, borrowing by dominant-language speakers and shift-induced interference by subordinate-language speakers, that directly illustrate the contrast between the two types of interference. The Yiddish–English bilingual group mentioned above is one striking example. In the group's Yiddish, their L1, where the process is borrowing, lexical interference is very strong, morphosyntactic interference is moderate, and phonological interference is weak; but in their English, the L2, we find the typical pattern of shift-induced interference – moderate lexical interference, but strong morphosyntactic and phonological interference.

Here are two similar cases. In the two languages of a group of bilingual Salar speakers in China, borrowing interference in Salar (the L1) from Chinese includes very strong lexical interference and moderate morphosyntactic and phonological interference; but shift-induced interference in the group's Chinese (the L2) shows weak lexical interference, strong morphosyntactic interference, and moderate phonological interference. A group of Quechua–Spanish bilinguals in Peru has the same pattern: borrowing into Quechua (the L1) involves more lexicon and less structure, while shift-induced interference in Spanish (the L2) involves less lexicon and more structure.

Two of the linguistic areas surveyed in Chapter 5, the Ethiopian highlands and South Asia, involve large amounts of shift-induced interference (although in South Asia, at least, borrowing has also contributed to the present state of the area). Because both of those cases require more detailed descriptions than would be appropriate for the present chapter, we'll wait until Chapter 5 for system-wide examples of the effects of imperfect learning.

Linguistic predictors of contact-induced change

The three main linguistic factors that affect the outcome of contact-induced change are listed in the outline at the beginning of this chapter: universal markedness, the degree to which features are integrated into the linguistic system, and typological distance between the source language and the recipient language. Markedness seems to be most important in cases of shift-induced interference. Marked features in a TL (because they are harder to learn) are less likely to be learned by a shifting group and therefore less likely to appear in TL_2; and marked features in the shifting group's original language are less likely to be learned by original TL speakers, and thus less likely to appear in TL_3. In borrowing, markedness probably plays a lesser role; once the borrowers have learned the source-language structures, no question of learnability is relevant, so in principle they can borrow marked features as easily as they can borrow unmarked features.

The prediction from differences in degree of integration is that features which are deeply embedded in elaborate interlocking structures are less likely to be borrowed and also less likely to be transferred from a shifting group's

L1 into their TL$_2$. In practice, this seems to apply especially to the inflectional morphology, and it is the main reason why inflectional morphology tends to lag behind other parts of the grammar in almost every case study of interference.

Typological distance leads to the following prediction: even features that are highly marked or highly integrated into an interlocking structure are readily exchanged between typologically similar systems. The most obvious instance of this is in dialect borrowing, where borrowing is common even in the inflectional morphology. But it also happens in borrowing between languages; for instance, in the Balkan linguistic area (described in Chapter 5), Megleno-Rumanian has added person/number verbal suffixes borrowed from the Slavic language Bulgarian to fully inflected Rumanian forms. That is, starting with verbs like *aflu* 'I find' and *afli* 'you (singular) find', the added – redundant! – Bulgarian suffixes *-m* 'first person singular' and *-š* 'second person singular' yield the forms *aflum* and *afliš*. The two systems started out with verbal systems that were similar in their means of expressing the person and number of a verb's subject, because they inherited the basic pattern from Proto-Indo-European: Rumanian is a Romance language, and Bulgarian is a Slavic language. So adding these particular Bulgarian suffixes caused no typological change in Megleno-Rumanian.

All these factors are important, but they are less important than the social factors we have already examined, and much less important than the influence of speakers' attitudes, which will be discussed in the next section. By 'less important' I mean that the linguistic factors can be overridden by social factors pushing in an opposite direction.

Speakers' attitudes: why contact-induced change is unpredictable

Although a relationship of dominance and subordination between two groups of speakers is a powerful predictor of contact-induced change, with intensity increasing as cultural pressure on the subordinate group increases, and although the contrast between borrowing and shift-induced interference accounts for a great many differences in the linguistic results of contact, these are not the most powerful force in contact-induced change. Speakers' attitudes can and sometimes do produce exceptions to most of the generalizations we have already drawn.

It is a truism in historical linguistics that language change is unpredictable: if you know that a change is certainly going to happen, it must already be under way. In cases of deliberate, conscious change this assertion is an overstatement (as for instance when someone changes a language trivially by coining a new word for a new invention, like *automobile* or *email*), but overall it holds true. Even the most 'natural' structural changes – common changes that occur frequently in diverse languages all over the world – often do not happen. This truism holds in the subfield of contact-induced change too. So although we can draw some useful generalizations about tendencies in this area, we cannot confidently predict that any particular changes will occur in a particular language in a particular contact situation. Stating constraints on contact-induced change is a more promising enterprise, but, as we saw in an earlier section, substantive constraints that rule out impossible changes tend to be as elusive as substantive predictions about inevitable changes.

At least one constraint can be stated with absolute confidence: as mentioned above, contact-induced language change cannot occur without language contact. So, to take just one of many examples, Swahili speakers cannot borrow any words or other linguistic features from Pirahã (a language spoken by a small group of people who live in a remote region of Amazonia in Brazil) if no Swahili speakers ever come into contact with any Pirahã speakers. Even here some hedges are needed: since a few Portuguese and English speakers are in contact with Pirahã speakers, and since other Portuguese and English speakers are in contact with Swahili speakers, it is conceivable, if unlikely, that a chain of borrowing could lead from Pirahã to Swahili; moreover, if Pirahã becomes a written language, Swahili speakers could in principle gain access to grammars and texts and teach themselves enough Pirahã to borrow things from the language. But as a matter of social probability, the chances that Swahili will ever have any borrowings from Pirahã are virtually zero. So this constraint is viable. Unfortunately, however, it is also completely trivial, and it therefore contributes nothing to our understanding of probabilities or processes of contact-induced change.

A more substantive constraint has to do with intensity of contact. As we saw above in the section on borrowing, certain kinds of changes can occur under conditions of casual contact, when most speakers of the receiving language do not speak (or read) the source language fluently; but other kinds can only occur when the contact is more intense – when there is extensive bilingualism among borrowing-language speakers. Consider the most obvious application of this constraint: it is quite possible to borrow a few words from a language you do not speak at all well, but in order to borrow syntactic or morphological structures you must know the source language quite well. In other words, you cannot borrow what you do not know. In spite of the fact that the notion of intensity of contact is necessarily vague, this constraint is valid and useful in predicting what kinds of features can be borrowed when.

A comparably substantive constraint applies in situations in which the changes are brought about by imperfect learning. The probability that shift-induced interference will become fixed in a target language is crucially dependent on the relative sizes of the two speaker groups. If the shifting group is large relative to the population of target-language speakers – either of the target language as a whole or of a subcommunity that is forming a single new speech community with the shifting speakers, isolated from the larger TL speech community – then the chances are good that at least some of the shifters' interference features will become fixed in the target language. This is what happened with Irish Gaelic features in what is now called Irish English: the shifters' variety of English was able to influence the English of Ireland as a whole because the shifters were numerous relative to the original native speakers of English in Ireland. But if the TL group is much larger, then – as with Greek speakers in the United States – the interference features are almost sure to be ephemeral, confined to the shifters themselves and not passed on to their offspring or picked up by original target-language speakers. Like the previous constraint, this one is vague; no numerical value can be assigned to the notion of 'relatively large', but again the vagueness does not render the constraint useless.

This constraint, however, is not as solid as the one about intensity of contact in borrowing contexts: although it is impossible to borrow a feature you do not know, there are exceptions to the relative-size rule. Exceptions are especially (and maybe only) likely when the shifting group is elite rather than subordinate. The most notorious exception is that of French influence on English after the Norman Conquest of 1066. The conquerors did not shift from French to English immediately, though the evidence indicates that they did become bilingual in English soon after the Conquest. The new ruling class continued to hold lands in Normandy as well as their new property in England, and they maintained their French language along with their ties to the Continent. But in 1204 King John, in a remarkable exercise of bumbling ineptitude, lost Normandy, and at that point the Norman nobles had to choose between their Norman possessions (and status as vassals of the king of France) and their English possessions (and status as subjects of the king of England). Those who chose to stay in England shifted from French to English.

The shifting French speakers in England numbered perhaps about 20,000, as against more than 1.5 million English speakers; nevertheless, because they were the ruling class, French speakers introduced many loanwords and a small but significant number of structural features into English when they eventually gave up French after 1204. Besides everyday words like *judge* and *mutton*, the French borrowings include suffixes like *-able*, which is added both to borrowed verbs like *remark* and to native English verbs like *know* to form adjectives (*remarkable, knowable*). Another example: several originally allophonic (nondistinctive) pairs of sounds were phonemicized (made distinctive) through French influence, as when the fricative pair [f] and [v] turned into a contrasting pair of phonemes, /f/ vs. /v/, in part because borrowings like *very* and *vain* retained the Old French word-initial [v], which then contrasted with word-initial [f] in native words like *fair* (in the meaning 'beautiful') and *fain*. (Before these loanwords entered the language, [v] occurred only in mid-word, never at the beginning, except in a handful of loanwords from another Old English dialect; and [f] occurred elsewhere, never in the same mid-word environments as [v].)

Some implicational predictions or constraints on interference can also be adduced, though these too are probabilistic rather than deterministic – that is, they are robust tendencies, but not absolute certainties. One prediction, as we saw above, is that nonbasic vocabulary is always borrowed first, and structure later (with increasing intensity of contact) or not at all. By contrast, in the majority of shift situations the most common interference features are phonological and syntactic, with vocabulary lagging behind. This yields an important prediction (or, rather, a backwards prediction: a retrodiction) about long-past contact situations: if we can establish significant structural interference, but there are few or no loanwords, then the interference must have come about via imperfect learning of a target language during shift, not through borrowing. Note that this is a one-way prediction: because of rather rare cases like medieval French-to-English interference, we cannot assume that the mode of interference was borrowing if we find both lexical and structural interference features in the receiving language. Shift-induced interference does often include quite a few words, and occasionally the number of words rivals that of phonological and syntactic transfers. There is also, of course, another and rather trivial retrodiction based on the same dichotomy: if we find only some loanwords and no structural interference, then the process must have been borrowing.

But even predictions like this one, rooted firmly in a large body of evidence and with no certain counterexamples, must be treated as probabilistic rather than deterministic. It is possible to point to potential counterexamples, at least, and these make it necessary to take the possibility of actual counterexamples into account in our theorizing. Consider, for instance, Montana Salish and its neighbor Nez Percé (a Sahaptian language spoken in Idaho). As we saw in Chapter 1, Montana Salish speakers have tended to construct new words out of native parts for items new to their culture, rather than borrowing words from English. The example given there was *p'ip'úyšn* 'automobile', which literally means 'wrinkled feet' – a name derived from the appearance of tire tracks – and is composed entirely of native Salish morphemes: *p'i-* (more basically *p'y-*), a reduced reduplicative form of the root; *p'uy*, the root, meaning 'wrinkle'; and *-šn*, a variant of a suffix meaning 'foot'. Nez Percé speakers have the same habit; so, for instance, the Nez Percé word for 'telephone' is *cewcew'in'es*, literally 'a thing for whispering', and it too is composed of native morphemes. Now, we know that these two words are recent creations in the two languages, because the automobile and the telephone are recent (well, relatively recent) cultural innovations, not traditional items. But although the objects are certainly borrowed from Anglo culture, the words themselves are wholly native, both in form and in literal meaning.

Some other new words in these languages are in fact due to semantic borrowing from English, but they do not betray their foreign origin because they are not attached to borrowed cultural items. One example is the

Montana Salish word *sút'-s* 'long face' (literally 'stretch-face'), as in k^w *sút's* 'you've got a long face, you look sad': according to current elders, this word is a literal morpheme-by-morpheme translation from English – a calque, to use the technical term – but Salish people used it. Another example provided by the elders is viewed as a joke, not used in ordinary Salish speech but only as an interlingual pun (and maybe only once): k^w *póc-qn!* 'you're a sorehead!' (literally 'you sore-head'), which was said early in the twentieth century by an eight-year-old child (who had learned English in school) to his mother when she was being grouchy. This kind of interference is quasi-invisible: all the building blocks are native Salish morphemes, so the foreign origin of the words might not even be suspected, and certainly could not be proved, without the speakers' explicit statements about their foreignness. An investigating linguist might well not happen to think about the metaphorical nature of expressions like 'long face' and 'sorehead', and even the realization of that nature would not prove borrowing – similar metaphors often arise independently in a variety of languages. The interference is lexical, but it is semantic, not formal: what has been borrowed is the juxtaposition of the roots for 'stretch' and 'sore' with the suffixes for 'face' and 'head', respectively, together with the meaning of the resulting combinations, not the English words as wholes.

Now, why is Montana Salish a potential counterexample to the prediction that, in borrowing situations, lexical borrowing always happens first and most? Well, if lexical borrowing is rare overall, and if almost all of the actual lexical borrowing is disguised by calquing, then any significant structural interference would be more prominent by far than lexical borrowing. This is still only a potential counterexample, not an actual one, because no structural borrowing can be detected in the language. There are, to be sure, recent and ongoing changes in Montana Salish, as in all other languages; for instance, four complex and hard-to-hear consonants – resonant pharyngeal sounds – are disappearing in the pronunciation of some fluent native speakers. But there is no evidence that these changes result from English influence, especially as none of the numerous other consonants that sound exotic to an English speaker's ear, such as glottalized consonants, the lateral affricate, labialized (rounded) consonants, and uvular consonants (pronounced far back on the velum), show any sign of change.

On one occasion, just one, I was working with an elder who, in response to requests for translations of English sentences, gave me Salish sentences which were technically grammatical but very unusual for Salish, and very close to word-for-word translations from English. Finally I asked if these sentences were not rather, uh, Englishy. His answer: Yes, they are, but I thought that's what you wanted. This elder's literal translations were akin in nature to the calquing discussed just above, only at the sentence level rather than the word level. If such sentences were to increase in frequency in everyday usage, at the expense of (or even replacing) more usual Salish constructions, the syntactic structure of the language would be quite drastically changed, and we could certainly say that Montana Salish had undergone syntactic interference from English. However, there is no sign that any such thing is occurring, either in this elder's natural speech or in any other elder's speech. The only hint that the process might be beginning comes from elicitation sessions, when I have asked elders to translate English sentences into Salish: in 1999, unlike previous years, I was given more translations with English-like SV(O) word order rather than more typical Salish VS(O) order. But these sentences came from just one elder; another objected, and a third commented, Well, you could say it this way (i.e. SVO) too – and indeed, the SV(O) order is not especially rare in naturally occurring Salish texts. So the Montana Salish case is still only a potential counterexample to the vocabulary-first-and-most generalization about borrowing contexts.

The most important question that arises here, and the one we have the least hope of answering adequately, is this: why do some communities borrow foreign words along with foreign cultural items, while others create native words for cultural borrowings? Of course in a general sense the difference between the two types of communities must derive from differences in speakers' attitudes, but 'attitudes' cover a lot of ground. Characterizing the notion more precisely, for instance by identifying attitudinal factors that could permit predictions about speakers' behavior in contact situations, is not feasible, at least not with our current state of knowledge (or, rather, ignorance). It's certainly not a matter of level of bilingualism, because all native speakers of Montana Salish are also completely fluent in English, and the process of word creation is still ongoing: if a young learner asks for a word for a very modern item, like a television set, the elders will make one up, always using native morphemes.

From a broader perspective, speakers' attitudes are ultimately responsible for the failure of other substantive predictions about contact-induced language change too. Here are a few more examples, not necessarily typical (who knows what's typical in this domain?) but at least illustrative of some of the attitudinal factors that get in the way of predictions about interference.

(i) Montana Salish speakers' nonborrowing from English is only one possible extreme response by bilinguals to strong cultural pressure from a dominant speech community. At the opposite pole are communities like Laha speakers of Indonesia and Ma'a speakers of Tanzania. Instead of avoiding borrowings, these communities have borrowed so much that their original languages have been swamped by foreign lexicon and grammar, with only some native vocabulary (including, at least in the case of Ma'a, most of the basic vocabulary) remaining. In Laha the original grammar has been replaced by borrowed Ambonese Malay grammar, and in Ma'a the original Cushitic grammar has been almost entirely replaced by grammar borrowed from two neighboring Bantu languages. Each of these communities, despite a fully bilingual population, has resisted the pressure to shift to the dominant language, showing a stubborn loyalty to the ethnic-heritage language and maintaining the most salient component of that language – the lexicon. The development of these languages underscores the point that we cannot predict with confidence what will happen to a language as a result of intense cultural pressure from a dominant group's language. (See Chapter 8 for further discussion of these cases.)

(ii) The intuitively plausible assumption that the likelihood of interference is increased by greater access to a sociopolitically dominant language is dramatically counterexemplified in certain superficially (but misleadingly) contrasting communities. Some years ago the linguist Paul Kilpatrick spent several months in Juchitán, a large town on the Pan-American Highway in the state of Oaxaca, Mexico. Thousands of speakers of Isthmus Zapotec live in Juchitán; formal education is (or was, at that time) mostly in Spanish, the national language, and of course the location on a major highway exposes the inhabitants regularly to visiting Spanish speakers. Some children learned Spanish, some did not; many children would begin school but then drop out because they did not learn enough Spanish to succeed in school. Influence from Spanish on Zapotec was minimal in Juchitán.

In sharp contrast, the nearby Zapotecan language on which Kilpatrick conducted fieldwork had undergone significant borrowing from Spanish. This language was spoken in a remote village in the mountains, about two hours from Juchitán by bus, where visitors from the outside were rare. But the only people he could find there who spoke Zapotec regularly were men over the age of 40, because, the villagers told him, the local women had decided to speak only Spanish instead of Zapotec so that their children would learn enough Spanish to get jobs at a cement factory an hour away. In this case, then, the language whose speakers had easier access to Spanish had undergone much less interference than the language with less access – and the difference lay in the speakers' attitudes toward Spanish. (Kilpatrick was told that Isthmus Zapotecs believe that they were never conquered by the Spaniards, only surrounded – an attitude that no doubt contributed to the low level of Spanish interference in the Zapotec of Juchitán.)

(iii) Although numerous languages have borrowed pronouns – the best-known example is English *they*, borrowed from Norse – pronoun borrowing is generally considered to be a rare phenomenon, and periodically the claim is made that pronouns, or at least whole sets of pronouns, cannot be borrowed. In some parts of the world, though, pronouns seem to be borrowed freely. William Foley has discussed examples of borrowed partial pronominal paradigms in non-Austronesian languages of New Guinea, concluding that in these languages pronouns 'are definitely not immune to borrowing, nor even particularly resistant'; he also observes that pronoun borrowing is rather common in Southeast Asia, citing the borrowing of English *I* and *you* in Thai and Indonesian. It turns out that Thai has other borrowed pronouns as well. For instance, Christopher Court reports that male Thai school friends, in speaking to each other, may use the Chinese pronouns for 'I' and 'you'. And Samang Hiranburana says that the entire complex set of Thai 'royal' pronouns is claimed to have been acquired from Khmer (the national language of Cambodia) in the fourteenth and fifteenth centuries.

Court proposes a very interesting distinction that may help to account for the ease with which pronouns are borrowed in this part of the world. He calls pronoun systems like the familiar European type 'closed', in that there is usually just one pronoun for a given person/number or person/number/ gender combination. English is a typical example, with *I* for first person singular, *you* for second person singular or plural, *he* for third person singular masculine, and so on. By contrast, Court argues, languages like those of Southeast Asia have 'open' pronoun systems, in which there may be dozens of ways to say 'I' and 'you', depending on (among other things) social relations between a speaker and a hearer – perhaps most notably age difference, degree of intimacy, and social status. A hint of this kind of socially determined pronominal usage is found in many European languages, in the distinction between 'polite' and 'familiar' pronouns for 'you'; but this pattern generally adds just one new category to the pronominal system, and it pales in comparison with the far more elaborate Southeast Asian systems. Court's point, in the present context, is that pronouns are more likely to be borrowed into an open system than into a closed system. In other words, the probability of pronoun borrowing in any given instance is determined by specific factors that cannot be predicted from general principles.

(iv) Sometimes languages are deliberately changed by their speakers – surely the most dramatic variety of attitude-driven change (see Chapter 6 for further discussion of deliberate change as a mechanism of interference). So, for example, Don Kulick has observed that certain 'New Guinean commu-nities have purposely fostered linguistic diversity because they have seen language as a highly salient marker of group identity . . . [they] have cultivated linguistic differences' as a way of emphasizing their differentness from their neighbors. Often such changes take the form of new words replacing old ones. This type of deliberate change is found elsewhere in the world too, though the motives vary: there is the familiar phenomenon of teenage slang, which also signals in-group membership and is, in addition, a kind of semisecret code; and the Delawares (Lenape) of the northeastern United States used to practice vocabulary replacement as a means of making their wartime conversations unintelligible to bilinguals among their Iroquois enemies. Vocabulary creation is known from all cultures, of course, so the only unusual thing about contact-induced lexical replacement would be its extent in the more extreme cases.

But at least one deliberate change, reported by Donald Laycock in 1982, would probably be considered an impossible linguistic change by any historical linguist: one New Guinea community whose language has agree-ment marking for masculine and feminine gender switched all the masculine and feminine markers so that its gender agreement system was the precise opposite of the system found in dialects of the same language spoken in nearby villages. This type of change is hard to imagine without the deliberate, conscious agency of speakers. It is worth noting that this is a contact-induced according to the definition I am using; but it is not an interference feature.

In Chapter 8 we'll see that some mixed languages, specifically certain types of two-language mixtures, also seem to have been created deliberately by their speakers. These cases too serve to erase any confidence in absolute constraints on contact-induced change.

Meanwhile, we can draw a few general conclusions from the kinds of examples given in this section. One is that attitudes can be either barriers to change or promoters of change. In other words, the reason contact-induced language change is unpredictable is that speakers are unpredictable. Second, there are no linguistic constraints on interference: any linguistic feature can be transferred to any language, given appropriate social conditions (intensity of contact, motivation, etc.), and any change can occur as an indirect result of language contact. This follows, more or less, from the existence of deliberate changes like the gender-agreement switches in the New Guinea village; but in any case, as we saw at the beginning of this chapter, all the specific constraints on contact-induced change that have been proposed have been counterexemplified. And third, the fact that social conditions make a particular change possible does not mean that that change will inevitably happen: appropriate social settings, like bilingualism in borrowing situations and a large shifting group in shift situations, can never guarantee that particular changes, or any changes at all, will occur. The distinction here is between necessary and sufficient conditions for change: we can state some necessary conditions for change (e.g. 'you can't borrow what you don't know'), but we can never state sufficient conditions for change. And this statement has a corollary: the fact that a particular change did not occur in a particular contact situation does not mean that it could not have occurred.

Effects on the recipient-language structure

Let's shift our perspective temporarily and look at a very broad picture of the effects of interference on the structure of the receiving language. According to the typology of typologies at the beginning of this chapter, there are just three basic effects: a receiving-language feature may be lost without replace-ment as a result of interference; or a new feature may be added to the recipient language's stock of linguistic material; or an interference feature may replace one of the recipient language's original features. Of course, as I warned early in the chapter, this typology – any typology! – is misleadingly simple. To mention just two of the many complications, a feature may be only partly lost or only partly replaced; and the three categories are not always clearly distinct, because (for instance) a phoneme that merges with another phoneme could be viewed either as a loss (the structure point previously occupied by that phoneme has disappeared) or as replaced (the old phoneme was replaced by another one).

Still, this short list of types of effects will help to highlight a point of great importance: when we focus on the structural effect of a contact-induced change, and on the process by which an interference feature becomes embedded in the receiving language's system, the difference between contact-induced changes and internally-motivated changes largely disappears. The main difference, from this viewpoint, is in the trigger for the change. In contact-induced change the trigger is found in the influence of another language, while in internally-motivated change the trigger lies in structural imbalances within a single linguistic system. We'll return to this point after examining the effects themselves.

First there's feature loss. In the lexicon, words are typically lost and not replaced when the concepts they express disappear from the culture. An English example might be the archaic slang word *munch-present*, which referred to a servant who, when ordered to take a gift of food to someone, instead ate the food on the way. (Servants still exist here and there in the English-speaking world, and they may even be ordered to deliver gifts of food occasionally, but I would be surprised to hear that there is still a word in the language for a servant who eats up the gift.) I have found no clear examples of contact-induced lexical loss, but there might be examples to be found: the best possibility might be a borrowed cultural item that made a previously existing cultural item so obsolete that it disappeared, along with the word that designated it.

The loss of phonological features through contact is common; here are four examples. Wutun, a Chinese language spoken in western China, has lost its inherited tones under the influence of at least two nontonal languages, Amdo Tibetan and the Mongolic language Monguor. Various dialects of Greek in Asia Minor lost the characteristic Greek voiced and voiceless interdental fricative phonemes through merger with other phonemes (usually /t/ and /d/, respectively) under the influence of Turkish, which lacks interdental fricatives. And in urban dialects of the Turkic language Uzbek in the former Soviet Union, the influence of Tajik, an Iranian language, has brought about the loss of the inherited vowel harmony rules. In a slightly different type of phonological loss, the number of possible syllable types was drastically reduced in Comox, a Salishan language spoken on Vancouver Island in British Columbia, under the influence of neighboring Wakashan languages: unlike other Salishan languages, which have some of the most elaborate consonant clusters of any of the world's languages, Comox – like Wakashan – lacks syllable-initial consonant clusters entirely.

Morphological and syntactic features are also lost very often as a result of language contact. Some Semitic languages of Ethiopia, for instance, have lost their inherited dual-number category almost entirely under the influence of Cushitic languages whose speakers shifted to Semitic. One dialect of the

Baltic language Latvian has lost grammatical gender as a result of shift-induced interference from Livonian, a Uralic language. The Dravidian language Brahui has lost its inherited distinction between inclusive and exclusive 'we' under the influence of Baluchi, an Iranian language.

The second type of effect is addition of linguistic features through contact-induced changes. Examples are easy to find in all grammatical subsystems, including the lexicon – loanwords like English *shah* (from Persian) and *potlatch* (from Chinook Jargon) are borrowed words for borrowed concepts, not replacements for previously existing English words. In the phonology we find added phonemes like glottalized stops, which occur in both loanwords and native Iranian words in Ossetic as a result of interference from Caucasian languages such as Georgian; and the click phonemes in some southern Bantu languages of Africa, among them Zulu, a result of borrowing from Khoisan languages. The borrowed clicks in Bantu languages are especially interesting because they apparently reflect a deliberate innovation: clicks introduced into taboo Bantu words cause enough phonological distortion that it is permissible for the speakers to use the words instead of having to replace them with different words (as happens in many other instances of verbal taboo). Phonological rules are also added, either directly or (probably more often) indirectly as a side-effect of lexical borrowing; for instance, some Asia Minor Greek dialects have acquired vowel harmony rules from Turkish.

In morphology and syntax, typical additions are the several new noun cases in Ossetic (Caucasian influence), new cases in Lithuanian (Uralic influence), a new inclusive vs. exclusive 'we' distinction introduced into several Indic languages (e.g. Marathi and Bengali) under Dravidian influence, new mood categories (presuppositional, inferential) in northern Tajik dialects under Uzbek influence – though not in the same areas where urban Uzbek dialects were influenced heavily by Tajik – and a new singulative number category acquired by the Indic language Shina as a result of influence from the isolate Burushaski. The English pronouns *I* and *you* were borrowed in Thai, as we saw above, but they did not replace the native Thai pronouns; instead, they were simply added to the sets of pronouns already in use in Thai.

The third type of effect is replacement of old native linguistic features by new interference features. This type too appears in the lexicon as well as in other grammatical subsystems. The English word *animal*, for instance, is a loanword from Latin, and it replaced the native English word *deer* in the general meaning – though obviously *deer* remains in a more specialized sense, to refer to a particular type of hoofed mammal. (The original general Germanic meaning of *deer* is still found in the German cognate *Tier* 'animal'.) The English pronoun *they*, as we saw earlier in this chapter, is a Norse loanword, which replaced the original English third person plural pronoun.

In the phonology, replacement is not clearly a separate category, because –

as noted above – lost phonemes typically merge with other phonemes rather than disappearing entirely, and added phonemes usually replace preexisting phonemes, at least in particular words. But in both morphology and syntax, replacements are different from, and much more common than, either simple losses or simple additions. Changes in a language's basic word-order patterns belong in this category, for instance, and they are (as we saw earlier) among the most common structural interference features. Here are a few typical examples: Akkadian, a Semitic language that inherited VSO word order from Proto-Semitic, acquired SOV word order from Sumerian; Ethiopic Semitic languages also replaced their inherited SVO word order, with SOV order, under the influence of Cushitic languages; and SOV word order was replaced by SVO order in Finnish (a Uralic language) under Indo-European influence. Not all morphosyntactic replacements are in word-order patterns, of course. In the Dravidian language Gondi, for instance, the characteristic Dravidian relative participle was replaced by an adopted Hindi (Indic) relative construction with a relative pronoun instead of a special participle.

Now that we have surveyed the various effects of contact-induced changes on a linguistic system, we can consider the point raised at the beginning of this section, about similarities in the processes through which contact-induced changes and internally-motivated changes become embedded within a linguistic system. The crucial fact has to do with the competition between an innovative feature and a previously existing feature. Competition between old and new forms occurs at least sometimes with all three of the basic effects, though with loss, in particular, it would have to be competition between the old form and nothing. But it is most evident with replacements, so I'll focus on replacement in this context.

First, consider lexical replacements. When *animal* first entered English as a loanword from Latin, it was presumably synonymous with the native Germanic word *deer*, and the two words must have competed for the semantic slot occupied temporarily by both. Eventually *animal* won the competition for the general meaning 'animal'; *deer* was not lost entirely, but it survived only in a restricted meaning. The very same process can be seen with internal replacements – internal, that is, in the sense that the new word did not come from another language. Thirty years ago, for instance, probably the most common generic term for a photocopy was *xerox copy*, derived from the name of a (or the) prominent maker of photocopiers. Subsequently, after and perhaps because the Xerox Corporation complained about the general usage, Xerox copy came to be largely restricted to copies made on a machine produced by Xerox, and *photocopy* replaced it as the most usual generic term. The transition period, when *xerox copy* and *photocopy* competed for the same semantic space, was essentially identical to the transition period during which *animal* and *deer* competed; the only difference in the two processes was the very beginning of the competition: *animal* was introduced from another language, while *photocopy* was invented within English by combining two morphemes already present in the language (though both originally came into English separately as borrowings, *photo-* from Greek and *copy* from Latin).

The same parallelism in process can be found in grammatical features. The change from VSO to SOV word order in Akkadian would have proceeded through competition between the two ordering patterns, just as the native English plural suffix -*en* was replaced through competition by the native English plural suffix -*s* in words like *brothers* (which replaced older *brethren*). The significant difference in the two processes lies in the source of the innovations – Sumerian interference in the Akkadian example, internally-motivated reduction of plural formations in the English example.

A final point should be made before we move on to the last section in this chapter. Some specialists in language contact have argued for two other types of contact-induced effect on a linguistic system, CONVERGENCE and RELEX-IFICATION. Convergence, at its simplest, would be any process through which two or more languages in contact become more like each other; but this very broad definition would make almost every contact-induced change a case of convergence, and it's not what people usually mean by the term. In practice, convergence is discussed primarily in two contexts. One is a contact situation in which both (or all) languages change in ways that make them more similar. In this context, the point of talking about convergence is to emphasize the fact that the interference is mutual, not unidirectional, and the fact that the resulting convergent structures have no single source: either they were already present, but less prominent, in both languages, or they resemble both languages in part but do not match either one completely. Talking about convergence in this context is a way of avoiding the inappropriate (for these particular situations) terms 'source language' and 'receiving language'.

A typical example of a change in frequency, in one or both (or all) languages, of previously existing constructions can be found in word-order adjustments. When Filomena Sandalo conducted fieldwork in Brazil on the language Kadiwéu, for instance, she found that her consultants usually translated Portuguese sentences into Kadiwéu with SVO word order, even though natural Kadiwéu discourse has all orderings – OVS, VOS, SOV, OSV, and VSO, in addition to SVO. Clearly, the increase of SVO ordering in translations was an adjustment to the basic SVO word order of Portuguese. (Of course, this example does not reflect a completed word-order change in Kadiwéu, or even necessarily an ongoing change; but it is certainly a potential change in the language, and a good illustration of the way in which a change in frequency might begin.) Although Portuguese is the cause of the potential frequency shift in Kadiwéu, the fact that SVO order is native to Kadiwéu makes the dichotomy between source and receiving language only partly applicable.

The dichotomy is even less relevant in cases where neither 'source' language has the resulting interference feature. One good example is the establishment of two different phrase-final intonation patterns in Turkish and German as spoken by a group of bilingual children in Germany. Monolingual speakers of Turkish and German have just one pattern each, with the same function; the bilingual children have kept both patterns in both of their languages, and have differentiated them semantically (see also Chapter 6, under Mechanism 6, for discussion of this example). Phonologically, each of the two patterns can be traced to a single source language, but since neither source language has the two different functions, neither Turkish nor German can be said to be the source of either pattern as a whole.

In spite of the problems with fitting examples like these into a conceptual framework that emphasizes a neat dichotomy, it seems to me that we do not need a new category for it. All the examples are partial replacements. Some, like changes in word-order frequencies, are straightforward, without semantic effects. Others, like the Turkish–German example, leave the receiving language(s) with a semantic differentiation where none existed before – just as English *brothers* and *brethren* still exist as plurals of brother, although *brethren* occurs only in a very restricted sense.

The other main context in which convergence is discussed is in Sprachbund situations, in which the sources of the various areal features are all too often impossible to determine. In some discussions in this context the appeal to convergence seems almost mystical – as if a structural feature were somehow hovering in the air, waiting to zap the languages in the area spontaneously. Usually, though, the term 'convergence' is used as a kind of shorthand for 'there is no evidence about how this areal feature arose'. The problem of establishing sources for areal features is a serious one, and it will be discussed at length in Chapter 5. What needs to be said here (in my opinion) is that absence of evidence about how an areal feature arose and spread is not a good reason to hypothesize a new and different process by which the feature might have arisen and spread.

The other proposed new category, relexification, presents a more complex set of analytic issues. The term refers to the replacement of most or all of a language's vocabulary by the vocabulary of some other language. The only linguistic difference between ordinary lexical borrowing and relexification is a matter of degree: if, gradually and over a very long period of time, so many words are borrowed from a particular source language that little or none of the receiving language's native vocabulary remains, ordinary lexical borrowing can be said to have turned into relexification. The trouble is, there don't seem to be any such situations anywhere in the world. English, for instance, has occasionally been claimed to have changed from a Germanic language into a Romance language because of its massive borrowing from French and Latin; but a close examination of the English lexicon shows that about 93 per cent of the basic vocabulary items are still of Germanic origin. True relexification is a borrowing process by the definition of borrowing given earlier in this chapter, and obviously belongs in the replacement category discussed in this section. The difference between the process of relexification and the process of ordinary borrowing is social, not linguistic: it is likely that relexification is always a deliberate change. In the analysis of effects on a linguistic system, however, it fits well enough into the usual categories.

How can we tell whether contact-induced change has occurred?

Establishing the fact of contact-induced change is usually easy when the focus is on loanwords, but it can be much harder, and often impossible, with structural interference. Loanwords are easier to establish because they betray their origin directly. The Latin and French loanwords in English, for instance, mainly occur outside the basic vocabulary and match their Latin and French sources much more closely than real English cognates with Latin and French words do: the Latin word *frater* 'brother' is identical to the root of the English loanword *fraternal* 'brotherly' but less similar to the native English cognate *brother*, and French *quartier* 'quarter, fourth part' is very close to the English loanword *quarter* but less similar to the native English cognate *fourth*. Sometimes, too, loanwords can be detected because they are phonologically unlike native words; English *alcohol*, a loanword from Arabic, has to be a borrowing, because it has too many syllables for a single native English morpheme.

It is true that some words can only be suspected, but not firmly established, as loanwords, because no source language can be found. We know, for example, that English *skunk* was borrowed from an Algonquian language; but even if we had no information at all about Algonquian languages, we would suspect it of being a loanword because there are no cognates elsewhere in Germanic and the animal it designates is native only to the New World. Not surprisingly, the further back we go in time the harder it is liable to be to find a source for a suspected loanword. One famous example is a word that occurs widely in Indo-European languages but is not native to Indo-European (like English *alcohol*, its root is too long to be a single native morpheme): the word turns up in Indo-European in such forms as Greek *cannabis* (as in marijuana) and English *hemp*.

Still, whatever difficulties we encounter in trying to decide whether a given word is native or borrowed, they are likely to be multiplied many times in efforts to decide whether particular structural features are native or due to contact-induced change. Unfortunately, several common types of arguments for and against proposals of contact-induced change turn out to be fatally flawed. It clearly is not justified, for instance, to assume that you can only argue successfully for a contact origin if you fail to find any plausible internal motivation for a particular change. One reason is that the goal is always to find the best historical explanation for a change, and a good solid contact explanation is preferable to a weak internal one; another reason is that the possibility of multiple causation should always be considered and, as we saw above, it often happens that an internal motivation combines with an external motivation to produce a change.

It also is not justified to argue against a contact explanation on the ground that if there are no loanwords, there cannot be any structural interference either. No one will deny that loanwords make it easier to argue for contact-induced structural change, because the presence of loanwords proves that there was contact, which is the obvious prerequisite for proving structural interference. But often, in cases of shift-induced interference, there are few or no loanwords from the shifting group's original native language in the target language, and in those cases there may well be structural interference without any significant lexical interference.

Yet another unjustified assumption is that contact-induced change should not be proposed as an explanation if a similar or identical change happened elsewhere too, without any contact or at least without the same contact situation. This has been suggested, for instance, as a counterargument to the proposal that Swahili lost its inherited tone phonemes because of massive lexical borrowing from Arabic: the claim is that because another Bantu language, Tumbuka, also lost its inherited tones, without any influence from Arabic, Swahili could also have lost its tones without any Arabic influence. Of course the conclusion of this argument is correct: Swahili could certainly have lost its tones without any Arabic or other foreign influence, just as Tumbuka did. But it is not historically realistic to assume that contact-induced change is responsible only for changes that have never occurred elsewhere through internal causation. This assumption would leave us with only truly exotic contact-induced changes, as if borrowers routinely selected only especially fancy bits of foreign structure for adoption. On the contrary, all the available evidence suggests that, although contact is indeed sometimes responsible for exotic changes, it is much more often responsible for garden-variety changes that are also common as strictly internal changes. To take perhaps the most obvious type of example, we saw in the previous section that lexical innovations that arise within a single language closely parallel lexical innovations that arise through contact: the third person plural English pronoun *they* is a loanword from Norse, but many Indo-European (and other) languages have third-person pronouns that arose language-internally, typically derived from demonstrative pronouns meaning 'this' or 'that'.

A final, and especially common, unjustified assumption is that a solid case for a contact origin can be made on the basis of a single feature. For example, it has been argued that an innovative inclusive/exclusive 'we' distinction must be due to contact because it is too exotic a feature to have arisen through internal causes alone. The trouble with a claim of this sort is that it is potentially untestable: what if there is no evidence that any neighboring language ever had the feature? In that case, the proposal of contact-induced change is no explanation at all; it simply replaces one unknown with another. And even if some neighboring language does have the feature, what if this distinction is the only feature that the two languages share? It doesn't make good historical sense to assume contact between two languages intense enough to cause one of them to adopt a single structural feature from the other, but no other material at all. So although this case is more promising than the one with no available source language at all for the structural innovation, it is still at best a very problematic case.

So much for how not to prove that contact-induced structural change has (or has not) occurred. Here's how to make a solid case for structural interference in a (proposed) receiving language. First, we need to look at the language as a whole, not just at one bit of it. Even if our interest is focused on a particular grammatical construction, an argument for a contact origin will only be convincing if it is supported by evidence of interference elsewhere in the language's structure as well. In particular, as we saw earlier in this chapter in both the borrowing scale and the discussion of shift-induced interference, phonological and syntactic interference usually go together: if one occurs, the other will probably occur as well. The point is that structural interference is unlikely to be so isolated that any one interference feature is the only one in a receiving language. This first point is not so much a requirement as a warning: no case for contact-induced structural change will be fully convincing if we cannot point to other instances of structural interference from the same source language in the same receiving language. The remaining four steps, however, should be taken as rigorous requirements for making a promising case.

Second, we need to identify a source language. If (as happens in some cases of shift-induced interference) the actual source language has vanished because all its speakers shifted to the receiving language, then we'll need to find relatives of that language, as closely related to it as possible. The source language must be shown to be, or to have been, in contact with the receiving language, and the contact has to be intimate enough to make structural interference possible. As we saw above, the presence of loanwords establishes the fact of contact, though not necessarily the intensity. Since loanwords are universal, or virtually so, in cases of borrowing but not in cases of shift-induced interference, and since the source language is more likely to be available for study in a borrowing situation than in a shift situation, it is not suprising that it tends to be easier to make a strong case for structural interference in a borrowing situation than in a shift situation.

Third, we need to find shared structural features in the proposed source language and the proposed receiving language. The shared features need not be identical in all respects, and often they will not be. It is well known that interference features often have different forms or different distributions or different functions from the source features in the donor language. In Proto-Dravidian and most modern Dravidian languages, for example, retroflex consonants do not occur at the beginning of a word; but in Indic languages, which acquired retroflex consonant phonemes through shift-induced inter-ference from Dravidian, these consonants do occur word-initially.

Fourth, we must prove that the shared features – the proposed interference features – were NOT present in the receiving language before it came into close contact with the source language. That is, we have to prove that the receiving language has changed by innovating these features. And fifth, we must prove that the shared features WERE present in the proposed source language before it came into close contact with the receiving language.

In many, possibly even most, contact situations around the world, we cannot at present satisfy both the fourth and fifth requirements, and in some cases we probably never will be able to. Some of the most striking examples of this problem occur in long-established linguistic areas; these will be discussed in considerable detail in the next chapter, but here are a few typical (and typically puzzling) examples from the Pacific Northwest linguistic area of the United States and Canada. A number of this region's most striking areal features must be reconstructed for all three of the core families' proto-languages. Among these features are lateral affricates and fricatives (which are quite rare elsewhere in the world), verb-initial word order, and a weak noun vs. verb distinction. There are other shared features as well, and it is easy to show that languages in all three families have been in close contact for a very long time, so extensive contact-induced change is a reasonable hypothesis. But because the most widespread areal features were already in the proto-languages (as far as we can tell), it is impossible to establish which, if any, of the three families acquired the features through contact-induced change.

If we can get over the hurdle of all five requirements, especially the last four, and make a strong case for interference in a particular case, we still are not finished. For the sake of completeness, we also need to look for plausible internal motivations for the changes (including universal structural tendencies, based on such factors as markedness considerations), given the very real possibility of multiple causation. But even without this added step, satisfying all five of the basic requirements means that we have succeeded in explaining the changes in question, at least in part. (We can rarely or never hope to explain any change completely, because, as we saw earlier in this chapter, social factors – especially speakers' attitudes – are not amenable to predictive generalization.)

We still need to consider our options in the worst case: what if we can't satisfy the four crucial requirements? The answer is bleak: if we can't satisfy all the requirements, then we can't make a solid case for contact-induced change. The Pacific Northwest area is one example: we can certainly prove that some contact-induced changes have occurred in the region, but for a sizable number of features we can't establish a contact source in any of the languages. A less complicated example is the isolate Chipaya, a language of Bolivia that is surrounded by and under strong cultural pressure from Aymara, one of the region's two major indigenous languages. Chipaya has borrowed many words and even, apparently, a plural suffix from Aymara, and its structure is generally quite similar to Aymara structure typologically. Here is a case, then, where we are certain about the long-term existence of close contact between the two languages, and about lexical interference from Aymara in Chipaya. We must suspect that there has also been considerable structural interference from Aymara in Chipaya. But we can't prove it: because Chipaya is a genetic isolate, i.e. a language with no known relatives, and because it is not documented from a period preceding its close contact with Aymara, we cannot prove that Chipaya has changed structurally at all.

A final caution: if we can prove that change has occurred but can't establish the other requisites for establishing contact as a cause, and if we also can't find a plausible internal motivation for a change, then we might be left with no explanation at all for the change. This is too bad, but it is a routine fact of the historical linguist's life: the number of linguistic changes that we cannot explain is vastly greater than the number of changes that we can explain.

Long as this chapter has been, there is still much more that could be said about the topics covered here. (Luckily for readers' patience, only so much of this immense topic can be covered in one book.) But in spite of the complexity of the issues we have looked at so far, two-language contact situations tend to be less intractable than contact situations with three or more languages, which are the topic of the next chapter.

Sources and further reading

Much of the discussion in this chapter reflects the analysis in Sarah Thomason and Terrence Kaufman, *Language Contact, Creolization, and Genetic Linguistics* (1988), though the analysis here is not identical to the one in the earlier book, and some sections here were not prefigured in that book. The distinction between interference with and without imperfect learning is very similar to a distinction proposed independently, also in 1988, by Frans van Coetsem, specifically for phonology (see his book *Loan Phonology and the Two Transfer Types in Language Contact*).

For examples of Yupik lexical and structural borrowing from Chukchi, see G. A. Menovščikov (1969: 124–30). The borrowing of a Baluchi conjunction by Brahui is from Murray Emeneau's 1962 article cited below (reprinted in 1980), and the example of Azeri borrowing from Iranian is from Comrie 1981, p. 84 (also cited below).

The Asia Minor Greek case is discussed in exhaustive detail in R. M. Dawkins's impressive 1916 study *Modern Greek in Asia Minor* (and see Thomason and Kaufman for a case study based on Dawkins' study); but see Even Hovdhaugen's 1976 article 'Some aspects of language contact in Anatolia' for cautions about accepting all of Dawkins's proposals. See also Hans-Jürgen Sasse's 1992 article 'Language decay and contact-induced change: similarities and differences' for examples indicating that in the Ulaghatsh dialect, at least, the changes noted by Dawkins have progressed even further since 1916. An important series of modern studies of Turkish–Greek contact phenomena has been carried out by Bernt Brendemoen (e.g. 'Turkish–Greek language contact on the eastern Black Sea coast', 1997, and 'Pronominalsyntax in den türkischen Schwarzmeerdialekten', 1993); see also, for more general discussions of Turkish in contact with Indo-European languages, the writings of Lars Johanson, most notably *Strukturelle Faktoren in türkischen Sprachkontakten* (1992), and see also 'The dynamics of code-copying in language encounters' (1998). Johanson also argues for the replacement of the term 'borrowing' with the notion of 'code copying' because, as he observes, the source language does not give anything up, and the receiving language does not give a 'borrowed' item back. Johanson is clearly right about this; still, in an effort to avoid proliferating terminology, I am keeping the traditional term (though not in its entire traditional usage) in this book.

I am grateful to Hans Hock (personal communication, 1999) for the platypus analogy. J. R. Rayfield's 1970 book *The Languages of a Bilingual Community* is a valuable case study of Yiddish–English bilinguals.

Antoine Meillet was one of the most prominent specialists in Indo-European linguistics during the first half of the twentieth century; his classic 1921 book *Linguistique historique et linguistique générale* ['Historical linguistics and general linguistics'] contains the essay – entitled 'Le problème de la parenté des langues' ['The problem of linguistic relationship'] – in which he discusses the possibility of grammatical loans. The typologically determined hierarchy reflected in the borrowing scale in this chapter, with loosely structured subsystems more susceptible to borrowing than more highly organized sub-systems, is prominently discussed by Meillet in the same book (p. 84). Edward Sapir, a linguist as prominent in America as Meillet was in France, emphasized the importance of developmental tendencies in a discussion of possible phonological interference, in his famous 1921 book *Language*. Roman Jakobson, a Russian-born linguist whose distinguished career was divided between Prague and the United States, wrote about language contact in various works; the quotation in this chapter is taken from his 1938 article 'Sur la théorie des affinités phonologiques entre des langues' ['On the theory of phonological resemblances among languages']. Edith Moravcsik, in her 1978 article 'Language contact', is one author who proposes that words are always the first interference features. T. Givón, in a section entitled 'Why languages do not borrow grammar' in a 1979 article, is one prominent author who argues that contact-induced change simplifies the grammar, and C.-J. N. Bailey (e.g. in a 1977 article) is probably the most prominent author who claims that interference always complicates the grammar.

The borrowing scale is based on the one in Thomason and Kaufman 1988. It is fairly typical, but it differs in two major ways from some of the other borrowing scales in the literature. First, according to this scale syntax is more easily borrowed than morphology, but some scholars, e.g. Romaine (1995:

64), make the opposite prediction. And second, most other borrowing scales do not distinguish between borrowing in the sense used here and interference via imperfect learning.

The point that typological congruence facilitates borrowing is made by Uriel Weinreich in his classic work *Languages in Contact* (1953: 33).

Russian loanwords in Southwestern Pomo and Siberian Yupik Eskimo are discussed, respectively, in a 1958 article by Robert Oswalt and a 1969 article by G. A. Menovščikov. However, later work by Oswalt suggests that at least some of the Russian words entered the language by way of Alaskan Yupik, not directly from Russian. Sanskrit influence on literary Dravidian languages is discussed (for instance) by S. N. Sridhar in his 1978 article 'Linguistic convergence: Indo-Aryanization of Dravidian languages'.

There are conflicting views on the extent of influence from French in English during the first two hundred years after the Norman Conquest. Some scholars have claimed that the influence was extreme; others deny these radical proposals. Claims and counterclaims about French influence on English are discussed in detail in the case study on English in Thomason and Kaufman 1988, and in other sources that are cited there. One work that deserves special mention is David Mellinkoff's 1963 book *The Language of the Law*, which offers a fascinating historical description of the origins and development of modern legal language in England and the United States.

I am grateful to John Peter Paul for the story about the child (his brother) who called his mother a sorehead, and to him and other Montana Salish elders for their contributions of other Montana Salish words and sentences.

Laha is discussed in James T. Collins's 1980 article 'Laha, a language of the Central Moluccas'. For the history of Ma'a, see the case study in Thomason and Kaufman (1988: 223–8) and also Thomason (1997), and for an opposing view see Maarten Mous's 1994 article 'Ma'a or Mbugu'. I am grateful to Paul Kilpatrick for sending me, via email, the Zapotec example that shows different linguistic outcomes of contact arising from different attitudes. Examples of pronoun borrowing are discussed in William Foley's 1986 book *The Papuan Languages of New Guinea*, pp. 210–11; in Yuphaphann Hoonchamlong's 1992 article 'Some observations on *phom* and *dichan*: male and female first-person pronouns in Thai'; and in postings on the electronic list SEALTEACH by Christopher Court (30 April 1998) and Samang Hiranburana (22 April 1998). Don Kulick's discussion of deliberate change in languages of New Guinea is in his 1992 book *Language Shift and Cultural Reproduction* (see especially pp. 1–3), and he also cites Foley (1986: 9, 27) on this topic. Donald Laycock's report of gender switching in a New Guinea community's language is in a 1982 article entitled 'Melanesian linguistic diversity: a Melanesian choice?' (see especially his p. 36). Peter Lindeström, writing in 1691, told of the Delawares' lexical replacement in their war with the Iroquois (see pp. 203–4 of the 1925 publication of his treatise).

The contact-induced loss of tones in Wutun is discussed by Charles Li

(1986); more recently, Keith Slater (2000) has argued that the numerous changes in Wutun and neighboring Chinese and non-Chinese languages arose through convergence in a well-established Sprachbund in western China. Dawkins (1916) proposes a wide variety of interference features in Asia Minor Greek from Turkish, and both one-way and mutual influence between Uzbek and Tajik are discussed in Karl Menges's 1945 article 'Indo-European influences on Ural-Altaic languages' and especially in Bernard Comrie's 1981 book *The Languages of the Soviet Union* (pp. 51f., 66, 167ff.). Comrie's book is also the source of the example of Livonian interference in Latvian (p. 147) and of the example of interference in Ossetic from Caucasian languages (pp. 167, 171, 179). The Comox example comes from Laurence Thompson's 1979 article 'Salishan and the Northwest' (1979: 732).

See the end of Chapter 5 for more detailed discussion of the Ethiopic linguistic area and for further sources on Ethiopic Semitic changes due to Cushitic interference. Chapter 5 also has a case study on the South Asian linguistic area, which prominently includes Indic–Dravidian influences. Interference from Baluchi in Brahui is discussed in a number of works by Murray Emeneau, among them his 1962 book *Brahui and Dravidian Comparative Grammar* (see pp. 56, 59) and his 1962 paper 'Bilingualism and structural borrowing' (reprinted in 1980). Emeneau has also written about interference from Dravidian in Indic, for instance in his famous 1956 paper 'India as a linguistic area' and in his 1971 paper 'Dravidian and Indo-Aryan: the Indian linguistic area' (reprinted in 1980). The Bengali example is from M. H. Klaiman's 1977 article 'Bengali syntax: possible Dravidian influences'. Burushaski influence on Shina was described by D. L. R. Lorimer in his 1937 article 'Burushaski and its alien neighbors: problems in linguistic contagion'. Sara Lickey's 1985 M.A. thesis is the source of the interpretation of click borrowing as a way to cancel out taboo restrictions.

The Akkadian change from VSO to SOV word order under Sumerian influence is described in Stephen A. Kaufman's 1974 book *The Akkadian Influences on Aramaic* (p. 132). The example of syntactic interference in Gondi from Hindi can be found in S. N. Sridhar's 1978 article 'Linguistic convergence: Indo-Aryanization of Dravidian languages' (p. 205).

The example of convergent Turkish–German intonation is from Robin Queen's 1996 University of Texas dissertation, *Intonation in contact: a study of Turkish–German bilingual intonation patterns*.

Edgar Polomé, in his 1980 article 'Creolization processes and diachronic linguistics', argues that the loss of phonemic tones in Swahili need not have resulted from Arabic influence because (for instance) the language Tumbuka in Malawi 'has lost tone though no dialect mixture or impact of another language can be adduced to account for the phenomenon' (p. 192). The example of word-initial retroflex consonants in Indic but not in Dravidian is from Lyle Campbell's 1996 article 'Phonetics and phonology' in the handbook *Contact Linguistics* (p. 102).

5 Linguistic Areas

Readers might want to reread the last sentence of Chapter 4, so that they will be prepared for the much less confident conclusions in this chapter: what we understand about linguistic areas is depressingly meager, compared to what we don't understand about them. The main strategy adopted in this chapter, therefore, is to go over some general points for orientation and then survey a variety of linguistic areas in order to highlight the similarities and differences among them. As we'll see, perhaps the most prominent similarity in most of the areas surveyed here is the lack of an explanation for many or most of the areal features.

A definition

The term 'linguistic area' is an English translation of the more colorful German term 'Sprachbund' (literally, 'language union'), which was apparently introduced by Nikolai S. Trubetzkoy in 1928. Linguists have struggled to define the concept ever since, mainly because it isn't always easy to decide whether a particular region constitutes a linguistic area or not. The general idea is clear enough, however: a linguistic area is a geographical region containing a group of three or more languages that share some structural features as a result of contact rather than as a result of accident or inheritance from a common ancestor.

The reason for requiring three or more languages is that calling two-language contact situations linguistic areas would trivialize the notion of a linguistic area, which would then include all of the world's contact situations except long-distance contacts (via religious language, published texts, email, etc.). This would be unfortunate. It's useful to distinguish two-language contacts from more complex contact situations because, as we will see in this chapter, the difficulties involved in analyzing the dynamics of contact are greatly increased when more than two languages have to be taken into account, and also because the linguistic results of contact may differ in certain respects. The reason for specifying a single geographical region is obvious: no direct contact among speakers, no linguistic area.

The specification of shared structural features in the definition is also meant to avoid all-inclusiveness. Linguistic areas are posited only where contact is, or has been, intense enough to involve structural interference because that is where the languages have significantly strong historical links (aside, that is, from genetic connections among them, if any). Loanwords are a frequent component of linguistic areas and are certainly worth mentioning where they occur, but they are so widespread even in casual contact situations that, by themselves, they provide only the most superficial information about the histories of the languages. If we were to use shared noninherited vocabulary as a primary criterion, we could probably claim the whole world as a linguistic area, given the worldwide spread of certain 'international' words (e.g. *hamburger*, *email*, *Coca Cola*, *democracy*, and even *linguistics*). .

The last part of the definition is there because language contact is only one of the three sources of shared features in a group of languages. So-called accidental similarities, many of which are ultimately due to the operation of linguistic universals of various kinds, are the only shared features that do not arise from a historical relationship among the languages. To take two trivial examples, all but a handful of the world's languages have both a consonant phoneme /t/ and a clear-cut lexical distinction between nouns and verbs, so the mere presence of a /t/ phoneme and noun and verb categories in a group of neighboring languages does not signal a historical connection among them. And genetically related languages inherit their lexicon and structural features from their common parent language, so that they share features at all levels of the lexicon and grammar, provided that the time depth of the relationship is not so great that most or all of the shared features have vanished or changed out of recognition. So, for instance, English and German inherited both the word for 'sing' and the vowel changes in its past tense and past participle: the English forms *sing*, *sang*, and *sung* correspond precisely to the German root forms in *sing(-en)*, *sang*, and *ge-sung-en* (though the German words have affixes that are lacking in the English words).

Of course it is quite possible for all three of these sources of shared features to produce similarities in the same group of languages. All languages in the world share some 'accidental' features, so any random group of languages will have some of these. And there is nothing in the definition of linguistic area that requires the member languages to belong to different language families; in fact, in most linguistic areas around the world, at least some of the languages are related to each other. The reason for this is obvious: language families develop by gradual diversification from the parent language, and although at least partial breakdown in communication among the subgroups of a speech community is needed for language split, the subgroups need not be, and very often are not, geographically distant from each other. Related languages in a linguistic area will therefore share inherited features as well as features acquired through contact-induced change, and they will inevitably also share some 'accidental' features. Probably the most challenging aspect of linguistic areas, and therefore the most interesting aspect, is the problem of establishing the source of any given feature that is widely shared among the languages in the area. We'll return to this problem later in this chapter.

So far the definition is straightforward, but it does hide a few tricky points. First, how many features must be shared before a linguistically diverse region can reasonably be called a linguistic area? Opinions on this point vary, and some specialists have argued for an extreme position at the low end of the continuum – namely, that in principle a linguistic area could be defined on the basis of a single shared feature. This is not a popular position, mainly because it requires such an unrealistic historical scenario: if a contact situation is intense enough to produce one shared structural interference feature in a group of geographically close languages, it is intense enough to produce other shared features too. It is conceivable that, given several millennia, all but one feature spread by contact-induced change could disappear in the languages of an ancient linguistic area (that is, assuming that the languages survived in a single geographical region but stopped being in intense contact). But in such a case, with so little evidence, few or no linguists would consider claiming the region as a linguistic area. Still, even if we agree that several features are needed before a region qualifies as a linguistic area, how many do there have to be? The answer has to be a judgment call, but the distinction that is sometimes made between 'strong' and 'weak' linguistic areas may be useful here: borderline cases can be considered weak areas, and the label 'strong linguistic area' can be reserved for areas in which there are many shared features due to contact. The main point, however, is that the absence of a clear dividing line between a region that is a linguistic area and a region that is not does not justify adopting the historically implausible position that one shared feature is in principle enough.

Second, do all the features that are shared as a result of contact-induced change in a linguistic area have to be found in all the languages within the area? Here the answer is clearly no. If we answered yes, the number of linguistic areas in the world would immediately shrink from many to zero, because in all linguistic areas the distribution of shared features varies widely across the entire area. In part the variation has to do with the general problem of establishing boundaries for a linguistic area. In the majority of cases, the boundaries are fuzzy; often there is a central group of languages that share a large proportion of the characteristic features, and scattered peripheral languages or groups that share a considerably smaller number of the features. Frequently, too, there are shared features that are found only in a small subset of the area's languages. We will see examples of all these distributional types below.

This variation is hardly surprising, since the way a linguistic area arises is through contact-induced changes that occur over a long period of time and spread widely through the region – but always from language to language in a series of events, not in some single mystical area-wide process that affects many languages at once. In a large area, thanks to social connections that will be closer for some language pairs than for others and that may also vary over time, contact-induced changes will occur in different languages at different times, spread in different directions, and ultimately affect different numbers and different groupings of languages. There is no reason to expect that (for instance) a contact-induced change from k to $č$ will occur at the same time or in the same language as a change that introduces a new feminine gender category; even if both features spread to several other languages in the linguistic area, therefore, their final distributions in the area as a whole are quite likely to differ. (In many respects the spread of changes in a linguistic area resembles the differential spread of changes in dialects of a single language; this is why some scholars consider the field of areal linguistics to include both dialect geography and linguistic areas.)

There is an additional reason for the uneven distribution of shared noninherited features in a linguistic area: parallel contact-induced changes may introduce a feature into two neighboring languages, one of which keeps the feature while the other one loses it again at some later time. The two-step process of innovation and then loss of the feature in the one language will probably be unrecoverable by historical linguistic methods, since the time scale is more likely to be millennia than centuries, so that the chances of finding adequate evidence for tracing the two changes are small. That is: it should be easy enough to prove that the feature is absent from the language, but proving that it once existed in the language as a result of contact-induced change is another matter entirely.

This point is worth underlining by a necessarily rather technical one-paragraph digression into historical linguistic methodology. Historical linguists have only two methods for establishing the former existence of a feature in a language (other than the rare cases in which features long gone from a modern language are present in old documents). The most important of these is the COMPARATIVE METHOD, which permits the partial reconstruction of a family's parent language; any feature present in the parent language must have been inherited by all its daughter languages. The other method is internal reconstruction, which in a given case usually permits the reconstruction of only a few features in highly organized parts of the grammar. Internal reconstruction is so limited in scope that it is unlikely to be helpful in a case like this. Our only real hope of proving the former existence of a contact feature in a language that does not have it now, therefore, would be if the contact-induced change affected the language's parent language, so that the feature appears in its sister languages too. But in that case, we are likely to have trouble proving that the change is due to contact in the language family as a whole, rather than being a feature that (for all practical purposes) always existed in the family. Of course in principle we can compare entire families in long-standing linguistic areas rather than just the individual modern languages, and we might hope to argue for contact-induced change during the period before the parent languages split into their respective sets of daughter languages. In fact, it is clear that some linguistic areas are old enough that at least some of the relevant changes must have occurred in parent languages before they split into two or more daughter languages. But if that's what happened, we will not be able to argue convincingly for it unless the parent language itself is demonstrably related to languages outside the area. The reason is that – as we saw in the last section of Chapter 4 – we can only prove that contact-induced change has occurred when we have evidence that the proposed receiving language has in fact changed; and if the oldest stage we can reconstruct has the feature, we cannot establish it as an innovation. In any case, to return to the point about varying distributions of contact features, detecting a history of introduction and then loss of a feature in a particular language will almost certainly be impossible if the feature is not reconstructable for the language's parent.

A final question hidden in the above definition of 'linguistic area' also concerns the distribution of the area's characteristic features: do they have to be confined to the linguistic area? To me it seems that the answer is again clearly no: the features that characterize a linguistic area need not be exclusive to it, any more than they need to be universal in it. But this is a controversial issue, because some scholars have argued that a feature that is not confined to the particular region does not count as evidence for the existence of a linguistic area, and (by implication) that it cannot be considered a characteristic of the area even if the area is well established on the basis of other features. The controversy concerns only features that appear as a result of contact-induced change in some languages of the proposed linguistic area and that also occur in languages outside the proposed linguistic area but in its general vicinity.

The nature of language history supports the claim that a linguistic area can be characterized by features that are also found outside the area. First, and most obviously, all the features that characterize a linguistic area come from one or more languages that are (or were) spoken in the area. But often languages that belong to the area are related to languages that are spoken nearby but outside the area. If a feature that was inherited by the languages in such a family spreads by diffusion from a family member that is spoken within a linguistic area to other languages in the area, then of course that feature will also be shared by languages outside the area – namely, all the languages that belong to the same family as the source language. But if the feature is common within the linguistic area because of spread through contact to languages outside that family, it surely meets the most reasonable definition of an areal feature: a feature that is shared by languages in the area as a result of contact. Moreover, it is very likely that some features will spread beyond the area. Social linkages among speakers of the area's languages are (or were) presumably closer than social links between those languages' speakers and speakers of nearby languages outside the area; otherwise the areal boundary would be in a different place. Still, there will be some contact across the boundaries of many linguistic areas, and so some changes can and do spread into neighboring languages outside the area itself.

At this point readers may be wondering how the boundaries of a linguistic area can be determined at all, if contact features sometimes spread beyond proposed boundaries. Here it must be acknowledged that deciding where the boundaries are can be a difficult task, that some cases will be truly indeterminate, and that (in the most complicated cases) an ancient linguistic area can be overlaid by a more recently emerged linguistic area with different boundaries. But in strong linguistic areas there is a concentration of shared features that indicates an unusual level of contact-induced change across the whole area, with overlapping and interlocking ISOGLOSSES – an isogloss is a line on a map, most typically a dialect map but also a map of a Sprachbund, that surrounds the area in which a particular feature is found – and these are the prototypical cases.

In the rest of this chapter we will be concerned primarily with the historical analysis of areal phenomena. There are two crucial questions here: first, how do linguistic areas arise? And second, how are their linguistic features to be interpreted historically – that is, where did the features arise, and how did they spread through the area? The answer to the first question is that they arise in any of several ways   through social networks established by such interactions as trade and exogamy, through the shift by indigenous peoples in a region to the language(s) of invaders, and through repeated instances of movement by small groups to different places within the area. Natural and political boundaries help to set the boundaries of a linguistic area, because they help to limit the spread of features to languages beyond the borders. To understand the variety of linguistic areas as a social and historical phenomenon, we need to have an idea of their distribution and their social and linguistic nature. Accordingly, the next section surveys the world to give a general idea of their distribution and variety, including brief descriptions of some of the linguistic and historical features of a few representative examples. The stage will then be set for addressing the second question, about the emergence of the shared linguistic features in a linguistic area. It must be admitted, though, that it will prove impossible to give a simple straightforward answer to either of the two basic questions.

Some linguistic areas around the world

The fact that diverse languages in a particular geographical region often share numerous structural features is not a modern discovery. In the late eighteenth century, for instance, a Swedish prisoner of war, sent by his Russian captors to Siberia, compiled a list of common features linking Uralic and Altaic languages of eastern Russia, among them the presence of vowel harmony and agglutinative morphology. And in the nineteenth century Bartholomäus Kopitar (in 1829 and 1857) and Franz von Miklosich (in 1861) launched the field of Balkan linguistics by publishing some areal features of the Balkan Sprachbund. Most work on linguistic areas belongs to the twentieth century, however. And although the Balkan Peninsula remains the world's most famous linguistic area by far – it is the topic of a vast scholarly literature in books, articles, and at least two journals – the old view that it was a unique phenomenon has been superseded by the realization that linguistic areas are actually rather common.

Because of the prominence of the Balkan Sprachbund in the literature on areal linguistics, we will start our survey with Europe in general and with the Balkans in particular. In this and subsequent descriptions of linguistic areas, areal linguistic features will be listed without much explanation. Readers who want more detail about what a particular feature is like can consult the glossary at the end of this book for definitions of some of them; for others (especially ones that are less common in general among the world's languages) further explanation can be found in the sources listed at the end of this chapter. This minimalist descriptive strategy is meant to avoid having the main historical issues lost in a mass of detail; the point of including the lists of features is to show that the various linguistic areas are characterized by a variety of widely or narrowly shared features that are independent of each other, belonging to different structural subsystems.

The Balkans

The Balkan linguistic area comprises six languages (either the entire language or some of its dialects) that represent several branches of the Indo-European family: Romance, Slavic, Albanian, and Greek (and possibly Indic, if the Indic language Romani is considered to be a seventh member language). Several phonological and morphosyntactic linguistic features characterize the area; each one occurs in most of the languages, but not always the same languages, and there is also considerable variation in the expression of the various features from language to language. Other structural features, also clearly due to diffusion, are confined to two or three of the languages.

The major member languages are Rumanian (except for the westernmost dialect, in Istria), Bulgarian, Macedonian, and Albanian. Some dialects of Serbo-Croatian, specifically the southeastern Serbian dialects of the Torlak dialect group, also belong here; but other dialects of Serbo-Croatian do not, although some other Serbian dialects (including Standard Serbian) have at least a few of the characteristic areal features. Greek is generally considered to belong to the area as well, not only geographically (which is not in doubt) but also linguistically; but Greek is clearly not a core member of the linguistic area, because it shares only some of the features. Some scholars also include Balkan dialects of Romani, the language of the Gypsies, in the Balkan linguistic area; Romani shares only a few of the areal features, but one of these, the future formation with 'want', is one of the most characteristic of all the Balkanisms. All these Balkan languages are Indo-European, but they belong to widely divergent branches of the family: Rumanian is a Romance language, descended from Latin; Bulgarian, Macedonian, and Serbo-Croatian are Slavic languages; Romani is an Indic language (the Gypsies left India after 1000 CE); and Albanian and Greek are the sole members of their respective Indo-European branches. Turkish dialects spoken in southeastern Europe, though not Turkish dialects (including Standard Turkish) spoken in Asia Minor, apparently share some of the Balkan linguistic features, but as far as I know those features have not yet been analyzed in detail. Those Turkish dialects would be the only non-Indo-European members of the Balkan Sprachbund.

Precise information on the social conditions which gave rise to the Balkan linguistic area is lacking, as it is in the great majority of other linguistic areas. Still, at least two relevant points can be made. First, the present occupants of the Balkan Peninsula replaced earlier occupants whose languages are recorded only in place names and in a few inscriptions which can be read but can't be translated. One possible source of Balkan areal features, then, is interference from the language(s) of earlier inhabitants, either as result of borrowing or (more likely) as a result of imperfect learning when the people shifted to the languages of the newcomers. This point is relevant for the core Balkan languages, but not for Greek, which has been spoken in its present territory since well before the development of the current Balkan linguistic area. Albanian has also been spoken for a very long time in its present location (and is in fact a candidate for a descendant of the earlier inhabitants' language, which is claimed by some Balkan specialists to have been Illyrian). But Rumanian was planted in the Balkans by Latin-speaking settlers by the fifth century CE (or possibly by the Roman legions early in the second century CE), the Slavs moved south into the Balkans in the sixth century CE, and Romani speakers arrived long after the Slavs.

If some Balkanisms were originally interference features from previous inhabitants' languages, however, we will never be able to prove it, because we have far too little information about those languages to pin down the source. And most or all Balkanisms must have spread much later (at least to Slavic), because tenth-century Slavic texts, written in a South Slavic dialect that was roughly the parent language of Bulgarian, Macedonian, and Serbo-Croatian, do not display such characteristic Balkan features as the loss of the infinitive. (The features could, however, have arisen in some non-Slavic Balkan language(s) considerably earlier: it is only the spread to Slavic that must have been later than the tenth century.)

Second, the Balkans have a very long history of interethnic strife, including, in some parts of the region, some five hundred years of conquest and occupation by Turkish troops. This turbulent history has led to extraordinarily complex movements by small groups in different directions at different times. Some people, for instance, would move into the mountains or flee in front of the invading armies to get away from the Turks, while other people moved out of their refuges in the mountains to avoid starvation; in some cases whole villages packed up and moved to distant regions. All this movement resulted in changing patterns of language contact over the centuries, and in intermingling of populations in some places during some periods.

Even within a single language the results can look chaotic. A dialect map of Serbo-Croatian territory, for instance, shows extensive crosshatching of isoglosses rather than the more orderly bundled or parallel isoglosses that are characteristic of more settled regions. The Serbo-Croatian dialect picture is not total chaos, however: the great majority of the dialects can be classified unambiguously into groups in which shared common innovations have occurred as each group diverged gradually from the earlier parent language. But within various dialect areas there are alien pockets where migrant groups settled many years ago. Occasionally isolated features from those migrant groups' dialects have spread into their neighbors' dialects; and some of the migrant groups have of course shifted to the local dialects, occasionally bringing about a bit of shift-induced interference.

The relevant point in the present context is that the history of Serbo-Croatian dialects is paralleled, to a limited extent, by the histories of all the core Balkan languages. Even now there are, for instance, pockets of Serbo-Croatian speakers in Rumanian territory; and various Rumanian dialects are spoken in other parts of the Balkans – Arumanian dialects in Greece, Albania, Macedonia, and Bulgaria, Megleno-Rumanian dialects in northern Greece and Macedonia, and Istro-Rumanian in the Istrian Peninsula, outside the Balkan linguistic area in extreme western Croatia. The resulting contacts no doubt provided one means – perhaps the primary means – for the spread of the Balkan areal features from one language to another.

Although the precise route(s) by which interference features arose and spread through the Balkans cannot be determined, then, it is overwhelmingly likely that at least the contacts resulting from Turkish invasions contributed to the spread of some of the features throughout the area. It is of course entirely possible that other factors entered into the picture too. But even with so many questions surrounding the sociolinguistics and dating of the emergence of the features and their subsequent spread, crucial aspects of the general picture seems fairly clear: the situation was one of mutual bilingualism and multilingualism, and there was almost certainly no single source language for all the Balkan features. (Some scholars have argued for Greek as the source of the areal features, because of widespread Greek cultural influence in the region; but this isn't a promising position as Greek lacks some of the most characteristic Balkanisms.) There is no evidence in the Balkans for large-scale asymmetrical dominance relations – other than

Turkish dominance, but since Turkish, as noted above, does not have the areal structural features, it cannot be a source, much less *the* source. There is also no evidence for large-scale shift, although, as we have seen, there might have been a large-scale shift when speakers of the current languages moved in. We do know that there was no large-scale shift to Turkish in the core of the linguistic area, and probably there was none from Turkish to other Balkan languages either.

The linguistic effects, in any case, are striking. The Turks, while primarily filling the role of a catalyst promoting language contacts in the Balkans, also left direct linguistic traces in the form of numerous loanwords, especially in the nonbasic vocabulary, which spread throughout the Balkans. These loanwords are most common in Bulgarian, Albanian, and Megleno-Ruma-nian, but there is (for instance) a fat dictionary of Turkish loanwords in Serbo-Croatian, and a few Turkish derivational suffixes have also achieved a limited level of productivity within Serbo-Croatian. Most of the Turkish loanwords are nouns, but there are also quite a few verbs and, in the most-affected languages, many adverbs, prepositions, and conjunctions as well. According to Kristian Sandfeld, Greek cultural influence has led to the spread of numerous Greek loanwords through the Balkans (Albanian, Bulgarian, Serbian, Rumanian, and probably also Macedonian), and all the non-Romance Balkan languages have undergone significant Latin/Ro-mance interference at different periods. A diminutive suffix of Slavic origin (Slavic *-ica*) is found in Greek, Romanian, and Albanian. Since Latin (together with its daughter languages), Slavic, Greek, and to a lesser extent Romani are well understood historically, it is established that none of the characteristic structural areal features was present in the parent language of the modern Balkan languages – namely, in Proto-Indo-European.

The main areal phonological features are the presence of an unrounded central vowel, either a mid-central schwa or a high central vowel, and some kind of vowel harmony in stressed syllables. But the vowel harmony patterns differ in different languages: in Rumanian a mid-back vowel ends in a low glide before a nonhigh vowel in the next syllable, and in Albanian and Bulgarian back vowels are fronted before *i* in the next syllable. This feature also occurs in Greek, but it is lacking in some of the other Balkan languages; the central vowel feature is present in Rumanian, Bulgarian, some dialects of Macedonian and Serbo-Croatian, and Albanian, but not in Greek or Standard Macedonian.

Less widespread phonological Balkanisms are the presence of word-initial syllabic *m* and *n* in Albanian and Rumanian; the frequent loss of *l* before *i*, also in Albanian and Rumanian, and in some dialects of Romani as well; alternation between *n* and *r* in the same two languages; a change from *l* to *r* in Rumanian, Greek, Albanian, and (though rarely) Bulgarian; raising of *o* to *u* in unstressed syllables in Bulgarian, Rumanian, and Albanian; and a change from *ea* to *e* before *i* in Bulgarian and Rumanian. (Some of the features that appear in Bulgarian may also occur in the other Balkan Slavic languages.)

There are several well-established morphosyntactic Balkanisms. The loss of the inherited infinitive construction is perhaps the best known of these: instead of constructions that would translate into English as (e.g.) 'I want to eat', Balkan languages typically have constructions like 'I want that I eat'. Macedonian, Torlak Serbo-Croatian dialects, and Megleno-Rumanian lack the infinitive entirely; Bulgarian and Greek have only a few minor traces of the infinitive; other Rumanian dialects (except Istro-Rumanian) and the eastern variant of Standard Serbo-Croatian (which does not otherwise have the characteristic Balkan features) have very restricted usage of the infinitive; and Albanian, though it lost its inherited infinitive, has developed a new one (there are different new formations in the two main Albanian dialect groups). An example from eastern Standard Serbo-Croatian (i.e. Standard Serbian, but with accents omitted) is *rada sam da govorim* 'I'm glad to speak' (lit. 'glad.FEMININE be.I that speak.I'), as opposed to western Standard Serbo-Croatian (i.e. Standard Croatian, also with accents omitted) *rada sam govoriti* (lit. 'glad.FEMININE be.I speak.INFINITIVE').

The other especially well-known Balkan feature is the postposed article, as in e.g. Rumanian *aur-ul* 'the gold' (lit. 'gold-the.MASCULINE'); compare French *l'or* (lit. 'the.MASCULINE gold') and Spanish *el oro* (lit. 'the.MASCULINE gold'). This feature is present in all the Balkan languages except Greek. Other Balkanisms are a merger of dative and genitive cases in nominal declension; a periphrastic future construction using the verb meaning 'want', comparable to the English periphrastic future tense, e.g. *I will go*; a periphrastic perfect aspect construction formed with the verb 'have', also comparable to English, e.g. *I have gone* (this feature was present in (post-Classical) Latin, the parent language of Rumanian); pleonastic ('extra') personal pronouns, as in an English translation 'To him I wrote to him John'; identity of locative and directional constructions, again comparable to English, e.g. *I went in the house, I am in the house* (but compare the purely directional *I went into the house*); and a construction translating as 'one over/ on ten' for the numerals 11–19. There are a few other widespread shared morphosyntactic features in languages of the area, and a larger number of features that are confined to two or three languages, e.g. a plural suffix of Greek origin in Arumanian, frequent replacement of the dative feminine pronoun *je* by the dative masculine pronoun *mu* in Macedonian as a result of Albanian influence, and an innovative vocative case in Rumanian as a result of Slavic influence.

The Balkan areal features, then, occur in different subsets of the languages and with different specific manifestations of the particular feature. As we shall see, and as we could predict from the nature of linguistic areas (as described earlier in this chapter) and the nature of contact-induced language change more generally, both types of variation are typical of areal linguistic features.

The Baltic

Although the Balkan Peninsula is the best-known linguistic area in Europe, it is not the only one. A second one is most commonly labeled Standard Average European, or SAE (though it essentially includes only Indo-European languages of western Europe), and a third is the Northern Eurasian Sprachbund. But probably the best-established linguistic area of Europe after the Balkans is in northeastern Europe in the region around the Baltic Sea, where several languages belonging to two, or possibly three, different families form a Sprachbund. One set is a group of Uralic languages of the Finnic branch, including at least Estonian, Livonian, and Karelian. The other main members of the linguistic area are Indo-European: several members of the Balto-Slavic branch – Latvian and Lithuanian (Baltic) and northwestern Russian dialects (Slavic) – and dialects of German spoken in the Baltic region. The Turkic language Karaim might possibly belong to this Sprachbund, though it lacks many of the characteristic features. Maria Koptjevskaja-Tamm and Bernhard Wälchli have listed fourteen features as Baltic area characteristics, but only two of the languages – Estonian and Latvian – have all of them in some form: objects in the nominative case; lack of a verb 'have' (a sentence like English *I have a book* will often be translated as the equivalent of 'to me (is) a book'); the subject of a modal verb like 'must' is marked by the dative or genitive case, not the nominative (which is the usual subject case); impersonal constructions expressed with passive participles; the use of participles to express an evidential mode (as in 'John will come to the party, I hear'; a partitive case (as in 'some tea, a cup of tea') in addition to a genitive case (as in 'the price of tea'); numerals with partitive, genitive, or accusative case forms in nouns; GN word order (genitive preceding head noun, as in 'John's book') with basic SVO word order (beside nonbasic SOV order); special case marking with nonverbal predicates; lack of a copula verb 'to be' (in sentences like 'John is a teacher'); adjectives which agree with head nouns in number; phonemic tones; phonemically long vs. short vowels; and fixed stress on the first syllable of the word, which probably comes originally from Germanic. Other features are shared by only a few of the languages; one example is the use of verbs with prepositional prefixes in Estonian, Livonian, some Karelian dialects, and German – which is surely the source of the feature, since it is not confined to Baltic German dialects (e.g. Standard German *weg-gehen* 'to go away, leave', lit. 'away-go'). Another feature that might be added to this list is the existence of a rich case system in which nouns are marked for such grammatical categories as accusative (typically the case of a verb's object) and specific locations (in, into, on, onto, from, out of, etc.); this is a general feature that subsumes the case features mentioned above, and in the Indo-European languages of the area, at least, it primarily represents nonchange, not change: the Baltic languages and most of the Slavic languages are the only Indo-

European languages that have not lost most or all of the inherited case inflection of Proto-Indo-European.

Overall, the Baltic area has the same characteristics as the Balkan area: areal linguistic features are distributed differentially among the languages, and the features themselves vary in details of their structure. As for the sources of the Baltic features, some can be traced to Uralic and some to Indo-European, especially Germanic. The Indo-European languages most likely acquired Baltic features of Uralic origin through imperfect learning of the Indo-European languages by Uralic speakers, with shift (as in the case of Baltic and Slavic) or without shift (as in the case of Germanic); features of Germanic origin probably entered the other languages by way of borrowing, though imperfect learning is a possibility too: some German speakers, apparently unwilling to let Estonian speakers learn German, spoke to Estonians in a kind of 'half-Estonian', i.e. imperfectly learned Estonian, and German features could have entered Estonian by this route (and similarly in other Baltic contacts involving German).

The Ethiopian highlands

In Africa the best-known Sprachbund is located in the highlands of Ethiopia, home to members of three branches of the Afro-Asiatic language family – Cushitic, Omotic, and Ethiopic Semitic – as well as a number of non-Afro-Asiatic languages. The earliest major study of this linguistic area is Wolf Leslau's 1945 article 'The influence of Cushitic on the Semitic languages of Ethiopia: a problem of substratum', and Leslau's subtitle points to the origin of the Sprachbund: it apparently emerged primarily (though not necessarily entirely) as a result of shift-induced interference from Cushitic speakers who adopted the languages of the more recently arrived Semitic speakers. The linguistic area may be taken to include all of Ethiopia, but it is certainly strongest in the South, and especially in the Gurage region, where areal features are most pervasive. Although subsequent authors have disputed a few of the areal features originally proposed by Leslau, all specialists who have studied the region agree that it is a genuine linguistic area.

Below, to give an idea of the extent of Cushitic influence on Semitic, is a list of proposed areal features shared by Semitic with Cushitic and at least some of the other language groups of the area. With one exception – the occurrence of ejective (glottalized) stops, which was formerly thought to be an innovation in Ethiopic Semitic but is now believed by specialists to have been inherited from Proto-Semitic – all the major proposed areal features are mentioned here, even the controversial ones; a few of these features might need to be dropped from an eventual definitive list. It is important to keep in mind that, as with most other linguistic areas, not all these features appear in all Ethiopic Semitic languages. (My focus on Ethiopic Semitic is dictated by the fact that the literature on the Ethiopian Sprachbund focuses squarely on contact-induced changes in these languages. It is of course possible, even probable, that contact-induced changes may also have affected Cushitic and non-Afro-Asiatic languages of the region; but, as far as I have been able to discover, there is no systematic research on contact-induced changes in non-Semitic languages in the area.) The most-affected Semitic languages, those of the Gurage, share many more of the features than the least-affected northern languages – e.g. Amharic, the official national language of Ethiopia, which is based well north of the Gurage and which has few of the interference features.

First, Ethiopic Semitic languages have many loanwords from Cushitic languages. Some of these are in lexical domains that are typical for lexical interference in the language(s) of invaders: animals, vegetation, geographical terms, and tools. Others are more surprising: kin terms, body parts, numerals (for 'one', 'hundred', and 'ten thousand'), and (in some of the languages) a verb meaning 'bury' and a vocative particle. Some derivational affixes, for instance for forming abstract nouns, have also been transferred into Semitic from Cushitic. These more intimate loanword categories, together with the particle and derivational affixes, may (but need not) indicate that Semitic speakers were borrowing from Cushitic speakers before Cushitic speakers had given up their native languages and shifted to Semitic.

In the phonology, one highly marked new phoneme category has been added to Ethiopic Semitic: a series of labialized dorsal consonants, i.e. consonants like *k* and *x* pronounced with lip rounding. Less striking additions to Ethiopic Semitic phonology under Cushitic influence are a series of alveopalatal consonants, e.g. *č*, *č'*, *ĵ*, and *ñ*, and glides before *e* and *o*.

Morphological innovations in Ethiopic Semitic include just one new morphological category, a distinct future tense; this amounts to a functional split in the 'imperfect' category, which is used elsewhere in Semitic to express both present and future tenses, into a present and a future. Other morphological innovations involve a new means of expressing a preexisting category. For instance, most Semitic languages express the causative by means of a single prefix, but Ethiopic Semitic uses a double prefix – modeled on the Cushitic double-suffix formation, and therefore a good example of the common nonidentity of identity between source-language and receiving-language structures. In a partly parallel example, the negative perfect is formed in Ethiopic Semitic by a prefix–suffix combination (using only native Semitic morphemes), unlike the prefix-only negative perfect formation in other Semitic languages. In some Ethiopic Semitic languages, at least some noun plurals are formed by reduplication of the root's final consonant, replacing the inherited Semitic plural formations in Semitic nouns. The frequentative stem, which expresses an action that occurs often, is expressed by a vowel followed by reduplication of the penultimate (second-to-last) consonant of the root, and intensive or attenuative adjectives are expressed by reduplication – all as a result of Cushitic influence. Finally for the morphology, Ethiopic Semitic has undergone losses and partial losses under

Cushitic influence: the loss of the dual number category (Cushitic has no dual), the erosion of consistent gender distinctions in South Ethiopic (gender is less important as a category in most Cushitic languages than in non-Ethiopic Semitic), and the partial loss of plural marking on nouns in western Semitic languages of the Gurage (plural marking is optional in most Cushitic languages).

In the syntax, the most noticeable changes (because they change the appearance of the sentence) are the word-order changes: Ethiopic Semitic has changed from a verb-initial pattern including VSO sentential word order, Aux–Verb (auxiliary verb precedes the main verb), probable NA (adjective follows the noun it modifies), N Rel (a relative clause like 'who saw Mary' follows its head noun, as in English *the teacher who saw Mary*), and prepositions to a typical verb-final pattern, with SOV, Verb–Aux, AN, Rel N, and postpositions (as in a construction like 'the park in'). There is word-order variation within Ethiopic Semitic in some of these features: some of the languages use a sequence 'preposition N postposition' (as in 'in the park in') instead of just postpositions, and some languages have AN, Rel N alternating with NA, N Rel. Other syntactic interference features in Ethiopic Semitic are a change from coordinate and subordinate clauses with finite verbs to nonfinite gerund (so-called 'converbial') constructions – a difference that is partly comparable to the difference in English between *while he was walking to the store, John saw Mary* and *walking to the store, John saw Mary* – and the development of compound verbs like 'verb + "say"'.

The Ethiopian linguistic area follows the pattern we have already seen in the Balkans and the Baltic: areal features with differential spread and different detailed linguistic patterns in the various languages. But unlike the Balkans and the Baltic (as far as we can tell about those cases), the Ethiopian area arose primarily through imperfect learning, during a process of group language shift from Cushitic to Semitic. Of course this picture might change once more is known of the occurrence or nonoccurrence of some of these features in Omotic and especially in non-Afro-Asiatic languages of the Ethiopian highlands – and, for that matter, once more is known about the linguistic makeup of Proto-Afro-Asiatic. But for the features listed here, judging by what we know now, the process of spread was uniform and unidirectional. (And even if, or when, it turns out that Cushitic acquired some of these features through contact with non-Afro-Asiatic languages, it will still be true that Ethiopic Semitic got them from Cushitic through shift-induced interference.)

There are surely other linguistic areas in Africa besides the Ethiopic one. But the amount of detailed historical investigation of African languages – except for some branches of Afro-Asiatic – is still quite limited, and so, apparently, is the amount of detailed typological information. Investigation of other African linguistic areas will probably have to wait until more of the necessary historical and typological information is available.

South Asia

There are at least three linguistic areas in Asia: the Asian part of the Northern Eurasian area, Southeast Asia, and South Asia (the Indian subcontinent). Of these, South Asia is by far the best known and most studied. The linguistic area comprises languages of three families: Dravidian, all of whose members are spoken in South Asia; the Indic subbranch of Indo-European, most of whose members are spoken there; and Munda, a branch of the Austro-Asiatic family which is mainly spoken in Southeast Asia. These are not the only language families represented in the subcontinent; a number of Sino-Tibetan languages are spoken in the northeast and the isolate Burushaski in the northwest, as well as some non-Indian languages (most prominently English). In addition, Iranian languages (members, with Indic, of the Indo-Iranian branch of Indo-European) are spoken in the northwest. But Indic, Dravidian, and Munda are the groups whose members share significant numbers of the characteristic areal features. Iranian and Burushaski also share a few of the areal features, but they are not central members of the Sprachbund.

The South Asian area is extraordinarily complex. There are, first of all, ancient shared features – features that are universal, or nearly so, in Indic and Dravidian, and are therefore assumed (reasonably) to be the oldest of the area's characteristic features. Most of these can be reconstructed for Proto-Dravidian but not for Proto-Indo-Iranian (or Proto-Indo-European), so they are generally believed to have entered Indic from Dravidian via imperfect learning by Dravidians who shifted to the Indic language(s) of invading Indic speakers. The evidence that supports this hypothesis is all indirect. It is known that Dravidians were in India before Indic speakers, and the hypothesis that the source of these features was Dravidian is supported by the fact that they can be reconstructed for Proto-Dravidian. Significantly, however, there are few ancient Dravidian loanwords in Indic; this means that any Dravidian-to-Indic interference was almost surely a result of imperfect learning during a process of language shift. The shift hypothesis is also supported (indirectly) by the fact that the south of India is almost solidly Dravidian-speaking, while the northwest, in particular, is largely Indic-speaking – but with a few Dravidian languages spoken in speech islands scattered around Indic-speaking territory. The Indic speakers entered India from the northwest; the inference is that they found Dravidian speakers there, and that, although some of the Dravidians might have moved south while a few Dravidian-speaking groups survived in the North, many or most of the Dravidian speakers in the north shifted to Indic and became absorbed into the invaders' population. Some of these features shared by all Dravidian and almost all Indic languages occur in Munda too; others do not, or appear only in some Munda languages. There is no evidence, direct or indirect, for large-scale shift of Dravidian speakers to Munda, so there is no indication of how areal features got into Munda, or when. The core of the South Asian Sprachbund is in the western, southern, and northwestern parts of the subcontinent, not in the northeast – where Southeast Asian areal features can be found in some of the languages.

The old South Asian areal features, according to most of the literature, are the presence of retroflex consonants, especially stops (these occur in Munda too); phonaesthetic forms (e.g. with reduplication) (these occur also in Munda and in other Austro-Asiatic languages); agglutination in noun declension, with case markers added after distinct singular and plural stems (Munda has lots of agglutination, but with both prefixes and suffixes, so the connection with this Dravidian–Indic areal feature is dubious); a system of echo-word formation (in Munda too); a particular quotative construction; absolutive constructions unlike the ones that would have been inherited by Indic from Proto-Indo-European; the syntax of the Indic particle *api* and the corresponding Dravidian particle *-um* 'still, also, and, indefinite' (this feature is not found in Munda); rigid SOV word order with postpositions and other word order features that typically accompany SOV order (this also occurs in Munda, though other Austro-Asiatic languages have SVO word order); morphological causatives (not in Munda; but shared by Iranian as well as Indic and Dravidian); a second causative construction formed by doubling the causative suffix (but this feature is not found in Eastern Indic); a lack of prefixes (not in Munda, which has prefixes); conjunctive participles; a particular type of compound verb; the absence of a verb 'have'; and a particular comparison construction. The existence of two stems for personal pronouns is sometimes mentioned as an areal feature of South Asia, but since the feature can be reconstructed for both Proto-Dravidian and Proto-Indo-European, it is not the direct result of diffusion in South Asia. (It is not found in Munda languages.) Another feature that is often mentioned is a system of numeral classifiers; but this feature is characteristic primarily of eastern Indic languages and northeastern Dravidian languages, not of either Indic or Dravidian as a whole, and it may not be an especially old feature. Moreover, its source in South Asia seems to be Indic, not Dravidian; the northern Dravidian language Malto, for instance, uses borrowed Indic morphemes as well as native Dravidian morphemes in its classifier system. Numeral classifiers also appear in some, but not all, Munda languages.

A few of these old areal features also occur to the north of the Indian subcontinent, leading to the hypothesis that (in Colin Masica's phrasing) 'in the larger context, the Indian area appears as a southward extension of the Northern Eurasian area'. Masica also points to overlapping shared features between the South Asian and the Southeast Asian linguistic areas. It is quite possible that South Asia as a whole is part of a larger Eurasian Sprachbund, and it is equally unsurprising – given the presence of languages belonging to families located primarily in Southeast Asia and/or East Asia (Munda, Sino-Tibetan) – that some languages of northeastern South Asia have links to languages farther east. Whether these links are genetic or primarily due to contact is still uncertain.

So far the Indian picture looks complicated, but not extraordinarily so. What makes the complexity extraordinary is the very large number of locally distributed – and probably more recent – areal features, features found in a few to numerous languages of the area but not area-wide. Masica comments, for instance, on diffusion between Malayalam (Dravidian) and Sinhalese (Indic, spoken in Sri Lanka), between Kannaḍa (Dravidian) and Marathi (Indic), between Telugu (Dravidian) and South Munda, and between Kurukh (Dravidian) and Oriya or Hindi (both Indic). Kurukh has acquired nasal vowels from Indic; Pengo (Dravidian) has acquired numerous loanwords, aspirated stops, a sentence-final question marker, and other features from Oriya; Gondi (Dravidian) has borrowed an infinitive suffix and a relative cause construction from Indic, including a borrowed Hindi relative pronoun; Bengali (Indic) has borrowed a personal/impersonal distinction in nouns, together with the plural noun suffixes *-ra* 'HUMAN' and *-gulo:/guli* 'NONHU-MAN', from Dravidian; Marathi and Bengali (Indic) have acquired negative inflection from Dravidian (and note that Munda also has conjugated negation); and so forth. There are Indic to Dravidian changes, Dravidian to Indic changes, and Indic to Indic interference too. All these instances of diffusion – most intense, or at least most visible, in the border region separating the Dravidian south from the largely Indic north of the sub-continent – combine to form a picture of overlapping isoglosses, a network of links which, to put it a bit fancifully, tie South Asia together into a single linguistic area.

What makes this a particularly strong Sprachbund is the fact that the (apparently) more recent patterns of localized interference are superimposed on a background of (apparently) more ancient area-wide interference features. The main process that produced the old diffusion was probably imperfect learning during Dravidian-to-Indic shift; the processes that contribute to the more recent and ongoing interference are more varied, but they certainly include a great deal of borrowing, and there has perhaps been some shift-induced interference as well.

But this discussion probably gives the impression that it is possible, on the basis of current knowledge, to be sure about how the South Asian Sprachbund emerged and developed. In fact, a considerable amount of controversy surrounds the historical interpretation of the shared South Asian features, though everyone (as far as I know) agrees that South Asia is a genuine linguistic area. In this respect South Asia is no different from most, or more likely all, other linguistic areas: the sources of the features and the patterns of their spread can only be tentatively established (at best). Moreover, given the age of at least some of the South Asian areal features, it is all too likely that some Indian languages have lost or greatly altered some areal features they acquired a very long time ago, so that today's picture does not match yesterday's. Again, this is hardly unique to the South Asian area: it is a problem with many, most, or all other linguistic areas around the world.

The Sepik River basin, New Guinea

The Pacific basin is home to many hundreds of languages – a third of all the world's languages, according to one estimate, for a total of about two thousand languages in this one region. The languages of the region, which includes Australia and New Guinea, fall into two sharply different categories from the viewpoint of areal linguistics. The great majority of the islands of the Pacific are populated by speakers of languages belonging to the enormous Austronesian language family (over six hundred languages in all, some of which are spoken on the Southeast Asian mainland and as far west as Madagascar). There may be some linguistic areas in Oceania, as the Pacific islands are called collectively, but if so they have not been analyzed in any depth to sort out inherited from diffused features. Shared features in Austronesian languages as a group, in any case, are attributable to inheritance from their common ancestor, Proto-Austronesian.

The situation is radically different in Australia and New Guinea. The roughly two hundred known languages of Australia, about half of which are no longer spoken regularly, are commonly grouped into a single family, but there is no general agreement on the accuracy of this classification. The major problem is that Australia is one huge linguistic area, the result, apparently, of thousands of years of intimate contact and multilingualism through exogamy and other social institutions; the amount of mutual interference between languages has been so very extensive that distinguishing inherited features from interference features is a daunting task. The task is not, or may not be, hopeless: the Comparative Method has not yet been fully exploited for Australian languages, and more evidence is sure to become available in future in the effort to determinine genetic lines of descent among Australian languages. A major study of the Arnhem Land linguistic area (or subarea, within the Australian Sprachbund) of northern Australia showed that, although interference could indeed often be detected and separated from internal changes, the direction of interference was sometimes impossible to establish. Arnhem Land has a much greater concentration of languages than one finds in most of Australia; but since northern Australia is the oldest populated region of the country, the entry point for the first human settlers 50,000 years ago or more, this is the place to look for the origins of the larger Sprachbund. A detailed analysis of the Australian area, however, must wait until further information is available to help distinguish inheritance from diffusion.

Unlike Australia, where linguistic diversity is limited enough, and shared lexical and structural features numerous and systematic enough, to make a hypothesis of genetic unity plausible, the thousand or so languages of New Guinea and its satellite islands fall into at least sixty different language families – or rather at least sixty-one, because about two hundred and fifty of the languages are Austronesian, spoken in coastal regions and clearly latecomers. The other seven hundred and fifty languages of New Guinea are sometimes called Papuan, but the term translates to 'non-Austronesian languages of New Guinea' and is definitely not a label for a single language family. There is no detectable connection between Papuan languages and Australian languages, although New Guinea is geographically close to Australia.

In New Guinea too – as in Arnhem Land and elsewhere in Australia – intimate contact, extensive multilingualism, and extensive contact-induced language change are the rule, not the exception. We already saw Arthur Capell's famous remark about the languages of the island's central highlands in Chapter 2: adjoining languages have very different vocabularies, but their grammatical features 'recur with almost monotonous regularity from language to language'. This situation is clearly of ancient standing, and, again as in Australia, the problem of distinguishing diffused from inherited features is acute in historical work in New Guinea. As William Foley puts it in his 1986 book on Papuan languages, 'because of . . . multilingualism, Papuan languages are generally in a state of permanent intimate contact with each other', and this state has led to such widespread lexical and grammatical interference that efforts to discover genetic relationships are seriously impeded.

New Guinea as a whole is sometimes considered a linguistic area, thanks to a few very widespread features such as SOV word order, which is innovative in the island's Austronesian languages. But in discussing areal linguistics, Foley focuses on much smaller linguistic areas, where there is some hope of establishing particular shared features as due to contact. He also provides very much more social information than one finds in most analyses of linguistic areas, describing cultural features that contribute to the development of areal groupings. In particular, he argues that 'Each community constructs its identity by drawing on the available pool of cultural and linguistic traits', and since each community's members are multilingual, the available pool always includes other villages' languages as well as their own village's language. But then why, Foley asks, has all this mutual interference not produced a single homogeneous culture and language, a complete merger of culture and linguistic structure throughout the island? The reason is that, in addition to the outward-looking attitudes that multilingualism entails and that lead to the adoption of linguistic material from other languages, New Guinea communities also have a 'self-directed' world view that 'regards one's own customs and language as best and others as inferior' – so that communities deliberately maintain their own linguistic (and cultural) differentness from their neighbors. And the ultimate result, in Foley's words, is 'dazzling diversity . . . in spite of the pervasive tendency toward convergence'.

One small linguistic area in New Guinea is comprised of three neighboring languages of the Sepik River basin in northern Papua New Guinea. (It is possible that other languages also belong to this area, and that these three are the only ones sufficiently well understood so far to analyze comparatively.) The languages, which belong to three different language families, are Yimas, Alamblak, and Enga. (That is, they are unrelated to each other, as far as present knowledge goes; as Foley observes, even if further research shows them to be distantly related, the relationship would be so distant as to be irrelevant for the emergence of the areal features.) The shared features do not follow a uniform pattern, though Yimas and Alamblak share more of the features listed by Foley than any other grouping of the three: of the twelve features Foley discusses, all three languages share three features, Yimas and Alamblak share six, Yimas and Enga two, and Enga and Alamblak one.

All three languages have a palatal series of consonants, a series that is otherwise not common in Papuan languages. This feature is reconstructable for Proto-Engan and innovative in Yimas and Alamblak, so if it diffused in the area, Enga is the original source (though not necessarily the direct source in both languages, because it could have diffused from Enga to Alamblak and then from Alamblak to Yimas, or – less likely – vice versa). But the feature might not be due to diffusion at all in Yimas and Alamblak; it could have arisen independently in each language, because in both it happened via a sound change in which an apical consonant coalesced with a neighboring /i/ or /y/ into a palatal consonant. (Multiple causation is probably the most likely explanation for the feature's emergence in the two languages.) All three languages also share a suffixing possessive construction, but this feature is not due to any recent diffusion, at least, because all three languages inherited it from their respective parent languages. And all three have complex tense systems consisting of at least five tenses – a present, a future, and three past tenses (immediate past, near past (yesterday), and remote past) – but expanded in Yimas to include two future tenses (near, remote) and four past tenses (adding a 'day before yesterday and back to about five days' tense). The five-tense system was probably acquired by Yimas through diffusion from Enga and/or Alamblak, but it is original in both Enga and Alamblak in the sense that it can be reconstructed for their respective parent languages. It is possible, of course, that one of the parent languages acquired it from the other by diffusion.

Yimas and Alamblak, as noted above, share more structural features than any other grouping of these three languages: two or more central vowels (due to independent inheritance in both languages, not to diffusion); a particular plural pronominal suffix (probably due to diffusion); an elaborate system of verb compounding; bound adverbial forms in the verb (probably diffusion from Alamblak to Yimas); a particular causative formation; and a type of temporal adverbial clause in which an oblique suffix is added to the inflected verb.

Yimas and Enga share two features, a causative formed with the suffix -*(a)sa* added to a specific small set of verbs (diffusion from Enga to Yimas) and an indirect causative construction using the verb 'say'.

Enga and Alamblak, finally, share one feature, a particular switch-reference construction, i.e. a construction that signals a change of actor from one verb to the next (as in a sentence like English 'John arrived and Mary left'). This feature diffused from Enga to Alamblak.

As the list indicates, Foley is able to make educated guesses about the histories of some but not all of these shared features. Several are interference features from Enga into Yimas and/or Alamblak; Yimas is not demonstrably the source of any diffused features in the other two languages. Other shared features are inherited from the respective parent languages. In these cases there is no way to tell – not now, and quite possibly not ever – whether they are truly independent, all the way back in time, or the result of ancient diffusion from one proto-language into another.

The Pacific Northwest of North America

A large number of linguistic areas have been identified in the Americas, areas that are of greater or lesser strength and that are supported by greater or lesser (mostly lesser) amounts of systematic evidence. Lyle Campbell recently listed the following linguistic areas for all the Americas: in North America, the northern Northwest Coast, the Northwest Coast, the Plateau, northern California, Clear Lake (California), South Coast Range (California), southern California–western Arizona, the Great Basin, the Pueblo region, the Plains, the Northeast, and the Southeast; in MesoAmerica, the MesoAmerican linguistic area (which covers Mexico and parts of Central America); in (Central and) South America, the Colombian–Central American area, the Venezuelan–Antillean area, the Andean area, the Ecuadoran–Colombian subarea, the Orinoco–Amazon, Amazonia (the Amazon), lowland South America, and Southern Cone. Most of these areas have been studied only sketchily (at least so far), but a few – notably the Pacific Northwest (or Northwest Coast) and the MesoAmerican areas – have been the subject of considerable systematic analysis.

The Pacific Northwest linguistic area, which extends eastward from the Coast region into the Plateau region, has three core families: Salishan (twenty-one languages), Wakashan (six languages), and Chimakuan (two languages). Languages belonging to other families are also spoken in the region, and most of them have at least a few of the areal features, especially Tsimshian, Chinookan, Sahaptian, and the isolate Kutenai, but also the few Athabaskan languages in the area (in the phonology only). The Sprachbund contains two different culture areas: the Northwest Coast area, which extends northward from northern California to Alaska and eastward to the Coast Range; and the Plateau area, bounded by the Cascades in the west, the Rockies in the east, the Great Basin (desert) in the south, and the upper

Fraser River region in the north. Contacts among the area's languages have been close, involving much intermarriage between tribes, extensive trade relations, wars that brought tribes together as well as pushing them apart, and other social connections between neighbors living in a relatively densely populated region. These contacts led both to multilingualism and probably to the emergence of at least one pidgin language, Chinook Jargon (see Chapter 7 for discussion of this pidgin, and note that widespread multi-lingualism and the emergence of a pidgin are not as incompatible as one might assume). Chinook Jargon was the major contact language in the nineteenth century (and possibly earlier) in the Northwest Coast culture area and the western Plateau culture area, while the major contact language in the eastern Plateau was the Plains Indian Sign Language. Some aspects of culture do, however, coincide with the (fuzzy) boundaries of the Pacific Northwest linguistic area; in ethnobotany, for instance, one finds such area-wide features as the use of soapberry as a whipped dessert (it is called 'Indian ice-cream' throughout the region), the use of cow parsnip as a green vegetable, and the use of devil's club as a medicine.

Multilingualism in the Pacific Northwest linguistic area led to the diffusion of numerous linguistic features, both throughout the whole area and in localized subgroups of the member languages. Some of the area's features are clearly ancient, because they can be reconstructed for the parent languages of at least the three core families; in these cases, it is impossible to tell whether all the parent languages already had the features or (in some cases) acquired them by diffusion. In the phonology, these features include glottalized stops and affricates; labialized dorsal consonants, e.g. $/k^w/$ and $/x^w/$; a uvular (or back velar) series of dorsal consonants as well as a velar (or fronted velar) series, e.g. $/k/$ vs. $/q/$; lateral obstruents, most often a voiceless fricative and a glottalized (ejective) affricate; and a $/ts/$ affricate. Some of these features are rare elsewhere in the world; for instance, ejectives occur in perhaps sixteen percent of the world's languages, but lateral obstruents (usually only a fricative) occur only in about nine percent of the languages of the world. Some widespread areal features are later developments, due to diffusion in some of the languages; one example is a change from velar to alveopalatal obstruents, e.g. $/k/$ to $/č/$ – a change that left the languages with no nonlabialized velars – which took place in most Salishan languages (but in separated areas, so independently in each group), in Wakashan, in Chimakuan, and in some other languages of the area.

In the morphology and syntax, all three core groups have complex morphological structure with relatively few prefixes but many suffixes; minimal case systems; verb-initial sentence structure (this also occurs in Chinookan and Tsimshian); sentence-initial negation (also in Chinookan and Tsimshian); a particle or suffix that marks yes–no questions (sometimes optional; also in Chinookan and Tsimshian); a weak noun vs. verb distinc-tion; possessive pronominal affixes added to a possessed word (also in

Chinookan and Tsimshian); optionality of plural inflection, and the use of reduplication to express a 'distributive' ('one by one') plural (also in Nez Percé); the use of numeral classifiers for counting such categories as people vs. animals vs. canoes vs. other things, or different shapes; pairs of roots referring to singular vs. plural actions or states; and a system of lexical suffixes (suffixes which have concrete meanings like 'hand', 'domestic animal', and 'small round object' rather than more purely grammatical meanings like 'first person singular agent' or 'continuative aspect' or 'location in').

Here are a few examples of these features, all from Montana Salish: for extensive use of suffixes, *qʷo č-taXʷl-m-n-cút-m-nt-m* 'they came up to me' (lit. 'me to-start-DERIVED.TRANSITIVE-TRANSITIVE-REFLEXIVE-DERIVED.-TRANSITIVE-TRANSITIVE-INDEFINITE.AGENT'), with one prefix and six suffixes; for verb-initial and negation-initial sentential word order, *Tam escucu'úms* 'He isn't hitting him' (the negative word *tam* becomes the main verb of the sentence); for yes–no questions, *Ha escucu'úms?* 'Is he hitting him?'; for a weak noun–verb distinction, *a-qL-anwí* 'it'll be yours' (lit. 'your-FUTURE/IRREALIS-you' – *anwí* is the emphatic second person pronoun, and the tense/mood prefix *qL-* is essentially a verbal prefix); for a more typical example of possessive pronominal affixes, *sl'áXt-s* 'his friend' (lit. 'friend-his'); for plurals, *estiyéši* 's/he's crawling, they're crawling (together)' vs. *estiyé'eši* 'they're crawling one by one' (with a plural infix); for numeral classifiers, *mús* 'four of anything but people' vs. *čmúsms* 'four people'; for paired singular–plural roots, *cqntén* 'I put one thing down' vs. *slntén* 'I put several things down'; and for lexical suffixes, *n-kʷtn = áqs* 'he has a big nose' (lit. 'in-BIG = nose'; the lexical suffix is preceded by =) and *kʷtn = álqw* 'a tall person' (lit. 'BIG = long.object'). Wakashan and Chimakuan languages have the largest numbers of lexical suffixes, typically several hundred; most Salishan languages have a hundred or more of them, and they are also present, to a lesser extent, in Kutenai; Nez Percé also has a few lexical suffixes, presumably due to Salishan influence. In general, in fact – another areal feature – word structure is very complex in Pacific Northwest languages, including for instance subject markers on verbs and often also object markers. An additional widespread feature that may occur in all three of the core families (and elsewhere) is the use of a periphrastic imperative construction meaning, literally, something like 'it would be good if you did such-and-such', as in Chinook Jargon *Lus (spus) mayka Latwa* 'go!' (lit. 'good (if) you go'). Finally, a lexical areal feature is the category of decedence in kin-term designations, with kin terms like 'daughter-in-law after son's death' – that is, the relationship that exists after the death of an 'intermediate' relative. A Montana Salish example is *č'éwe'* 'grandparent after death of parents'.

Many other areal features in the Pacific Northwest have a much more limited distribution with the linguistic area. There are some loanwords that have been borrowed widely around the area, e.g. trade items and animal and plant names – often with discontinuous distribution, suggesting either long-distance trade (which happened often) or borrowing throughout a particular region and then loss by intervening languages. A few words are area-wide, such as a word for 'fence, corral'; most are more locally distributed, e.g. 'turtle' (several coast and interior Salishan languages, the Sahaptian languages Sahaptin and Nez Percé, and also Cayuse; on internal evidence, the source is Sahaptin). Another example is words for 'six' in Chinookan and coastal Salishan languages. But often the source of a word cannot be determined, because complex areal words may be analyzable into separate morphemes in two or even three of the languages or language families.

One of the two most striking phonological feature with limited distribution is the presence of pharyngeal consonants. These are striking because they are so very rare in languages of the world generally; they are found in languages of the Caucasus and in the Semitic branch of the Afro-Asiatic language family, but almost nowhere else in the world. They occur in three unconnected areas of the Northwest: all seven interior Salishan languages (but none of the coastal languages) have four or more pharyngeal consonants, which are phonologically sonorant; two Wakashan languages, Nootka and Nitinaht, and also northern Haida, have a voiceless pharyngeal fricative and a pharyngealized glottal stop (historically derived from a uvular fricative and a uvular stop, respectively); and Stoney (a Siouan language spoken in western Alberta) has two pharyngeal fricatives, a voiced and a voiceless one. Only one of these occurrences, the Wakashan one, is in the coastal area that is the center of Pacific Northwest areal features generally, and moreover the phonetics and phonology of the pharyngeals differ significantly among the three areas where they occur. Since the areas are unconnected, it is hard to argue successfully for diffusion of this trait from one area to the next; but, as Dale Kinkade has pointed out, it is also difficult to accept the proposition that this extremely rare phoneme type developed completely independently in languages that belong to the same linguistic area. (A hypothesis of more widespread pharyngeals at an earlier period, with subsequent loss in all but these few languages, is certainly conceivable, especially as two of the areas where they occur are peripheral within the area; but there is no solid evidence to support such a hypothesis.)

The other especially striking feature is also extremely rare worldwide: in five languages in two noncontiguous areas, nasal stop phonemes changed into corresponding voiced oral stops, e.g. /n/ to /d/, so that the languages lack nasal stop phonemes entirely (though some have nasal allophones). The languages are Makah and Nitinaht (Wakashan) and Quileute (Chimakuan) on the outer coast, and Twana and Lushootseed (both Salishan) on Puget Sound. Dale Kinkade has argued that this feature arose as a result of widespread variation and even 'intermediate' pronunciation between nasals and voiced oral stops in all coastal languages of the Pacific Northwest, when speakers of these five languages settled on an oral variant as the basic phoneme type. The question of origin still remains: that is, why did these particular languages settle on the oral variants? As so often happens in investigations of areal features, it is difficult to tell whether we are looking at two independent innovations with spread to neighboring languages or at an originally more widespread diffused feature with subsequent loss of the feature in the languages between the two nasalless areas.

Other phonological features of limited spread occur in continuous parts of the area (and are also less highly marked crosslinguistically), so explaining them as an independent innovation followed by diffusion to neighboring languages makes good sense. Here are some examples – by no means a complete list: very extensive consonant clusters in most Salishan and some other languages (e.g. Montana Salish); lack of /l/ (Klallam, Nootka, Tlingit); partial or total lack of labials in the northern part of the area; glottalized resonants, especially /l'/, /n'/, /m'/, /w'/, and /y'/ (Haida, Tsimshian; Kwakwala, Nootka (Wakashan); Bella Coola, Squamish, Twana (Salishan); Tolowa (Athabaskan)); interdental fricatives (Halkomelem, Comox (Salishan), Chasta Costa (Athabaskan)); tone or pitch-accent systems (Upriver Halkomelem (Salishan), Bella Bella (Wakashan), Quileute, Kalapuya, Takelma, Tlingit, Haida); vowelless words (Bella Coola (Salishan) and Bella Bella (Wakashan)); and alternations between *w* and *k* and between *y* and *č*, as a result of change from the VOCOIDS to the stop and affricate, respectively (a small subarea on the northern edge of the Olympic Peninsula – a regular change in Klallam (Salishan) with spread to Makah (Wakashan) and Chimakum, and related changes in two other Salishan languages as well). Even more restricted features are a nonglottalized lateral affricate borrowed by Quileute from Wakashan (first in loanwords, but later in native Quileute words as well), a glottalized lateral affricate and perhaps uvulars borrowed by Sahaptin (presumably from Salishan), and a lack of syllable-initial consonant clusters borrowed by Comox from Kwakwala (called Kwakiutl in the older literature).

Morphosyntactic areal features with limited distribution are similarly common and diverse. Examples (just a few) are feminine vs. masculine pronominal gender (Coast Salishan, Quileute, and Chinookan); inclusive vs. exclusive 'we' (Kwakwala (but not Nootka), Quileute (but not Chimakum), Chinookan, some dialects of the Salishan language Shuswap, and the possible Penutian language Coos); evidential markers; and classificatory verbs. A more varied but still characteristic feature is the occurrence of somewhat to extremely elaborate demonstrative systems, e.g. (on the extreme end of the continuum) Kwakwala categories near the speaker/near the hearer/near a third person; visible/invisible; masculine/feminine; and singular/dual/plural. This feature occurs in Wakashan, Chimakuan, Chinookan, Takelma, Tlingit, Siuslawan, Tsimshian, and Haida.

All these features, both the ones that are characteristic of the entire linguistic area and the ones with limited distribution within the area, reflect diffusion (most likely via borrowing rather than shift-induced interference, given the large numbers of loanwords around the area, but it is impossible to be sure). Even the ancient features, the ones that can be reconstructed for all three core-family parent languages, probably reflect some ancient diffusion, but establishing contact-induced changes at that time depth is almost sure to remain impossible. As with the other linguistic areas we have looked at, therefore, the general picture is clear enough in this case, but the detailed histories of the features cannot be determined.

The complex histories of linguistic areas

Now that we have examined several different linguistic areas, with quite different mixes of languages and language families, differing numbers of languages and of areal features, and demonstrably different overall historical developments, the main historical conclusion is not very optimistic: in most cases the detailed histories of the languages and their features have not been worked out, and in most or possibly all cases the details will never be worked out, because not enough information is (or will be) available. The social circumstances of past contacts in the areas can sometimes be assessed – shift from Cushitic to Ethiopic Semitic, ancient shift from Dravidian to Indic, and probably borrowing in certain other cases – but in other areas they can't be. In short, 'linguistic area' is not a uniform phenomenon, either socially or linguistically.

One feature that characterizes all well-established linguistic areas is a tendency, in a long-term Sprachbund, toward isomorphism, or convergence, in everything except the phonological shapes of morphemes. But it is important to stress that this does not justify an assumption that a natural outcome of a long-term Sprachbund is total merger of the grammatical structures of the languages. In fact, there is no evidence whatsoever that such a thing has occurred in any linguistic area anywhere in the world, so that arguing for it as a realistic possibility seems rash.

One reason, surely, is that although a high level of multilingualism and long-term close contact may lead to a large amount of structural interference, there is still a very long way to go before that adds up to total merger. The only contact situations that have led to total structural merger, as far as I know, are cases where the speakers of one language are under intense pressure to assimilate to a dominant culture, but are stubbornly determined to avoid total assimilation, and they ultimately borrow more and more from the dominant language until their original grammar is completely replaced. But those amount to a few extraordinary situations, and all are two-language contact situations (see the discussions of Ma'a and Laha in Chapter 8). In linguistic areas, what we find more often – perhaps always – is institutionalized bilingualism or multilingualism involving constant but not overwhelming contact with neighbors. In these situations there are countervailing tendencies:

speakers may tend to reduce the degree of separation between their two or more repertoires, but they also tend (as William Foley noted for New Guinea) to maintain cultural and linguistic boundaries.

It is also important to stress the fact that contact-induced change reaches an extreme level in parts of New Guinea, to the point where it has so far been impossible, and may remain so, to determine the lines of genetic descent in some languages. But even here there is no sign of total structural merger; and in other linguistic areas, with the possible exception of parts of Australia, the degree of convergence is much less. In most places, such as the Pacific Northwest and the Balkans, areal features tend to be variations on a common theme – quite different in structural detail, though unified by an overall commonality. The different specific phonetic and phonological manifestations of the pharyngeals of the Pacific Northwest is an example; the very different degrees and nature of infinitive loss in the Balkans is another. These differences in themselves argue against overall structural convergence. Instead, they seem to reflect the diffusion of a general pattern which is then often instantiated in entirely different ways from language to language.

A final point needs to be made in this connection: it is not safe to assume that degree of cultural diffusion will correlate with degree of linguistic diffusion. Cultural features can be and sometimes are adopted so extensively and rapidly that cultural convergence is extreme; structural linguistic features typically diffuse less rapidly and less completely. This is easiest to see in two-language contact situations. Montana Salish speakers, for example, have to a very large extent adopted the dominant European-American culture of their environment, maintaining aspects of their traditional culture with difficulty; but their language, as we have seen, has adopted few English words and no English structure – it is still in all respects a typical Salishan language. In some linguistic areas, too, the level of cultural congruence is very high, much higher than the level of linguistic diffusion.

Sources and further reading

This chapter is to a large extent an expansion of a brief paper entitled 'Linguistic areas and language history' (Thomason 2000). Among the most useful general sources on linguistic areas are Catherine Bereznak's 1996 dissertation *The Pueblo Region as a Linguistic Area*, Lyle Campbell's article 'Areal linguistics and its implications for historical linguistic theory' (1985), and Lyle Campbell, Terrence Kaufman, and Thomas Smith-Stark's 1986 article 'Meso-America as a linguistic area', which also provides some details about the Balkan linguistic area.

Nikolai S. Trubetzkoy introduced the term 'Sprachbund' in Proposition 16 at the First International Congress of Linguists in Leiden, Holland, 1928.

Among the most useful general sources on the Balkan Sprachbund are Jouko Lindstedt's 2000 article 'Linguistic Balkanization: contact-induced change by mutual reinforcement' and Kristian Sandfeld's 1930 book *Linguistique balkanique: problèmes et résultats*. Franz von Miklosich was a proponent of the view that Balkanisms are the result of shift-induced interference from an Illyrian or Thracian substrate (see Miklosich 1861). For a very thorough discussion of the loss of the infinitive in Balkan languages, including arguments for the importance of both internal and external factors in motivating the changes, see Brian Joseph's 1983 book *The Synchrony and Diachrony of the Balkan Infinitive: A Study in Areal, General, and Historical Linguistics*. I am very grateful to Saskia Moraru-de Ruijter for information about the distribution of varieties of Rumanian.

For the Baltic area, see especially Östen Dahl and Maria Koptjevskaja-Tamm, *Language Typology around the Baltic Sea: A Problem Inventory* (1992). Maria Koptjevskaja-Tamm and Bernhard Wälchli list Baltic Sprachbund features in 'An areal typological perspective on the circum-Baltic/North-East European languages: Sprachbund vs. contact superposition area' (a paper presented at the Annual meeting of the Deutsche Gesellschaft für Sprachwissenschaft, Halle, 1998). See Éva Ágnes Csató, 'Some typological properties of North-Western Karaim in areal perspectives' (1996) for a discussion of whether Karaim belongs in this linguistic area.

Bernd Heine discusses African linguistic areas briefly in his 1992 article 'African languages'. Information on the Ethiopian linguistic area comes primarily from two articles by Wolf Leslau (1945, 1952), but also from articles by Robert Hetzron (1975), Martino Mario Moreno (1948), and Greta D. Little (1974). Charles A. Ferguson (1976) gives a broader picture of the area. Both Moreno and Hetzron argue that some of the areal features listed by Leslau are mistaken, but all these authors present evidence that supports the existence of the linguistic area itself.

The South Asian linguistic area is described and analyzed in a number of important articles that are collected in Murray B. Emeneau's book *Language and Linguistic Area* (1980). Another important source on the area is Colin Masica's 1976 book *Defining a Linguistic Area: South Asia*. There is in fact a very large literature on this Sprachbund, but these two books are probably the best place to start reading about it. But see Hock 1975 and 1984 for arguments against hypotheses of ancient Dravidian substratum interference in Indic.

Jeffrey Heath's 1978 book *Linguistic Diffusion in Arnhem Land* (Canberra: Australian Institute of Aboriginal Studies) provides the most detailed and comprehensive look at perhaps the most important Sprachbund in Australia.

For New Guinea, see William Foley's excellent 1986 book *The Papuan Languages of New Guinea*; the quotation about permanent intimate contact is from p. 210, the comments on opposite tendencies toward linguistic amalgamation with neighbors and linguistic differentiation from neighbors are on pp. 26–7, and the description of the Sepik River Sprachbund is on pp. 263–7. Arthur Capell was one of the first students of the languages of New Guinea;

the quotation from him is cited in Stefan A. Wurm's 1956 article 'Comment on question: "Are there areas of *affinité grammaticale* as well as *affinité phonologique* cutting across genetic boundaries?" '.

The best general source on linguistic areas in the Americas is in Lyle Campbell's 1997 book *American Indian Languages: The Historical Linguistics of Native America*. On the MesoAmerican linguistic area, see Lyle Campbell, Terrence Kaufman, and Thomas C. Smith-Stark, 1986, 'Meso-America as a linguistic area'.

Some areal features of the Pacific Northwest Sprachbund were mentioned at least as early as 1911, in Franz Boas's 'Introduction' to *The Handbook of American Indian Languages*; for instance, Boas mentions the periphrastic imperative construction as widespread in the Northwest. But the first systematic discussion of this linguistic area is Melville Jacobs's 1954 article 'The areal spread of sound features in the languages north of California'. Mary R. Haas discusses some Pacific Northwest areal features in her 1969 book *The Prehistory of Languages*. Nancy Turner discusses the ethnobotany of the area in a 1997 conference paper 'Patterns in Pacific Northwest ethnobotany'. The estimates of percentages of languages with ejectives and lateral fricatives are William Poser's, from his 1997 conference paper 'Areal phonological features in languages of the Pacific Northwest'. Two papers by M. Dale Kinkade, 'More on nasal loss on the Northwest coast' (1985) and 'The emergence of shared features in languages of the Pacific Northwest' (1997), explore the distributions and histories of various Northwest areal features.

6 Contact-Induced Language Change: Mechanisms

In Chapters 4 and 5 we saw examples of various kinds and degrees of contact-induced language change, with a focus on a major dichotomy between two very general modes of change: contact-induced changes in which imperfect learning plays a role (shift-induced interference) and contact-induced changes in which imperfect learning is not a significant factor (borrowing). The crucial distinction between these two sociolinguistic types of change, as we have seen, correlates with a distinction in their typical linguistic results: less transferred vocabulary and more structure in shift-induced interference vs. more transferred vocabulary and less structure in borrowing.

But although this salient social distinction provides generally valid predictions of different linguistic results under each of the two conditions, and is therefore useful in efforts to sort out very general processes of contact-induced change, it does not help us in our efforts to understand exactly how contact-induced change occurs. A full account of the specific processes through which foreign material gets into a language would require attention to innumerable social and psychological details, and linguists are nowhere near any comprehensive understanding of all the relevant processes.

Still, some progress can be made even if a full understanding is beyond us. In this chapter we will approach the 'how?' question by examining seven mechanisms of contact-induced change – mechanisms which operate, singly or in combinations, to produce contact-induced changes of all kinds. (These may well not be the only mechanisms that exist; but they are the only ones that I have been able to identify so far.) Some of the labels for the seven mechanisms will not make much sense until they are defined in later sections, but for ease of reference, here they are: code-switching, code alternation, passive familiarity, 'negotiation', second-language acquisition strategies, bilingual first-language acquisition, and change by deliberate decision. These are all broad mechanisms; a comprehensive analysis of the processes would require combining these mechanisms with the results of the detailed research that is being carried out by many scholars on both psychological and social aspects of the problem. Those lines of research, having to do with such issues as the activation of one or two languages in a bilingual speaker's brain and the spread of a linguistic change through a speech community, were discussed very briefly in Chapter 3.

The relationships between the seven mechanisms and the dichotomy based on presence or absence of imperfect learning will also be considered in this chapter. As we will see, the fit between them may not be precise. In fact, only code-switching and second-language acquisition strategies definitely correlate robustly with the predictions that arise from the major dichotomy; all the other mechanisms except change by deliberate decision might also fit well, but the available evidence is inconclusive.

Before we begin our survey, three preliminary observations must be made. First, it is important to recognize that our chances of tracking the full course of any linguistic change, from the first speaker's initial innovation to the spread of the innovation throughout a speech community, range from slim to none. In practice, even the most sophisticated sociolinguistic methods – and modern methods of studying ongoing change are very sophisticated indeed – cannot begin tracking a change until the change is already well under way. There is no way to tell in advance whether a child's *I goed home early* or a tired (or inebriated) adult's *Have you already aten?* (instead of *eaten*) will catch on and turn into a morphological change; the only way to find out would be to follow the speaker around for ten or twenty years to see if s/he uses the innovative form consistently and, if so, if the people s/he talks to begin to use it too.

Unfortunately, this is not a promising research project, because the chances of interesting results are vanishingly small: the vast majority of innovations do not catch on, even in the innovator's speech. For instance, in the fall of 1999 a class of twenty first-year undergraduate students at the University of Michigan collected dozens of innovations – speech errors, potential language changes! – in just a few hours; none of us had ever heard most of the innovative forms before, and it is quite possible that none of us will ever hear most of those innovations again. Moreover, even if an observer were to detect the very first use of an innovative form, there would be no way to be sure that it was the first instance. Because a discussion of mechanisms of interference implicitly focuses on how one speaker adopts a foreign feature, the whole topic therefore requires us to draw inferences about processes that we can only observe in part. This is true for all aspects of language change, of course, including internally- as well as externally-motivated (i.e. contact-induced) changes. The proper intellectual stance is not despair, but instead a recognition of the inevitable gap between innovation in one person's speech and change in an entire language, and (therefore) caution in drawing inferences.

The second preliminary comment is that the question of whether or not a change is linguistically possible is settled as soon as an innovation appears just once in a single speaker's speech. Speech errors made by people who are tired or drunk or just generally inclined to tongue-stumbling are all possible changes. The question of whether a change is linguistically probable and/or socially possible is quite another matter, of course. In this chapter we will look at a number of examples that are one-time speech events, a single speaker's usage on a single occasion, rather than completed changes in a language. The use of such examples is justified by this second observation, which in this chapter serves as a background assumption.

The third observation concerns a claim that was made in Chapter 4, namely, that there are no absolute linguistic constraints on interference. Certain kinds of contact-induced changes are more probable than others, certainly, and extreme degrees of contact-induced change are not very common; but all kinds and degrees of linguistic interference are possible, and can be illustrated from well-documented examples. This claim also serves here as a background assumption, and it carries implications for the analysis of mechanisms of interference: if the no-constraints assumption is correct, then either every mechanism also lacks absolute linguistic constraints, or the different mechanisms have different constraints such that, when taken all together, the mechanisms as a group do not rule out any particular kind or degree of interference.

It should be noted immediately, therefore, that there are no well-estab-lished linguistic constraints on any mechanism of interference. Constraints have been proposed, especially on code-switching, but there is no consensus among specialists that any of the proposed constraints are valid. It's hard to tell, in the present state of research, whether the lack of constraints on any mechanism is the way things are in the world or simply a result of the fact that not one of the mechanisms is fully understood.

Below is a survey of each mechanism in turn. At the end of the chapter we'll examine one specific process that can't be clearly assigned to one or more mechanisms: double morphological and/or syntactic marking during a process of contact-induced change.

Mechanism 1: Code-switching

Code-switching deserves the first position in a survey of mechanisms of interference because it is by far the most studied of the seven mechanisms. This may or may not mean that code-switching is the major mechanism by which contact-induced changes are introduced; it is quite possible that the predominance of code-switching in the scholarly literature has to do instead with the fact that it is especially noticeable in many bilinguals' conversation, or with the possibility is that it is more easily studied than most of the other mechanisms. What is clear is that code-switching has been the topic of numerous books and innumerable articles, and the focus of many theories. Inevitably, then, the treatment of the topic in this section will be much too brief to capture the full flavor of the code-switching literature, and interested readers should refer to works such as those mentioned at the end of the chapter for more detailed consideration. Still, brief though it is, this section is much longer than the others in this chapter, because much more is known about code-switching than about the other mechanisms, with the possible exception of Mechanism 5.

Code-switching is the use of material from two (or more) languages by a single speaker in the same conversation. By implication, 'the same conversation' means that all the other participants also speak, or at least understand, both (or all) the languages. The general topic is sometimes subdivided into two categories, code-switching – intersentential switching, which is switching from one language to another at a sentence boundary – and code-mixing or intrasentential switching, in which the switch comes within a single sentence. These two categories are used in many sociolinguistic analyses of switching. In this book, however, the term 'code-switching' will be used to refer to both categories, because for the analysis of change mechanisms they seem to be roughly equivalent.

Here are two typical examples of intrasentential code-switching from Yiddish–English bilinguals, one from each of their languages: *When I come in I smell the kugel* (*kugel* is a kind of pudding) and *Di kinder geen tsu high school* ('the children go to high school'). In both of these examples a single lexical item from one language is inserted into a sentence that is otherwise entirely in the other language; the inserted words refer to concepts – *kugel, high school* – that are unknown, and therefore without a native equivalent, in the other culture. Code-switching serves many different conversational functions. I will not try to list all of them here (there is no complete list available, or even possible), but one obvious function, as in the examples just given, is to adopt a word from the one language to fill a lexical gap in the other language. Two other functions can be illustrated from the same Yiddish–English bilingual community as the above examples. In the first, a Yiddish word is inserted into an English sentence as a kind of euphemism, to soften the effect of something unpleasant: *One is already geshtorbn* ('dead'). In the second, a Yiddish clause is inserted into an English sentence in mid-conversation when someone is mentioned who is identified with Yiddish: *Is warm. Is wool. Dos hot meyn shvester gemakht a long, long time ago* ('my sister made it', lit. 'that has my sister made').

Strong claims have been made about the relationship between code-switching and contact-induced change. At one extreme are scholars who deny any connection between the two – who claim, in effect, that code-switched elements will never turn into borrowings; at the other extreme are scholars who believe that code-switching is the only mechanism through which foreign morphemes are incorporated into a language. As is usually the case with extreme and all-encompassing claims in a domain as complex as contact-induced language change, neither of these positions can be made to fit all the available data.

There is solid empirical evidence for a transition between code-switching and permanent interference, for instance in Jeffrey Heath's 1989 book *From*

Code-Switching to Borrowing: A Case Study of Moroccan Arabic. This finding is not surprising: among the most frequent code-switched elements are nouns and discourse markers (such words as English *so*, *well*, and *anyway*). But nouns and discourse markers are also among the most common types of loanwords, an agreement that is hard to explain as mere coincidence. It is also difficult to see how a principled distinction could be drawn between (say) a code-switched element and a loanword: how many times can a code-switched foreign element appear in bilinguals' speech? If it is very common, and if monolingual speakers of the language have adopted it from bilingual speakers, surely it must be assumed to have become a loanword.

On the other side, assigning universal relevance to code-switching makes it hard to account for the undoubted examples of interference in which code-switching is demonstrably not a factor – for such reasons as community disapproval of code-switching or because the bilinguals in a particular contact situation usually talk to monolinguals, not to other bilinguals. It is also difficult to propose code-switching as the mechanism for interference in cases where the interference features do not correspond to results that have been found in code-switching contexts, for instance the deliberate introduction of a voiceless lateral fricative *ł* by Ma'a speakers (Tanzania) into Bantu words when speaking the Bantu language in which they are all bilingual (see below for discussion of this example).

Even if it is not a universal factor in contact-induced change, however, code-switching is certainly an important element in many cases of lexical and structural interference. Several issues complicate the analysis of the transition from a code-switch to an interference feature, but they can all be subsumed under one question: how are the two phenomena to be distinguished? Various criteria have been proposed, and some of them are quite useful, but no set of criteria can be counted on to give a definitive answer to the question in all cases. The reason, ultimately, is that the boundary between code-switch and permanent interference feature is necessarily fuzzy: as in other types of gradual language change, clear cases can be found on each side of the boundary, but near the boundary different criteria will give different results. In other words, although code-switches and interference features are two different things, they lie at opposite ends of a continuum; the difference between them is not categorical. In the following discussion of some major criteria for making the distinction, I will refer to the language in which code-switches and interference features appear as the receiving language, and to the language the features come from as the source language.

First, if monolingual speakers of the receiving language use a source-language element in speaking their language, it is probably safe to conclude that that element has become an interference feature: speakers cannot code-switch to or from a language they do not know at all. This criterion is not very useful, though, in contact situations where everyone is bilingual or multilingual.

Second, it has been proposed that code-switched elements are not inte-grated into the receiving language's structure, whereas borrowed elements are NATIVIZED – adapted to the structure of the receiving language. Shana Poplack and Marjory Meechan have phrased the distinction as follows, adding a third category, nonce borrowing, to their classification:

> '[C]ode-switching' may be defined as the juxtaposition of sentences or sentence fragments, each of which is internally consistent with the morphological and syntactic (and optionally, phonological) rules of its lexifier language . . . . 'Borrowing' is the *adaptation* of lexical material to the morphological and syntactic (and usually, phonological) pat-terns of the recipient language. Established 'loanwords' (which typi-cally show full linguistic integration, native-language synonym displacement, and widespread diffusion, even among recipient-lan-guage monolinguals) differ from 'nonce borrowings' only insofar as the latter need not satisfy the diffusion requirement.

But like the first criterion, the usefulness of this one is asymmetrical: if an element is nativized, it is probably an established interference feature; but if it is not nativized, it could be either a code-switch or an established interference feature. The reason is that structure can also be transferred from one language to another, so an unassimilated structure could be either a code-switch or a permanent interference feature. So, to take a relatively trivial example, the name of the German composer Bach is a loanword for all English speakers, not a code-switch, but its pronunciation varies: some English speakers pronounce the name with a final velar stop /k/ (nativized) and others, including some who do not speak German at all, pronounce it with the final German consonant, a velar fricative /x/. The name may or may not have entered English via code-switching; but if code-switching was the mechanism for the interference, nativization is clearly useless as a criterion in this case. True, the borrowing of German /x/ is not a general phenomenon in English – it may even be confined to this one word – but it is easy to find contact situations in which many words and other elements are borrowed with their original source-language structural features intact.

Third, if a foreign element appears just once in a bilingual speaker's discourse, then it is presumably safe to assume that it is a code-switch, not a borrowing. (I do not mean to suggest here that anyone is likely to be able to find out that the element appeared just once! Determining the frequency of appearance is a hopeless task, but the principle, though nonempirical, is still valid.) And conversely, if it appears very frequently, it is most reasonable to classify it as a borrowing. But all too often this criterion is difficult or impossible to apply in practice: unless an element occurs very frequently, how can one determine whether a speaker has used it once, occasionally, or frequently? This problem is essentially the same as the problem of tracking a linguistic change from the first speaker's original innovation, in that much of the process, especially at the beginning stages, is invisible (or inaudible) to scholars.

A fourth criterion arises from the structural constraints on code-switching that have been proposed in the literature – most notably, in this context, the Free Morpheme Constraint, which predicts that code-switches will not occur within a word, i.e. between a stem and an affix or between two affixes. The argument is that if one finds elements from the source and receiving language combined within a word, the source-language element must be a borrowing, not a code-switch. As numerous authors have pointed out, however, some instances of word-internal language alternation look very much like code-switching. One example is the presence of hybrid English–Maori words with un-Maori phonology in bilinguals' Maori speech in New Zealand. English stems like *inject* are combined with Maori suffixes like *-ngia* 'PASSIVE' to produce words like *injectngia* 'be injected', which has segments and consonant clusters that would never be found in Maori itself – a sign that the English elements are more likely to be code-switches than borrowings. And there is corroborating evidence for this analysis, because English loanwords in Maori are nativized, so that they do not have such segments or clusters. English stems like *inject* in *injectngia* are therefore best analyzed as code-switches, in spite of the fact that the switch occurs in mid-word.

A warning is in order here, however: we cannot be absolutely certain that this analysis is accurate. It is possible that, although older English loanwords were nativized into Maori phonology, newer loanwords are no longer being nativized, with the eventual result being a changed Maori phonological system. As we saw in Chapter 4, for instance, early Russian loanwords into Siberian Yupik Eskimo were fully nativized, but later Russian loanwords – those that entered the language after Yupik speakers became fluent bilinguals – retained the (previously) non-Eskimo phonological features of the Russian source words.

What, exactly, is the process through which code-switches turn into permanent interference features in a receiving language? This is again a question that cannot be answered fully without much more knowledge than is currently available about psychological and sociological processes. But the general outline of the process is fairly clear. Suppose, for example, that the code-switched English word *inject* becomes a loanword in Maori. If Maori has no native verb with a similar meaning, then *inject* will simply be added to the language's lexicon to refer to the new concept, perhaps with phonological nativization. This process is similar to lexical innovation in a monolingual context, as with *email* or *photocopy*: someone thinks up a new word and introduces it and then, if it catches on, it eventually spreads throughout the community. If Maori already has a verb with roughly the same meaning, then *inject* enters into competition with the native verb, just as *photocopy* competed with *xerox* for the same semantic domain. Competition between old forms and innovative forms was discussed in Chapter 4, and I will not repeat it here, but I will underline the basic point in the present context: code-switching is a mechanism whereby new forms and new structural features are introduced into a receiving language; once a code-switched element is present, it progresses to permanence along the same path followed by other innovations, including internal ones.

A final question about code-switching has to do with its relevance in each of the two major modes of contact-induced change. Code-switching is certainly a major mechanism for borrowing interference, that is, for inter-ference in which imperfect learning does not play a significant role. This is most obvious for the borrowing of vocabulary, given the very high frequency of single-word code-switches. Within this category, the insertion of words that have no precise equivalent in the receiving language is especially common – as is lexical borrowing of such words. Structural interference can also result from code-switching. Maori–English bilinguals, for instance, use the English conjunction *and* as a code-switched element in Maori sentences – apparently because the simple English coordinating construction with *and* is so much easier to use than the much more complex Maori system of coordination. And there is evidence that this English feature is connected with ongoing change in Maori, as the Maori preposition *me* 'with' expands its range of usage to converge with the use of *and* in English.

What about code-switching as a mechanism of shift-induced interference, when imperfect learning does play a significant role? Probably code-switch-ing is not a major mechanism of this type of contact-induced change. By far the most common code-switched elements are single words and short phrases, but in shift-induced interference structural features – especially phonology and syntax – predominate. Of course this does not mean that code-switching is never operative in shift-induced interference, but it is unlikely to be of much importance. It is certainly true that words from shifting speakers' first language get incorporated into a target language; Turkish immigrants in the Netherlands, for example, insert Turkish words into Dutch sentences when they do not know the right Dutch word for the context, or in order to give an ethnic flavor to their Dutch. But many of these inserted words may be ephemeral even in the immigrants' speech, and probably few of them will become permanent features of any variety of Dutch.

Mechanism 2: Code alternation

Code alternation is the other common type of behavior among fluent bilinguals. Like code-switching, code alternation is the use of two (or more) languages by the same speaker. But unlike code-switching, code alternation does not occur in the same conversation with the same speaker. Instead, bilinguals use one of their languages in one set of environments and the other language in a completely different set of environments. In the simplest case, the bilingual speaker would speak only to monolinguals, so that code-switching would not be useful for purposes of intelligible communication.

Perhaps the most typical context for code alternation is the use of one language at home and another at work. This sets the stage for code alternation rather than code-switching in communities where (for instance) the men work outside the home and are bilingual, while the women stay home and are monolingual; but it may well occur even when everyone at home or even in both settings is bilingual. Code alternation is also common in cases of language death, when the last fluent speakers of the dying language speak it only with the few other remaining fluent speakers, but speak the dominant language of the surrounding community with everyone else. In such a case the bilinguals may code-switch when talking to other bilinguals, but in some communities they do not engage in any code-switching. In fact, in some communities code-switching is frowned upon as socially unacceptable, so that code alternation is the only option for speakers who regularly use two different languages.

Examples of changes brought about by code alternation are not easy to find in the literature. The reason is probably not that they are rare, but that in many or most cases it is hard to be sure that the mechanism was code alternation rather than code-switching (or a combination of code-switching and code alternation). The problem is that changes resulting from code-switching and code alternation may well be very similar or even identical, so that the two processes can be distinguished sharply only where we have evidence that only one or the other is present. Since code alternation is so much less prominent in the literature than code-switching, it bears the burden of proof: the only convincing examples will be those in which code-switching can be ruled out. The examples I have found so far of changes due to code alternation are anecdotal, and the results are not clearly fixed as permanent interference features in anyone's speech, much less in an entire language. Still, they show that this mechanism must be considered in any effort to determine the route by which an interference feature entered a language.

The first example is a report by Ad Backus, a Dutch–English bilingual, about his conversations with a group consisting of one American (who did not know Dutch) and two other Dutch speakers. On these occasions he alternated between Dutch and English, always speaking English to one friend and Dutch to the other two; that is, he did not code-switch. He noticed that this code alternation led to extensive though temporary interference in both his Dutch and his English in this setting, in the lexicon as well as in the grammar: he had trouble thinking of the right words when using either language, and he found himself using grammatical constructions from one language when speaking the other.

The second example comes from a native speaker of Italian (and French) who, after spending twelve years in school in the United States, heard with dismay compliments from Italians to the effect that she spoke Italian quite well, for an American. She then paid close attention to her Italian speech and realized that it had been influenced by English in phonology: she used English intonation patterns, alveolar instead of dental stops, and aspirated instead of unaspirated initial voiceless stops. There were also some changes in her lexical semantics, for instance in her use of Italian *libreria* in the sense of English 'library' instead of 'bookstore', as in Italian (in Italian the word for 'library' is *biblioteca*.) She thought there might be changes in her Italian syntactic patterns as well. Code-switching could be ruled out as a mechanism: she spoke only Italian in Italy and, except for a few occasions when Italian friends visited her in the United States, only English in the United States. Code alternation, then, must have been the mechanism by which English interference features entered her Italian.

The third example is similar to the second. An Estonian speaker who had lived in Finland for eight years, returning regularly to Estonia with her family for summer vacations, was complimented on speaking Estonian very well for a foreigner. Estonians found her accent strange, and her word-order patterns had become closer to Finnish than Estonian. She reported trying very hard to keep her vocabulary pure Estonian, with some success. She said that the mechanism was code alternation, not code-switching, although her home language even in Finland was Estonian.

A point worth emphasizing is that all of these bilingual speakers were unwilling participants in the processes of linguistic interference: the Dutch–English bilingual speaker was annoyed, the Italian–English bilingual speaker felt humiliated, and the Estonian–Finnish bilingual speaker was embarrassed by the changes that had occurred in their native languages. The Estonian–Finnish speaker was apparently able to prevent lexical interference from affecting her Estonian, but like the other two bilinguals she experienced involuntary incorporation of second-language features into her first language. She and the Italian–English speaker were unconscious victims of these changes, noticing them only when other native speakers of their first languages commented on them. Not so the Dutch–English speaker, who was fully aware of what was happening to him during his code-alternating conversations with English- and Dutch-speaking friends.

Regardless of what educated and linguistically trained bilinguals think of this process, however, it is clear that interference features introduced in this way can easily become fixed in a whole language. This is most likely to happen if many members of a community are bilingual in the same language and also involved in code alternation, so that similar changes will arise and then spread throughout the community.

These examples bring to mind a point mentioned in Chapter 3 above, about a proposal by François Grosjean and Carlos Soares. Grosjean and Soares argue that, when bilinguals speak one of their languages, the other language 'is rarely totally deactivated, even in completely monolingual situations'. This proposal suggests the way code alternation might work:

regular use of the two languages in different situations might make deactivation of each one more difficult, so that bits of each language would leak into the other. This could, of course, happen in code-switching contexts too; but code-switching is different, because in effect it licenses the activation of either language at any time. That is, if a bilingual speaker is talking to another bilingual in language A, and when articulating some concept thinks of the B word first instead of the A word, he or she can simply insert the B word into a sentence that is otherwise in A – and likewise with grammatical constructions. The code-switching bilingual can also switch entirely from A to B at will. In code alternation, a B word could presumably be inserted into A discourse occasionally without disrupting the process of communication, but the complete-switch option is not available, because only one of the two languages is appropriate in a given context. Activation of B in an A context is therefore a problem without an easy solution. But structural changes might make the problem less acute, at least sometimes, by bringing about structural convergence and thus reducing the effort required to deactivate either language.

The last thing we should consider in this section is the connection between code alternation, on the one hand, and borrowing and shift-induced interference on the other. Unfortunately, not much can be said about their interrelationships, because there is still too little information available about code alternation to provide a clear picture of its scope and frequency. My impression is that lexical interference is considerably less prevalent in code alternation than in (for instance) code-switching, but this impression is based on such a small amount of data that its validity must be considered doubtful.

Mechanism 3: Passive familiarity

The third mechanism of interference is even less visible in the language contact literature than code alternation. Contact-induced change through passive familiarity occurs when a speaker acquires a feature from a language that s/he understands (at least to some extent) but has never spoken actively at all. Most of the examples I have found so far are in situations where the source and receiving languages share much of their vocabulary – mainly cases where the languages are fairly closely related to each other or even dialects of the same language. But there is not enough evidence available to know whether the mechanism might be restricted to such situations. Like code alternation, this mechanism presumably involves partial activation of a foreign system. Also as with code alternation, it is often difficult to prove that a particular change came about in this way, but there are cases where the process seems reasonably clear. Let's begin with two anecdotal examples.

In Danish, the word order for polite imperatives like 'Please close the door' differs from English word order in that the Danish adverb *venligst* 'kindly' is obligatorily placed after the imperative form of the verb, as in *Luk venligst døren* (lit. 'close please door.the'). Karen Anne Jensen, a Danish linguist, recently saw the following sign posted in her apartment building: *Venligst brug gadedørsnøglen* 'Please use the front door key' (lit. 'please use street.-door.key.the'). The caretaker who wrote the sign does not speak English, but like most Danes he understands some English. Jensen has also seen this word order used in shops managed by people who might know a little English; her guess is that the English-influenced construction will spread, although other areas of Danish syntax are not influenced by English. Although it is impossible to be certain that the caretaker and the shopkeepers came up with the innovative pattern on their own, rather than hearing them first from Danish–English bilinguals in the community, the fact that the construction was first noticed in non-English-speakers' writing makes passive familiarity a probable mechanism for the innovation.

The second anecdote, which is likely to reflect a common type of situation, is a change that definitely came about through this mechanism. In spoken Standard English, the use of the interrogative pronoun *whom* at the beginning of a sentence has been declining for many years. It is the accusative case form, obligatory when the question word is the object of the verb, as in *Whom did you see?* But most Standard English speakers today have never used it in such constructions in speaking (as opposed to formal writing); it has been replaced within the last hundred years by *who*, as in *Who did you see?* (*who* is the subject form etymologically and has always been correct Standard English in sentences like *Who is going there?*). The change was well under way when I was a child, but I grew up with the old rules for *who* and *whom* usage intact in formal speaking situations, such as classroom lectures. A tricky distinction prescribes *whom* in *Whom do you think he saw?* but *who* in *Who do you think saw him?* – because in the former sentence *whom* is the object of the verb *saw*, while in the latter sentence *who* is the subject of *saw*, not the object of *think*.

The trickiness did not trip me up when I was very young. But by the time I was in my twenties, there were three groups of Standard English speakers with respect to the sentence-initial *who/whom* distinction: a very large group who never used *whom* at the beginning of a sentence, a very small group (including me) who used the forms according to the old rules, and a growing group who used *whom* by preference for elegant effect, even where it was ungrammatical according to the old rules – for instance, in *Whom do you think saw him?* Since this last group included many professors and other university staff members, I heard this non-Standard construction frequently at work, and it always sounded pretentious and ignorant to me. Then I began to catch myself almost using it. This happened more and more often, and it was striking because I had never spoken the pretentious-sounding dialect to which it belonged; the problem was that I heard it so often that it interfered with my native *who/whom* rule.

Like some of the other examples we've seen in this chapter, this one shows that speakers whose speech undergoes contact-induced change can be involuntary or even unwilling participants. It does not necessarily show, however, that speakers cannot prevent interference. Perhaps they cannot; or perhaps speakers may always be able to prevent interference if they want to, provided they have a strong motive. In this particular case, I had no powerful motive to keep my *who/whom* rule; it marked me as a rather archaic speaker anyway. Given the prevalence of sentence-initial *who* in American English, and its consequent familiarity, it was easy for me to avoid the offensive non-Standard use of *whom* by switching overnight (almost literally) to universal sentence-initial *who*.

If these examples seem a bit exotic, the sorts of changes that might not happen very often, consider the very frequent transfer of words from one language to another when the borrowers do not speak the source language. In American English, for instance, many words are adopted from African American Vernacular English (AAVE) by people who do not speak AAVE and who have no knowledge of its structural features. AAVE words and phrases are particularly frequent in urban dialects, and they are even more frequent in certain subcultures – for instance among inmates in the State Correctional Institution at Pittsburgh, a maximum-security state penitentiary for men. The local prison slang has numerous lexical items that originated in AAVE, in spite of the fact that it would be socially inappropriate and quite possibly dangerous for white inmates to try to speak AAVE. Examples are *hittin'* 'very good' (as in *That ice cream was hittin'!*), *punk panties* 'jockey shorts' (which many black inmates consider fit only for sissies), *dude buggin'* 'he's acting insane', and *strapped* 'armed; well off' (as in *You can afford it, you're strapped*). Many white inmates also use AAVE pronunciations for certain words, like *police* with heavy stress on the first syllable.

AAVE of course shares most of its vocabulary and structure with other dialects of American English, so lack of active fluency in AAVE would not in any case be a barrier to lexical borrowing. But in some cases, though possibly quite rarely, words can be adopted by monolinguals from an otherwise unintelligible language. A prime example is the word *taboo*, which was introduced to English speakers in the writings of Captain James Cook, the famous English navigator and explorer, who learned it from Tongan speakers in the Tongan islands (Polynesia, South Pacific) in the late eighteenth century. Captain Cook did not speak Tongan; but he would have been able to learn the meaning 'forbidden' from gestures and other nonlinguistic behavior of people saying *tabu* repeatedly. This was therefore an instance of change through passive familiarity that did not involve much familiarity.

Perhaps the most common type of situation in which passive familiarity is a significant mechanism of structural interference is in a shift situation when some features are adopted by original target-language speakers from the version of the target language (i.e. the TL_2) spoken by members of the shifting group. In the formation of TL_3, the more or less unified language of an emerging integrated community, original TL speakers do not, according to the scenario outlined in Chapter 4, learn to speak TL_2; but they hear TL_2 spoken around them and talk to TL_2 speakers, and eventually their TL_1 variety changes through passive familiarity with TL_2. Members of the shifting group, meanwhile, give up those TL_2 features that are not adopted by the original TL speaker group, and the outcome is TL_3.

None of the examples we have looked at in this section is obviously influenced by imperfect learning: in each case the interference features match the source-language model, although some AAVE-origin phrases used by white inmates at the State Correctional Institution at Pittsburgh did display a mixture of AAVE and other English grammatical features. Still, the mode for all the examples appears to be borrowing, not shift-induced interference. But again, as with code alternation, the lack of extensive evidence about the scope of this mechanism makes any generalizations about it risky.

Mechanism 4: 'Negotiation'

The quotation marks that surround the name of this mechanism are meant as a warning that the term is not to be taken literally, in the sense of deliberate, conscious negotiation between speakers of languages in contact, with discussions and mutual decisions about changes. Speakers probably are not conscious of most contact-induced changes in which this mechanism plays a role. The 'negotiation' mechanism is at work when speakers change their language (A) to approximate what they believe to be the patterns of another language or dialect (B). Crucially, this definition includes situations in which speakers of A are not fluent in B, as well as situations in which they are. If they are bilingual, the changes they make through this mechanism will make A more similar to B: the structures of A and B will converge. If they are not fluent in B, the changes may or may not make A more similar to B. If both A speakers and B speakers engage in the 'negotiation' process, the result will be either two changed languages (A and B) or an entirely new language (though the second outcome is much more likely if more than two languages are in contact).

The most striking cases of 'negotiation' are those in which nobody in the contact situation knows anybody else's language, because that is where A speakers' beliefs about B's structure are most likely to be mistaken. Prototypical pidgin genesis situations are the classic examples – namely, those in which a pidgin arises in a brand new contact situation where there is no effective bilingualism or multilingualism to facilitate communication between the groups in contact, for instance foreign traders and indigenous peoples. As people try to communicate with each other, they will make guesses about what their interlocutors will understand. When they guess wrong, that particular word or construction will not be repeated often; but right guesses are likely to become part of the emerging pidgin. The pidgin is more likely to resemble its creators' languages in unmarked than in marked features, because unmarked features – which in principle are easier to learn than marked features – are more likely to be understood by all the interlocutors than marked features (see Chapter 7 for a more detailed discussion of pidgin genesis).

The effects of 'negotiation' are also evident in contexts involving a whole group's acquisition of a second language – namely, shift situations where imperfect learning is a significant factor. In these situations, members of the shifting group acquire some knowledge of the target language as they learn it, but that knowledge is far from complete. Their version of the TL, i.e. the TL_2, incorporates their mistaken guesses about TL_1 structure. Note that the A language, the language that the speakers are changing, is their emerging version of the TL – they are creating TL_2 – not the shifting group's original ethnic-heritage language. The B language in this context is TL_1.

Here's a typical example. In a northern region of the former Yugoslavia near the Hungarian border, a sizable number of local speakers of Hungarian, which is not related to Slavic, shifted to the local dialect of Serbo-Croatian. In learning Serbo-Croatian they perceived correctly that the stress was not placed on the first syllable, as it is in Hungarian; but because their original native language had fixed stress, they believed that stress would have a fixed position in Serbo-Croatian too. It does not; stress is free in almost all Serbo-Croatian dialects. But not in this one, because the shifting Hungarian speakers' TL_2 turned out to have fixed stress on the penult, the second syllable from the end of the word. And since the community became integrated linguistically, the entire dialect (the TL_3) now has fixed penultimate stress. The noteworthy point here is that the shifting group's stress pattern matches neither their original language nor the original target language (the TL_1).

Finally, bilingual speakers who engage in 'negotiation' adjust features of their language's structure (A) to approximate those of another language (B). They make no errors, and the result is convergence. An example is a potential word-order change in Kadiwéu, a Waikurúan language spoken in Brazil. Six different word-order patterns occur in Kadiwéu discourse: OVS, VOS, SOV, OSV, VSO, and SVO. But when translating sentences from Portuguese to Kadiwéu, bilingual speakers usually use SVO word order, which makes their sentences more similar to Portuguese, an SVO language. This tendency does not necessarily mean that Kadiwéu is changing in the direction of Portuguese in this feature; it might be, but also it might not be. Even if it is not an actual ongoing change, however, it is certainly a potential change.

An especially elaborate and sophisticated instance of bilingual 'negotiation' was discussed briefly in Chapter 4: a Montana Salish elder, on one occasion only, translated several English sentences into Salish with sentential calques – deliberately, because he thought the linguist wanted something as close as possible to the English sentences. When asked for a translation of 'Johnny stole huckleberries from Mary', for instance, he gave *Čoni naq$^{w'}$ t* *st'ša tl' Mali* (lit. 'Johnny steal PARTICLE huckleberry from Mary') – with word order and uninflected main words quite close to the surface patterns in the English sentence. Such sentences, though fully grammatical in Montana Salish, are very odd stylistically, except in certain discourse contexts. A more usual translation of this sentence would differ in numerous ways, most notably in having a morphologically complex verb form: *T Čoni naq^w'-m-l-t-s Mali ci t st'ša* (lit. 'PARTICLE Johnny steal-DERIVED.TRANSITIVE-RELA-TIONAL-TRANSITIVE-he Mary that PARTICLE huckleberry').

This example shows that bilingual speakers are able to manipulate one language's resources quite consciously to approximate the structure of another language. In some cases, interference may occur if speakers start exploiting this mechanism systematically. Montana Salish morphology and syntax would change drastically, for instance, if all the speakers began producing such English-like sentence structures outside the restricted discourse contexts where they are appropriate.

Some insight into processes of 'negotiation' is provided by the phenomenon of CORRESPONDENCE RULES (or borrowing routines). Correspondence rules are (mostly) phonological generalizations drawn, consciously or unconsciously, by bilinguals, though full fluency in both languages is not required. They are especially evident when they link two languages that are closely related and thus share much of their vocabulary. The generalizations are of the form 'Your language has *x* where my language has *y*', and the rules are generally applied to nativize the phonology of loanwords.

Wherever correspondence rules exist, they are largely invisible. Nativization of loanwords is extremely common in borrowing, and it is generally impossible to tell when nativization is produced by a set of correspondence rules and when it is not. Correspondence rules only become visible when they fail – when they 'nativize' a word by producing *y* when there was in fact no *x* in the source language. Here is a typical example, a case of borrowing between two Canadian languages belonging to the Salishan family. Thompson River Salish (south central British Columbia) has borrowed a number of words from Chilliwack (southwestern British Columbia). Because they are related to each other, Thompson and Chilliwack have many cognates, words that are descended from the same proto-language forms. But these cognates do not always agree phonologically. In Chilliwack, both Proto-Salishan */l/ and Proto-Salishan */n/ have merged into /l/, while in Thompson both of these Proto-Salishan phonemes have remained unchanged. As a result, Thompson words with *n* correspond to Chilliwack words with *l*, and Thompson words with *l* also correspond to Chilliwack words with *l*. At least one Chilliwack loanword in Thompson shows that speakers of Thompson must have a correspondence rule for the *n/l* correspondence: Chilliwack *k^{w}úk^{w}əls* 'high cranberry' was borrowed into Thompson as *k^{w}úk^{w}ns*. In fact the proto-language had an *l*, not an *n*, so in this case the existence of the correspondence rule is revealed by its 'wrong' application.

A correspondence rule also accounts for the pronunciation of the word *latam* 'table' in Upper Chehalis, a Salishan language spoken in the state of Washington. The ultimate source of the word is Chinook Jargon, a pidgin once spoken all along the Northwest Coast, where the word is *latab* (or, in some varieties of the pidgin, *latap*). The Chinook Jargon word originally derives from French *la table* 'the table', so /b/ is the original final consonant. Why, then, does Upper Chehalis have *latam* instead? The reason is that Upper Chehalis speakers must have borrowed the word not directly from Chinook Jargon, but rather from one of the nasalless languages of the area – languages in which, as we saw in Chapter 5, the nasal stops /m/ and /n/ had changed to /b/ and /d/, respectively. The nasalless languages, having a /b/ natively, would have borrowed the Chinook Jargon word as /latab/. And the Upper Chehalis speakers must then have applied a correspondence rule, 'their /b/ is our /m/', in borrowing the word from a nasalless language.

Not all correspondence rules are entirely phonological, however. Here is a (rather embarrassing) personal anecdote to illustrate a more complicated rule. Early in my career, desperate for a job, I agreed reluctantly to teach Russian, in spite of the fact that I was far from fluent in the language. (I did warn my prospective employer; he said that since I was a linguist I could certainly give grammar lectures adequately. Little did he know . . . .) At the time I was quite fluent in another Slavic language, Serbo-Croatian, because I had recently spent a year in then-Yugoslavia carrying out dissertation research. All Slavic languages are very closely related; most of the basic vocabulary items are cognate throughout the family, and there are many close correspondences in the grammar too.

But not everything matches. Among the nonmatches is the numeral for 'forty', which is *sorok* in Russian and *četrdeset* in Serbo-Croatian. The Serbo-Croatian word follows a regular pattern for counting in tens, which consists of the lower numeral followed by 'ten': the word for 'four' is *četiri*, and the word for 'ten' is *deset*. Russian generally has the same basic pattern, though there are phonological differences between the two languages: compare, for instance, Russian *sem'* 'seven', *desjat'* 'ten', and *sem'desjat* 'seventy' with Serbo-Croatian *sedam* 'seven' and *sedamdeset* 'seventy'.

The Russian word for 'forty' is different, however; its original meaning was apparently 'a bundle of forty sable pelts' (because forty pelts made a fur shirt), a traditional measure of value, and the word eventually came to be used to designate forty of anything. My embarrassment arose from my mistaken application of a set of correspondence rules when I was teaching numeral words to a class of second-year Russian students. In a careless moment, while drilling the class on twenty, thirty, forty, fifty, . . ., I rephonologized Serbo-Croatian *četrdeset* into pseudo-Russian *četyredesjat* (which is what the word would have been – should have been! – if it hadn't been replaced by *sorok*) and gave them that as the word for 'forty'. An alert student protested; I blushed; but that mistake now provides a good example of a correspondence rule that exploits both the Serbo-Croatian/Russian phonological correspondences and a pattern of numeral formation that is otherwise valid for both languages.

Note too that the speaker in this case was not completely fluent in either of the two relevant languages. My knowledge of Serbo-Croatian was much greater than my knowledge of Russian at the time, but only one rather deaf native speaker ever mistook me for a native speaker of Serbo-Croatian.

A question arises here: are bilingual speakers likely to be aware of applying correspondence rules when speaking one (or both) of their languages? Sometimes no, sometimes yes. I knew what I had done with 'forty' as soon my mistake was pointed out, but I certainly didn't do it on purpose, and I wasn't aware of it until afterward. But speakers are often able to manipulate correspondence rules consciously, with full awareness, and they may even comment on them to linguists (as in, 'Well, in that language the word is *x*, so in our language it ought to be *y*').

For phonological interference, at least, a way of viewing the process is to see a change as the result of a failure to apply a correspondence rule – that is, a speaker simply stops applying the rule, consciously or otherwise. Upper Chehalis, for example, would acquire new /b/ and /d/ phonemes if its speakers stopped applying the rule that replaces source-language /b/ and /d/ with Upper Chehalis /m/ and /n/, when borrowing words from nasalless languages. Siberian Yupik Eskimo speakers may have applied a correspondence rule like 'their *č* is our *s*' in borrowing words like 'tea'; if so, they stopped applying it later, when contact with Russian became much more intense and, as we saw in Chapter 4, the earlier Yupik form *saja* 'tea' (from Russian *čaj*) was replaced by Yupik *čaj*).

As the examples discussed in this section indicate, the 'negotiation' mechanism figures both in changes due to borrowing and in changes due to shift-induced interference. Those changes in which the speakers are not fluent bilinguals show the usual effects of imperfect learning in their perceptions of the structure of the source language; those changes in which the speakers are fluent bilinguals do not show any effects of imperfect learning. In fact, 'negotiation' seems to be an active part of a great many contact-induced changes in which other mechanisms are also at work, perhaps most prominently code alternation and second-language acquisition strategies, and perhaps also bilingual first-language acquisition, but also (for instance in the Montana Salish case) change by deliberate decision.

Mechanism 5: Second-language acquisition strategies

As we saw above, 'negotiation' is one major strategy used by second-language learners to help make sense out of the sometimes confusing second-language (L2) input that they receive. But it is clearly not the only learners' strategy that leads to shift-induced interference. Another is what might be called a gap-filling approach – using material from the native language, while speaking the target language, to plug the holes in knowledge of the TL. This is perhaps most obvious with lexical insertions, but it also, and more prominently, involves structural features. So, for instance, English speakers who are learning French will often pronounce a French /r/ as if it were an English /r/, a sound that does not exist in French, and French /t/ as an English-style aspirated alveolar stop rather than a true French unaspirated dental stop. And English-speaking learners are quite likely to use their native SVO word order in a subordinate clause when trying to speak German, which actually has SOV order in subordinate clauses.

A third strategy is to maintain distinctions and other patterns from the learners' native language (their L1) in constructing their version of TL grammar, by projecting L1 structure onto TL forms. This is the mechanism responsible for some of the Cushitic interference in Ethiopic Semitic as a result of imperfect learning by shifting Cushitic speakers (Chapter 5), e.g. the double-prefix construction used to form the causative (vs. a single prefix in other Semitic languages and a double suffix in Cushitic). Note that 'negotiation' is also a component of this change.

A more complex illustration of this strategy, also with a 'negotiation' component, is the development of the so-called 'second genitive' case in one of the masculine noun classes of Standard Russian. The distinction is between a general genitive case, as in *cena čaj-a* 'the price of tea' (where 'tea' has the general genitive case suffix -*a*), and a partitive genitive case meaning 'some of' or 'a part of', as in *čaška čaj-u* 'a cup of tea' (with the partitive suffix -*u* on 'tea'). Now, the general genitive suffix -*a* is the old Proto-Slavic genitive singular suffix for this noun class; the suffix -*u* was originally the regular (and only) genitive singular suffix of a different masculine noun class, a much smaller one. As Russian developed out of Proto-Slavic, these two masculine noun classes merged, after a period of competition between their conflicting suffixes for each case. Mostly the suffixes belonging to the bigger noun class won out and replaced the suffixes of the smaller class; in the genitive singular, however, both suffixes remained, though with an innovative functional distinction – one regular genitive, one special partitive genitive.

Why did this happen? The answer seems to be that shifting Uralic speakers, who would have encountered the partly merged noun classes and the extra options for suffixes at certain points in the declensional system, assumed that the suffixes had different functions and concluded that the functions must match some from their own native languages; and the relevant Uralic languages have a distinction between a general genitive case and a partitive case. Since Uralic lacks noun classes altogether, assigning a class distinction to the competing suffix pairs would not have been so likely to occur to the shifting speakers. And since the other competing suffix pairs did not map easily onto a native Uralic distinction, it is not surprising that Uralic speakers did not introduce other new functions elsewhere in the system. The final step in the process was taken when the shifting speakers were integrated into the Russian-speaking community, so that original TL speakers adopted this feature from the TL_2 of the shifting Uralic speakers, thus fixing the partitive construction in the TL_3 – namely, the dialects that became Standard Russian.

A final strategy used by second-language learners is to ignore distinctions, especially marked distinctions, that are present in the TL but opaque to learners at early to middle stages of the learning process. These errors of omission – failure to learn certain TL features – are among the most common of shift-induced interference features. A typical example is the loss of gender in a dialect of Latvian under the influence of shifting Uralic (especially Livonian) speakers.

Mechanism 6: Bilingual first-language acquisition

Like several of the other mechanisms discussed in this chapter, this one has not yet been investigated systematically enough to encourage confidence in our understanding of the breadth and depth of its effects. However, there is experimental evidence that suggests its importance as a mechanism of interference. The clearest examples are relatively superficial and easily borrowed syntactic features like word-order patterns and nonsalient phonological features like intonation patterns.

An example of a subtle change in word order comes from research on children growing up bilingual in French and German. The children in one study did not mix their two first languages and never produced sentences in one of their L1s with word orders that were completely foreign to that language. What they did do was to increase the frequency of word order patterns that, while present in both of the adult languages, were more restricted in their occurrence. This is a process of 'negotiation', but its domain is the acquisition of two first languages simultaneously.

The prime phonological example in the literature to date concerns a phrase-final intonation pattern; it was already mentioned in Chapter 4 above: a group of children of Turkish parents, growing up in Germany and learning both Turkish and German as L1s, learned an intonation pattern that differed phonetically but had the same function in their two languages. As with the Uralic speakers shifting to Russian, these bilingual children kept both of the competing forms and introduced a functional distinction between them (but in this case, unlike the two genitives in Russian, the two patterns came from two different languages). Interestingly, neither their Turkish-speaking parents nor their German-speaking teachers noticed the existence of the two different intonation patterns; still, although the change was apparently too minor to be detected by monolingual adults, the children had created a new structure in each of their two languages, in each case using material originally drawn from both languages.

This phonological example is quite exotic, but it is not unique in the literature. A strikingly similar example from Finnish–Swedish bilinguals has been discussed in the literature; and although the source gives no indication of the mechanism involved, bilingual first-language acquisition is at least a possibility (though not the only possibility). Speaking of bilinguals in Turku, in the part of Finland where both Swedish and Finnish are routinely spoken, Ilse Lehiste reports that 'both groups of Turku speakers exhibit a combined prosodic system that contains more contrasts than either of their two languages': specifically, they have introduced extra length distinctions in vowels and/or in consonants into both their Finnish and their Swedish.

Mechanism 7: Deliberate decision

The idea that speakers can change a whole language simply by deciding to do so is not novel. But in general, deliberate decisions have been taken to be relevant only for trivial changes – mainly for the adoption of loanwords, as far as contact-induced change is concerned. For instance, the words for local animals like skunks and moose were taken over from Algonquian languages by English speakers as they moved into and across what is now the United States. Deliberate contact-induced change has mostly been unrecognized as a possibility for less superficial parts of a language's lexicon and structure.

There are a few exceptions to this generalization. Eighteenth-century English grammarians introduced several Latin-inspired rules into Standard English, such as the ban against split infinitives: compare the prescribed standard sentence *He intends never to go there* with the proscribed non-standard sentence *He intends to never go there*, in which the two words of the infinitive construction *to go* are split by the adverb *never*. (In Latin, the infinitive is marked by a suffix rather than by a separate word, so it is impossible to split an infinitive by inserting another word between verb stem and infinitive marker.) Still, these invented grammarians' rules remain relatively superficial, in that they are obeyed only by the most self-conscious writers and (less often) speakers – a small and relatively elite group. With the rise of mass education, Standard English is losing (or has lost) some of the invented rules, including the anti-split infinitive rule.

Although grammarians' power to change English turned out to be limited, the same cannot be said of everyone who tinkers with a standard language. An impressive example is the Estonian language reformer Johannes Aavik, who, early in the twentieth century, invented about two hundred new words and a number of morphological and syntactic innovations for Standard Estonian. At least thirty of the new words came into general use among Estonian speakers, and so did some of the grammatical features, including such productive morphological constructions as a morphological superlative formation (equivalent to English *handsomest*, as opposed to the phrasal superlative *most handsome*). Some of Aavik's innovations were completely new words and structures, not modeled on any other language, so that they cannot be called contact-induced changes; but others, such as the one-word superlatives, were surely inspired by structures he knew in other languages, notably Indo-European ones, and these are indeed contact-induced changes in Estonian.

Standard languages are not the only ones that undergo significant deliberate contact-induced change. Sometimes a group of people – usually quite a small group – will deliberately change their language in order to differentiate their language more sharply from those of neighboring communities. So, for instance, the 1,500 speakers of Uisai (Bougainville Island, Papua New Guinea) apparently decided at some point to make their language less like the other dialects of the same language, Buin (*ca.* 17,000 speakers). To accomplish this, they reversed all their gender agreement markers – in pronouns, verbs, numerals, deictics ('this', 'that', etc.), and adjectives – so that nouns with masculine agreement in Uisai have feminine agreement in other Buin dialects, and vice versa. This change was contact-induced, according to the definition given at the beginning of Chapter 4, because it would have been much less likely to happen if the Uisais were not in contact with speakers of other Buin dialects; but of course it does not involve linguistic interference, because only the grammatical rules have changed.

A phonological example in this same general category is found among the Ma'a people of Tanzania. Ma'a speakers are fully fluent in the Bantu language(s) of their basically Bantu communities, but they retain about half of their original non-Bantu vocabulary and a very few non-Bantu structural features for use as an in-group language (see Chapter 8 for discussion). Their Ma'a language has just one phoneme that is not found in the local Bantu languages: a voiceless lateral fricative, in which the air escapes around the sides of the tongue. This sound is considered by the Bantu speakers in the community to be difficult and exotic – as it would be (for instance) for English speakers too, but not for Cushitic speakers, because it is a common phoneme in Cushitic. Historically, this phoneme was found only in non-Bantu Ma'a words; but to emphasize the differentness of their other language, they sometimes introduce it into Bantu words when speaking to their Bantu-speaking neighbors.

Sometimes people distort their language in order to make it unintelligible to outsiders. This motive is akin to the motive for inventing secret languages, like Pig Latin or one of the many secret languages invented by children in various cultures. But sometimes distortions involve changing words by less rule-like processes, and sometimes the grammar is changed. Again, these are contact-induced changes, but they usually do not include actual interference features. An example of systematic lexical distortion is a dialect of Lambayeque Quechua in Peru, whose speakers altered their vocabulary by switching the order of certain vowel–consonant sequences in the word, a process called METATHESIS: for instance, *yawar* was changed to *yawra*, *-taq* became *-tqa*, *-pis* became *-psi*, and *kabalta* became *kablata*.

Examples like these can easily be multiplied. But the most spectacular cases of deliberate manipulation of linguistic resources by bilinguals are the mixed languages formed relatively abruptly as symbols of a new ethnic identity, such as Michif, in which French noun phrases are combined with Cree verb phrases and sentential syntax, and Mednyj Aleut, a mixture of Aleut lexicon and structure with Russian verb inflection. These and other examples of bilingual mixed languages will be discussed in Chapter 8.

Deliberate change as a mechanism of interference (that is, when it does result in actual interference) does not obviously correlate with either shift-induced interference or borrowing. True, creating a new bilingual mixed language (for instance) requires a relatively high level of community bilingualism; but it is also entirely possible that some instances of shift-induced interference, especially those involving carryover of structural features from the shifting group's original native language, are deliberate changes, made because shifting speakers wanted to keep certain distinctions not originally present in the target language.

One important implication of all these kinds of deliberate changes is that they greatly reduce the already slim chances for finding any nontrivial absolute linguistic constraints on contact-induced language change. It was already evident, from the fact that counterexamples to all the constraints proposed so far are so easy to find, that absolute constraints are not very likely; but the range of deliberate contact-induced changes is great enough to suggest that speakers can (and occasionally do) make changes in any area of structure that they are aware of. This would leave only aspects of language structure that speakers aren't (and can't become) aware of invulnerable to deliberate change. Linguists are far from any general agreement about what, if anything, might be included in that category.

Another implication is that generalizations based on broad social factors cannot be relied on absolutely. For a start, this is true of the correlation between transferred features with and without imperfect learning: since some cultures rigorously avoid lexical borrowing, there may well be languages without significant numbers of loanwords but with significant structural interference. But it is also true of the commonly stated generalization linking level of bilingualism with amount of interference: very often, in fact most often, more bilingualism will correlate with more interference; level of bilingualism is one aspect of the intensity of contact, as we saw in Chapter 4. But sometimes it doesn't. Findings from a number of contact situations, for instance Karelian/Russian in Russian Karelia and Pennsylvania German/ English in Pennsylvania, have shown that some fluent speakers of the pressured language (Karelian, Pennsylvania German) keep their two languages quite separate, while others have freely adopted both lexicon and structural features from the surrounding community's language (Russian, English). If there are individual differences in levels of borrowing among equally fluent speakers, it would not be surprising to find similar differences

among languages in contact situations involving comparable levels of bilingualism.

Two final points about mechanisms of interference

Two loose ends need to be tied up before we move on to Chapter 7. One is the
question of multiple mechanisms operating to produce the same change; the
other is a phenomenon that cannot easily be pinned down to any mechanism.
First, consider cases in which multiple mechanisms are at work at the same
time. We have already seen that 'negotiation' operates together with other
mechanisms, perhaps especially code alternation, second-language acquisition strategies, and bilingual first-language acquisition. Deliberate decision
potentially works in conjunction with all six of the other mechanisms on
occasion. Code-switching and code alternation could certainly be operative
in the same contact situations, in which case both could be responsible for
certain changes – although, as noted above, their typical results do not match
very closely. Passive familiarity will not exist in a code-switching or code-
alternation context, at least not in the same speakers, for obvious reasons;
but it could combine with change by deliberate decision, and also with
'negotiation'. And so forth. The seven mechanisms can be distinguished in
principle, and sometimes a mechanism will operate alone (except perhaps for
'negotiation'); but in real-life contact situations it will frequently, or even
usually, be impossible to discover which mechanism(s) produced a given
change.

   All this complexity of course complicates the analysis of contact-induced
changes immensely. Here's an example that illustrates the complexity. In the
famous case of the village of Kupwar in India, where speakers of all four of
the community's languages have been multilingual for a long time, it has
been reported (though not in these exact terms) that code-switching occurs in
some social contexts, while code alternation is the norm in other social
settings. It seems reasonable to assume, therefore, that at least these two
mechanisms contributed to the extensive grammatical convergence (via
borrowing) that characterizes the four languages; 'negotiation' must also
have been at work, and possibly also deliberate decision and bi-/multilingual
first-language acquisition.

   The second loose end presents a different sort of analytic problem: it is not
clear where the phenomenon belongs in a catalogue of mechanisms of
contact-induced change. It clearly is not a separate mechanism, but it does
seem to fit into this chapter; it may be something that happens in conjunction
with some or all of the seven mechanisms. The phenomenon is double
marking of particular grammatical categories in contact-induced change –
sometimes a transitional phenomenon that occurs when one construction is
being replaced by another, but sometimes a permanent fixture in the
receiving language.

   One example of the transitional type was mentioned in Chapter 4: when

Siberian Yupik Eskimo borrowed conjunctions from Chukchi, they were used at first in combination with the inherited Yupik nonfinite clause types. Before the borrowing of *ŧnkam* 'and', for instance, the sentence 'Beasts and birds live on the tundra' would have been *Nunivaɣmi kijaxtaqut tɨɣiɣat-ɬju qawaɣɨt-ɬju*. Literally, the words mean 'on.the.tundra live beasts-with birds-with'; *-ɬju* is a comitative suffix meaning 'with', and it is used to conjoin two noun phrases. Once *ŧnkam* was borrowed from Chukchi, Siberian Yupik speakers used sentences with both kinds of conjunction: *Nunivaɣmi kijaxta-qut tɨɣiɣat-ɬju ŧnkam qawaɣɨt-ɬju*, literally 'on.the.tundra live beasts-with and birds-with'. But this double marking – both the native Yupik suffix and the borrowed Chukchi conjunction – apparently was not permanent, because the linguist who investigated the contact situation also found sentences with just the conjunction, as in *Nunivaɣmi kijaxtaqut tɨɣiɣat ŧnkam qawaɣɨt*.

Other examples of double marking are, or at least may be, permanent; and there is no doubt that double marking is a possible permanent situation, because there are numerous examples in internal change. As soon as the double marking exists in a language, therefore, the fact that one marker may have a foreign source is irrelevant to the question of whether both markers will remain (to be interpreted eventually as a single complex construction). An example is a set of personal endings on verbs in Megleno-Rumanian (as discussed above in Chapter 5, under the Balkan Sprachbund): Rumanian verbs such as *aflu* 'I find' and *afli* 'you find' have suffixes that indicate the person and number of the subject (in these instances, first person singular *-u* 'I' and second person singular *-i* 'you'). When this dialect of Rumanian came under strong Bulgarian influence, it added the Bulgarian suffixes *-m* 'I' and *-š* 'you' to the original forms, yielding new double-marked forms *aflum* and *afliš*. The fact that Rumanian and Bulgarian already had suffix sets with the same meanings must have facilitated the borrowing; but the fact remains that the added Bulgarian markers did not fill a structural gap of any kind in the receiving language.

Clearly, the whole topic of mechanisms of interference is far from adequately understood. Still, the survey above at least gives some idea of the kinds of general factors that must be considered in any analysis of processes of contact-induced change.

Sources and further reading

This chapter is based in part on the article 'On mechanisms of interference' (Thomason 1997), though the chapter and the article differ significantly in a number of ways.

Two good examples of psycholinguistic research on bilingual speakers are François Grosjean's 1982 book *Life with Two Languages* and a 1986 volume edited by Jyotsna Vaid, *Language Processing in Bilinguals: Psycholinguistic and Neuropsychological Perspectives*, though neither of these works focuses on contact-induced change. A good introduction to the sociolinguistic study of the spread of changes within a community can be found in James Milroy and Lesley Milroy's works, for instance 'Linguistic change, social network and speaker innovation' (1985) and 'Exploring the social constraints on language change' (1997).

The point about the impossibility of studying a change from its inception is reminiscent of a comment made by Einar Haugen many years ago: 'Since the actual moment of borrowing is rarely observable, most conclusions about interference are based on inferences' (1958: 777). I am grateful to the twenty students in my University of Michigan first-year seminar in the Fall Term of 1999, for their diligence and success in collecting speech errors.

The scholarly literature on code-switching is vast. An excellent place to begin is the set of papers in Lesley Milroy and Pieter Muysken's 1995 edited volume *One Speaker, Two Languages: Cross-Disciplinary Perspectives on Code-Switching*. Probably the area of this literature that is most relevant to this chapter (and this book) is the topic of constraints on code-switching. Here two now-classic articles, Carol Pfaff's 'Constraints on language mixing' (1979) and Shana Poplack's 'Sometimes I'll start a sentence in Spanish Y TERMINO EN ESPAÑOL' (1980), are still well worth reading. (Poplack proposes the Free Morpheme Constraint in this 1980 article.) The work of Carol Myers-Scotton (e.g. 1993) is also prominent, though controversial; Myers-Scotton attempts to explain code-switching and other language-contact phenomena as governed by psycholinguistic constraints. And the interested reader should also consult works critical of the various claimed constraints, for instance Eliasson's 'English–Maori language contact: code-switching and the free-morpheme constraint' (1990). An article that explores the distinction between code-switching and code-mixing is Suzanne Moffatt and Lesley Milroy's 'Panjabi/English language alternation in the early school years' (1992).

The examples of Yiddish–English code-switching are from J. R. Rayfield's 1970 book *The Languages of a Bilingual Community* (pp. 55–7). Rayfield also gives numerous examples of interference features that look like fossilized code-switches – features that began as code-switches but have become fixed as permanent parts of the speakers' English or German.

Writers who draw a sharp distinction between code-switching and permanent interference features are Aravind Joshi (1985: 190) and David Sankoff and his colleagues (1990: 97). Carol Myers-Scotton argued in 1998 (p. 290) that intrasentential code-switching is a necessary condition for all structural interference that includes transferred morphemes. The quotation about code-switching vs. borrowing (and nonce borrowing) is from p. 200 of Shana Poplack and Marjory Meechan's 1995 article 'Patterns of language mixture: nominal structure in Wolof-French and Fongbe-French bilingual discourse'. Stig Eliasson has investigated Maori–English code-switching, for instance in his 1995 article 'Grammatical and lexical switching in Maori-English 'grasshopper speech' (see especially pp. 48, 55–6); see also his 1990 article (cited above).

I'm grateful to Ad Backus for the observation about Turkish words inserted into immigrants' Dutch and for the anecdote about code alternation (personal communication, 1996).

I am most grateful to Nancy Dorian, who first suggested the idea of code alternation as a mechanism of contact-induced change to me in 1989. The example of Italian–English code alternation is from Michela Shigley-Giusti (personal communication, 1993), and the example of Finnish–Estonian code alternation is from Eve Mikone (personal communication, 1999). Karen Anne Jensen provided the Danish word-order example (personal communication, 1999). Research on prison slang at the State Correctional Institution at Pittsburgh was carried out by Greg DeMichele in 1990.

The concept of 'negotiation' described in this chapter was first proposed in a 1975 conference paper that was the forerunner of Thomason and Kaufman 1988. In part it resembles 'accommodation theory', which has received a great deal of recent attention in sociology and sociolinguistics (see for instance Giles 1984). The two concepts also differ significantly, however.

The Serbo-Croatian dialect with the Hungarian-influenced stress pattern was described by Pavle Ivić in his course 'Balkan Linguistics', taught at the 1964 Linguistic Institute at the University of Indiana. The Kadiwéu example is from Filomena Sandalo's 1995 University of Pittsburgh dissertation. Mark Durie and Malcolm Ross, in introducing their 1996 book *The Comparative Method Reviewed*, discuss correspondence rules (though not by that name) on p. 29; Jeffrey Heath, in the 1989 book mentioned above, discusses them under the label 'borrowing routine'. The Chilliwack–Thompson example is from Kinkade 1995: 35. The Siberian Yupik Eskimo examples of phonological adaptation in lexical borrowing and (in the last section of this chapter) double marking in morphosyntactic change are discussed in a 1969 article by G. A. Menovščikov; they are also discussed in Chapter 4 above.

The example of loss of gender in Latvian under Uralic influence is from p. 147 of Bernard Comrie's excellent 1981 book *The Languages of the Soviet Union* (which is outdated only in its title).

The example of French and German bilingual children subtly altering each language's word order patterns is from a talk given in 1996 by Annick De Houwer and Jürgen Meisel, 'Analyzing the relationship between two developing languages in bilingual first language acquisition'. The Turkish-and-German-speaking children's innovative intonation pattern is from Robin Queen's 1996 University of Texas dissertation. The example of Swedish–Finnish prosodic contrasts is from pp. 375–6 of Ilse Lehiste's 1997 article 'Cross-linguistic comparison of prosodic patterns in Finnish, Finland Swedish, and Stockholm Swedish'.

Syntactic rules introduced into English by eighteenth-century grammarians are discussed in various handbooks on the history of English, among them Albert Baugh's *A History of the English Language* (see pp. 330 ff.); for a specific discussion of the rule against split infinitives, see for instance pp.

300–4 of Stuart Robertson and Frederic Cassidy's book *The Development of Modern English*, 2nd edition.

I am grateful to Ilse Lehiste for examples and references to changes introduced by Aavik into Estonian; the changes are discussed further, with examples, in the section 'Linguistic innovation in Estonian' in Paul F. Saagpakk's introduction to his 1982 Estonian–English Dictionary (pp. lxxix–lxxxvii), and in Els Oksaar's 1972 article 'Bilingualism' in a volume surveying linguistic studies in western Europe. The Uisai gender-switch example is from a 1982 article by D. C. Laycock, 'Melanesian linguistic diversity: a Melanesian choice?' (p. 36). The Ma'a lateral fricative example is from p. 199 of Maarten Mous's 1994 article 'Ma'a or Mbugu'. I am very grateful to David Weber, who – citing Dwight Shaver's research as the source of the example – told me in July 1999 about systematic lexical distortion in Lambayeque Quechua. Discussions of differential amounts of borrowing by individual fluent bilinguals can be found in Anneli Sarhimaa's 1999 book *Syntactic Transfer, Contact-Induced Change, and the Evolution of Mixed Codes: Focus on Karelian–Russian Language Alternation* and in Marion Lois Huffines' 1989 article 'Case usage among the Pennsylvania German sectarians and nonsectarians'.

The contact situation in the village of Kupwar is described in the 1971 article 'Convergence and creolization: a case from the Indo-Aryan/Dravidian border', by John J. Gumperz and Robert Wilson; see Chapter 3 for further discussion of this famous case.

7 Contact Languages I: Pidgins and Creoles

'The Negroes who established themselves on the Djuka Creek two centuries ago found Trio Indians living on the Tapanahoni. They maintained continuing relations with them . . . The trade dialect shows clear traces of these circumstances. It consists almost entirely of words borrowed from Trio or from Negro English.' (*Verslag der Toemoekhoemak-expeditie*, by C. H. de Goeje, 1908).

'The Nez Perces used two distinct languages, the proper and the Jargon, which differ so much that, knowing one, a stranger could not understand the other. The Jargon is the slave language, originating with the prisoners of war, who are captured in battle from the various neighboring tribes and who were made slaves; their different languages, mixing with that of their masters, formed a jargon . . . . The Jargon in this tribe was used in conversing with the servants and the court language on all other occasions.' (*Ka-Mi-Akin: Last Hero of the Yakimas*, by A. J. Splawn, 2nd edn., 1944, p. 490)

The Delaware Indians 'rather design to conceal their language from us than to properly communicate it, except in things which happen in daily trade; saying that it is sufficient for us to understand them in that; and then they speak only half sentences, shortened words . . .; and all things which have only a rude resemblance to each other, they frequently call by the same name'. (*Narratives of New Netherland 1609–1664*, by J. Franklin Jameson, 1909, p. 128, quoting a comment made by the Dutch missionary Jonas Michaëlius in August 1628)

The list of language contact typologies at the beginning of Chapter 4 had three entries under the heading 'extreme language mixture': pidgins, creoles, and bilingual mixed languages. All of these are types of contact languages; they are three separate phenomena, but pidgins and creoles go together naturally, in contradistinction to bilingual mixed languages. The distinction is basically the same as the one between contact-induced change with and without imperfect learning: pidgin/creole genesis is akin (though not identical) to shift-induced interference, and bilingual mixed language genesis is akin to, and in effect actually is, borrowing. That is, pidgins and creoles develop in social contexts where few or no members of the groups in contact are bilingual or multilingual in each other's language(s), while imperfect learning plays no significant role in the development of bilingual mixed languages. This characterization is oversimplified, as we will see below (and in Chapter 8), because contact-induced language change is not the only component of contact-language genesis; but the dichotomy between two basic categories of contact language is valid in spite of the oversimplification. Because of this dichotomy, pidgins and creoles will be discussed together in this chapter, and bilingual mixed languages will be covered in Chapter 8.

Before beginning any detailed discussions, we need a definition of 'contact language'. There is unfortunately no uniform definition of the term in the scholarly literature, but there are two main kinds of usage. Some people apply it always and only to languages of wider communication, i.e. to all LINGUA FRANCAS. Under that definition, any language that is used for intergroup communication is a contact language – including not only pidgins and creoles, but also nonpidgin/noncreole languages like English, which is certainly the most widely used lingua franca in the modern world. (See Chapter 2 for examples of other lingua francas around the world.)

In this book a different definition will be used. Here, a contact language is any new language that arises in a contact situation. Linguistically, a contact language is identifiable by the fact that its lexicon and grammatical structures cannot all be traced back primarily to the same source language; they are therefore mixed languages in the technical historical linguistic sense: they did not arise primarily through descent with modification from a single earlier language. By definition, therefore, contact languages are not members of any language family and thus belong in no family tree – except perhaps as the ancestor of a language family: a contact language has no single parent language in the historical linguist's usual sense, but it may have descendants. In other words, I am defining 'contact language' on the basis of the type(s) of historical connections to other languages.

It follows from this definition that contact languages need not be lingua francas at all, and in fact some are not. Pidgins and creoles emerge in contexts in which people from different linguistic backgrounds need to talk to each other regularly, and they are therefore lingua francas in origin; but bilingual mixed languages are in-group languages, not languages of wider communication. We'll return to some of the implications of this definition of contact language below, and again in Chapter 8.

The organization of this chapter is as follows. We'll begin in the next section with definitions of pidgins and creoles, and then move on to their history and current or attested former distribution around the world. In the following section we'll consider two common beliefs, partly true and partly false, about pidgins and creoles: that they are maximally simple (especially pidgins) and that they are all alike (especially creoles). The last major section covers the major origin theories for pidgins and creoles – historical scenarios that have been proposed and defended for their emergence.

What, when, where?

The first step in investigating pidgins and creoles as a contact phenomenon is to place them in historical and geographical context. Again, we need to begin with definitions. As with just about everything else in the field of pidgin/ creole studies, all the available definitions of 'pidgin' and 'creole' are controversial. I'll present and discuss the definitions that seem most work-able to me, but readers who want to explore the controversy can find references to other definitions in the 'Sources and further readings' section at the end of the chapter.

What?

Let's start with pidgins. Traditionally, a pidgin is a language that arises in a new contact situation involving more than two linguistic groups. The groups have no shared language – that is, no single language is widely known among the groups in contact – and they need to communicate regularly, but for limited purposes, such as trade. For some combination of social, economic, and political reasons, they do not learn each other's languages, but instead develop a pidgin, with vocabulary drawn typically (though not always) from one of the languages in contact. The new pidgin's grammar does not come from any one language; instead, it is a kind of crosslanguage compromise of the grammars of the languages in contact, with more or less (usually more) influence from universals of second-language learning: in particular, ease of learning helps to determine the linguistic structure of a pidgin. The process by which a pidgin is created is 'negotiation', as outlined in Chapter 6.

Adopting this view of pidgins carries several implications. One is that a pidgin is nobody's native language: pidgins are always spoken as second languages (or third, or fourth, or . . .) and are typically used for limited purposes of intergroup communication. A second implication is that, thanks to their limited social functions, pidgins have less linguistic material than nonpidgin languages – fewer words, limited grammatical and stylistic re-sources in syntax and discourse. In addition, for reasons that are probably connected mainly to ease of learning, pidgins tend to lack elaborate mor-phological structures.

A creole, by contrast, is the native language of a speech community. Like pidgins, creoles develop in contact situations that typically involve more than two languages; also like pidgins, they typically draw their lexicon, but not their grammar, primarily from a single language, the LEXIFIER LANGUAGE. (The terminology for labeling the lexifier language varies: in particular, the terms 'English-lexifier creoles' and 'English-based creoles' are used interchangeably.) The grammar of a creole, like the grammar of a pidgin, is a crosslanguage compromise of the languages of its creators, who may or may not include native speakers of the lexifier language. (That is: the lexifier language has to be available to pidgin or creole creators at least to the extent that they take most of the new language's vocabulary from it; but L1 speakers of the lexifier language are not always involved in 'negotiating' the structure of the contact language itself.) In fact, some creoles are nativized pidgins. Such a creole was originally a pidgin which later became the main language of a speech community, learned as a first language by children and used for general community activities; its linguistic resources expanded with the expansion in its spheres of usage. Other creoles seem never to have gone through a pidgin stage at all, but to have developed gradually by increasing divergence from the lexifier language, and still others apparently arose abruptly, also without going through a well-defined pidgin stage. We'll examine all these possibilities below.

In the present context, what's important is that the definitions just given apply to some, but not clearly to all, pidgins and creoles. It may be reasonable to say that the pidgins and creoles that best fit these definitions are prototypical – that they are the basic type, and that other kinds of pidgins and creoles diverge in one or more respects from this fundamental type. This is reasonable, of course, only to the extent that one agrees with the basic definition; some scholars would propose quite different definitions. Much of the controversy stems from competing theories of how pidgins and especially creoles arise in the first place – theories of pidgin and creole genesis – so we'll postpone consideration of the controversies to the section below on pidgin/creole genesis.

Meanwhile, here are two ways in which some pidgins and creoles differ from the picture supplied by the definitions. First, there are a few two-language pidgins and creoles. One is described in typical nonlinguist's language in a quotation at the beginning of the chapter: Ndyuka-Trio Pidgin, spoken in Suriname in northern South America, is an example of a two-language pidgin. It probably dates from the early eighteenth century, when many slaves escaped from coastal plantations, fled into the interior of the country, formed a creole-speaking community, and later came into contact with the Trio Indians of southern Suriname. Its main function is the classic one for pidgins: it is used primarily for trade between the Ndyukas (whose language is an English-lexifier creole) and the Trios. Berbice Dutch Creole is a rare example of a two-language creole. Like Ndyuka-Trio Pidgin, it is (or was – only four or five speakers remained as of 1993) spoken in northern South America, but in Guyana rather than Suriname. It was created by speakers of Dutch and the West African language Eastern Ịjọ after Berbice was founded in 1627 as a Dutch colony; it became a British colony in 1796. Another two-language creole is Baba Malay, which is spoken by about 15,000 ethnic Chinese and ethnically mixed people in Melaka and

Singapore. Lexically based on the Austronesian language Malay, Baba Malay has as its other component Hokkien Chinese.

Second, some pidgins expand in both functions and linguistic resources without, or at least before, being learned as a first language by a population of speakers. An example is Tok Pisin (the name means 'pidgin language', and its components ultimately come from English *talk* and *pidgin*), now one of the official languages of Papua New Guinea: although it is currently a creole by the above definition, with a population of native speakers, Tok Pisin had expanded into all spheres of New Guinea public life long before it acquired native speakers; and its transition to a native language therefore involved little or no significant linguistic change at all. Expansion without nativization is hardly surprising, given the right social circumstances; but the requisite social circumstances obtain relatively rarely, so that the classic trade pidgin, restricted in functions and in linguistic material, remains the prototype for pidgins. Some scholars prefer to use the term 'creole' for an expanded pidgin like Tok Pisin before it had native speakers; others (including me) prefer to stay with the traditional definitions, while recognizing that the correlation between linguistic expansion and nativization will not hold in every single case.

Another point needs to be made before we turn to the 'when' and 'where' of the section title. A notion that is implicit in most of the pidgin/creole literature and explicit in some of it is that pidgins and creoles arise because speakers of the various other languages in the new contact situation have too little access to the lexifier language to learn it 'properly'. Certainly imperfect learning plays a role in the genesis process, as noted above, but lack of access is too simplistic a notion, as it is usually presented. For one thing, there is no reason to assume that the lexifier language is always a target language in the sense that speakers of the other languages strive or even want to learn it; in at least one case, that of Chinese Pidgin English, Chinese speakers are said to have created it in part because they were unwilling to learn the inferior foreigners' language, English – and even more unwilling to permit English or other foreigners to learn Chinese.

For another thing, even if they would like to learn the lexifier language as a whole, learners are sometimes actively prevented from doing so by speakers of the lexifier language. Two of the quotations at the beginning of this chapter illustrate slightly different motives for withholding the lexifier language from would-be learners: the Nez Percé Jargon was clearly used by the Nez Percé people as one means of keeping their slaves in a separated position in the community, so that the slaves could not understand their masters when the masters were talking among themselves. As in some other Northwest communities, speaking Jargon may also have been one way in which slaves were expected to make their inferior position clear to everyone.

The Delaware people's attitude reflects a situation that is found here and there around the world: they deliberately withheld their full language from outsiders (at least from Europeans) in order to maintain social distance between themselves and others, to prevent others from getting too close to their culture. It was in this context that the now extinct Pidgin Delaware arose, probably in the seventeenth century. Similar comments have been made by other frustrated outsiders in other contexts. Here are two more examples, one from fieldworkers among Hamer speakers in Ethiopia and one from an early missionary's experience among the Motus in what is now Papua New Guinea:

> For the next seven months we lived in Hamer villages without any interpreter or intermediary between ourselves and the Hamer . . . at the end of the seven months, we felt we had achieved a working knowledge of Hamer . . . . Today we realize that the language which we had learned . . . was a kind of 'Pidgin Hamer' which is used only for and by policemen, traders, and non-Hamer settlers. In the past year we have succeeded in having our Hamer friends and companions talk to us in proper Hamer.

> The first references of any sort to any 'unusual' language spoken by the Motu is that contained in references to W. G. Lawes' early attempts to learn Motu from villagers in Port Moresby harbour where he and his wife first settled in 1874. According to several recent reports, the Motu were never keen on teaching him their 'true' language but instead attempted to communicate with him and later to teach him 'a simplified form of their language' . . . . However, it was not until some time later that his son, Frank, who played with the boys of the village and learned the 'true' language from them, drew his father's attention to the deception. Even so it was only with difficulty that Lawes was able to learn the true language, because many of the villagers were still opposed to imparting the knowledge to strangers.

When and where?

How long ago did pidgin and creole languages first arise, and where are they spoken now and in the recent past? The first question cannot be answered definitively: we have little or no hope of discovering very old pidgin or creole languages, both because mentions of languages of any kind are sparse in ancient documents and because pidgins and creoles have been marginal languages for most of their history, thanks to their universal status (until very recently) as unwritten languages.

In most of the literature on the history of pidgins and creoles, the famous Lingua Franca has pride of place. This was an Italian-lexifier pidgin that arose sometime during the Crusades, which were carried out from 1095 CE until the mid-fifteenth century. It was used for intergroup communication in the lands bordering the Mediterranean Sea; in the western Mediterranean it acquired much Spanish lexicon as well. Some scholars believe that it underlies at least some later pidgins and creoles elsewhere as well. This view has been especially popular, in a global form encompassing most or all pidgins and creoles, among scholars who believe that pidgins and creoles are rare phenomena, confined largely to areas of European exploration, trade, and colonialism. But others, probably by now the majority of specialists, believe that such contact languages are likely to have arisen rather frequently all over the world, and that the reason so few are reported from outside the range of European activities is that most histories have been written by Europeans and their New World descendants.

In any case, the Lingua Franca is not in fact the earliest documented pidgin or creole language. That distinction goes to an eleventh-century Arabic-lexifier pidgin that was reported by the great Arab geographer Abu 'Ubayd al-Bakrī (*ca.* 1028–94 CE), whose magnum opus, *Roads and Kingdoms* (in Arabic, *al-Masālik wa 'l-Mamālik*), was completed in 1068. Al-Bakrī himself did not undertake the travels he describes in his book; he was born in Andalusia in southern Spain and spent his entire life there. He gathered stories from travelers and used secondary sources as well. He frequently prefaces a story with 'someone told me', as he does in his report of what appears to have been an Arabic-based pidgin:

> Someone told me that a dignitary from the people of Aswan used to travel a lot. One day he reached a small town called Maridi. Upon his return, he said to the prince of the believers [the ruler in Islamic faith, presumably in this case the Fatimid Caliph of Egypt], 'Sir, may God give you plenty of good and honour your face, here is my case! Its goal is to preserve and spread the word of God. The Blacks have mutilated our beautiful language and spoiled its eloquency with their twisted tongues. During my visit, Sir – may God protect you – only God's guidance helped me escape the dangers and understand their miserable Arabic. Sometimes, and may God forgive me if I did wrong, I could only laugh at what they called Arabic; and may God forgive me if I call what they uttered Arabic.

These prefatory remarks are followed by a ten-sentence story given to illustrate the 'bad Arabic' spoken by the people of Maridi; in this story the lexicon is almost entirely Arabic but the grammar is not like that of any ancient or modern variety of Arabic. The structural features do, however, match those of modern Arabic-lexifier pidgins in a number of respects, so it seems safe to conclude that the short text represents a pidginized form of Arabic, though of course there is no way to tell whether it was a stable pidgin language or not.

The traveler's comment about 'Blacks' twisted tongues' shows that racist assumptions about how and why pidgins and creoles arise go back to the earliest recorded example; similar comments are all too easy to find in quite recent literature as well. All such remarks reflect a profound misunderstanding of processes of pidgin and creole genesis: even if we assume that the inhabitants of Maridi wanted to learn Arabic itself rather than just to construct a pidgin to use in conversing with Arab traders, it is hardly likely that anyone, of any color, could achieve fluency in a language after hearing it spoken briefly by an occasional traveler once a year or so. (It is not certain exactly where Maridi was, but the village apparently had no significant permanent Arab population; it was probably either in what is now the Sudan or in what is now Mauritania.)

Thanks to al-Bakrī's account of Maridi Arabic, we know that pidgins were spoken during the early Middle Ages in at least two places, Africa (probably either in the Sahara Desert or the Sudan) and the Mediterranean. There may have been many other pidgins and even creoles all over the world by then, but the next ones we have any knowledge of arose during the Age of Exploration, which was inaugurated by Prince Henry the Navigator of Portugal (1394–1460). Prince Henry sent his first expedition down around the coast of Africa in about 1418, and many other exploring expeditions along the West African coast. Europeans reached the mouth of the Congo River in 1482; in 1488 they rounded the Cape of Good Hope at the southern tip of Africa, and soon after 1515 they reached the port of Canton in southeastern China. From there Europeans spread to the entire Pacific, and they crossed both the Pacific and the Atlantic to the New World. Traders and colonists followed (or, in some cases, accompanied) the explorers; soon the European presence was worldwide. Meanwhile, Arab traders and conquerors also expanded far beyond the Arabian Peninsula of southwestern Asia, to northern and then sub-Saharan Africa and eastward into Asia.

All these activities eventually gave rise to pidgins and creoles all over the world, especially – given the sea routes that most explorers followed – on and near the world's seacoasts. Maridi Arabic was apparently not near a coast, but the Lingua Franca was. There are Arabic-lexifier pidgins on islands near the Arabian Peninsula as well as in the interior of northeastern Africa, but most known pidgins and creoles are connected with European expansion and trade, and of these the great majority have European lexifier languages. In Africa there are several Portuguese-based contact languages, among them West African Pidgin Portuguese (fifteenth to eighteenth centuries), Cape Verde Creole (Crioulo), and São Tomense Creole (spoken on an island in the Gulf of Guinea); in Asia there are several others, e.g. Sri Lanka Creole Portuguese and (in Macao–Hong Kong) Macanese Creole Portuguese.

English-lexifier pidgins and creoles are more numerous and more widespread; in fact, English is by a large margin the most frequent lexifier language for known pidgins and creoles. Here are a few examples, chosen to illustrate the geographical range: in the New World, American Indian

Pidgin English in the northeastern United States, the African-American creole Gullah in the coastal southeastern United States, Jamaican Creole English in the Caribbean, Miskito Coast Creole English in Nicaragua, Sranan and Ndyuka (both are English-lexifier creoles) in Suriname; in Africa, Cameroonian Pidgin English; in the Pacific, Chinese Pidgin English, Tok Pisin in Papua New Guinea, Hawaiian Pidgin English (now nearly extinct), Hawaiian Creole English, Pitcairnese (a creole), Kriyol in the Northern Territory of Australia. Some of these are trade pidgins (American Indian Pidgin English, Cameroonian Pidgin English, Chinese Pidgin English, probably Hawaiian Pidgin English); others arose in the Atlantic slave trade (Gullah, Jamaican Creole English, Miskito Coast Creole English, Sranan, Ndyuka), and still others arose when free, or semifree, workers were imported to plantations (Tok Pisin, Hawaiian Creole English, and perhaps Kriyol – all three of these are creolized pidgins). One creole, Pitcairnese, stands out from all the rest, and indeed from all other known creole languages, because we know precisely both the date on which the stage was set for its formation and the backgrounds of its creators: it developed after nine mutineers, having evicted Captain Bligh from the *Bounty* in 1790, settled on Pitcairn Island with sixteen speakers of the Polynesian language Tahitian. (It's possible that a few of the sixteen Polynesians spoke languages other than Tahitian natively, and most of the male Polynesians died or were killed too soon after the group arrived on Pitcairn to have contributed much to the emerging creole. Still, we have much more information about the starting point for this creole than for any other.)

Similar lists of languages and circumstances can be given for pidgins and creoles with French, Spanish, and Dutch lexicons, though these are neither as numerous nor as wide-ranging geographically as the English-lexifier languages. There are also a few German- and Russian-based pidgins and creoles, for instance the Pidgin German that was once spoken in New Guinea and the Chinese Pidgin Russian that was used for trade on the Russo–Chinese border, e.g. in Kyakhta, south of Lake Baikal. One trading pidgin, Russenorsk, was used in northern Europe in trade between Russians, Norwegians, and (to a lesser extent) Sámis (Lapps), Low German speakers, and Swedes. Two Basque-lexifier pidgins were used for trade in the Atlantic, one in Iceland and one in Newfoundland.

Most known pidgins and creoles with non-European lexifier languages also arose as a direct result of European expansion. In the northeastern United States, for instance, Pidgin Delaware was used between European traders and missionaries, on the one hand, and Delaware Indians on the other. Pidgin Inuit (Eskimo) was used for trade with Europeans in Alaska; Sango – a pidgin-turned-creole with the Ubangian language Ngbandi as its lexifier language, spoken in the Central African Republic – apparently arose as a pidgin among local Africans and then African workers who accompanied Frenchmen and Belgians as they traveled up the Ubangi River; the now extinct Nootka Jargon (actually, probably, a pidgin language) developed on Vancouver Island in what is now southwestern Canada, between European explorers and Nootkas; and Fanagaló, a Zulu-lexifier pidgin, arose (like several other Bantu-lexifier mining pidgins) in Europeans' African mines, specifically, in this case, in South Africa.

There may have been, and there may even still be, a great many pidgins and perhaps creoles that did not originate through Europeans or European expansion. As noted above, our chances of finding out about such contact languages are relatively slim: in most cases most of the speakers would have been illiterate, so the languages can attract scholars' attention only if they happen to be noticed and identified by outsiders. Nevertheless, although we cannot know how many there have been, we do have evidence and direct attestations of quite a few of these languages. Bazaar Malay, for instance, is used in Malaysia for intergroup communication in the market squares. Hiri Motu (also called Police Motu), which takes its lexicon from the Melanesian language Motu and which arose through trade relations with neighboring groups, is one of the major national languages of Papua New Guinea. Chinook Jargon, a pidgin once spoken widely in the Pacific Northwest of the United States and neighboring British Columbia, probably arose before European contact through trade with Native neighbors and (as with the Nez Percé Jargon mentioned above) in communication between the Lower Chinook people and their slaves. The Nez Percé Jargon itself, if it was a full-fledged pidgin language, also falls into this category. The Pidgin Inuit that was used in trade with Athabaskan speakers is not directly attested, but apparently it differed greatly from the Pidgin Inuit that developed in European–Inuit contacts.

A final comment on the distribution of pidgins and creoles: contrary to what common sense might suggest, it is not safe to assume that the presence of one contact language ensures the absence of one or more others. Sometimes, to be sure, overlap seems to be avoided. It is a striking fact that the pidgin Chinook Jargon stopped spreading eastward at about the same point that the Plains Indian Sign Language – which fulfilled a pidgin's functions – stopped spreading westward; in northwestern Montana, for example, the Montana Salish people knew the sign language but not Chinook Jargon, while the tribes just west of Montana knew Chinook Jargon but did not use the sign language.

Nevertheless, there are several known instances (and possibly many unknown instances) of coexisting pidgins in the same areas, and there are also cases of coexisting, coterritorial pidgins and creoles. During the seventeenth century, Pidgin Delaware and American Indian Pidgin English coexisted in parts of their territory in the northeastern United States, for instance, and Pidgin Hawaiian and Hawaiian Pidgin English apparently overlapped in Hawaii in the nineteenth century. In their trade relations (though perhaps not with the same trading partners) Motu speakers used

both Hiri Motu and two or more pidgins based lexically on non-Austrone-
sian languages (Toaripi Hiri Trading Pidgin, Koriki Hiri; *hiri* in the names of
these languages comes from the term for the Motus' annual trading voyages
along the New Guinea coast). In maps in the *Atlas of Languages of
Intercultural Communication in the Pacific, Asia, and the Americas*, Pidgin
Fiji and Pidgin Hindustani overlap in parts of Fiji (vol. 1, map 30), as do
Pidgin Chukchi and Pidgin Russian in northern Siberia (map 110), and Inuit-
Russian Pidgin and Alaskan Russian Pidgin in Alaska (map 110). Other
examples of overlapping pidgin territories can also be found. And perhaps it
should not be surprising that the same set of languages in contact can give
rise to more than one lingua franca: as we have seen, there are different
motives for developing a pidgin, and it is easy to imagine more than one
motive being present in the same groups of speakers, or even the same motive
pushing the groups to form and then use different pidgins.

   As for pidgins coexisting with creoles, every pidgin that became a creole
by nativization must have passed through a stage in which some people
spoke the language natively while others spoke it as a second language. So,
for instance, through most of the twentieth century Hawaiian Pidgin
English was spoken side by side with Hawaiian Creole English; the same
is true of Tok Pisin, although (unlike the Hawaiian languages) its creolization process was strictly social, with no significant linguistic consequences,
because it had already expanded linguistically long before it acquired native
speakers.

Pidgins and creoles are not maximally simple and not all alike

The title of this section may be a bit puzzling: why should anyone expect
pidgins and creoles to be either supersimple or identical? The two expectations are connected and belief in them is common, but it is asymmetrical for
pidgins and creoles. Pidgins (but not creoles) are widely believed to be
maximally simple, while both pidgins and creoles are widely believed to be
very similar to each other structurally. Each of these widespread beliefs stems
from two main sources.

   Both beliefs surely arose in the first place because pidgins in particular
seemed to early investigators to be 'reduced' – simplified – versions of their
lexifier languages, and because of perceived similarities in the structures of
pidgin and creole languages. Early specialists noticed a number of similarities
immediately and found them important enough to motivate the hypothesis
that all these contact languages are in fact alike and simple. The features that
are most often proposed as pidgin/creole universals are a lack of morphology, a lack of 'exotic' sounds and complex consonant clusters, SVO word
order, and, in creoles only, a particular distribution of particles indicating
tense, mood, and aspect (TMA). Or, to put it more generally, since all these
features (except perhaps the TMA patterns) are universally unmarked, the
typical hypothesis is that pidgins and (at least if they emerge abruptly, rather

than evolving from well-established pidgins) creoles specialize in unmarked linguistic features.

This hypothesis, based as it is on the empirical evidence of perceived similarities, makes good intuitive sense too when one is making predictions about the linguistic outcome of processes of pidgin/creole genesis. First, for the maximal simplicity claim, there is the standard view of the social conditions under which a classic trade pidgin arises: new contact situation, no shared language, need for intergroup communication, very limited communicative functions (like the stereotypical 'you give me gun, me give you beaver pelts'). Under these conditions, one might reasonably expect that an emergent pidgin will have only the most rudimentary structure and a minimal vocabulary. That does not, of course, entail a prediction that creoles will also have rudimentary structure and lexicon: a creole, by definition, serves as the main language of a speech community, so it ought to have all the lexical and structural resources of any other language – and all known creoles do in fact meet this expectation.

The nature of a new pidgin's expected rudimentary structure is in part predicted by the second main reason for the belief in similarity across all pidgin and creole languages. This is essentially the reason outlined in Chapter 6 under Mechanism 4, 'Negotiation': when nobody in a contact situation knows anybody else's language – that is, in a classic pidgin or (abrupt) creole genesis situation – guesses about what the other person will understand are most likely to be accurate when they involve universally unmarked features, both because all the languages in contact are likely to share numerous unmarked features and because unmarked features are easier to learn than marked features. The idea, then, is that if all pidgins and creoles develop through communication among groups that share no common language, their structures will all have predominantly unmarked features; and since unmarked features are supposed to be universal, this in turn should mean that all pidgins and creoles will be structurally similar. Pidgins should be similar to each other in their rudimentary structures, and creoles, though not limited in their range of structures, should resemble each other closely.

Neither prediction holds up completely to close scrutiny, however. They are certainly not totally wrong; pidgins that are used for limited functions do have less overall morphosyntactic structure than any of the languages whose speakers created them, and markedness does clearly play an important role in the linguistic outcome of pidgin and creole genesis processes. Most pidgins and creoles either lack morphology entirely or have very limited morphological resources compared with those of their lexifier and other input languages. Morphology also tends to be extremely regular when it does exist in pidgins and creoles, without the widespread irregularities that are so very common (to the distress of students of foreign languages) in other languages' morphological systems.

Nevertheless, in their strong form, both predictions are false. The empirical basis of the hypotheses turns out to be misleadingly limited, primarily to languages that have western European lexifier languages and (for creoles) primarily to languages that have related and often typologically similar languages of western Africa as their substrate languages. The western European lexifier languages are typologically similar in a number of respects, as almost all of them are both genetically related to each other and members of the Standard Average European linguistic area. So on typological grounds alone, it is not surprising that Caribbean creoles share a sizable number of structural features. In any case, once one looks beyond the most-studied pidgins and creoles, and especially at those with non-European lexifiers, it is immediately clear that pidgins and creoles display much more structural diversity than specialists used to envision.

Some of the problems with the common-sense predictions about pidgin/creole structures have to do with processes of pidgin and creole genesis, and these will be discussed in the next section. Some obvious general points can be made here, though. For one thing, the communicative purposes for which pidgins are used are usually not confined to basic trade transactions; either from the beginning or soon after the pidgin CRYSTALLIZES, a pidgin is very likely to serve at least a few other purposes as well, for instance for domestic conversations between slaves and masters. The structure of a pidgin at the time of crystallization may therefore not be minimal. (A vexing practical problem is that determining what structural features a pidgin or creole had when it first arose ranges from difficult to impossible, because the language that is available for study is all too likely to have changed between its time of origin and its time of attestation. Most known creoles have a presumed history of three to five hundred years, ample time to allow for structural changes, and even some pidgins are two hundred years old or more. But using the standard methods of historical linguistics makes it possible to support hypotheses about initial pidgin and creole structures – except in those cases for which we have relatively early attestations, such as Sranan.)

In addition, even the most rudimentary pidgin structures might not be similar, because the creators' native languages play a role in the selection of features that go into the emerging pidgin. To justify the title of this section, therefore, let's look at some examples of nonsimple, nonsimilar pidgin and creole structures.

One recurring claim about these contact languages is that their phonological structures are simple, consisting of unmarked consonants and vowels arranged in simple syllables with at most one consonant at each end; it is often proposed that pidgins and creoles tend to have CV structure, with no syllable-final consonants at all. This fits with the markedness prediction, since CV is generally considered to be the least marked syllable type cross-linguistically. The consonant phoneme inventory of Chinook Jargon, together with the pidgin's highly marked consonant clusters, offers perhaps the most striking violation of this prediction; and since it is unlike the consonant system of any other known pidgin or creole, it also violates the all-structures-equal prediction about pidgins and creoles. The system does, however, make areal sense in view of the fact that its features match those of the Pacific Northwest Sprachbund, which was outlined in Chapter 5. Table 1 gives the basic consonant inventory (each item in the table is a single unit phoneme; columns 3–5 contain affricates).

p	t		ts	tš	k	k^w	q	q^w	?
p'	t'	tł	ts'	(tš')	k'	$k^{w'}$	q'	$q^{w'}$	
b	d				g				
		ł	s	š	x	x^w	X	X^w	
m	n				(N)				
	r	l							
w			y						

TABLE 1. Chinook Jargon consonant phonemes

As with all pidgins (indeed, as with all languages), there was some variation among Chinook Jargon speakers: many Native American speakers of the pidgin did not use either /b/ or /d/, for instance, and only the most talented and perceptive whites used glottalization, uvulars, the /ts/ affricates, and the lateral fricative and affricates. But there is enough consistency in nineteenth- and twentieth-century documentation of the pidgin to justify this elaborate inventory, with such marked (and non-Standard Average European) consonants as the ones most white speakers of the pidgin did not learn. Similarly, there is ample evidence to support the claim that Chinook Jargon had unusual non-SAE-ish consonant clusters like /tq'/ in /tq'ix/ 'want, like' and /ptš/ in /ptšəx/ 'green'. Nor is this the only pidgin or creole with highly marked phonological features; both the English/Portuguese-lexifier New World creole Saramaccan and the creolized African pidgin Sango, for instance, have double-articulated stop phonemes /kp/ and /gb/ (in addition to /p/, /k/, /b/, and /g/). All these unusual phonological features occur in at least some of the languages spoken by the contact languages' creators, indigenous languages of the Pacific Northwest and of West Africa, respectively.

Another common claim about pidgin and creole phonological systems is that tone distinctions, even if present in some or all of the languages spoken natively by the creators of a pidgin or creole, are typically absent in the new contact language. This too is false, though it is certainly true that many pidgins and creoles created by native speakers of tone languages have no tones. It is also true that, even when pidgins and creoles have tones, the tones often have fewer functions than in any of the input languages that have tone phonemes. But tone languages are not especially hard to find among contact languages. Ndyuka, for example, has at least two phonemic tones, unlike its lexifier language (English) but like the African languages spoken by its creators; Saramaccan is also a tone language, like the African languages spoken by (some of) its creators. Sango has tone phonemes, as does its lexifier language Ngbandi, though in Sango the tones serve fewer functions than in Ngbandi: they distinguish words in both languages, but they are used much more extensively in Ngbandi to make grammatical distinctions. The same is true of Kitúba, a Kikongo-lexifier creole spoken in the Democratic Republic of the Congo (formerly Zaire and Congo); but in Kitúba only a minority of the lexical items have distinctive tones. Tây Bôi, the French-lexifier pidgin once spoken in French-occupied Vietnam, was said to have two different phonologies that matched the systems of the two input languages; French speakers thus presumably lacked tones in their version of the pidgin, but for Vietnamese speakers Tây Bôi was presumably a tone language.

Perhaps the best place to look for nonphonological structures that are not maximally simple is in pronominal systems, and one of the best places to look for elaborate pronoun systems is in islands of the Pacific Ocean, where many Austronesian languages and some others too have such pronominal categories as inclusive vs. exclusive 'we' and dual, trial, and occasionally paucal number as well as singular and plural ('paucal' means 'a few').

In Tok Pisin, for instance, all the pronominal morphemes are ultimately derived from English, but the system certainly is not. It lacks the English gender and case distinctions (which are unknown in the languages of the original pidgin's Austronesian-speaking creators) but has typical local categories of person and number, with exclusive vs. inclusive 'we' and a system of pronominal number divided into singular, dual (two people or things), trial (three people or things), and plural (more than three people or things – as opposed to a simpler system like that of English, where plural refers to more than one). Table 2 gives the forms.

	SINGULAR	DUAL	TRIAL	PLURAL
1st exclusive	mi	mitupela	mitripela	mipela
1st inclusive		yumitupela	yumitripela	yumipela
2nd	yu	yutupela	yutripela	yupela
3rd	em	tupela	tripela	ol

TABLE 2. Tok Pisin pronouns

The English sources of the morphemes in the Tok Pisin pronouns are *me*, *you*, *him*, *two*, *fellow* ('*fella*'), *three*, and *all*, combined in very un-English ways. It is worth noting that this system was in place before Tok Pisin expanded dramatically in its functions, i.e. while it was still an ordinary nonexpanded pidgin. In spite of the absence of the English pronominal categories of case and gender, no one would want to claim that this is a simple system: it is as complex as the pronominal systems of the Austronesian input languages, though somewhat more transparent in its formation than most of them.

It's easy to find other fairly complex grammatical subsystems and individual features in pidgin and creole languages. The African creole Kitúba, for example, is based lexically on the Bantu language Kikongo, and it was apparently created by speakers of various Bantu languages with possible input also from West Africans who accompanied Europeans in their journeys to what later became Congo and the Democratic Republic of the Congo. Unlike most other Bantu-based pidgins and creoles, Kitúba has a number of Bantu morphosyntactic features. The two that are most striking are a fairly elaborate system of prefixal noun classes, fewer than in Kikongo but still quite complex, and a tense/aspect system basically like that of Kikongo in categories, though not in form: the Kitúba tense/aspect system is regularized, and, though two tenses are formed with suffixes, most of the other tense/aspect categories are expressed by free particles – which, however, is also in part a feature of relevant dialects of Kikongo.

Yet another claim that is often made about pidgins and creoles is that they lack morphology, especially inflectional morphology; as noted above, these contact languages do tend to lack morphology, but the strong claim is nevertheless unjustified. The two Kitúba tense suffixes are counterexamples to this claim; other examples are the transitive suffix of Tok Pisin, the transitive suffix and causative affix of Hiri Motu, the participial suffix -*ing* of Pitcairnese, the reflexive suffix (from Russian) and the imperfective aspect suffix (from Mongolian) of Chinese Pidgin Russian, the diminutive and augmentative prefixes of the Portuguese-lexifier creole Fa d'Ambu, the negative prefix of Sranan, and the three aspect suffixes (perfective, imperfective, and iterative, all from the substrate language Eastern Ịọ) of Berbice Dutch Creole. These examples are only a sample; morphology is not particularly uncommon in pidgins and creoles, although no pidgins or creoles have morphological systems as elaborate as those of their most elaborate input languages.

The consonant phonemes of Chinook Jargon, the tone phonemes of Ndyuka and several other pidgins and creoles, the personal pronouns of Tok Pisin, the noun classes of Kitúba, and most of the specific examples of morphology also provide evidence against claims about similarity among all pidgins and creoles, since none of these features is common in these contact languages worldwide. Other examples of structural diversity can be found in word order features of various pidgins and creoles. In particular, it has sometimes been claimed that SVO sentential word order is universal among creoles, even those which developed with major input from languages with other word order patterns (usually SOV); the claim has sometimes been extended to pidgins as well. Certainly this seems to be true of all well-studied languages that are generally agreed to be creoles, in the Caribbean and elsewhere: all the Caribbean creoles have SVO word order, as do the creoles of the Indian Ocean and elsewhere, e.g. Tok Pisin and the Arabic-lexifier creole Nubi, which is spoken in Kenya and Uganda. (The universal-SVO word order claim applies only to the initial word order pattern, of course. Once they are crystallized into languages, creoles, like all other languages, will undergo both internally- and externally-motivated changes, and these changes may include word order alterations; so, for instance, Sri Lanka Portuguese Creole has changed from SVO to SOV order under the influence of neighboring Dravidian languages.) Many pidgins have SVO order too, among them Russenorsk, Chinese Pidgin English, and Fanagaló.

But it isn't true of all pidgins. The Ndyuka-Trio pidgin, for instance, is SOV in sentences with noun subjects but usually OSV in sentences with pronoun subjects – like one of its input languages (Trio) but unlike the other (Ndyuka, an SVO creole). In Hiri Motu (whose lexifier language, Motu, has rigid SOV order, as do most or all of the other input languages), the word order is SOV when both S and O are nouns; OSV or, more rarely, SVO when S is a noun and O is a pronoun; OSV when S is a pronoun and O is a noun; and either OSV or SVO when both S and O are pronouns. Pidgin Delaware had both SVO and SOV order, neither obviously predominant, and Chinook Jargon typically had VS order with adjectival predicates (in a translation of English *I'm hungry*, for instance) and SVO order with all other predicates. Chinese Pidgin Russian has (or had) SOV order, as does Nagamese, an Assamese-lexifier pidgin spoken in northern India (Assamese belongs to the Indic subbranch of the Indo-European language family). The situation is more complicated in Pidgin Yimas(-Arafundi), a trade pidgin with mainly Yimas lexicon but also with numerous Arafundi words that is spoken in the Sepik River basin in northern New Guinea (see Chapter 5 for a discussion of the Sprachbund in this region): this pidgin has verb-final sentential word order but free ordering of subject and object, so that both SOV and OSV occur frequently.

Another word-order feature that varies widely among pidgins and, in this case, among creoles too is the placement of the negative element(s) in a sentence. In many creoles, the negative element appears at the beginning of the verb phrase, as in Papiamentu *mi no ta bini* 'I'm not coming' (lit. 'I NEGATIVE FUTURE come'), French Guiana Creole *mo pa té travaille* 'I hadn't worked' (lit. 'I NEGATIVE TENSE work'), and Tok Pisin *yu no kan go long biglain* 'you can't go to the work-group' (lit. you NEGATIVE can go to work-group'). Some pidgins also have this ordering, as in late nineteenth-century Chinese Pidgin English *maj no hav kači buk* 'I haven't borrowed a book' (lit. 'I NEGATIVE have caught book'). But other creoles and pidgins have different orders. In Berbice Dutch Creole, for instance, the negative element is clause-final, as in ɛk suk mu lasan eni ka 'I didn't want to leave them' (lit. 'I want go leave 3pl NEGATIVE'). In Chinese Pidgin Russian the negative element usually follows the verb. Fa d'Ambu has double negation, with one negative element

before the verb and the other attached to the last word of the sentence, as in
Odyai amu na be mem = bo xama-kumu = f 'I didn't see your mother at the
market today' (lit. 'today I NEGATIVE see mother = your place-food = NEGA-
TIVE'). In Chinook Jargon, as in all of the Native Pacific Northwest
languages, negation is almost always sentence-initial, as in *Halo nika kumtux*
'I don't understand' (lit. 'NEGATIVE I understand'), and in Pidgin Delaware
the negator also usually precedes the subject, as in *Matta ne kamuta* 'I didn't
steal it' (lit. 'NEGATIVE I steal').

The purpose of this section has not been to convince readers that pidgins
and creoles differ from each other in all possible respects. There are some
striking similarities among these contact languages, for instance in the
famously uniform, or at least similar, placement of tense, aspect, and mood
markers in many creoles. These markers typically occur in the order tense–
mood–aspect, as in the following examples with anterior tense ('before the
event under discussion'), irrealis mood ('unreal'), and nonpunctual aspect:
Saramaccan *Mi bi-o-tá-nján dí fisi* 'I would have been eating the fish' (lit.
'ANTERIOR-IRREALIS-NONPUNCTUAL-eat the fish' and Fa d'Ambu *Ineni bi ske
xa tabaya* 'they would have been working' (lit. 'they ANTERIOR IRREALIS
NONPUNCTUAL work'). At a less specific level, nonexpanded pidgins in
particular typically share such general linguistic features as a small lexicon,
lack of extensive morphology, and lack of such (morpho)syntactic resources
as clearly marked subordination and a fully elaborated tense/aspect system;
as noted above, they also tend to lack a full range of social functions, being
restricted to such limited functions as trade or master–slave communication.

The goal of the section, instead, has been to emphasize the fact that
similarity and (in pidgins) simplicity are not the whole story, as some
traditional approaches to the study of these contact languages have suggested. This emphasis is needed when we move on to a consideration of the
major theories of pidgin and creole genesis, because the diversity in pidgin
and creole structures reduces the appeal of some of the theories under debate:
any successful pidgin/creole genesis theory must account for the diversity
within this set of languages as well as for the similarities among them.

Pidgin/creole genesis theories: where does the grammar come from?

Again we need to begin with a definition: in this book, 'pidgin/creole genesis'
is any process through which a pidgin or creole language comes into being.
The rather clumsy phrasing of the definition has a purpose that will become
evident when we examine gradualist genesis theories.

In any consideration of pidgin and creole genesis, the problem is to figure
out the source(s) of the languages' structures, since the lexical items are
(usually) easy to trace to one or more sources. In most cases there is one main
lexifier language, with a small to medium-sized set of words from one or
more other languages. Some pidgins and a few creoles have more heterogeneous lexicons, but here too there is no great difficulty in finding the

sources. Saramaccan, for instance, has about 50% English words and about 35% Portuguese words, together with a sizable number of words from African languages, in particular the Bantu language Kikongo and the Kwa languages Ewe, Fon, and Twi. Most of the lexicon of Chinook Jargon, including the bulk of the basic vocabulary, comes from the Lower Chinook language, but two or three dozen words (some of them quite basic) come from Nootka, a smaller number of words come from Salishan languages, and quite a few words entered the pidgin from French and then English, especially after the mid-nineteenth century. There is no mystery, therefore, about the lexical sources of pidgins and creoles. All the controversy centers on the route(s) through which the languages' grammars emerged.

Treating this complex set of issues in one section of one chapter risks obscuring a major topic of debate: can the question of pidgin and creole origins reasonably be considered as a single problem, or should they be considered separately? This question has no simple answer, for at least two reasons. First, it depends on what type of creole we are talking about: the development of a creole out of a stable pidgin via nativization has no direct parallel in pidgin genesis, so any parallels that exist in processes of pidgin and creole genesis must be sought in creoles that develop without going through a stable pidgin stage. Second, and this is related to the first reason, it appears that both pidgins and creoles have emerged through a variety of developmental processes, so that a search for *the* genesis process for either or both sets of languages is misguided. And, as we shall see, most of the processes involved do appear to have been operative both in pidgin genesis and in creole genesis.

I believe that some, perhaps many or even most, of the controversies surrounding the topic of pidgin and creole genesis will vanish if we recognize that the common assumption of a single universal developmental route to creole genesis – which is the main locus of the controversies – is unmotivated. If specialists agree that there are several ways in which creoles (and pidgins) arise, then it may turn out that several theories are viable, but for different languages. An empirical question that arises here is whether different genesis routes lead to different linguistic results; unfortunately, and this no doubt accounts in part for the uniform-genesis assumption, they apparently do not always do so (see below for a bit more discussion of this point).

From a historical linguist's viewpoint, a vitally important consideration is that an origin theory that includes both pidgins and creoles is to be preferred, all other things being equal, to a theory that requires totally different routes of development for pidgins and creoles. This is a standard principle in any historical linguistic analysis, as it is in historical sciences generally: if two theories account equally well for the data, then, all other things being equal, the simpler and more comprehensive theory wins. In the case of pidgins and creoles, an approach that comprehends both will be simpler than an approach that requires separate genesis scenarios for these two types of contact language. Of course scholars can and do disagree sharply about what counts as 'all other things being equal'. But in the present context, the appeal of a theory that accounts equally well for pidgin and creole genesis is that pidgins and creoles obviously do share certain linguistic and social features, as we have seen; in particular, both arise under circumstances in which at least some of the groups in contact do not learn any of the other groups' languages – that is, under conditions where we would expect to find linguistic effects of imperfect learning.

I should acknowledge my own bias as a historical linguist: given the things that pidgins and creoles have in common, I prefer to try for a simpler unified approach to the genesis problem, rather than starting from the assumption that pidgins and creoles follow entirely different developmental paths. That is why I'm treating both in a single section. As I'll argue below, this approach works well in many cases, but it doesn't always work, because clearly there are also some significant differences between pidgin and creole genesis processes.

With these preliminary comments out of the way, we'll begin our examination of pidgin/creole genesis theories by surveying some of the major former and current approaches.

Monogenesis

One of the oldest theories about pidgin and creole genesis is the MONOGENESIS HYPOTHESIS. In its strong form, this hypothesis states that all pidgins and creoles are descendants of the original LINGUA FRANCA of the Mediterranean, albeit with RELEXIFICATION – lexical replacement – for all pidgins and creoles that do not have Italian lexicon, i.e. almost all known modern pidgins and creoles. Most proponents of the hypothesis posit as the first step the development (out of the Lingua Franca, or at least under the influence of the Lingua Franca) of a Portuguese-lexifier pidgin, which became well known in West Africa. The idea is that European explorers, traders, colonizers, and slavers learned West African Pidgin Portuguese and took it along in their travels around the globe, replacing its Portuguese lexicon with that of their own native language. Relexification also happened, according to the hypothesis, in the formation of non-European-lexifier pidgins and creoles. This would not be descent in the historical linguist's framework of genetic linguistics, because a process of lexical replacement does not fit the standard notion of descent with modification; but, if correct, the hypothesis would nevertheless link the Lingua Franca directly to the vast majority of the world's pidgins and creoles. One obvious exception would be Maridi Arabic, which predates the Crusades; other exceptions would be pidgins and creoles that arose completely independently of European expansion, such as the indigenous trade pidgins of New Guinea. Moreover, the monogenesis hypothesis can account for creoles only if all creoles arose via nativization of well-established pidgins; but, as we'll see below, this doesn't seem to be the case.

The appeal of the monogenesis hypothesis is that it would account nicely for the structural similarities among pidgins and creoles. This no doubt explains its popularity in the 1960s and 1970s, when most specialists viewed pidgins and creoles as grammatically very similar. But that was early in the history of pidgin/creoles studies – the field is quite new, in spite of early pioneers like Hugo Schuchardt in the late nineteenth and early twentieth centuries and Robert A. Hall, Jr., in the middle decades of the twentieth century. The last few decades have seen greatly increased intensive study of pidgin and creole languages all over the world, so that we now know much more about their structural diversity than we used to, and also much more about the fairly numerous pidgins that lie well off the beaten track of European exploration and colonization. The monogenesis hypothesis cannot account for any of the structural diversity that is now known to exist, and it also lost much of its initial appeal once its claim to (near-)universality turned out to be unjustified. Modified versions of the hypothesis are still taken seriously, for instance for all English-lexicon Caribbean creoles, which some scholars believe to be direct descendants, in the standard historical linguist's sense, of a pidgin that arose on the coast of West Africa. But the strong form of the hypothesis is no longer considered a viable candidate in the search for a global route to pidgin and creole genesis.

Abrupt genesis scenarios

The major current views of pidgin/creole genesis fall into two major categories, with several subcategories in each. The focus of theoretical research has long been on creole genesis rather than on pidgin genesis, in part because Caribbean creoles and, to a lesser extent, the European-lexifier creoles in Africa still receive much more attention than pidgins. The reason for this emphasis probably has to do ultimately with numbers of speakers: many of the most interesting pidgins are now extinct or nearly so, while most known creoles are flourishing as the primary languages of large speech communities. In any case, most people who propose contact-language genesis theories talk only about creole genesis.

The two categories of theories can be characterized as abrupt vs. gradual genesis scenarios. The simplest way to think of contact-language genesis seems to me to be abrupt creation, because it fits the traditional view of the onset of the appropriate kind of language contact, especially for pidgins: a new pidgin arising in a new multilingual contact situation for use in limited domains, a new creole arising in a new multilingual contact situation for use in all domains. In this scenario, the creole arises without going through a stable pidgin stage. The idea of 'abrupt' has to be somewhat elastic here; it isn't meant to suggest an overnight event. Estimates of the time required for abrupt contact-language genesis range from a few years to twenty-five years, because time is needed for full crystallization of the language in the contact community – development of a shared vocabulary and grammar that must be learned by anyone who wishes to speak the language, including native speakers of the lexifier language.

Abrupt creolization scenarios in turn fall into three different subcategories. Derek Bickerton's Language Bioprogram Hypothesis (LBH), one of the earliest important theories in this category, treats creole genesis as the outcome of first-language acquisition in a context of restricted linguistic input from the surrounding community. According to Bickerton, creoles – specifically plantation creoles – arise in new contact situations where a new community-wide language is needed immediately for all purposes. The adults in the community communicate with each other in a macaronic prepidgin – no stable shared grammar at all – and their children, growing up with only the unstable prepidgin as input for their language-learning task, construct a grammar derived from grammatical structures that are literally genetically programmed, hard-wired in every newborn human infant's brain. (He allows for some time, a generation or two, to crystallize the new creole's grammar.) Bickerton finds support for his theory in aspects of ordinary first-language acquisition as well as in creole genesis, and he argues that children who learn languages with normal input do not display the Bioprogram features because those features are overlaid by the grammatical features of their community's language, English or Quechua or Tagalog or whatever it is. The LBH could account for the shared features in the classic creoles, especially the tense/aspect/mood features; it cannot of course account for the diversity found in plantation creoles, and it is not meant to account for any grammatical features of nonplantation creoles like Pitcairnese and Tok Pisin, or for grammatical features of fully crystallized pidgins, which in everyone's views are adults' (or at least not primarily children's) creations. The LBH also does not account for shared nonsyntactic features of plantation creoles, though it could in principle be extended in that direction.

The LBH was especially popular in the 1980s, but is now considered a viable theory mainly by formally-oriented linguists who are not creolists. The reasons for skepticism about it are partly historical: detailed investigations of the demographics of slave populations in numerous Caribbean colonies have revealed that there were few or no slave children for the first fifty years or more – it was cheaper to import adult slaves, and in any case women slaves were all too often barren after suffering the rigors of slave ships in the journey from Africa to the Caribbean. Presumably because of such findings, Bickerton now refers mainly to Hawaiian Creole English as an example of a creole resulting from the operation of the LBH.

Other reasons for skepticism about the LBH are social: it seems very unlikely that whoever raised slave children (when there were any) would have spoken to them exclusively in a macaronic prepidgin; all the adults in the community, after all, knew at least their native languages, and they would inevitably have talked to children in those languages. So the input received by infants was surely never restricted to a prepidgin. In addition, slaves who were born and raised in the Caribbean were likely to have relatively privileged positions in the plantation societies, with greater access to the lexifier language.

Still another reason for skepticism has to do with the lack of generality, even for plantation creoles: if the LBH cannot account for syntactic structures of many Caribbean creoles because there were too few children on hand to manifest the LBH features there, and if Caribbean creoles nevertheless share the typical plantation-creole syntactic features (like the widespread TMA patterns, which were first noticed in the Caribbean), then obviously those creoles had to acquire the shared features in some other way. We still need an explanation for those shared features; the LBH is not available for those languages, so why suppose that it was operative in the Hawaiian Creole English context, where there apparently were children early enough to make its operation possible? Why not try, instead, to find a single explanation that works for the shared features in Hawaiian Creole English and also in Caribbean and other plantation creoles? Such reasoning has led most creolists to reject the LBH. But, although Bickerton's strong claims for the LBH seem shaky on the empirical evidence, his notion of universal innate features is by no means a dead issue: this is one version of a major component of several pidgin/creole genesis theories.

Another theory in the abrupt creation category is Claire Lefebvre's Relexification Hypothesis. Although the strong version of the monogenesis hypothesis has vanished from the creolization debates, relexification continues to be discussed; it is the basis of the theory explored by Lefebvre and her colleagues in a long-term research program, the Haitian Creole Project. According to Lefebvre's hypothesis, 'creoles are created by adults who develop a new lexicon by combining the phonetic shapes of one language with the semantic and syntactic information of another language'; she proposes this as 'the central process in creolization'. Her method of searching for evidence to support this hypothesis is to compare syntactic structures of Haitian Creole, a French-lexicon Caribbean creole, with syntactic structures of Fon, a West African language that was spoken by a significant proportion of the slaves in Haiti during the creole's formative period. The time frame for the relexification process is not specified, but of course it must have been completed while Fon was still spoken by the slaves, which argues for an abrupt rather than a gradual process. Proponents of the relexification hypothesis have not discussed its possible relevance for pidgin genesis, but in principle, if correct for creoles, it could be extended to account for pidgins too. Like Bickerton's LBH, Lefebvre's Relexification Hypothesis is grounded in formal syntactic theory; also like the LBH, it has met with considerable skepticism from creolists, though not primarily on demographic grounds.

In the framework presented in this book, the creole genesis process envisioned by Lefebvre is borrowing: speakers of Fon graft French phonetic strings onto their native Fon grammar. Imperfect learning plays no role in the process, because this is incorporation of French material into Fon by native Fon speakers, not Fon interference creating a Fon-influenced variety of French. The process envisioned by Lefebvre and her colleagues does not match other known instances of relexification. Those few pidgins that seem to have undergone relexification are, by hypothesis at least, cases where (for instance) native speakers of Spanish relexified a Portuguese-based pidgin that they already spoke; and the case cited by Lefebvre herself as a parallel, the Media Lengua of Ecuador, is a case of language creation by bilinguals for use as an in-group language (see Chapter 8). In other words, in other cases of relexification the relexifiers have been bilingual, and they have not needed a new medium of communication for a new contact situation. The Media Lengua, in particular, is not at all similar to Haitian Creole (or any other creoles) as a social phenomenon. Moreover, the Relexification Hypothesis takes no account of any tendency, or need, for 'negotiation' in the process of creating a new contact language: its proponents do not consider the effects of other languages in the new creolizing context, but instead assume that Fon speakers will simply use their native grammatical structures in trying to communicate with other members of the community. This assumption seems simplistic in light of what is known about second-language acquisition, where even the first efforts of learners tend not to match their native-language structures exactly, and about shift-induced interference, where interference features very often don't match the source features in the shifting group's language exactly.

The third major line of research on abrupt creolization, in contrast to Bickerton's exclusively universalist/innatist approach and Lefebvre's relexification approach, is based on the assumption that both pidgin genesis and creole genesis are akin to second-language acquisition and thus to processes of shift-induced interference. There are several versions of this approach; I'll describe my own, but it's compatible with most of the other approaches. This approach encompasses both pidgin and creole genesis; the basic scenario can be constructed by combining the discussions of Mechanisms 4 and 5 in Chapter 6, 'negotiation' and second-language acquisition strategies. All the strategies used in pidgin/creole genesis according to this hypothesis will usually involve 'negotiation', however, because in most cases there is probably no serious effort to learn the lexifier language as a whole: instead, the learning process is one in which the people in the new contact situation learn to communicate with each other by deploying the new vocabulary with grammatical structures they hope will be understood by their interlocutors. The idea is that people's 'right' guesses about what the others will understand become part of the emerging contact language. The hypothesis does not predict that they will simply make use of their native structures; on the contrary, it predicts that they will be likely to abandon those native structures that are not understood by speakers of the other languages. The structures they settle on will be those best understood by all the other people – primarily unmarked structures, but also marked structures that are common in most or all of the languages in contact. The resulting pidgin or creole grammar, on this hypothesis, is a crosslanguage compromise among the languages of the pidgin/creole creators.

This approach can account for features that are widely shared among pidgins and creoles, to the extent that those features are universally un-marked and/or derivable from most of the native languages spoken by the creators of the contact languages. The approach has been criticized because the famously shared features (for instance the tense/aspect/mood patterns in creoles) do not all seem to be shared by the languages of the creoles' creators; they may be universally unmarked in some sense, but that has not been demonstrated. But caution is needed in interpreting the patterns historically. First, Caribbean creoles all have members of the 'Standard Average European' (SAE) linguistic area as lexifier languages (see Chapter 5), and there is considerable typological congruence among some groups of substrate languages as well, e.g. the Kwa languages that were so prominently represented at the relevant period in the history of Haitian Creole. Even Hawaiian Creole has an SAE language as its lexifier; and nobody has compared its substrate languages systematically to find out whether they share relevant features with the substrate languages underlying Caribbean and other plantation creoles.

Second, the notion of a crosslanguage compromise via 'negotiation' does not predict that the structure of the resulting contact language will be a lowest common denominator of the structures of the input languages; instead, it is the cumulative result of different speakers' perceptions of shared structures or of their interlocutors' unshared structures. A superficial analysis of the shared features is likely to miss crucial connections. Consider, for instance, the SVO word-order pattern of Caribbean creoles. This word order is present in most of the European lexifier languages (English, French, Spanish) and in many of the African substrate languages, so it requires no special explanation for those languages. But Berbice Dutch Creole has SVO order in spite of the fact that it is based lexically on Dutch, an underlying SOV language, and has as its only important substrate language Ijọ, which is also SOV. At first glance this seems to argue for a universalist, perhaps an innatist, explanation for the SVO order. But Silvia Kouwenberg argues instead for a process of 'negotiation' on the basis of a detailed analysis of relevant structures in the two input languages:

[T]he development of [SVO] properties of BD [= Berbice Creole Dutch] is reconstructed from the application of compromise strategies in a situation in which speakers of Du and EI [Eastern Ijọ] were involved in a process of linguistic negotiation. These strategies are aimed at the creation of a linguistic system which optimally exploits perceived similarities between Du and EI. Surface structures of different languages may be comparable, even when underlying structures are in fact irreconcilable. Also, marked strategies of one language may be comparable to unmarked strategies in another . . . . The development of VO ordering in BD can plausibly be explained as continuity of comparable superficial orderings in Du and EI.

Similarly, the English-lexifier pidgin Bislama, spoken in Vanuatu, has developed a number of structures that are shared by English and the local Austronesian languages, although it also has structures that are found in the local languages but not in English.

It must be emphasized that there is no reason to assume that speakers of the lexifier language will always participate in the creation of an abrupt pidgin or creole: sometimes they do, as in the case of Berbice Creole Dutch, Bislama, Pitcairnese, and Pidgin Delaware, but sometimes they don't, as in the case of Hawaiian Creole English (if Bickerton is right about its being an abrupt creole). If the lexifier language's speakers do participate, then one can reasonably expect the crosslanguage compromise to reflect that participation; if not, then the lexifier language should have little or no nonlexical impact on the emergent pidgin or creole.

An approach based on 'negotiation' can also account without difficulty for diversity in pidgin and creole structures. The elaborate consonant system of Chinook Jargon, the elaborate system of personal pronouns in Tok Pisin, and the noun classes of Kitúba are all quite reasonable as crosslanguage compromises, given that the crucial features are widely shared among the local languages spoken by the pidgins' creators. The notion of crosslanguage compromise cannot be taken as a rigid prediction, however. For instance, the double-articulated stop phonemes /kp/ and /gb/ that appear in Saramaccan and Sango do not provide evidence that every input language had these phonemes: they indicate only that some of the input languages (or perhaps even just one prominent input language) had the phonemes. The idea of 'negotiation' leading to a crosslinguistic compromise is indeed predictive, but it is loosely predictive. As with ordinary contact-induced language change, social factors that cannot be discovered after the fact will inevitably influence the specific outcome of a process of pidgin or creole genesis.

This completes the roster of major approaches to the explanation of pidginization and creolization that assume an abrupt-genesis scenario. These approaches make good sense for some pidgins and creoles, for instance the English-lexifier language Pitcairnese, which was certainly an abrupt creation that crystallized as a language within one or at most two generations. (A quibble is possible here, as it is possible that one or more of the Bounty mutineers already spoke a pidgin or even a creole before the mutiny; a likely candidate would be the mutineer who came originally from

St. Kitts in the Caribbean. Still, Pitcairnese itself surely arose on Pitcairn Island; it certainly has some striking Tahitian structural features, and it has not been reported to share features with Caribbean creoles that would be surprising in a two-language English–Tahitian creole.) There is also no reason to suppose that functionally restricted trade pidgins like Pidgin Delaware and Chinook Jargon arose gradually; such pidgins are likely to have begun forming as soon as contact was established and to have crystallized with their eventual (rudimentary) grammars soon afterward. But it is becoming increasingly obvious that abrupt creation is not the only way in which pidgins and creoles arise, and maybe not even the major way, at least for creoles.

Gradual genesis scenarios

Of course one type of nonabrupt creole has always been recognized in the literature, namely creolized pidgins – creoles that develop from fully crystallized pidgins, often after the pidgin has undergone considerable lexical and grammatical expansion as a result of acquiring new social functions. In such cases, e.g. in Tok Pisin, the creolization process is typically gradual socially, as mixed marriages produce native speakers of the parents' only shared language, the pidgin – and as the pidgin gradually acquires more functions even in adults' daily lives. Linguistically, the effects of creolization in these cases may be negligible, depending on how expanded the pidgin was before it acquired native speakers. The linguistic expansion process itself is almost sure to have been gradual, of course.

But creolized pidgins are not the focus of the current boom in gradualist creolization theorizing. Instead, all these theories concern plantation creoles, mostly in the Caribbean but also in the Indian Ocean and in Africa – creoles which, in the opinion of most creolists, did not emerge from a stable pidgin. Pidgins and pidgins-turned-creoles are only rarely discussed in this literature. Several different lines of research have recently led to theories of gradual creole genesis, but these theories don't necessarily all fit together: different authors often mean quite different things by 'gradual creolization', although probably all would subscribe to the characterization of creolization in at least some cases as 'a gradual process, extending over a number of generations of speakers'.

Almost all the authors who espouse a gradualist position make extensive use of detailed demographic information about the patterns of settlement and the importation of slaves in various (eventual) plantation settings. Perhaps the most important demographic fact, as far as creole-genesis theories are concerned, is the finding that there were two distinct stages in the development of the relevant agricultural societies: at first, agriculture was practiced on a small scale, and the population comprised European masters, African slaves, and (in some places) indentured Europeans who worked side by side with the slaves. Later – the time of the change varies from colony to colony, but it was sometimes thirty to fifty years after the founding of a colony – the economy shifted to large-scale plantations, usually sugar plantations. The workers on these plantations were overwhelmingly African slaves, who were imported in large numbers. The switchover from small farms to large plantations figures in most of the gradualist theories: with the advent of large plantations, the slave population rapidly came to outnumber its masters greatly (and indentured Europeans mostly vanished from the scene).

One prominent gradualist creole-genesis hypothesis is Robert Chaudenson's. Chaudenson's main focus is on French-lexifier creoles in the Indian Ocean, but he argues for the general application of his theory to other French-based creoles (and indeed to all creoles). On his view, the first slaves to arrive in the colonies worked and lived with native French speakers and therefore learned French (specifically regional dialects of French) – but no doubt imperfectly, so that their variety of French incorporated shift-induced interference features from their native languages. Once the economy switched from small farms to large plantations, newly arrived slaves no longer had much (if any) contact with their French-speaking masters; they therefore learned French from the first group of slaves, so that the later arrivals' target language was a variety of French that already showed changes from the masters' French. Subsequent waves of slaves learned increasingly divergent varieties of French, until at last the general language of the slaves, shared by all of them, was a creole language, not French at all. The process, on this hypothesis, was gradual divergence from the masters' French; each new wave of imported slaves learned a TL, but the TL was in effect a moving target, with more and more (shift-induced) interference features with each new wave of imported slaves. At each stage, the process was ordinary L2 acquisition, with perfectly ordinary contact-induced change; the only unusual aspect was the fact that it happened again and again until the resulting language could no longer be called a variety of French.

Chaudenson himself sees the resulting creoles as extensively modified French, allowing little scope for interference from the slaves' languages; he rejects theories that propose significant structural contributions from African (or other non-French) languages. He has been sharply criticized for this insistence on French as the source of many, most, or all creole structures, given the large amount of evidence for African-language influence. He has also been criticized for his assumption that French itself (in whatever form) was the target language for successive waves of newly arrived slaves; it seems likely that, as in many other pidgin/creole-genesis contexts, there was no target language in the usual sense. But his scenario for gradual creolization does not in itself require a French-structure focus; it is compatible with theories that claim extensive structural contribution from the slaves' languages and/or from universal structural tendencies based on markedness considerations. And in fact other gradualists do allow a greater role for substrate-language structural contribution.

The major appeal of all the current gradualist theories, including Chaudenson's, is that they provide a reasonable way of dealing with a fact that is very awkward for any theory that assumes abrupt creolization for all plantation creoles: in colonies where slaves at first worked closely with their masters, and often with indentured Europeans as well, for thirty or more years, they must have had adequate access to the masters' language for language-learning purposes; so why would a creole emerge at all? The answer, for a gradualist, is that it didn't – not until much later, after the shift to a large plantation economy. The major appeal of Chaudenson's particular theory is that it requires no special assumptions at all about the process of creolization: for him, creole genesis is simply a matter of repeated instances of imperfect language learning of French (and, by extension, of other European slavemasters' languages). A possible problem for Chaudenson's theory has to do with the size and timing of the influx of new slaves after the shift to a sugar economy: if the influx was large and fast enough, the resulting new slave society might have fit an abrupt-creolization scenario better than a truly gradual genesis scenario: the new slaves might have learned their lexicon from French-speaking earlier slaves, but they might not have learned much if any of the modified French grammar of those earlier slaves. That is, the earlier contingent of slaves might not have been large enough to provide sufficient access for the newcomers to learn French. Other problems for Chaudenson's hypothesis, especially if it is claimed to account for all French-lexifier or even all European-lexifier creoles, are demographic. In the Indian Ocean, for instance, the island Réunion may fit his scenario rather well (though there are doubters), and its creole, Réunionese, has numerous French structural features; but on the nearby island Mauritius, slaves outnumbered whites within ten years of the initial French settlement.

Other gradualist theories do not posit such a seamless progression that starts with a European language learned imperfectly from Europeans, then proceeds to an altered European language learned imperfectly from Africans, and finally results in a variety so distant linguistically from the original European target language that it qualifies as a separate creole language. Instead, these authors analyze particular linguistic features (in practice, the features are always syntactic) and conclude either that the typical (later) creole features did not emerge for quite a while after the founding of a colony or that the features showed a lot of variation until quite a while after the founding of a colony. The proponents of these theories usually make extensive use of early textual data, emphasizing the structural differences between early data (e.g. the earliest Sranan text, of 1718) and later data (e.g. Sranan after 1750). Sometimes authors argue that linguistic change in a creole (or pidgin) may occur faster than linguistic change in a noncreole (nonpidgin) language. Sorting such factors out, as everyone acknowledges, is no easy matter; there is, for instance, too little crosslinguistic information available about the time required for any general kind of linguistic change to justify an argument that creoles change more rapidly than other languages. This is especially true given that ordinary contact-induced change often proceeds quite rapidly, and many changes in young creoles are sure to be contact-induced. It is even more difficult to decide when a speech form has enough structure to be called a language: as with any other linguistic phenomenon that can change into something else, the boundary between language and not-yet-language will inevitably be fuzzy. In any case, this approach raises a crucial question: how can we distinguish between a process of creole genesis and a process of ordinary language change in an existing language? In Chaudenson's approach, of course, there is no distinction, as creole genesis is simply contact-induced language change taken to an extreme; but in other gradualist approaches the question arises and must be dealt with somehow.

Yet another variant of gradualism is John V. Singler's. Singler, arguing from demographic evidence about (among other things) the ethnographic origins of slaves at different periods and the numbers of people of color relative to the numbers of whites at different periods, holds that 'the principal agents of creole genesis in the sugar colonies of the Caribbean were those present in the period immediately following the sugar boom' – for instance, in Haiti, speakers of Gbe dialects (including, but not only, speakers of the Fon dialect), who comprised the dominant linguistic group during the first fifty years after the start of the sugar-plantation economy. The relevance of Gbe speakers is that Haitian Creole displays a number of Gbe features in its structure, a fact that makes sense only if Gbe speakers played a prominent role in its formation.

In spite of the considerable appeal of gradualist theories for at least some creoles, they seem to leave important questions unanswered. Most crucially, how were African slaves communicating with each other during the transitional period between the founding of a new colony and the onset of the sugar plantation? Was everyone speaking some version of the European slavemasters' language? If so, when each colony shifted to a sugar economy, did the sudden influx of slaves cause a sharp break in the transmission of the language, so that what occurred was in fact abrupt creolization, in spite of the delay in its onset? Chaudenson believes there was never a sharp break in the transmission of the European language; Singler suggests the possibility of an abrupt genesis after the shift to sugar. If everyone wasn't speaking the European slavemasters' language in the pre-sugar economy, what were they speaking? A fully crystallized pidgin developed in the colony? A fully crystallized pidgin imported from Africa? (In such cases, of course, the process of creolization would be nativization of a pidgin, not the emergence of a creole language without a stable pidgin stage.) This issue has been addressed occasionally; there is for instance, growing evidence for the continued use of African languages in some colonies where large numbers of slaves did share a native African language. But most of these questions remain unanswered.

Another question arises here: if we agree that some creoles arose gradually (in some sense of gradual), is this route to a mixed language exclusively relevant to creoles, or does it apply sometimes to pidgins as well? The answer, interestingly, is that some pidgins seem to have arisen by a gradual process that is comparable to the genesis scenario proposed by Chaudenson for creoles. For these pidgins, the starting point is a foreigner-talk version of a lexifier language; this variety (simplified by native speakers of the lexifier language and perhaps modified also by interactions with people who do not speak the lexifier language) later crystallizes into a new contact language as the speaker group expands and diversifies. An example is Hiri Motu. As we saw above, the Motu people avoided using their 'true' language in talking to outsiders; instead, they used foreigner talk. Their position in and around Port Moresby in New Guinea was prominent enough that newcomers had to depend on them for (among other things) food, and foreigner-talk Motu became the region's lingua franca – probably with different variants used by and with different non-Motu groups in the community. The community itself grew rapidly after the first Europeans settled there in 1874, with an influx of various foreign groups. Foreigner-talk Motu was widespread in Port Moresby before it crystallized into Police Motu (now called Hiri Motu) as a result of its use in training the ethnically diverse police force, whose members took the language along with them in their travels throughout British New Guinea.

Although the social process in a case like the development of Hiri Motu was presumably different from the social dynamics among slaves on a sugar plantation, the linguistic processes – in which an ethnically mixed society takes a lexicon (and in this case some grammar) from a single prominent language in the community and forms a contact language – seem parallel to a considerable degree: the emerging contact language becomes less and less like the lexifier language as it is learned and changed by speakers of different languages, who 'negotiate' a shared grammar in the process of communicating with each other. One difference between the two processes might be the deliberate distortion of their language by Motu speakers; but even that, for all we know, could have a parallel in plantation creole genesis. Another feature of plantation creole genesis is that isn't at all clear that it makes sense to speak of a target language in the usual sense of second-language acquisition (though the linguistic processes are similar, the goals differ); this too was quite likely a feature of the genesis of Hiri Motu, once the training of police became institutionalized.

What can we conclude from our survey of all these theories? It seems to me that the main conclusion is that it's a serious mistake to search for *the* route to pidgin and creole genesis. On the contrary, there is solid evidence for more than one route. The development of many pidgins was probably abrupt, but Hiri Motu emerged gradually from foreigner-talk Motu. The development of Pitcairnese must surely have been abrupt, with no fully crystallized pidgin stage. Haitian Creole may or may not have developed abruptly; if it is an abrupt creole, the demographic evidence indicates that its abrupt genesis did not begin until thirty years after the settlement of Haiti by French speakers and their slaves (because the relevant Africans were not there until the shift to sugar after thirty years); if it is a gradually developed creole, it might or might not have arisen from a fully crystallized pidgin. Tok Pisin certainly emerged from a fully crystallized, and indeed an expanded, pidgin.

Do different genesis routes have different linguistic outcomes?

A vital question is whether different genesis processes correlate with different linguistic results. If they do, then we can infer the process retrospectively from the structure of the resulting pidgin or creole; if they don't, we cannot tell what the process was unless we have external information. Unfortunately, there doesn't seem to be any strong indication that we can expect different linguistic outcomes from different genesis processes. Scholars were struck by the structural similarities among pidgins and especially creoles way back when the standard view was that all creoles developed from stable pidgins – i.e. long before the diversity in genesis routes was recognized – and those similarities remain. Pitcairnese is structurally similar to Tok Pisin in some striking respects, for instance. True, we can point to a few significant differences: pidgins, presumably because their speakers continue to use their native languages as well as the pidgin, tend to have more structural contributions from the substrate languages than creoles have; this tendency also seems to be shared to some extent by two-language creoles. These effects can be seen in languages like Chinook Jargon, Tok Pisin, Pitcairnese, and Berbice Dutch Creole. But even this generalization doesn't lead to firm predictions, given the large amount of substrate languages' contribution to (for instance) Haitian Creole.

Even more unfortunately, adequate external information to support a particular claim about just how a pidgin or creole arose is all too often lacking. (But this may be an overly pessimistic assessment, given the increasingly sophisticated analysis of demographic data in creole-genesis contexts that is helping to clarify many previously obscure points.) At present, at least, we can be certain that diverse genesis processes have produced pidgins and creoles, but these processes usually cannot be distinguished retrospectively, either in principle or in fact. This means that the controversies about how pidgins and creoles arise will surely continue. As we get more detailed historical information, we will be able to refine existing theories further, and we may be forced to abandon some theories that turn out to be incompatible with the external historical evidence. Still, it is probably wise for pidgin/creole specialists to admit the possibility that the controversies may be unresolvable due to the permanent absence of adequate historical information.

The rest of the field

This chapter is already very long, but it has barely scratched the surface of the immense complexity of pidgin/creole studies. It has, I hope, given something of the flavor of the lively theoretical discussions in this corner of academia: readers who enjoy the intellectual stimulation of sharply differing scholarly opinions – not to mention the interactions in print of colorful and uninhibited scholars – will find further exploration of the field rewarding. Other intriguing and important issues must be left untouched here, among them the notion of a creole continuum, with varieties closer to and more distant from the lexifier language's grammar; the recurring question of whether English, with its enormous component of French and Latin lexicon, is a creole (it isn't); the issue of fuzzy boundaries and their relevance to proposed semicreoles like Afrikaans, which is spoken by descendants of Dutch immigrants in South Africa; and the roots of African-American English (is it a creole in origin?). The social functions of pidgins and creoles have only been touched on in passing in this chapter. This is a pity, because many (but not all) of these languages have traditionally been viewed with contempt even by their own speakers, and especially by speakers of the lexifier language – partly because they seem to laymen to be bastardized versions of the lexifier language, and partly because most speakers of most creoles are descended from slaves, so the languages are seen as fit only for slaves. These attitudes have been changing dramatically in recent decades, however; examples of the trend are Haitian Creole, which became one of Haiti's official languages in 1987, and Seselwa (or Seychellois, the French-lexifier creole of the Seychelles in the Indian Ocean), which has been the country's first official language, with English and French, since 1981. There is also the question of whether, or how, pidgins and creoles are connected with bilingual mixed languages; but this topic, at least, will be addressed in the next chapter.

Sources and further reading

There is an enormous scholarly literature on pidgin and creole languages. An excellent general introduction to the subject is the 1995 book *Pidgins and Creoles: An Introduction*, edited by Jacques Arends, Pieter Muysken, and Norval Smith. Besides the usual general sections on pidgins and creoles (including genesis theories), the book covers such topics as oral and written creole literature and five specific grammatical features, and it also has sketches of one pidgin and seven creoles. Overall, as the mix of pidgin and creole sketches suggests, the book's coverage is better for creoles than for pidgins. Another especially valuable source is the two-volume work *Pidgins and Creoles* by John Holm (1988, 1989), which covers general topics and surveys a large number of pidgin and creole languages. Both of these works contain lists, as complete as the authors could make them, of pidgins and creoles around the world. *The Journal of Pidgin and Creole Languages* (published by John Benjamins Publishing Company, Amsterdam and Philadelphia) is an excellent source of both general articles and specific case studies on pidgins and creoles.

Parts of this chapter draw on material in Thomason and Kaufman 1988 and on my 1997 article 'A typology of contact languages'.

The observation from de Goeje 1908 is taken from p. 102 of George Huttar and Frank Velantie's 1997 article 'Ndyuka-Trio Pidgin'.

The definition of contact languages given at the beginning of the chapter is controversial: it is not accepted by all language-contact specialists. One alternative view is that creoles, at least, can be defined by a list of characteristic features that they contain; this view was much more popular in earlier decades than it is now, but for a recent example, see John McWhorter's 1998 article 'Identifying the creole prototype: vindicating a typological class'. Another is that creoles, at least, cannot be defined at all in contradistinction to noncreole languages – that is, that they do not differ significantly in either synchronic or diachronic respects from other languages; see especially various writings by Robert Chaudenson (e.g. his 1992 book *Des îles, des hommes, des langues* ['Islands, people, languages'] and by Salikoko Mufwene (e.g. his 1996 article 'The founder principle in creole genesis'). On this view, creoles (at least) do not comprise a coherent class of languages, either synchronically or diachronically; they may be identified by (for instance) political criteria, but not by any set of linguistic criteria. Most specialists would probably agree with the pioneer creolist Robert A. Hall, Jr., who wrote in 1966 that 'there are no structural criteria which, in themselves, will identify a creole as such, in the absence of historical evidence' (p. 122); and most specialists would probably also agree that pidgins and creoles do form a class (or perhaps two separate classes) of languages, even if some languages seem to fall on the borderline between contact language and 'ordinary' language.

Many pidgins and creoles are mentioned in this chapter, and I will not provide references to detailed discussions of all of them. Instead, references are given here only to the languages mentioned most prominently in the chapter. Sources for information about other pidgins and creoles can be found in general works, especially Arends *et al.*, eds., 1995, and Holm 1988, 1989.

The structure and history of Ndyuka-Trio Pidgin are described by George Huttar and Frank Velantie in their 1997 article 'Ndyuka-Trio Pidgin', and Ndyuka itself is described in the 1994 book *Ndyuka*, by George Huttar and Mary Huttar. Berbice Dutch Creole is analyzed most fully in Silvia Kouwenberg's 1994 book *A Grammar of Berbice Dutch Creole*. See also her article 'Berbice Dutch' on pp. 233–43 of the 1995 book edited by Arends *et al.*; the example of a negative Berbice Dutch Creole sentence is from p. 237 of Kouwenberg's 1995 article. The Ịjọ component of Berbice Dutch Creole is discussed in a 1987 article by Norval Smith, Ian Robertson, and Kay Williamson, 'The Ịjọ element in Berbice Dutch'. Umberto Ansaldo and Stephen Matthews argue, in their recent paper 'The Minnan substrate and creolization in Baba Malay', for the status of Baba Malay as a two-language creole; the estimate of its number of speakers is from p. 358 of Norval Smith's annotated list of contact languages in Arends et al., eds., 1995. The scholarly literature on Tok Pisin is very large; one of the most prominent specialists is Gillian Sankoff, who has published numerous articles on the language, among them 'The genesis of a language' (1979) and, with Suzanne Laberge, 'On the acquisition of native speakers by a language' (1974, reprinted in Sankoff's 1980 book *The Social Life of Language*).

The claim that Chinese speakers created Chinese Pidgin English because they were unwilling, not unable, to learn English is from p. 8 of Robert A. Hall, Jr.'s, classic 1966 book *Pidgin and Creole Languages*.

The only information I have about the Nez Percé Jargon is from the source quoted at the beginning of the chapter, but there is some literature on Pidgin Delaware: the most comprehensive structural and historical analysis is in Ives Goddard's 1997 article 'Pidgin Delaware'. The quotations about Pidgin Hamer and Pidgin Motu are, respectively, from p. 397 of Jean Lydall's 1976 article 'Hamer' and pp. 95–6 of Percy Chatterton's 1970 article 'The origin and development of Police Motu', as cited by Tom Dutton and H. A. Brown on pp. 760–1 of their 1977 article 'Hiri Motu: the language itself'. The best source for information about Hiri Motu is Tom Dutton's 1985 book *Police Motu: iena sivarai*; the first half of the book's title refers to the spread of the pidgin by policemen who traveled into the interior of Papua New Guinea to carry out their duties, and the second half is a Hiri Motu phrase meaning 'its story'. For a summary of his research results on the pidgin, see Dutton's 1997 article 'Hiri Motu'.

There have been various claims over the years about which Romance language was the main lexifier of the medieval Lingua Franca. Robert A. Hall, Jr., argued for a Provençal lexifier, for instance, in *Pidgin and Creole Languages*. Convincing evidence for Italian as the lexifier for the Lingua Franca has been presented by Guido Cifoletti in his 1989 book *La Lingua Franca Mediterranea*; Jacques Arends (personal communication, 2000) observes that western Mediterranean varieties of the language acquired much Spanish lexicon as well. Maridi Arabic is discussed in a 1986 article by Sarah G. Thomason and Alaa Elgibali, 'Before the Lingua Franca: pidginized Arabic in the eleventh century A.D.'. For a broader view of Arabic-lexifier pidgins and creoles, see Jonathan Owens' 1997 article 'Arabic-based pidgins and creoles'. The location of Maridi is disputed, because the textual and linguistic indications conflict: Thomason and Elgibali argue for a location in modern Mauritania on the basis of internal evidence in al-Bakrī's text, and Owens argues for a location in Upper Egypt or northern Sudan on the basis of linguistic features that point to an eastern dialect source of the Arabic material in the pidgin.

For a good recent list of pidgins and creoles around the world, see Norval Smith's 1995 article 'An annotated list of creoles, pidgins, and mixed languages' in the book edited by Arends et al. (For Smith and the other authors in that book, the term 'mixed languages' is used only for what I call 'bilingual mixed languages'; in my usage, and therefore throughout this book, the term encompasses pidgins and creoles as well as bilingual mixed languages.) A recent survey of lingua francas, with good coverage of pidgins (more than of creoles), is the *Atlas of Languages of Intercultural Communication* edited by Stephen A. Wurm, Peter Mühlhäusler, and Darrell T. Tryon (1996).

For information on Pitcairnese, see Alan S. C. Ross & A. W. Moverley's 1964 book *The Pitcairnese Language*. A good recent source on Pidgin Eskimo is Hein van der Voort's 1996 article 'Eskimo pidgin in West Greenland'. The history and structure of Sango were described recently by Helma Pasch in her 1997 article 'Sango'. Pasch describes the creole variety of Sango; this is presumably different from the pidgin variety, for which, she says, data are not readily available. William J. Samarin has also discussed Sango in numerous articles, most prominently in his 1967 book *A Grammar of Sango*. Chinook Jargon is the subject of a large scholarly and popular literature; for a survey of its structure and history, together with references to data sources and other analyses, see my 1983 article 'Chinook Jargon in historical and areal context'. A good recent sketch of Saramaccan is the article 'Saramaccan', by Peter Bakker, Norval Smith, and Tonjes Veenstra, in Arends et al., eds., 1995.

Calling Hawaiian Creole English a creolized pidgin is a controversial statement; the opposing view is that Hawaiian Pidgin English was never a fully crystallized pidgin, and that the creole arose largely independently, without significant grammatical contribution from the pidgin. The most prominent advocate of this position is Derek Bickerton, who has argued for lack of grammatical input from a fully crystallized pidgin in numerous writings, e.g. his 1999 article 'How to acquire language without positive evidence: what acquisitionists can learn from creoles'. Bickerton discusses the issue from a more general perspective in his 1981 book *Roots of Language*; this book is also a very good source of information on features shared widely among creole languages, especially Caribbean creoles and in particular in the tense/aspect/mood system in verb phrases.

Tây Bôi was discussed in John Reinecke's 1971 article 'Tây Bôi: notes on the Pidgin French spoken in Vietnam'. A good recent source on the structure and history of Kitúba is Salikoko Mufwene's 1997 article 'Kitúba', which also contains much useful bibliography on the language. Two useful sources on Chinese Pidgin Russian are Gunter Neumann's 1966 article 'Zur chine-sisch-russischen Behelfssprache von Kjachta' (in German) and Johanna Nichols' 1980 article 'Pidginization and foreigner talk: Chinese Pidgin Russian'. I'm grateful to Jacques Arends (personal communication, 2000) for the news that Lingua Franca noun phrases had agreement inflection. Among the language sketches in the volume edited by Arends et al. are 'Fa d'Ambu', by Marike Post, and 'Sranan', by Lilian Adamson and Norval Smith; the example of a negative Fa d'Ambu sentence is from p. 197 of Post's article. I owe my information about Nagamese word order to Robbins Burling (personal communication, 1999). Information about Pidgin Yimas(-Arafundi) comes from an undated handout, 'On a non-European based pidgin', from a talk given by William A. Foley; the pidgin is discussed in print in Foley's 1986 book *The Papuan Languages of New Guinea* and his 1988 article 'Language birth: the processes of pidginization and creolization'.

The examples illustrating the ordering of tense, aspect, and mood markers is from the 1995 article 'TMA particles and auxiliaries', by Peter Bakker, Marike Post, and Hein van der Voort, in Arends et al., eds. Their account in turn relies in part on Derek Bickerton's well-known work, in particular his 1981 book *Roots of Language*.

Here are a few references to theories of pidgin and creole genesis. A good starting point is the section on 'Theories of genesis' in Arends et al., eds.; the four articles in this section are 'Theories focusing on the European input', by Hans den Besten, Pieter Muysken, and Norval Smith, pp. 87–98; 'Theories focusing on the non-European input', by Jacques Arends, Silvia Kouwen-berg, and Norval Smith, pp. 99–109; 'Gradualist and developmental hy-potheses', by Jacques Arends and Adrienne Bruyn, pp. 111–20; and 'Universalist approaches', by Pieter Muysken and Tonjes Veenstra, pp. 121–34. The monogenesis hypothesis was proposed by R. W. Thompson in his 1961 article 'A note on some possible affinities between the creole dialects of the Old World and those of the New' and espoused in 1973 by Jan Voorhoeve in 'Historical and linguistic evidence in favor of the relexification theory in the formation of creoles'; see also Keith Whinnom's proposals for the Lingua Franca as a source for at least some creoles, e.g. his 1977 article 'Lingua Franca: historical problems' (and compare his 1956 book *Spanish Contact Vernaculars in the Philippine Islands*).

Derek Bickerton's Language Bioprogram Hypothesis is discussed in numerous works, of which the most prominent is his 1981 book that is mentioned above. For extended discussion of his views, see his 1984 article 'The language bioprogram hypothesis', which was published together with critical responses by several other scholars and then Bickerton's response to the responses. An excellent recent critical article that focuses on Bickerton's LBH and Claire Lefebvre's relexification hypothesis is John V. Singler's 1996 article 'Theories of creole genesis, sociohistorical considerations, and the evaluation of evidence: the case of Haitian Creole and the Relexification

Hypothesis'. The point about plantation-born slaves often having greater access to the lexifier language is from p. 196 of Singler's article.

The relexification hypothesis is discussed in various writings by Claire Lefebvre and her colleagues, e.g. in Lefebvre's 1993 article 'The role of relexification and syntactic analysis in Haitian Creole: methodological aspects of a research program' and in her 1999 book *Creole Genesis and the Acquisition of Grammar: The Case of Haitian Creole*. The quotations stating the hypothesis are from Lefebvre's and John S. Lumsden's announcement of a 1994 conference, The MIT Symposium on the Role of Relexification in Creole Genesis: The Case of Haitian Creole; they are cited by John V. Singler on p. 186 of his 1996 article (cited above). In this article Singler also offers various criticisms of the hypothesis.

Pidgin/creole genesis as a kind of second-language learning – also called the substratum theory of pidginization and creolization – is proposed by such specialists as John Holm (see his 1988–89 work), Norbert Boretzky (in his 1983 book *Kreolsprachen, Substrate und Sprachwandel*) and Thomason & Kaufman (in our 1988 book, as well as in other writings of mine). The quotation about the origins of SVO word order in Berbice Dutch Creole is from p. 296 of Silvia Kouwenberg's 1992 article 'From OV to VO: linguistic negotiation in the development of Berbice Dutch Creole'. The information about Bislama comes from W. G. Camden's 1975 paper 'Parallels in structure of lexicon and syntax between New Hebrides Bislama and the South Santo language spoken at Tangoa'.

The quotation characterizing 'gradual creolization' is from p. 111 of Jacques Arends & Adrienne Bruyn's 1995 article 'Gradualist and developmental hypotheses' in Arends et al., eds.; Arends & Bruyn also discuss a gradualist model of creole genesis, based on a combination of demographic information and the time of emergence of particular syntactic features, and apply it to Sranan. Chaudenson's writings are almost entirely in French; for a clear statement of his position (on both gradual creolization and proposed French sources for structural features of French-lexifier creoles), see his 1992 book (cited above). One of Chaudenson's most devoted critics is Philip Baker; see, for instance, his 1996 review article of Chaudenson's 1992 book. See Salikoko Mufwene's 1996 article 'The founder principle in creole genesis' for a good summary of a gradualist view that is closely related to Chaudenson's. Derek Bickerton has addressed the problem of distinguishing between creole genesis and change in an existing creole in his 1991 article 'On the supposed "gradualness" of creole development'. The quotation about the agents of creolization is from p. 226 of John Singler's 1996 article (cited above). The gradual emergence of Hiri Motu is discussed by Tom Dutton in his 1985 book *Police Motu: iena sivarai* and his 1997 article 'Hiri Motu'.

See Thomason & Kaufman's 1988 book (cited above) for a lengthy discussion of the English-as-a-possible-creole issue. Thomason & Kaufman also has a case study on Afrikaans, concluding that it is a semicreole; but since the publication of that book I have decided that the category 'semi-creole' doesn't really exist (see my 1997 article 'A typology of contact languages' for discussion). An excellent recent study of African-American English is John R. Rickford's 1999 book *African American Vernacular English: Features, Evolution, Educational Implications*.

8 Contact Languages II: Other Mixed Languages

'All speakers of Laha are fluent speakers of Ambonese Malay . . . Laha has maintained its indigenous language in the face of increasing pressure from Ambonese Malay but only at the expense of drastic revision of its grammar . . . Bit by bit the grammar of Laha has become nearly interchangeable with Ambonese Malay grammar. This adaptability in the Laha language has contributed to its survival.' ('Laha, a language of the Central Moluccas', by James T. Collins, 1980, pp. 13–14)

The Métis 'usually settle near the borders of the towns of the Whites or they form separate colonies such as Camperville at Lake Winnipegosis, where a language is spoken that is a mixture of French and the language of the Crees.' (*In de canadeesche wouden*, by Anne de Mishaegen, 1947)

'Mōkkī, the cant of the Lōṛīs, . . . is an artificial jargon, which the Lōṛīs have mechanically invented on the basis of the language of the people among whom they live, and which they more especially employ when they want to keep their meaning to themselves . . . And yet so universally and successfully is the jargon used, that it seems doubtful whether its artificiality suffices to debar it from being classed as a language . . . it is at any rate acquired naturally and as a matter of course by Lōṛī children; it is no longer, it would seem, simply a secret patter; it is becoming a language for the home-circle.' (*Census of India*, vol. 4: *Baluchistan*, by Denys de S. Bray, 1913, pp. 139–40)

At the cost of some possibly unnecessary repetition, this chapter will begin with a review of the main linguistic similarity and the main linguistic distinction between pidgins and creoles, on the one hand, and other mixed languages – almost all of them bilingual rather than multilingual – on the other hand. As we saw in Chapter 7, all mixed languages share the property of comprising grammatical subsystems that cannot all be traced back primarily to a single source language. And all of them are contact languages, by the definition of a contact language as any new language that arises in a particular contact situation. The mixtures in the two of contact languages differ in nature, however. In pidgins and creoles the lexicon usually comes mainly from one source language, while the structural subsystems can be viewed in large part as a crosslanguage compromise among the creators' languages (and the creators may or may not include speakers of the lexifier language); the grammar and lexicon of other mixed languages are taken directly from each source language in large chunks, usually without any significant compromises or indeed any other significant changes.

The characterizations of 'pidgin' and 'creole' in Chapter 7 might perhaps be called prototypes. A prototypical pidgin emerges abruptly in a new contact situation involving three or more languages, with limited contact and no full bi-/multilingualism among the groups in contact, and with need for a contact medium only in restricted social circumstances (e.g. trade), so that the new pidgin has limited lexical and structural resources; most of its structural features are not derived from any single previously existing language. A prototypical creole emerges abruptly in a new contact situation involving three or more languages, with no full bi-/multilingualism among the groups in contact, and with need for a contact medium for all ordinary purposes of everyday life, so that the resulting creole does not have restricted lexical or structural resources; most of its structural features are not derived from any single previously existing language. I would not press the claim that these are in fact the prototypical cases: as we have seen, that claim would be highly controversial. And, of course, 'prototypical' refers to something like the basic case, the ideal case; we examined a number of languages in Chapter 7 that departed from the proposed prototypes, for instance the nonabrupt creoles. However, these suggested prototypes do reflect the cleanest split from their creators' linguistic traditions before the onset of the contact situation that led to pidgin or creole genesis, so from that point of view they are the simplest cases.

In sharp contrast, the prototypical other (nonpidgin, noncreole) mixed language arises in a contact situation involving just two languages, where there is widespread bilingualism (though usually one-way, not mutual, bilingualism), so that there is no need for a new language to serve as a medium of communication between the two groups in contact. The resulting mixed language is a first language for some learners, it has no lexical or structural restrictions, and every component is easily traceable to a single source language. Bilingual mixed languages are not lingua francas linking the two speech communities that provided their linguistic material.

The basic linguistic distinction is between mixed languages that arise in circumstances where imperfect learning plays a prominent role in the genesis process (pidgins and creoles) and mixed languages in which imperfect learning plays no role (other mixed languages).

This distinction correlates robustly with a social distinction: whereas pidgins and creoles arise from a need for a medium of communication among groups that share no common language, the other mixed languages arise instead within a single social or ethnic group because of a desire, or perhaps even a need, for an in-group language. All members of the group already speak at least one language that is used as a medium of communication with the other group(s) in the contact situation and that could be used for all in-group communicative functions as well. The new mixed language is likely to serve one of two functions – keeping group members' conversations secret from the other group(s), or being an identity symbol of an ethnic or subethnic group within a speech community. (The latter motive for creating a new mixed language may have applied in at least some pidgin/ creole-genesis contexts as well, as some creolists have argued.)

One more preliminary note: in the rest of this chapter I will refer to all these nonpidgin, noncreole mixed languages as BILINGUAL MIXED LANGUAGES. The label refers to the fact that they are created by bilinguals; but it is somewhat misleading, because there is in principle no upper limit to the number of languages that could be combined to form one of these mixed languages. That is, there is no reason why a group of multilinguals could not form a mixed language by drawing on three or more of the languages they speak, although I do not know of any stable mixed language with whole components drawn from more than two languages. (The label is also awkward in that it is not of course the languages that arc bilingual, but rather the creators of the languages.)

What, when, where?

The systematic study of bilingual mixed languages has a short history: several valuable studies appeared in the 1960s, but there is very little before that. Tantalizing hints about them can be found in earlier writings by both laymen and linguists – the quotation at the beginning of this chapter about the mixed language of the Métis is one example – but it is only in the past few decades that they have been described in sufficient, and sufficiently convincing, detail to quiet most skeptics' doubts about the possibility of such a thing.

Skepticism about language mixture was the overwhelmingly dominant view of historical linguists for over a century, starting in the second half of the nineteenth century, because it was seen as a threat to the historical linguist's much-prized (and justifiably so) COMPARATIVE METHOD. So, for instance, in 1871 the linguist Max Müller wrote dogmatically, 'es gibt keine Mischsprache' ('there is no (such thing as a) mixed language'). All mixed languages were generally considered to be impossible, but bilingual mixed languages were not viewed as a problem until very recently, because no reports of them had been widely circulated. Instead, the skepticism focused on pidgins and creoles, which were usually assumed to be related to, and descended from, their lexifier languages. Given the difficulty of figuring out exactly how pidgin and creole grammars develop, the increasingly wide-spread insistence that they could not reasonably be claimed to be lineal descendants of their lexifier languages was fairly easy for traditional historical linguists to ignore. Bilingual mixed languages, when they began to be reported more visibly and reliably, were another matter: it is hard to view a language like Michif, with noun phrases from French and verb phrases from Cree, as a lineal descendant of either French or Cree. There are now few skeptics left. As one early investigator of a bilingual mixed language commented after surveying the language's structure, 'there is something slightly amiss with the common assumption that mixed languages simply do not exist'.

Still, the brevity of the history of research on bilingual mixed languages means that we cannot survey them as readily as we can pidgins and creoles, and it is even more difficult to draw generalizations about them than it is with pidgins and creoles. It's true that one section of Norval Smith's 1995 list of contact languages includes bilingual mixed languages: he lists 135 of these in all, a sizable number (compare, for instance, the total of 372 pidgins and creoles in his list). But many of the speech forms in Smith's list are not well enough known to permit a confident assessment of their status as fully crystallized languages, and many others may not be mixed in the strong sense intended in this chapter. Instead of attempting a representative geographical sample, therefore, I shall describe very briefly six bilingual mixed languages that are especially well understood. These are not the only ones that are relatively well documented, but there are very few others.

Ma'a (sometimes called Mbugu, especially in the older literature) is spoken in the Usambara Mountains of northeastern Tanzania. The Ma'a people are, or were, an ethnic group quite distinct from their Bantu-speaking neighbors, whose languages, Shambaa (or Shambala) and Pare, are also spoken by all the Ma'a people. According to oral traditions of the Pares and the Shambaas, the Ma'as were cattle-herders who arrived in the Pare Mountains several centuries ago; there, some clans eventually settled among Pare speakers and shifted to Pare, but other clans moved to the southeast, to the Usambaras, the Shambaas' homeland, in an effort to preserve their separate ethnic identity. The clans that maintained Ma'a also maintained their ties with their Pare-speaking kinfolk, however, migrating en masse to the Pares for many years for the annual initiation rites. Structurally, the Ma'a language is now almost entirely Bantu, including all the elaborate Bantu morphology as well as its phonology and syntax. Ma'a does have a few non-Bantu structural features, apparently from a Cushitic language – three phonemes, agreement patterns in demonstratives and pronominal possessives, the lexical semantics of color terms, the structure of 'have' expressions, and (an indication of incomplete Bantuization) inconsistent usage of Bantu class prefixes on nouns. But the Ma'a language described in earlier sources, from the 1930s through the early 1960s, has more vestiges of non-Bantu structure than the current language has, and less consistent use of Bantu morphology; the most recent investigators who have carried out fieldwork among the Ma'a people have found very few traces of non-Bantu structural features. (One trace is the voiceless lateral fricative phoneme that Ma'a speakers insert into Bantu words sometimes for the exotic effect; see Chapter 6, under Mechanism 7, for discussion.) The lexicon of Ma'a is extremely mixed. According to one estimate, about half of the vocabulary is Bantu; but most of the basic vocabulary is not Bantu. The non-Bantu vocabulary of Ma'a is traceable mainly to Cushitic, though not all to the same Cushitic language; a sizable number of words come from Masai, which is related neither to Cushitic nor to Bantu.

Anglo-Romani, one of several varieties of mixed Romani-lexicon languages spoken in Europe, is used as a secret language by Rom (Gypsy) people in England. All of its speakers are native speakers of English; Anglo-Romani is primarily or entirely learned as a second language. Real Romani is the Indic ethnic-heritage language of the Rom people, whose ancestors left northwest India around 1000 CE and arrived in Europe several centuries later. Their English descendants do not speak Romani, which is most definitely not the same language as Anglo-Romani. However, real Indic Romani was recorded as late as the nineteenth century in England, together with Anglo-Romani, so it is clear that both the full ethnic-heritage language and the mixed language coexisted for a period of time. The grammar of Anglo-Romani is full English grammar; the lexicon is also mostly English, but it includes hundreds of words, including many basic vocabulary items, from the group's original Romani language. Linguistically, Anglo-Romani is similar to Ma'a, except that whereas Ma'a does have a few remaining traces of non-Bantu grammar, Anglo-Romani has no traces at all of non-English grammar. In this chapter it stands as a typical representative of all Romani-lexifier mixed languages; what is said below of Anglo-Romani may (or, of course, may not) be true of all of them.

Kormakiti Arabic is the language of Maronite Christians whose ancestors migrated to Cyprus in 1191 CE. When it was investigated in the early 1960s, it was still the main home language in the village of Kormakiti; all its speakers were also completely fluent in Cypriot Greek. The village's school had Greek as the medium of instruction. Thirty-eight percent of the vocabulary of Kormakiti Arabic, in a sample of six hundred and thirty common words, was borrowed from Greek, including some basic vocabulary items and also some function words. The grammatical mixture arose directly from the lexical mixture: words of Arabic origin are used with Arabic phonology, morphology, and syntax, while words of Greek origin are used with Cypriot Greek phonology, morphology, and syntax. There is some leakage from the Greek component of Kormakiti Arabic into the Arabic component, but apparently not vice versa. For instance, a few Greek suffixes are added to Arabic words, some Arabic phonemes that do not occur in Cypriot Greek have been lost from the Arabic component of the Kormakiti Arabic lexicon, some Greek morphophonemic rules are used in Arabic words, and a number of Greek syntactic features are pervasive in the mixed language. Kormakiti Arabic resembles Ma'a and Anglo-Romani in having much vocabulary from both of its source languages, but it differs from Ma'a and Anglo-Romani in that it has sizable numbers of grammatical features from both source languages.

Michif is spoken on the Turtle Mountain reservation of North Dakota and, as a home language only, in Manitoba and Saskatchewan. It is one of the traditional languages – now seriously endangered – of the Métis people, a mixed-blood population that emerged sometime during the middle decades of the eighteenth century in the Red River valley of what is now southern Manitoba. The original Métis were the offspring of white fathers, employees of the North West Company (mostly French, but also Scottish, fur traders), and Indian mothers; political maneuverings by the rival British enterprise, the Hudson's Bay Company, encouraged the coalescence of a Métis Nation that would (the British hoped) oppose the activities of the French trading company. Many or most Métis were at least bilingual from the beginning: they spoke French and the Algonquian language Cree, which was the native language of many of the Indian mothers and a lingua franca for the others (most of whom spoke closely-related Algonquian languages). Some of the early Métis also spoke English. Many of the white fathers and the Indian mothers of the original Métis population were also bilingual or multilingual. In addition to Michif itself, which is a fully crystallized mixed language in regular use in certain Métis communities, the Métis people speak (or spoke) a distinctive dialect of Canadian French, Métis French; this dialect provided the French component of Michif. However, most modern Michif speakers do not know either French or Cree, though they all speak English fluently. The linguistic mixture in Michif is unusual even in the small class of bilingual mixed languages: Michif is comprised of French noun phrases and Cree verb phrases and sentential syntax. There are a few exceptions to this characterization: for instance, Michif has a few Cree nouns and numerous Cree nominalizations (used in noun phrases with French determiners and syntax), and a few French verbs that are used with all the elaborate Cree verb morphology. Each component matches its source language closely in lexicon, phonology, morphology, and syntax. There is, however, some leakage from Cree into the regular French noun phrases: although the nouns, adjectives, and determiners are all French, the demonstratives are Cree; in addition, certain categories of French nouns are marked with the Cree obviative suffix, which indicates a third-person form that is less important (in the context) than some other third-person form in the same discourse. There is much less leakage from French into the Cree component of Michif, but the most common negative element in the verb phrase is *nu*, which is probably from French *non* 'no, not'; a Cree negator also appears sometimes in Michif noun phrases, though, so negative markers leak in both directions. In spite of the apparent half-and-half distribution of Cree and French elements in Michif, the elaborate verb phrase and sentence structure show that the language is basically Cree, with incorporated French noun phrases. As with Mednyj Aleut, neither component of Michif is seriously distorted: the French is on the whole perfectly good Métis French, and the Cree is perfectly ordinary Plains Cree. There is some distortion in the French component, but not much.

Structurally, Michif differs strikingly from Ma'a, Anglo-Romani, and Kormakiti Arabic: in those three languages the lexical mix is distributed throughout the lexicon, while in Michif the lexical mix is compartmentalized in different grammatical subsystems. The grammatical mix also differs: only in Michif is there a compartmentalization of grammatical features in different subsystems. By contrast, in Ma'a and Anglo-Romani the grammar comes entirely (or nearly so) from just one source language, and in Kormakiti Arabic both source languages contribute to the language's grammar in all grammatical subsystems. The other two languages to be surveyed, Mednyj Aleut and Media Lengua, resemble Michif in having the contributions of the two source languages distributed according to grammatical subsytems, not spread more or less evenly throughout the mixed language.

Mednyj Aleut (also called Copper Island Aleut), now almost extinct, was created on Russia's Mednyj (Copper) Island by the mixed-blood offspring of Russian–Aleut unions. Direct information about the language is drawn from the writings of just three fieldworkers, G. A. Menovščikov (before 1963) and Evgenij V. Golovko and Nikolai B. Vakhtin (1982, 1985, and 1987). It was the main language of its speech community until the last speakers were moved to nearby Bering Island in the late twentieth century. Mednyj Island was first settled by employees of the Russian-American Company, a fur-seal trading company, who brought Aleuts there in 1826. Since Mednyj Aleut was obviously created by Aleut–Russian bilinguals, it must have arisen sometime between 1826 and the disappearance of the Russian population after the fur-seal trade fell off in the second half of the nineteenth century. The mixed-blood population on the island outnumbered the Aleut population by the end of the nineteenth century, which would have given the mixed language extra prominence between about 1900 and the 1940s, when Russians again arrived on the island to impose Russian administration and education. The linguistic mixture in Mednyj Aleut is quite different from that of the other mixed languages we've examined, and indeed from all other known bilingual mixed languages: the structure of Mednyj Aleut is basically Aleut in most respects, but the enormously elaborate Aleut finite verb morphology has been replaced with Russian finite verb morphology. Other grammatical subsystems, including not only nouns but also nonfinite verbs, retain the extensive Aleut inflectional categories and morphemes. The language has numerous Russian loanwords as well, including such function words as conjunctions and prepositions; but an analysis of Mednyj Aleut texts showed that 94 percent of the verbs and 61.5 percent of the nouns were native Aleut, and Alaskan Aleut also has many Russian loanwords (about eight hundred in one count). There has also been some interference from Russian in Mednyj Aleut syntax. Overall, however, the Russian interference features outside the finite verb morphology are quite typical of structural borrowing under moderately intense contact conditions, and most or all of them are also found in unmixed varieties of Aleut. A vitally important point is that the creators of Mednyj Aleut had to be fluent speakers of both Russian and Aleut, because neither the finite verb morphology nor the Aleut grammatical features are seriously distorted (though a variant type of past tense formation does use Russian morphemes in a decidedly non-Russian way, adding Russian present-tense person/number affixes after the Russian past-tense suffix -*l*).

Media Lengua, a mixture of Quechua and Spanish, is spoken as a first language by hundreds of people in central Ecuador. The community in which it is spoken is ethnically Quechua; it is close enough to the country's capital, Quito, to encourage members of the community to seek work in the city and in closer Spanish-oriented towns. There they learned Spanish and adapted culturally to the Spanish culture of the towns. Speakers of Media Lengua are neither fully Quechua nor fully Spanish culturally: they have abandoned some of their Quechua cultural heritage but have not adopted all of the Spanish-oriented city culture. They therefore comprise a separate ethnic (sub)group, and their mixed language is an in-group symbol of the new ethnic identity. Although it is not a secret language, it is not used with outsiders. The lexicon of Media Lengua is almost entirely Spanish, while the grammar is almost entirely Quechua. Some changes and regularizations can be found in the Spanish lexical items, and some minor changes have also occurred in the Quechua grammar, but the basic mix is clear. Unlike the situation with (for instance) the French lexicon of Michif and the Greek lexicon of Kormakiti Arabic, the Spanish lexical items are phonologically adapted to Quechua; Spanish phonology is not retained. Since some other varieties of Quechua have very large numbers of loanwords from Spanish – up to 40 percent in all in some regions, and including some basic vocabulary items as well as a great many other nouns and rather large numbers of verbs – Media Lengua, with its 90 percent Spanish lexicon, looks like a case of lexical borrowing gone wild; the main investigator of the mixed language interprets it, reasonably enough, as a case of relexification.

Two routes to bilingual mixed-language genesis

What do these six languages have in common? There is the fact that they all have material from two different languages combined in ways that show that the people who did the combining were fluent in both languages. But otherwise they do not obviously have much in common at all. Different languages show different linguistic mixtures, and even where the mixtures

look parallel, looks can be deceiving. For instance, Anglo-Romani and
Media Lengua could perhaps be claimed to have the lexicon of one language
and the grammar of another (using 'the lexicon' loosely, since in Anglo-
Romani most of the lexicon actually comes from English); but in Anglo-
Romani the basic lexicon comes from the group's ethnic-heritage language,
while in Media Lengua the lexicon comes from the European colonists'
language, i.e. from the outsiders' language. Another example: both Michif
and Kormakiti Arabic have grammatical structures derived from both their
source languages; but in Michif the two different sets of grammatical features
are restricted to separate subsystems, while in Kormakiti Arabic they are
distributed relatively evenly throughout the language, because the lexicon is
highly mixed and the lexical items determine the grammatical properties of
any particular phrase. And so on: even the generalizations that are available
often turn out to be less general than they appear at first glance.

One possible conclusion we could draw from this nonuniformity of the
linguistic mixtures is that bilingual mixed languages result from a variety of
different processes. In some sense this must be true, of course. But I believe
that the correct conclusion lies in a somewhat different direction: it seems
likely that deliberate decision, Mechanism of interference 7 of Chapter 6,
plays a prominent role in the genesis of all bilingual mixed languages. We saw
in Chapter 4 that contact-induced language change is fundamentally unpredictable, both because we can never hope to explain how a multitude of
major and minor social factors combine to produce a particular change and
because speakers can and do make deliberate choices about changing their
language. The same is true, and even perhaps more true, of the genesis of
bilingual mixed languages.

Nevertheless, there is one striking division within the class of bilingual
mixed languages, a social distinction that correlates with a linguistic distinction. Three of the languages sketched above, Ma'a, Anglo-Romani, and
Kormakiti Arabic, are the languages of persistent ethnic groups. Their
speakers live within a dominant speech community, and they also speak
the dominant group's language – natively, in the cases of Ma'a (along with
Ma'a itself) and Anglo-Romani. ('Dominant' in this context means numerically or socioeconomically superior, or both.) All three languages have
suffered encroachment from the dominant group's language – Ma'a and
Anglo-Romani to the extent that (almost) the only remnant of the ethnic-
heritage language is a part of its vocabulary, including much or most of the
basic vocabulary, Kormakiti Arabic to a lesser extent but still with significant
erosion of the original Arabic grammar and lexicon. Moreover, distortions in
the Romani-origin lexicon of Anglo-Romani makes it clear that its current
speakers lack any systematic knowledge of true Romani. All three of these
speaker groups have been under intense cultural pressure for hundreds of
years from the dominant community; but instead of acculturating entirely to
the dominant community and abandoning their ethnic-heritage language

entirely as part of the process, they have stubbornly resisted total assimilation, maintaining what they could of their original language and culture. What they have been able to maintain is, obviously, very little, culturally as well as linguistically. A fieldworker in the 1930s, for instance, was told by the Ma'as that they 'no longer possess songs and folk-tales in their own language' – a striking fact in view of the existence of traditional stories even in some pidgins, e.g. Chinook Jargon, whose speakers told stories (presumably originally from their native cultures) to early fieldworkers, and sang songs that were probably first composed in Chinook Jargon. The stubbornness of these persistent ethnic groups has not tended to make them popular among members of the dominant group; Rom people have long been viewed with suspicion and hostility by other Europeans, and some time ago the Shambaa neighbors of the Ma'a people attempted to enrich themselves by selling Ma'a people to Arab slavers. The mixed language is the visible, or rather audible, symbol of the nonassimilation of its speakers to their neighbors' culture.

One route to a bilingual mixed language, then, is the gradual loss of a group's language under relentless pressure, over a period of hundreds of years, to assimilate to a surrounding dominant community. For at least some of these languages, the linguistic correlate of this process is pervasive interference from the dominant group's language in the receding group's language: a great many interference features are found throughout the lexicon and structure, with only some lexicon remaining in the most extreme cases. For all of them, crucially, no subsystem is descended intact from the group's original language, neither the lexicon nor any grammatical subsystem.

The other route to a bilingual mixed language is abrupt creation by people who are active bilinguals in both languages. This is what must have produced the other three languages surveyed above, Michif, Mednyj Aleut, and Media Lengua. In each of these cases a new ethnic group – or possibly a subethnic group, in the case of Media Lengua – arose because of intimate cultural and linguistic contact between two other ethnic groups. Michif and Mednyj Aleut were both created by new mixed-blood populations in the context of European/Native contacts; Media Lengua speakers are Quechuas, not a mixed-blood population, but they are partly deculturated from traditional Quechua society because of their close contact with the dominant Spanish-speaking culture of Ecuador. There is solid evidence in each case that these three populations stand (or stood) apart from both the European population and the full-blood, culturally unassimilated natives: the Métis and the mixed-blood Aleut/Russian population had a legal and economic status that differed from both of the pure-blood populations from which they arose, and the Quechuas who created Media Lengua had economic opportunities that differed considerably from those of nearby communities of stay-at-home Quechuas. In this group of languages too the mixed language serves as a symbol, but here it is a symbol of a new ethnic identity, one that separates the speakers from both source groups.

Two kinds of evidence support the claim of abruptness in the creation of this set of languages. One is in the dates: the Métis community in which Michif arose did not exist before the mid-eighteenth century; the mixed-blood Aleut/Russian population in which Mednyj Aleut arose did not exist until sometime after 1826, and the mixed language must have arisen before the Russians left about fifty years later; and the first sustained intimate contact between the Quechuas of central Ecuador and Spanish speakers – contact intimate enough to lead to partial acculturation of these particular Quechuas to Hispanic culture – was established after 1909, when a rail link was established between the relevant Quechua territory and Quito, and especially after 1967, when young Quechua men began working in Quito and returning to their villages with money and fluent Spanish. All these periods, even the earliest, are too short to permit enough gradual change to produce such dramatic restructuring. As we saw in Chapter 4, some perfectly ordinary contact-induced changes proceed quite rapidly; but most of these were in cases of shift-induced interference with imperfect learning during a rapid group shift to another language, not in cases which (like the ones under consideration here) involved fluent bilinguals. The second kind of evidence has to do with the nature of the linguistic mixture: there are no cases of ordinary, nonextreme, contact-induced change that involve the replacement of entire subsystems (like finite verb inflection or all noun phrases) by intact subsystems from a different language. Given a long enough period of time, some hundreds of years, contact-induced change can certainly lead to dramatic restructuring (see, for instance, the various examples from Asia Minor Greek in Chapter 4, or the discussion of the Ethiopian highlands Sprachbund in Chapter 5). But the dramatic restructuring that sometimes occurs over centuries of intimate contact still does not produce whole subsystems lifted out of a source language. Parts of subsystems, yes; but not whole subsystems. So even if there were enough time for ordinary contact-induced change to accumulate gradually in these three cases, the expected result would not be languages like these.

This points to the linguistic correlate of the abrupt creation route to a bilingual mixed language: whereas the mixed languages of persistent ethnic groups are massively affected throughout all their subsystems by the dominant group's language, the mixed languages that arise as symbols of new ethnic groups have compartmentalized sets of structures from their source languages – noun phrases vs. verb phrases (and sentential syntax) in Michif, finite verb morphology vs. everything else in Mednyj Aleut, and lexicon vs. grammar in Media Lengua. Although the particular mix in a mixed language created by a new ethnic group is unpredictable, it can at least be predicted safely that the language will not reflect pervasive interference throughout the language's systems. It's worth noting that the abrupt bilingual mixed languages parallel most pidgins and creoles in this respect: in most pidgins and creoles too, there is compartmentalization of material from the source languages – almost the entire vocabulary comes from one source language (the lexifier language), while the grammar does not come from that language (or from any other single language). There is no such parallelism between pidgins and creoles and the bilingual mixed languages of persistent ethnic groups: on the one hand, languages like Ma'a and Anglo-Romani (though not Kormakiti Arabic) also show a sharp split between lexicon and grammar, but on the other hand – unlike most pidgin and creole lexicons – the lexicons of both these bilingual mixed languages are full of words from the dominant group's language as well.

How?

Of the basic questions about bilingual mixed languages, only the 'what' question can be dealt with adequately, and even there we can only discuss a handful of languages in any detail. As we saw above, we have no long recorded history to provide any insights about the 'when' of these languages – nothing like the thousand-year historical documentation of pidgins (and, by extension, creoles), for instance – and there are too few well-established cases for us to be confident about any answer to the 'where' question. Answering the 'how' question presents some of the same kinds of difficulties for the mixed languages of persistent ethnic groups as for theories of pidgin/ creole genesis, but, surprisingly, it is easier to understand how the abrupt bilingual mixed languages could have arisen. Easier, that is, in that at least some of the processes of change and creation seem fairly clear in these cases. As with all contact-induced (and other!) language change, however, our understanding of the psychological processes involved is still weak. That is: we can figure out some of the things people do in creating these languages, but we don't really know what goes on in their heads while they're doing them.

In this section we'll consider the bilingual mixed languages of persistent ethnic groups first and the abrupt creations second. One point needs to be kept in mind throughout the discussion of both types: if we want to compare the genesis of bilingual mixed languages with contact-induced language change, the only kind of contact-induced change that could possibly be relevant is borrowing in the narrow sense outlined in Chapter 4 – incorporation of material from a language one knows well into another language one knows well. There is no evidence that imperfect learning played a major role in any of these genesis processes.

The genesis of bilingual mixed languages in persistent ethnic groups

In the previous section, the genesis of languages like Ma'a and Kormakiti Arabic was referred to as gradual loss of the ethnic-heritage language, and as involving interference features – as in borrowing – from the dominant group's language in the ethnic-heritage language. These two points require some discussion. The second characterization, at least, is controversial, and it may not apply to Anglo-Romani at all.

The idea that these stubbornly persistent ethnic groups have lost their full ethnic-heritage language is not in itself controversial. That the loss was gradual is also certainly true in the social sense. Oral histories collected from the Bantu-speaking neighbors of the Ma'a attest to a long history of avoidance by the Ma'a of cultural assimilation both to the surrounding Bantu-speaking cultures and to (for instance) Western culture, and the history of the Rom people in Europe also attests to gradual assimilation to the host countries' cultures over hundreds of years. The degree of cultural assimilation varies among Rom communities; in some European countries, for instance, real Romani is still spoken, albeit with moderate to very extensive interference from the dominant group's language. And, as we saw above, real Romani was still spoken in England in the nineteenth century, alongside Anglo-Romani. We have no old documentation for Kormakiti Arabic, but it is at least plausible that the situation as described in the 1960s reflected a thousand-year process of gradual cultural and linguistic assimilation.

The question is whether the process through which these mixed languages arose was also gradual, a matter of borrowing first nonbasic vocabulary, then structure and some basic vocabulary, then more vocabulary and structure, until at last the inherited ethnic-heritage linguistic material was partially or totally swamped, except for some of the vocabulary. If this is what happened, then it is reasonable to talk about the introduction of more and more interference features from the dominant group's language, with an eventual extreme degree of accumulation. The hypothesis is that a pressured group, resisting strong pressure to assimilate completely to the dominant culture, including giving up its language, nevertheless ended up preserving nothing (in the most extreme cases) but some of its original lexicon, including most of the basic vocabulary. The quotation about Laha at the beginning of this chapter gives a capsule account of the hypothesized process – and also of the speakers' determination to maintain something of their traditional language in the face of enormous pressure to give it up. It is easy enough to understand why the only linguistic remnant of the group's original language would be part of the lexicon: the lexicon is by far the most salient subsystem of a language. If you keep your words, you can imagine that you have kept your language; if you replace all your words and keep your grammar intact, you cannot imagine that you have kept your language.

This seems to me to be the simplest genesis hypothesis for this set of bilingual mixed languages, for three reasons. First, the process of cultural assimilation in all these languages was demonstrably gradual, as we have just seen, and it would hardly be surprising to find that gradual but incomplete cultural assimilation was accompanied by gradual but incomplete linguistic assimilation. Second, we saw in Chapter 4 that anything can be borrowed, and indeed all the individual types of features of these mixed languages that originated in the dominant groups' languages can be found as interference features in cases of ordinary borrowing. The examples of borrowed features in Chapters 4 and 5 include basic vocabulary, derivational and inflectional morphological categories and affixes, phonological features, syntactic features, and lexical semantic features, in addition to the more common nonbasic vocabulary. So the only difference between the interference features in ordinary borrowing and the (suggested) interference features in these bilingual mixed languages would be in the quantity: moderate to extensive in ordinary borrowing, extreme in the mixed languages. That is, we already know that it is possible to borrow all these kinds of features; and there is no known principle that would limit the quantity of borrowed items. Here, as with so many other things in the field of language contact, the determining factors must be social, not linguistic.

The third and most important reason for considering gradual replacement of inherited by borrowed linguistic material to be the simplest genesis hypothesis is the linguistic evidence for a certain amount of gradual change – not for the whole range of changes, because none of the languages has a long enough documented history to offer any hope of tracing long series of changes, but for some of the relevant changes. Indirect evidence comes from Romani: because all varieties of real Romani in Europe have undergone a lot of interference over the centuries from dominant groups' languages, it makes sense to assume such a process in the case of at least some of the several bilingual mixed Romani-lexicon languages as well. Anglo-Romani itself does not look like a good candidate for this scenario, given its documented coexistence with real Romani in the nineteenth century: the gradual-replacement process hypothesized for Ma'a and Laha would rule out any coexistence between the group's original language and the mixed language.

Direct evidence comes from an analysis of Ma'a, both a comparison of earlier documents with the most recent attestations and an analysis of the internal evidence within Ma'a. As noted above, modern Ma'a has a very few Cushitic grammatical features, but published Ma'a data from the 1930s through to the 1960s has a few more. This is of course the most direct evidence for incremental Bantuization: Ma'a has lost most of its apparently residual non-Bantu structural features since the 1960s. Close examination of the Ma'a lexicon also reveals further traces of non-Bantu structure. Most strikingly, some non-Bantu affixes are added to stems that have already undergone Bantu-influenced phonological reshaping, which proves that at least some aspects of non-Bantu grammar were still active after Bantu structural features entered Ma'a. In addition, Bantu affixes are added both to non-Bantu stems that have been reshaped – Bantuized – and to non-Bantu stems that were not yet reshaped, proving that the Bantu affixes did not all enter Ma'a at the same time. There are also a few nouns that occur variably (in the earlier scholarly literature on Ma'a) with Bantu singular/plural prefixes and with Cushitic plural suffixes, and even one form with double plural affixation, both Bantu and Cushitic; this is another indication of a gradually changing grammar, with competition between the replacing Bantu system and the vanishing Cushitic system. And finally, there is a prophetic comment from 1960 by an observer who studied Ma'a at a time when the progress of Bantuization was apparent in the contrast between younger and older speakers within the Ma'a community:

> Here it is certainly true that the affix-system is better established among younger people than among the older generations, and it may well be that if they do not become wholly assimilated by the Shambala, they will in time not only operate the affix-structure of a Bantu language but will also acquire a sufficient number of Bantu stems and roots for them to be considered speakers of a Bantu language.

This quotation is prophetic in more than one respect. Not only does it foretell the further linguistic evolution of Ma'a, but it also predicts correctly the view of some later scholars who view Ma'a as a Bantu language, with some non-Bantu vocabulary added on. Some people who espouse this view believe that the Ma'as added the non-Bantu lexicon to their already fully Bantu language, in order to create a secret, in-group language; the idea seems to be that there was no preexisting Ma'a ethnic group, but rather that the added vocabulary created a new (sub)ethnic group. On that view, Ma'a would belong to the abrupt category of bilingual mixed languages. One difficulty with this approach is that it does not explain where the non-Bantu lexicon came from: in a totally Bantu milieu, where did the Ma'as-to-be come across Cushitic and Masai vocabulary? Bantu speakers in the Pares and the Usambaras are unlikely to have close enough contact with either linguistic group to learn their vocabulary; one would also want to explain why those particular languages might have been chosen as lexical contributors. In addition, this approach does not take into account either the oral histories of the Pares and Shambaas, which clearly identify the Ma'as as an old distinct ethnic and linguistic group, or the linguistic evidence of incremental incorporation of Bantu lexicon and structure into a preexisting non-Bantu language. This interpretation of Ma'a history also would not account for other bilingual mixed languages of persistent ethnic groups – Laha, Anglo-Romani, Kormakiti Arabic, and a few others. (Of course, this does not make that interpretation wrong for Ma'a; it does, however, mean that it is not generalizable to other cases that appear to be comparable to Ma'a.)

Another proposal that would move Ma'a and also Anglo-Romani (but not Kormakiti Arabic) into the category of abrupt creations is that these languages arose when a group of speakers first shifted to a dominant group's language and then incorporated some of their lost language's lexicon – in a kind of 'partial relexification' – into their new language. Proponents of this approach agree that these are persistent ethnic groups, but deny that there was incremental borrowing over a long period that ultimately replaced all the inherited grammar and much of the lexicon. Instead, they envision a shift to the dominant language instead of massive or even, perhaps, moderate structural borrowing. Their reasoning, in part, is that speakers would be more likely to shift than borrow much structure, especially morphological structure. It's true that many groups that come under intense pressure to acculturate to a dominant culture do shift to the dominant group's language before (and therefore instead of) borrowing much structure from it. But the noteworthy social fact about the Roms and the Ma'as is precisely their unusually persistent resistance to total assimilation, a resistance that has now lasted for centuries; they are quite different from most ethnic groups in that respect, as evidenced by the apparently very small number of groups that have preserved their ancient ethnic identity in spite of centuries of dominance by alien cultures. In any case, although this approach accounts nicely for the lack of structure from the ethnic-heritage languages in the mixed languages, it cannot explain the linguistic evidence of gradually accumulating inter- ference features in Ma'a. But it is likely to be correct for Anglo-Romani, given the known coexistence of that with real Romani.

In other words, it is quite possible that a shift-with-partial-relexification process actually followed gradual borrowing of lexicon and structure from the dominant group's language; the two approaches are by no means mutually exclusive. That would help explain the coexistence of real Romani and Anglo-Romani in nineteenth-century England: real Romani, presum- ably with some structural interference from English, may have been spoken by older community members while younger people, learning only English as their first language and failing to learn real Romani at all, nevertheless learned enough of its lexicon to use it with English grammar as a secret in- group language. (The younger people would have been semi-speakers; see Chapter 9.) Something similar could have happened with Ma'a, but if so it must have happened quite recently, because a few non-Bantu grammatical features were used actively by Ma'a speakers until very recently, and (as argued above) there is also other evidence of gradual Bantuization of an earlier non-Bantu language. Certainly the adoption of a special lexicon to produce a secret language, or for that matter to produce a nonsecret in-group language, is not implausible; in the next section we will see several such examples. Equally certainly, 'real Ma'a', presumably a Cushitic language but completely unattested, cannot be shown to have coexisted with Ma'a the mixed language; only the mixed language is attested.

As with pidgin and creole genesis, there is no reason to suppose that the exact same route was followed in the genesis of all bilingual mixed languages of persistent ethnic groups. So, for instance, the Lahas replaced their grammar bit by bit while the speakers of Kormakiti Arabic retained their

Arabic grammar but restricted its usage to Arabic lexicon and used Greek grammar with Greek lexicon. The Roms of England may well have shifted from Romani to English without first accumulating massive interference from English, while the Ma'as shifted to Bantu only after accumulating massive interference from Bantu. The creation of Anglo-Romani is likely to have been abrupt, even though it is the language of a persistent ethnic group and shares with other languages in this category the property of having one language's grammar combined with part of the lexicon of another language. There may also be other ways, not yet identified, in which bilingual mixed languages have arisen during a long slow process of acculturation to a dominant surrounding culture.

The abrupt genesis of bilingual mixed languages in new ethnic groups

Unlike the bilingual mixed languages of persistent ethnic groups, the abrupt creations cannot be compared directly to ordinary borrowing. Not only is the available time too short for incremental borrowing to have accumulated to a sufficient degree, but also the mixtures themselves often do not resemble the effects of ordinary borrowing. Ordinary borrowing (within the limits of the borrowing scale given in Chapter 4) normally leads to across-the-board interference in all grammatical subsystems, but languages like Michif and Mednyj Aleut have only moderate interference in the native lexicon and structure, combined with one subsystem adopted intact from the European language (noun phrases in Michif, finite verb inflection in Mednyj Aleut). The relexification in Media Lengua, as we saw above, does look like lexical borrowing run wild; but in cases of ordinary borrowing, even with 40 percent of the lexicon borrowed (as has occurred in some varieties of Quechua), the borrowed vocabulary will be accompanied by a significant amount of borrowed structure, whereas Media Lengua has 90 percent Spanish lexicon and very little structural interference from Spanish. There are thus qualitative as well as quantitative differences between ordinary borrowing and the abrupt creation of a bilingual mixed language. In an important sense, however, the genesis of all three languages is akin to borrowing: in each case, as with ordinary borrowing, material from one language has been incorporated into another language by bilinguals. It is reasonable in these cases to view the European language as the source language of the material and the native language as the receiving language: Mednyj Aleut is mostly Aleut, Michif is more Cree than French – especially given the fact that in Algonquian languages (including Cree) the verb phrase is much more important than the noun phrase – and Media Lengua, as the term relexification indicates, reflects the incorporation of Spanish lexicon to replace original Quechua lexicon. I do not mean to suggest that any of these languages is the Native language; clearly, they are all new languages. But the starting point is the Native language.

Although the abrupt bilingual mixtures do not reflect ordinary borrowing, they can nevertheless be compared usefully with other linguistic phenomena, though not necessarily all of them with the same phenomena. Media Lengua has the most common type of abrupt bilingual mixture – lexicon mainly from one language, grammar from another. The particular mixes in Michif and Mednyj Aleut are unique, in that no other stable mixed languages are known with these particular combinations of subsystems (though see below for a brief description of a possibly emerging parallel to Michif). Since Media Lengua exemplifies the common type, we'll start with that.

First, let's look at a few more examples that resemble Media Lengua in the lexicon/grammar split. One is a stable mixed language called Steurtjestaal, which arose in the former Dutch East Indies (present-day Indonesia) in an orphanage founded in 1885 by a Dutch missionary named de Steur (the name of the language means 'Steur's language'). A total of seven thousand children – many of them the offspring of Dutch–Indonesian marriages who had been abandoned by their Dutch fathers – were raised there, five hundred at a time; they came from all over what is now Indonesia, but especially from Java. Most of them spoke Malay. The mixed language emerged abruptly, within a few years of the founding of the orphanage; it was used as an in-group language, and children had to learn it as soon as they arrived at the orphanage in order to fit in. Lexically, Steurtjestaal is mixed, but most of the lexicon is Dutch; the grammar is basically Malay. The language has both Dutch and Malay function words, some of them with identical or over-lapping functions (for instance the negative markers); different speakers differ in their use of Dutch and Malay function words, in such categories as conjunctions, prepositions, and question words (e.g. 'what', 'where', 'how'). Steurtjestaal is quite stable: a Dutch linguist was recently able to collect data from speakers, even though the language ceased to be learned after Indonesian independence in 1945. It is not as neat a split as Media Lengua, because it has a more mixed lexicon, but it is similar. It is also similar, apparently, in the motivation for its formation: like Media Lengua, Steurtjestaal was invented (and created abruptly) as a symbol of a new group within the larger Indonesian community.

Another example, from the same country but in a different region and involving very different populations and motivations, is the unnamed mixed language spoken in Ternate in North Maluku, Indonesia. Probably this is not a stable mixed language, although appropriate speakers' attitudes could certainly make it one. Ternatean itself is a non-Austronesian language with possible links to some of the languages of Irian Jaya, the western (Indonesian) half of the island of New Guinea. The unnamed mixed language consists of Ternatean lexicon and Malay grammar. It is used by younger community members on the island of Ternate in certain social circumstances, for instance for courtship; older community members are said to understand the mixed language too, since they are all bilingual in Malay. The mixed language arose because parents on Ternate now talk to their children only in

Malay, and that is the children's first and only language until they reach an age when they find themselves in social situations where Ternatean is the appropriate language. They then learn some Ternatean, but they replace its grammar with Malay grammar – or rather, much more likely, they do not bother learning Ternatean grammar, but instead simply attach Ternatean lexicon onto Malay grammar so that they can imagine that they are speaking Ternatean. (If this is correct, the label 'bilingual mixed language' obviously needs to be taken with a grain of salt, because the creators were not true bilinguals. But imperfect learning still played no role in the mixing process, as the lexicon is proper Ternatean, not significantly distorted by a failure to learn it properly. And it is probably equally likely that the young creators of the mixed language did learn full Ternatean and chose not to use its grammar, finding the lexicon enough for their purposes, and finding it easier to combine the new lexicon with Malay grammar.) In spite of the lack of any genetic affiliation between the non-Austronesian Ternatean language and the Austronesian Malay language, there has been long-term mutual influence between the two languages in the region, so that typological differences between the two were already minimal when the mixed language was formed. Still, all Ternatean structural features are replaced by Malay structure in the mixed language. Ternatean is not dead as a full language with inherited lexicon and grammar, because it is still spoken elsewhere in the region, for instance along the coast of North Halmahera, where parents still speak Ternatean to their children.

Ternate is not far from Ambon, the island in Central Maluku where Laha is spoken (see again the quotation about Laha at the beginning of this chapter). Although Ternatean, like Laha, is a traditional language that is under very strong pressure from Malay, the linguistic situation is rather different in Ternate: here, the convergence between Malay and Ternatean has been mutual, not one-way as in Laha; and the mixed language clearly arose abruptly on Ternate, a creation of young people who are Malay speakers but who want to use their community's traditional language for certain traditional purposes. The creation of the Ternatean–Malay mixed language parallels one of the hypotheses for the creation of Anglo-Romani, though it is impossible to tell just how similar the two genesis processes actually are.

Another phenomenon which resembles Media Lengua in some respects, but which is more similar in its motivation to Anglo-Romani, is Mōkkī, the deliberately created secret language of the Lōṛīs of Baluchistan that was mentioned in the quotation at the beginning of the chapter. The Lōṛīs' goal in creating their secret language was to prevent outsiders from understanding them, and the language must also have served as a symbol of their ethnicity. The process they used in creating Mōkkī was lexical replacement, but instead of simply adopting words from another language, as in Media Lengua (words adopted from the outsiders' language) and Anglo-Romani (words adopted abruptly, according to one hypothesis, from the ethnic-heritage language), the Lōṛīs constructed their Mōkkī lexicon by adopting and distorting words taken from two or more of the languages that they already spoke.

The resulting creation is not exactly a bilingual mixed language; but it is a different language from the languages used to form it, just as Media Lengua is neither Spanish nor Quechua and Anglo-Romani is neither English nor Romani. Only the source of the new lexicon differs in this case. The motive for distorting words rather than adopting another language's lexicon is easy enough to understand: the Lōṛīs' neighbors, like the Lōṛīs themselves, were multilingual, so simply replacing their native lexicon with the lexicon of one of the other languages they knew would not serve the purpose of secrecy. To make a new language unintelligible to their neighbors, they were forced to develop a truly novel lexicon. What Mōkkī proves is that speakers have the ability to construct a new lexicon and graft it onto a preexisting grammar – an ability that is also exploited by the creators of abrupt new bilingual mixed languages. For that matter, this same ability underlies the secret languages invented by children (well, usually by children) by applying a simple distorting phonological rule to their native lexicon. Pig Latin is the best-known secret play language in the English-speaking world (*Ancay ouyay eadray isthay entencesay?*).

In-group fads, even if they are quite ephemeral, also produce examples that can shed light on speakers' abilities and motives in the creation of bilingual mixed languages. According to one report, some groups of Dutch teenagers – all of whom know at least some English – lard their Dutch sentences with English words, to such an extent that many sentences will have more English words than Dutch words. This is not a mixed language, or any language; it almost surely is not crystallized into a speech form with set rules of combination that must be learned, but is rather produced in an ad-hoc way, sentence by sentence and speaker by speaker, without any consistency in the choice of particular English inserts. It also may not reach the 90 percent level of English lexicon that (for instance) Media Lengua has with its Spanish lexicon. But the fact that the teenagers can do this deliberately, for reasons of fashion, provides further evidence that speakers can combine the lexicon of one language with the grammar of another whenever they wish to. All they need is a motive; and all that's needed to produce a fully crystallized bilingual mixed language by this means is a strong motive that is shared by a group of people.

The ephemeral Dutch–English mixture, if examined in detail, might turn out to resemble code-switching. This suggests the possibility that speakers might create a bilingual mixed language by fixing, or 'fossilizing', the code-switching mechanisms that already form part of their linguistic repertoire; and the mixed language that immediately comes to mind as a candidate for such a process is Michif. The reason is that the particular mix in Michif, with French noun phrases inserted into otherwise Cree sentences, is a common code-switching pattern, found in a wide variety of code-switching contexts. In French–Moroccan Arabic code-switching, for instance, French noun phrases are much more common as code-switches than complete French verb phrases. (My use of the term code-switching includes alternation of two languages within a single sentence – a pattern that some scholars call 'code-mixing', reserving the term 'code-switching' for language alternation between sentences.) In fact, the emergence of a bilingual mixed form with this mix is not unique to Michif in bilingual Algonquian–French contact situations, as indicated by the following report of a new mixed language that seems to be developing in northern Quebec among speakers of Montagnais (Mt.) – like Cree, an Algonquian language – and French (Fr.):

> Mt. is the normal language of daily intercourse and is learnt by virtually all children as a first language . . . However, tests of bilingual dominance administered to children between 9 and 13 years of age show that these children are dominant in Fr. on items of the core nominal lexicon, suggesting that Fr. nouns are replacing Mt. ones even in core areas . . . Moreover, the study of Mt. speech . . . reveals an intricate picture with code-mixing emerging as a discourse mode. Mt./ Fr. code-mixing (intrasentential) is characterized by the incorporation in Mt. sentences of Fr. tags, adverbs, and some verbs . . ., but typically, the preferred strategy for code-mixing is the insertion of full Fr. N[oun] P[hrase]s or P[repositional] P[hrase]s into an otherwise Mt. sentence.

Yet another example, this one a sort of private bilingual mixed language, was reported in a recent newspaper article about a young Chinese-American whose parents had immigrated to the United States in the 1950s. Describing his bilingual upbringing, the young man said that he 'grew up speaking a hybrid language with English verbs and Mandarin Chinese nouns'. Now, it isn't at all clear that social circumstances will promote the stabilization and crystallization of the Montagnais–French mixture, and the young man's Chinese–English mixture is surely ephemeral. But these reports, together with the evidence from more ordinary code-switching situations, attest to speakers' ability to manipulate two languages in creating a mixture that, given the right social conditions, could turn into a stable mixed language. The right social conditions don't often come together, however, and that is what makes Michif so unusual.

And finally, what about Mednyj Aleut? Unlike Michif, Mednyj Aleut appears to be truly unique in its linguistic mixture. Also unlike Michif, Mednyj Aleut is hardly a promising candidate for a fossilized code-switching phenomenon: although proposed absolute constraints on possible code-switches (like proposed absolute constraints on contact-induced changes) seem to serve mainly as a magnet for counterexamples, it would be very surprising indeed to find a prominent code-switching pattern in which all and only the finite verb morphology of one language was switched into sentences that were otherwise completely in another language. Can we hope to find a close parallel to Mednyj Aleut anywhere else among contact phenomena? The answer is no, at least at present. There are cases in which morphological patterns have been borrowed, but I've never heard of the replacement of an entire verbal inflectional system except in Mednyj Aleut. Still, we can at least point to deliberate contact-induced changes that are as apparently arbitrary as the mix in Mednyj Aleut. Perhaps the most spectacular of these is another change mentioned in Chapter 4: speakers of Uisai, spoken on Bougainville Island in Papua New Guinea, reversed all their masculine and feminine gender agreement markers in order to make their language more different from that of their neighbors, who speak other dialects of the same language, Buin. This change affected the most intricately interconnected patterns in a morphological and syntactic system, and it was certainly deliberate and abrupt. If these speakers were able to manipulate their own language in such a way, it isn't hard to see how Aleut–Russian bilinguals were able to manipulate their languages' intricately interconnected morphological systems in a similarly arbitrary way. (It should be mentioned here that the mix in Mednyj Aleut might not actually have been entirely arbitrary. Although the creators of the language must have been bilingual, given the lack of distortion in both the Russian and the Aleut components of the language, they might well have found Russian finite verb morphology less burdensome to use than Aleut, and that might have provided a motive for replacing the more cumbersome Aleut finite verb morphology – with over four hundred different endings! – with the much less elaborate Russian finite verb morphology.)

What can we conclude from this collection of partial parallels to abruptly created bilingual mixed languages, and the resulting hints about how the mixed languages arose? The main conclusion, clearly, is the same as for the genesis of the bilingual mixed languages of persistent groups: they didn't all arise in the same way. Some came about through lexical replacement, one or more emerged from a code-switching pattern, and Mednyj Aleut, at least, must have been created by a more or less conscious and deliberate decision. Deliberation was probably a feature of the other abrupt creations as well; but the other creators might not have been fully aware of the triggers for the processes, in lexical borrowing or code-switching.

Prospects for future study

In this chapter we have surveyed several bilingual mixed languages, and we have divided them into two basic categories – languages that arose as symbols of stubbornly persistent ethnic groups (sometimes for use as secret languages), and languages that arose as symbols of new ethnic groups. The former category involves gradual loss of an ancestral culture, and at least sometimes gradual loss of the ancestral language too, through replacement by lexicon and grammar of a dominant group's language. The bilingual mixed languages in this category have features of the dominant group's language in both lexicon and grammar, with no special concentration of those features in particular subsystems. Languages in the latter category arise as abrupt creations; they show compartmentalization of the components drawn from different languages, with asymmetrical distribution of the features in particular subsystems. There is some overlap between these two categories. Some mixed languages spoken by persistent ethnic groups, for instance (or perhaps in particular) Anglo-Romani, may have arisen abruptly, although both the history of their speakers and the nature of their linguistic makeup makes them fit into the persistent-group category. In neither category do we find a simple picture pointing to a single uniform creation process for all the languages. Instead, there appear to be a number of ways in which bilingual mixed languages of both kinds arise. We also saw a number of different motives for creating a bilingual mixed language. All the languages in both categories share a vital sociolinguistic feature, however: they are all symbols of their speech communities – either badges of retention of part of a formerly more independent ethnic identity, or indicators of a newly independent ethnic identity. Linguistically, they share the property of being members of no language family: they cannot be analyzed as descendants, with modification, from any single ancestral language. This last feature is also shared with pidgins and creoles; the symbolic status of the abrupt creations by new ethnic groups may also be shared with at least some creoles and possibly with some pidgins as well.

Probably the most obvious lesson to be learned from the contents of this chapter is that the study of bilingual mixed languages is still in its infancy. The second most obvious lesson is that the wide range of variation already evident in the languages currently available for study is likely to be the proverbial tip of an iceberg. To judge by the anecdotal examples that audiences produce whenever someone gives a public lecture on this topic, we can confidently expect that the future will reveal still more variation in structural mixtures, in modes of genesis, and in motives for creating these languages. One glimpse of the future is provided by a 1999 conference paper on a trilingual mixed language, Kelantan Peranakan Chinese of Malaysia, said to be a linguistic synthesis of Chinese, Malay, and Thai. An example like this points to the third most obvious lesson here for students of bilingual mixed languages: anyone who believes that sweeping generalizations or strong predictions about these languages are possible in our current state of knowledge is at best overoptimistic.

Sources and further reading

The literature on bilingual mixed languages is not extensive – not surprisingly, since the widespread recognition that they exist is recent. Among the earliest convincing reports of them are Wilfred Howell Whiteley's 1960 article 'Linguistic hybrids' (on Ma'a), Brian Newton's 1964 article 'An

Arabic-Greek dialect' (on Kormakiti Arabic), and G. A. Menovščikov's 1969 discussion of Mednyj Aleut in his article 'O nekotoryx social'nyx aspektax evoljucii jazyka' ['On some social aspects of the evolution of language']. More and more articles on the topic have recently been popping up in journals and books, however. Thomason and Kaufman's 1988 book has both general discussion of the phenomenon and three case studies (on Ma'a, Michif, and Mednyj Aleut). One recent book is devoted entirely to the topic of bilingual mixed languages: *Mixed Languages: 15 Case Studies in Language Intertwining*, edited by Peter Bakker and Maarten Mous (1994). Another, *Contact Languages: A Wider Perspective*, edited by me (1997), has five case studies on these contact languages (Michif, Media Lengua, Callahuaya, Mednyj Aleut, and Ma'a).

The quotation at the beginning of the chapter about Michif, one of the languages of the Métis of Canada, is cited from de Mishaegen by Peter Bakker and Robert A. Papen on p. 301 of their 1997 article 'Michif: a mixed language based on Cree and French'.

An important book on the topic of creole genesis is devoted to the exploration of an ethnic-identity-creating motive: *Acts of Identity*, by Robert B. Le Page and Andrée Tabouret-Keller (1985).

The Max Müller quotation is from p. 86 of vol. 1 of his 1871–2 book *Lectures on the Science of Language*. The quotation about something being wrong with Müller's position is from p. 51 of Brian Newton's 1964 article (cited above). Norval Smith's annotated list of contact languages in Arends *et al.*, eds., 1995, has mixed languages in two categories: eighty-seven 'symbiotic mixed languages' (pp. 364–70, including secret languages and professional jargons) and forty-eight 'mixed languages proper' (pp. 370–3).

For a good discussion of Ma'a grammar and a theory about its origin, see Maarten Mous's 1994 article 'Ma'a or Mbugu'; for a comparison of its typological features with Bantu and Cushitic typological features, and also a competing theory of the language's origin, see my 1983 article 'Genetic relationship and the case of Ma'a (Mbugu)', and also my 1997 article 'Ma'a (Mbugu)'. The quotation about the Ma'as having lost all their traditional songs and stories is from p. 243 of B. D. Copland's 1933–4 article 'A note on the origin of the Mbugu with a text'. For surveys of Romani-lexicon bilingual mixed languages, see the very brief survey on pp. 47–9 and then p. 50 in Peter Bakker and Pieter Muysken's 1995 article 'Mixed languages and language intertwining' in Arends *et al.*, eds.; a longer discussion of these languages is in Norbert Boretzky and Birgit Igla's 1994 article 'Romani mixed dialects'. Kormakiti Arabic is described in Brian Newton's 1964 article (cited above). About twenty years after Newton's article appeared, Alexander Borg published a book arguing that Newton was mistaken, and that Kormakiti Arabic was never a language – just a rather elaborate code-switching phemonenon, with more or less Greek mixed in with the Arabic, depending on the context. But because of political turmoil and tensions on Cyprus at the time, Borg was unable to visit Kormakiti itself; it is not clear that the people he interviewed were typical speakers; and it is also possible that, in the twenty years intervening between Newton's research and Borg's, Kormakiti Arabic had begun a slide into extinction – a slide that can proceed very rapidly once it starts (see Chapter 9). The title of Borg's 1985 book is *Cypriot Arabic: A Historical and Comparative Investigation into the Phonology and Morphology of the Arabic Vernacular Spoken by the Maronites of Kormakiti Village in the Kyrenia District of North-Western Cyprus.*

The major sources of information on Mednyj Aleut structure are the 1969 Menovščikov article cited above and a 1990 article by Evgenij V. Golovko and Nikolai B. Vakhtin, 'Aleut in contact: the CIA enigma'. For more extensive historical background and a proposed origin theory, see my 1997 article 'Mednyj Aleut'. The count of native words in Aleut texts is from p. 29 of Irina Sekerina's 1994 article 'Copper Island (Mednyj) Aleut (CIA): a mixed language', and the figure eight hundred for Russian loanwords in Alaskan Aleut is from p. xxxiii of Knut Bergsland's 1994 *Aleut Dictionary / Unangam tunudgusii: An Unabridged Lexicon of the Aleutian, Pribilof, and Commander Islands Aleut Language.* For information on Michif, see Peter Bakker and Robert A. Papen's 1997 article 'Michif: a mixed language based on Cree and French', and also Bakker's 1997 book *'A Language of Our Own': The Genesis of Michif, the Mixed Cree–French Language of the Canadian Me'tis*; see also the case study on Michif in Thomason and Kaufman 1988. Pieter Muysken is almost the only linguist who has studied Media Lengua. The language is sketched briefly on pp. 43–5 of the 1995 Bakker and Muysken article cited just above; a detailed case study of the language can be found in Muysken's 1997 article 'Media Lengua'. Muysken's 1997 article is the source of the estimate of 40 percent lexical borrowing (pp. 372–3).

The quotation about younger vs. older speakers' degree of Bantuization is from p. 96 of Wilfred Howell Whiteley's 1960 paper 'Linguistic hybrids'. Maarten Mous, in his 1994 article 'Ma'a or Mbugu', argues that Ma'a is a Bantu language with an alternative lexicon added to its fully Bantu lexicon, and Wilhelm J. G. Möhlig claims in his 1983 article 'Mbugu' that Ma'a is a Bantu language. A shift-with-partial-relexification hypothesis was proposed for Anglo-Romani by Norbert Boretzky in his 1985 article 'Sind Ziegeuner-sprachen Kreols?' ['Are Gypsy languages creoles?'], and essentially the same hypothesis was proposed for Ma'a by Matthias Brenzinger in his 1987 M.A. thesis *Die sprachliche und kulturelle Stellung der Mbugu (Ma'a)* and by Hans-Jürgen Sasse in his 1992 article 'Theory of language death'.

The information about Steurtjestaal is from a conference presentation delivered in March 1998 at the Deutsche Gesellschaft für Sprachwissenschaft by Hadewych van Rheeden, 'The role of functional categories in language contact and change'. The Ternatean mixed language was described by Robert B. Allen, Jr., in 'The present situation of local languages in an

Indonesian region', a paper presented at the Workshop on Language Maintenance and Death: Reports from the Field and Strategies for the Millennium (University of Illinois, 1999). I am grateful to Marjolyn Verspoor for telling me about the Dutch teenagers and their mixed Dutch–English speech (personal communication, 1999). The example from French–Moroccan Arabic code-switching is from p. 38 of Jeffrey Heath's 1989 Book *From Code-Switching to Borrowing: A Case Study of Moroccan Arabic*. The quotation about the Montagnais–French mixture is from the abstract of Lynn Drapeau's 1991 presentation 'Michif replicated: the emergence of a mixed language in northern Quebec' at the 10th International Conference on Historical Linguistics in Amsterdam. The private Chinese–English mixed language was reported in *The New York Times* on 15 September 1995, p. B4; the person quoted in the article is Eric Liu, who was then twenty-five years old. The example of gender switching in Uisai is from Donald Laycock's 1982 article 'Melanesian linguistic diversity: a Melanesian choice?' (see especially his p. 36). The suggested motive for replacement of Aleut finite verb morphology can be found, with slightly more detailed discussion, on p. 237 of the 1988 Thomason and Kaufman book. Kok Seong Teo is the author of the 1999 conference paper 'The language of Malaysia's Kelantan Peranakan Chinese: the issue of the classification of a mixed code', which was presented at the ninth annual meeting of the Southeast Asian Linguistic Society (SEALS) in Berkeley, California.

9 Language Death

'This study is based primarily on materials I collected in Carnarvon and Onslow . . . The corpus consists of vocabulary and sentences elicited from six speakers . . . I was unable to record any text material . . . The competence of the speakers I interviewed ranged from semi-speaker abilities through to limited fluency. All speakers had knowledge of some other languages of the area, and there are inconsistencies in the data which suggest interference. Other inconsistencies may result from the erosion of contrasts which may occur as a language dies, or which may reflect earlier dialect variation which can no longer be recognised by speakers. In any case, the quality of the data is not comparable with that which may be collected from the fluent speakers of fully viable languages, and the current analyses must be considered in this light.' (From a descriptive grammar of a language of western Australia, *Yingkarta*, by Alan Dench, 1998, p. 9)

'When we were buying, there's things we can't say in Gaelic, we'd have to say that in English.' (A comment by a speaker of Scottish Gaelic in Nova Scotia, quoted in 'Sociolinguistic creativity: Cape Breton Gaelic's linguistic "tip"', by Elizabeth Mertz, 1989, p. 108)

'me djéljtë nëkë fljásëm moré; pljákat se cë jémi' ['we don't speak [Arvanitika] with the children; only with old folks like ourselves']. (A comment by an elderly woman about the dying variety of Albanian spoken in Greece, quoted in 'Skewed performance and full performance in language obsolescence', by Lukas D. Tsitsipis, 1989, p. 122)

'White Thunder, a man round forty, speaks less English than Menomini, and that is a strong indictment, for his Menomini is atrocious. His vocabulary is small; his inflections are often barbarous; he constructs sentences on a few threadbare models. He may be said to speak no language tolerably. His case is not uncommon among younger men, even when they speak but little English. Perhaps it is due, in some indirect way, to the impact of the conquering language.' ('Literate and illiterate speech', by Leonard Bloomfield, 1970 [1927], p. 154).

'The language is of great importance to our tribe, and we must be careful about how we use it. Elders keep the words long but younger people chop them off, and this must stop, or the words will disappear entirely' (a comment by a Montana Salish tribal elder and prayer leader, at a ceremony in the Longhouse in St. Ignatius, MT, 26 July 1995)

Language death is as melancholy as its label, a culturally devastating loss to every speech community whose language dies and a loss to the scholarly community too. Every loss of a language deprives us of a window into the human mind and the human spirit; every language that dies deprives us of a unique repository of human experience and thought. Loss of a language deprives its speech community of much more, because a large part of a culture must inevitably vanish with the language. Language death is not a modern phemonenon – historical records are littered with names and sometimes attestations of dead languages – but current rates of language loss are alarmingly high, and are a matter of urgent concern to linguists as well as to speakers of endangered languages. In the next chapter we will look at language death from a worldwide perspective, and at some responses to the threat of language loss. This chapter, however, will be devoted to an examination of the linguistic processes through which language death comes about. Its relevance to this book is obvious: language death is almost always a result of intensive language contact.

Defining language death

As usual, we need to begin with a definition. It seems at first glance as if defining language death ought to be trivially easy: a language must be dead when it no longer has any speakers. There are problems with this definition, though. For instance, what if only one person still has any practical knowledge of a dying language? Can we say that the language still lives? Tricky: it lives in that person's head, in a sense, but it is not in use as a means of communication, because its one 'speaker' has nobody to speak it to. Can we say, then, that a language dies when it is no longer used as a means of regular communication? This too is tricky. Most linguists would agree that Latin is a dead language, and yet it was the main language of international European diplomacy for centuries after it ceased to be spoken as a first language. Consider, too, the way in which Latin 'died': it never lost speakers. Instead, its speakers spread out through much of western Europe and, over several centuries, their speech diverged until they were speaking the several Romance languages, not Latin itself. By the time Latin evolved into several separate languages, it had vanished as the primary language of any speech community; Old French is not Latin but a descendant of Latin, and likewise for the other early Romance languages. There was no moment at which the language people were speaking ceased to be Latin and became Italian, French, Spanish, Rumanian, and other Romance languages, so pinpointing the death of Latin is clearly impossible. (Some linguists, in fact, will disagree with the claim that Latin is a dead language, arguing that – like the dinosaurs that turned into birds – Latin evolved instead of dying.)

A different set of problems arises when we try to settle on criteria for deciding what it means to be a speaker of a language. If we insist on full fluency, then many languages that are still spoken regularly within their traditional speech communities would have to be considered dead. And who gets to decide whether someone is fluent enough to count as a 'real' speaker or not? Someone who learned a few words of her grandparents' language would not be regarded by everyone as a speaker of the language, but she might regard herself as a speaker, and members of her community might (or might not) agree with her. Someone who knows some phrases and numerous words might be able to carry on conversations about certain topics in the language; is she a speaker? It's also easy to imagine a situation where the sole remaining speaker of a language does still use it – speaking it to a grandson, perhaps, who understands it but doesn't speak it (and who therefore responds in a different language). So even if we were to agree that a language is dead when no one uses it for communication, then, we would still have difficult decisions to make when classifying languages as dead or alive.

These are only some of the issues that complicate the task of determining the point of a language's death, and many or most of the issues are truly indeterminate; there is really no objective way of arriving at a definition that will satisfy everyone and work on all occasions. We can give a definition that will be generally useful, but it won't cover all the possibilities. Here it is: a language dies when it ceases to be used for any purposes of regular spoken communication within a speech community. Old English and Middle English are both dead, because no one has spoken them for centuries. Latin died when it stopped being the regular language of any speech community (because it turned into the Romance languages), although it survived as a spoken lingua franca among educated people for a long time afterward. Pidgins pose a problem for this definition: they must surely be considered living languages as long as they continue in use, but they fit the definition only if we use a rather elastic concept of 'speech community'; and if we do that, it's hard to exclude Latin.

Hebrew presents yet another set of analytic problems. It is the most famous example to date of language revival: according to the usual view, it was dead for many centuries and was then revived in modern Israel, where it is now the nation's main spoken language. The question is, was it ever really dead, or did it live throughout the centuries of exile? As the language of a major religion, it was always learned for religious purposes, and it was even spoken regularly in certain formal religious contexts, but it wasn't used for ordinary everyday communication within any speech community. Instead, Jewish people in Europe ordinarily spoke Yiddish and other Jewish languages, and/or the language(s) of the countries they lived in. Everyone will acknowledge that Hebrew entered into vigorous life when it became a widely spoken everyday language after two thousand years of very restricted usage. But not everyone will agree that it ever died at all, because it did continue in regular, though limited, use.

Still, in spite of the various problematic cases, the phenomenon of language death is usually easy enough to recognize. No one studies Latin as a case of language death; the cases people study are those in which a once viable language loses ground to a dominant language until finally it is no longer a fully functional living language. A typical example is the case of Yingkarta, which is featured in a quotation from Alan Dench's grammatical description at the beginning of the chapter. The difficulties reported by Dench plague many, many fieldworkers who investigate dying languages.

A theoretical framework

A comprehensive theoretical model of language death was proposed in 1992 by Hans-Jürgen Sasse, based primarily on the information available in two exceptionally detailed case studies: his own long-term study of the dying Arvanitika variety of Albanian, spoken in Greece, and Nancy Dorian's long-term case study of East Sutherland Scottish Gaelic. He does not claim that his model is valid for all cases of language death, but rather urges that other cases be compared with these two in light of the model's predictions.

Sasse summarizes his model schematically in a flow chart with three interacting columns: the external setting, the speech behavior of the dying language's speakers, and the structural consequences in the dying language. His schema does not specify a majority/minority relationship between two language groups in contact, but I'll assume that for convenience here (since it's the most likely relationship). The first, or external setting, column is headed by a reference to 'historical events which lead to uneven distribution of languages in multilingual setting'; this in turn leads to pressure on the minority population, and then a negative attitude toward the minority group's language develops, which ultimately culminates in a decision to abandon that language – to shift away from it to the language of the majority group. In the second, or speech behavior, column, the historical events of column one dictate restriction of the community's languages to different domains, and the analyst's task is to discover (in the words of the sociolinguist Joshua Fishman) 'who speaks what language to whom and when'. This encourages increasing levels of bilingualism among members of the minority group (since they need the majority group's language for use in certain domains of daily life – as, for instance, in the quotation about having to use English instead of Cape Breton Gaelic for some purposes in Nova

Scotia). Once the minority language is negatively stigmatized, its speakers develop still more competence in their other language. And as part of the decision to abandon their ethnic-heritage language, they are likely to avoid transmitting it to their children, resulting in a sharp break in transmission and at best incomplete acquisition of the language by the youngest generation. The quotation at the beginning of this chapter about Arvanitika being spoken only among 'old folks' exemplifies this step. At this point the majority's language is the entire community's main language; the domains in which the minority language is used shrink further, until at last nobody uses it regularly for everyday communication. Community members may retain some residual knowledge of it in a few domains, for instance some lexicon for use in a secret language or for group identification, or some formulaic sentences and texts for use in religious services. (In this brief description of the model, I am omitting mention of a few of the directional arrows in the flow chart.)

Sasse's first two columns provide a brief overview of the social processes that combine to trigger the linguistic consequences – his third column, the one of greatest interest for this chapter. The first step is loss of lexicon or, if the domains are new, a failure to develop lexicon for domains in which the majority group's language is used exclusively. Borrowing, Sasse predicts, will increase as time goes on and more speakers of the minority language become more fluent bilinguals in the majority language. Even while the minority language continues in regular use in its appropriate domains, Sasse says, it will keep acquiring more majority-language features and will also undergo structural simplification, losing linguistic features that are not replaced. Once transmission of the minority language to children is interrupted, the linguistic result is predicted to be 'pathological reduction in the speech of "semi-speakers"' (namely, the children who fail to learn the minority language fully). At the final stage, if the minority language continues to fulfill emblematic religious or social functions, knowledge of it will likely be restricted to unanalyzed words and phrases. Sasse also predicts, however, that a variety of the majority language influenced by the minority group's original language will persist in the now monolingual community.

Sasse's theoretical model is extremely useful, because it makes explicit predictions about the course of language death. In the next section, we'll examine several linguistic routes to language death and consider whether they all fit neatly into Sasse's framework.

How do languages die?

Focusing on the linguistic effects of processes of language death raises a new set of complex issues. A perusal of the literature will reveal various predictions about the kinds of changes that do and do not happen in dying languages, and exceptions to most of the predictions. The typology of typologies at the beginning of Chapter 4 listed three routes to language death: attrition, grammatical replacement, and no change at all. Like most typologies, this one won't fit all cases, and even for the cases it does fit, it looks much neater than the actual dying languages do; still, it highlights an important set of distinctions in the linguistic correlates of language death. The typology is intended to characterize the dying language as a whole in its final stages, when there are still at least a few speakers but – barring some drastic change in social circumstances – extinction is imminent. This 'moment' is of course an idealization, perhaps even more so than with most abstractions from the messiness of real-life language: dying languages notoriously display a continuum of more and less lexical and structural deviation from the language state before the beginning of the slide toward death. As one might expect, a sharp break in transmission – when (another idealization) children suddenly stop learning the dying language as a first language – puts the younger generation at a great distance from the pre-decline language state; in such a case, treating the parents' version of the dying language and the children's version as a single language is of dubious validity. In fact, for some of the same reasons why a language like Tok Pisin or Jamaican Creole English cannot reasonably be claimed to be a variety of English, it doesn't seem to make much sense to claim the speech of the less proficient semi-speakers as the 'real' language; the semi-speakers have not learned the full language, just as the creators of (abrupt) pidgins and creoles, even if they wish to learn the full lexifier language, do not succeed in doing so. This observation reflects a strictly linguistic perspective, of course. From the community's perspective, as noted above, things may look very different. Here, though, the linguistic perspective will be adopted, and the typology will be treated as relevant for the last reasonably fluent speakers of the dying language. We'll look at each of the three categories of the typology in turn.

Before we begin our survey, a preliminary comment is in order. Throughout this chapter I'm assuming a general type of contact situation in which a dominant group's language is replacing that of a numerically and/or socio-economically subordinate group. Language shift is not confined to situations of this precise type. Nevertheless, since the focus here is on linguistic results, I will follow the bulk of the language-death literature in assuming this one context and so avoid getting into the intricacies of social conditions for language shift.

Attrition

As far as we can tell from the still small number of detailed case studies, this category is by far the most common linguistic route to language death, and it is the one that Sasse's model envisions. Attrition is a gradual process in which a language recedes as it loses speakers, domains, and ultimately structure; it is the loss of linguistic material that is not replaced by new material (for instance, by material borrowed from a dominant group's language). By the definition given at the beginning of Chapter 4, attrition is of course contact-induced change: any given change in attrition would be less likely to happen outside a particular contact situation.

First, as Sasse predicts, lexicon is lost when a language is excluded from domains where it used to be employed, such as religion. Lexicon is also lost when assimilation eliminates former cultural practices in the dying language's speech community. So, for instance, Montana Salish elders now have difficulty remembering certain words in the elaborate system of kinship terminology – such as the term for one's son-in-law after the death of one's daughter – because the kinship system itself has eroded within the culture over the past few generations. And as knowledge of traditional uses of plants has faded within the Montana Salish community, current elders can no longer bring to mind the names of some plants and the terms for their former uses. Another aspect of attrition, this one perhaps universal, is shrinkage in the range of stylistic resources. In the Montana Salish community, story-telling in the tribe's language is no longer a common activity, so the traditional devices of oral performance have been lost; similarly, in the quotation at the beginning of the chapter about conducting fieldwork on Yingkarta, Alan Dench reports that he was unable to record any texts from his six consultants. Of course, lexical losses of these types can also be found in viable languages, because culture change is hardly confined to language death situations; to give just one of many obvious examples, most current English speakers have no knowledge of terminology for parts of horse harnesses (and many of us have not replaced this lost knowledge with lots of words for parts of automobile engines). Lexical loss is peculiar to language death only when it is so pervasive as to lead to significant reduction in the language's overall vocabulary – which may or may not be true for the last fluent speakers in a language death situation.

In any case, the main emphasis in research on attrition is on loss of structure – mainly phonology, morphology, and syntax, but also discourse structure. Analyzing data from a dying language presents special difficulties, because there are several different sources of innovations, and they do not all have anything to do with the process of language death. Attrition is the focus of interest because it is unique to language death. One typical kind of attrition is reduction of rule-governed alternations by analogic generalization of one variant. For example, in some varieties of Nubian, a dying Eastern Sudanic language (Nilo-Saharan family) spoken in southern Egypt and the Sudan, speakers tend to generalize one of several plural endings, eliminating the rule that governed alternations in plural endings and thus simplifying the plural marking system. In the Australian language Dyirbal, examples of attrition include regularization of an irregular verb inflection and generalization of one case affix so that it fulfills several different case functions. A phonological example is found in a dying variety of the Uto-Aztecan language Pipil, Teotepeque Pipil, spoken in El Salvador. This dialect of Pipil inherited a rule that devoiced word-final resonant consonants, specifically /l/, /w/, and /y/. The rule has been generalized for /l/, so that all instances of /l/ are voiceless, not just word-final occurrences; but the voiced allophones of /w/ and /y/ have been generalized instead, so that all instances of those two phonemes are voiced, in all positions. The result, of course, is loss of the final-devoicing rule, although the particular generalizations differ for the lateral and the two glides.

A slightly different but also typical kind of attrition is merger or elimination of morphosyntactic categories. In the Australian language Warlpiri, for instance, there is an ongoing merger of pronominal forms for inclusive and exclusive 'we'. The process is not unidirectional – sometimes an exclusive form is replacing an inclusive form, but sometimes inclusive is replacing exclusive – and it is more advanced among younger speakers. The widely-reported tendency to replace morphologically complex constructions with analytic constructions – that is, with constructions making use of separate words rather than such morphological processes as affixation – also fits into the general category of attrition. Another tendency that has caught the attention of a number of fieldworkers is the loss of complex syntactic constructions. Leonard Bloomfield's story of White Thunder, quoted at the beginning of the chapter, illustrates this tendency – White Thunder, according to Bloomfield, 'constructs sentences on a few threadbare models'.

As Sasse's model indicates, however, another prominent category of change in a dying language is borrowing of both structure and lexicon from the dominant group's language. Borrowing itself cannot be symptomatic of language death, because – as we saw in Chapters 4 and 5 in particular – it occurs in all sorts of languages, including fully viable ones. Even heavy borrowing is found in viable as well as dying languages; we have seen examples in linguistic areas and also in such places as New Guinea (and other regions in and around the Pacific), where multilingual speakers readily adopt linguistic material into their native languages from other languages they speak. There is a widespread belief that borrowing proceeds more rapidly in dying languages than in viable languages, but no one has presented solid evidence to support this belief. Gradual language death is only one of numerous contexts where extensive lexical and structural borrowing are likely to occur. Although borrowing must be considered in any analysis of changes in a dying language, then, it cannot be considered part of the dying process.

Like other languages, dying languages will undergo ordinary internally motivated changes as well as contact-induced changes. These cannot be assumed to have any direct connection with language death. One special type of supposedly internal change, however, has been claimed to be specifically a characteristic of language death: these are innovations introduced by semi-speakers, perhaps deliberately, into an imperfectly learned dying language. Unlike attrition, these changes do not always reduce or simplify the system;

sometimes they complicate it. An example is the overextension of a marked, and markedly non-Spanish, feature in Jumaytepeque Xinca, a Guatemalan language belonging to the small (and perhaps by now completely extinct) Xincan language family: in this language, glottalization of consonants has run rampant, so that all possible consonants are glottalized – apparently a means of emphasizing the community's differentness from the dominant group's Spanish language. This sort of deliberate exaggeration of different-ness is not in fact specific to language death, however. In the framework of this book, these innovations would not count as internally motivated changes, because they would be much less likely to occur outside the contact situation that made speakers want to emphasize their differentness from the dominant group. Moreover, we saw examples of deliberate changes in Chapter 6, under Mechanism 7, that are comparable – and that have the same difference-enhancing motive. Here again, changes that at first seem to be closely linked to language death turn out to be more general contact phenomena.

It appears, therefore, that most of the linguistic processes that are common in language death situations are also common in contact situations in which no languages are dying. Lexical loss in particular domains takes place in every language in the world over time, though overall dramatic reduction of the lexicon is probably known only in language death. Borrowing, including heavy borrowing, has been shown in previous chapters to be common in many contact situations, not only those leading to language death. Internally motivated change affects all living languages, including dying ones. This leaves attrition as the only type of change that is exclusive to language death.

In analyzing changes in dying languages, though, we need to consider all the above types of change. If we simply look at a change in a dying language, decide that it simplifies the language's structure, and then label it an example of attrition, we are in serious danger of overlooking crucial features of the change. We need to look carefully for multiple causation, with both attrition and interference from the dominant group's language contributing to the change, because this combination seems to be very common in dying languages. The particular type of interference may well differ from case to case. It will be borrowing if the people introducing an interference feature are in fact fluent in the dying language, but shift-induced interference if the people introducing the feature are semi-speakers who learned the dying language as a second language – or, of course, both, if both fluent speakers and semi-speakers help to introduce the change.

One study that attempts to sort out some of these issues is Anna Fenyvesi's 1995 investigation of structural changes in a dialect of American Hungarian that is spoken in McKeesport, Pennsylvania. The community includes both fluent speakers and semi-speakers; the numbers of deviations from Hungar-ian as spoken in Hungary varied in the two groups, but the patterns of types of errors were similar for the two groups. Fenyvesi classified the changes in her data into three categories: (1) borrowing alone – changes that did not simplify the language and did bring it closer to the dominant group's language, English; (2) attrition alone – changes that simplified the language but did not make it more similar to English; and (3) both borrowing and attrition – changes that simplified the language and made it more similar to English. Her argument was that a change that could be either borrowing or attrition was quite likely to arise from both sources, since two possible causes pushing in the same direction ought to make a change more likely to happen. And even if this is not always true, it will be difficult or impossible to make a solid case for one of the two possibilities as the sole cause of the change. It should also be noted that Fenyvesi's borrowing category includes both the incorporation of some morpheme or structural feature from the other language (e.g. the SOV word order of Hungarian replaced by the SVO word order of English) and what is sometimes called 'negative borrowing', the loss of Hungarian features that do not correspond directly to anything in English, such as voicing assimilation in clusters of obstruent consonants.

Fenyvesi's results were as follows. First, there were very few changes in category (2), attrition alone. More changes belonged to category (1), borrowing alone, but there were still more (though not too many more) changes in category (3), both attrition and borrowing as causes of change. Some of the changes in category (2) actually complicated the grammar – for instance the frequent but not complete shift of word stress from the initial syllable to the verb's root. Typical changes in her category (2) were the loss of case suffixes (English has almost no case system) and degemination of double consonants between vowels.

Of course some questions can be raised about Fenyvesi's results. For one thing, it's by no means always easy to decide whether a particular change simplifies a language's structure or not. For instance, in her data some case suffixes were replaced by others in certain constructions – diminishing the range of usage for a replaced case suffix (a possible simplification) but increasing the range of usage for a replacing case suffix (not necessarily a simplification, because the rules for its usage may be complicated). Historical linguists believe that a change that simplifies the grammar in one place is likely to complicate it somewhere else. This doesn't necessarily happen; there are exceptions in all languages, not just in dying languages; but it is a generally justified expectation. Now, we expect to find a good deal of real attrition in a dying language, without concomitant complication elsewhere in the grammar to compensate for the loss of (say) an exclusive–inclusive 'we' distinction. Still, this expectation does not justify an assumption that every change in a dying language will result in a net structural simplification, because exceptions can arise from borrowing, from internally-motivated change, and from creative innovations introduced by reasonably fluent semi-speakers. In addition, it is certainly not safe to assume that Fenyvesi's results for an immigrant language in the United States will be generalizable even to other dying immigrant languages in the United States, much less to dying languages in other types of contact situations around the world. Her study is, however, one of the very few investigations to date that directly address the issue of multiple causation in an effort to establish sources for a large complex of changes in one dying language. It is likely (though I don't know of any empirical evidence on this point) that there is a higher percentage of structural borrowings that also simplify the system in a dying language than in viable languages. That is, it seems likely that attrition plays a greater role in the borrowing process in a dying language.

Grammatical replacement

In this linguistic route to language death, the original grammar of one language is gradually replaced by the grammar of another; in the few cases we know about, there has also been a great deal of lexical borrowing. At first glance, this route looks like a variant of the first and more general route, attrition, only with much more structural borrowing than in ordinary cases of gradual language loss with attrition. But there's a difference, and a simple two-part thought experiment will help make it clear. Imagine a dying language that has undergone much attrition as well as some lexical and structural borrowing from a dominant group. Now imagine that, through some cataclysmic social upheaval, its speakers are completely separated from the dominant group and settled on a previously uninhabited island. What is their linguistic situation? Their own traditional language has lost domains, stylistic resources, lexicon, and structure, and much of the lost structure and lexicon have not been replaced by borrowings from the dominant group's language. Their language is therefore severely impoverished. As Sasse's model predicts, their main language – and the first language of their children – is now the dominant group's language; so even though they are no longer dominated by that group (or by any other group), they are quite likely to continue using that language, and let their traditional language disappear. Alternatively, they might settle on a mix of that language with some vocabulary from their traditional language, if they want to retain a linguistic piece of their ethnic heritage; if they do that, it is the mixed language that will be learned henceforth by children in the community, because they will have no use for a second language.

Now imagine a group whose language has undergone gradual massive grammatical replacement from a dominant group's language, and is likely to be given up entirely in the not too distant future. Again let us separate the two groups by placing the speakers of the dying language on an uninhabited island. What language will they choose to speak on their island? Their in-group language is now a mixture of the dominant group's grammar and what is left of their own traditional language – mostly lexicon, including most of the basic vocabulary. This mixed language may have lost some domains, but it is still learned as a first language by their children (though not necessarily as the children's only first language). It fulfills many functions of their daily lives. It's not clear whether it is their main language – all its speakers are fully bilingual in the former dominant group's language – but it is not impoverished overall: it has changed by borrowing and more borrowing, and has not undergone any significant attrition; it has all the complexity of the former dominant group's language, because it has that language's grammar.

The most obvious difference between the two situations is that only the first one involves attrition, loss without replacement of lexicon and structure. But there are also other obvious differences. The language that has undergone grammatical replacement retains more domains of usage, including use with small children, than the language that has undergone attrition; as Sasse's model predicts, attrition, lack of transmission to children, and loss of domains of usage go together. All these differences can ultimately be explained by a vitally important attitudinal feature: the only languages that undergo massive grammatical replacement are those whose speakers stubbornly refuse, over a long period of time and under intense cultural pressure, to shift to the language of a numerically dominant group. We are in fact talking here about one of the sets of languages that were discussed in Chapter 8, namely, bilingual mixed languages that developed gradually in persistent ethnic groups. In Chapter 8 the question of language death was not emphasized. But clearly, once they have lost their original grammars by replacement, the original Laha and Ma'a languages no longer exist: they have died, though the communities that spoke them are still ethnic groups with their own distinctive languages. Whether the mixed languages that result from grammatical replacement survive is a different question. With stubborn enough resistance to total assimilation, the groups might be able to maintain their languages (without a social upheaval as drastic as the one in my thought experiment). But the most recent fieldwork on Ma'a, at least, suggests that the speakers have almost abandoned their resistance and shifted completely to Shambaa.

As James Collins suggests in discussing Laha (in the quotation at the beginning of Chapter 8), Laha speakers have maintained their language at the cost of giving up its grammar by adopting Ambonese Malay grammar 'bit by bit'. Although Laha and Malay belong to the Malayo-Polynesian branch of the Austronesian language family, they are not closely related; Ambonese Malay and local languages of Ambon have converged, so that typologically Ambon and prechange Laha were probably quite similar. But even so, the process of change would have been grammatical replacement, not a mere leveling out of dialect differences.

As we also saw in Chapter 8, there are several types of evidence supporting the claim of gradual grammatical replacement in Ma'a, including the observation that the full Bantu morphological system was, as of 1960, established among younger speakers but not yet among older speakers.

The problem mentioned in Chapter 8 remains, however: if we have two languages – say, Anglo-Romani and Ma'a – that consist (almost) entirely of the grammar of a dominant group's language combined with part of the lexicon of a persistent ethnic group's language, how can we tell whether the emergence of the mixed language was abrupt or gradual? That is, how can we tell whether the mixture arose through attrition or as a last stage in a process of gradual but eventually massive grammatical replacement? The answer is that we can't always tell. We assume that Anglo-Romani was a typical case of attrition, with all the social and behavioral concomitants of Sasse's model, because both Anglo-Romani and real Romani are attested in England in the nineteenth century; if Anglo-Romani had arisen by gradual grammatical replacement, it could not have coexisted in the same place with real Romani. (Here we must also assume that the two languages are attested in the same group of speakers, with real Romani spoken by the last fluent speakers and Anglo-Romani spoken already by the least proficient semi-speakers.) Arguments for the gradualness of the Bantuization of Ma'a were presented in Chapter 8. The main point is that, for at least the past seventy years and by inference for over two hundred years before that, elements of the non-Bantu grammar of Ma'a were being replaced by elements of Bantu grammar, with no overall attrition, no semi-speakers, and in particular with no shift from a 'real' Ma'a with non-Bantu grammar to a Bantu language with lexical residue from the group's original language: there has been no lack of transmission of Ma'a to younger generations.

A question arises here: if there are languages which (like Laha and Ma'a) have gradually borrowed the entire grammar of another language as well as much of its lexicon, are there any instances of the logical next step, borrowing of the whole language, lexicon and all, so that language death comes about by complete transformation into another language? The answer appears to be yes, at least when the two languages involved are closely related. Extensive data showing precisely how such a process might unfold are hard to find, but some such process seems to have operated in the death of some varieties of Votic, a member of the Finnic branch of the Uralic language family that is (or was) in intimate contact with a closely related Finnic language, Ižora (also called Ingrian): 'Ižora words and grammatical features made their way into Votic almost imperceptibly, until they achieved preponderance. Then the language of these Vots was no longer Votic, but Ižora.' In other words, although Sasse's model fits a large number of language death contexts, it doesn't fit Ma'a or Ižora, and it presumably also doesn't fit Laha. It is difficult to estimate how many other languages have died as a result of massive gradual grammatical (and occasionally even lexical) replacement; but the number might be small, because so many groups of people do shift to a dominant group's language when they come under intense long-term pressure to do so. (It is important to remember that, as we saw in earlier chapters, there are many quite stable contact situations in which everyone is bilingual and no one is shifting away from any of the languages. But sometimes, especially in the modern world, people do indeed come under intense pressure to shift to another language.) And even if there are fairly numerous cases of death through replacement, we may never know about them: the case is strong for Ma'a mainly because it happens to be attested over several decades, with significant changes visibly occurring during that period, and also because the oral histories of their Bantu-speaking neighbors attest to the Ma'a people's unusually strong desire to hang onto their ethnic identity. And we are lucky enough to know about the continuing close ties between the Ma'as and their kinfolk whose clans did shift to Bantu, providing an ideal context for the incorporation of Bantu features into Ma'a. The trouble is, we don't have such detailed information for most ethnic groups that might be candidates for this apparently rare class of bilingual mixed languages that replaced now-extinct unmixed languages.

No loss of structure, not much borrowing

Two kinds of cases fall into this category. First, some languages die so abruptly that there is no time for them to undergo attrition or any other significant changes as part of the dying process. The most tragic cases are those in which an entire ethnic group dies suddenly, either through illness or in a massacre. Even in these cases, of course, there are often a few survivors, so that the language survives for a little while in very limited usage. An example is the Lower Chinook language of the Pacific Northwest of the United States: the great majority of its speakers died rapidly after whites arrived in the region, mainly of introduced diseases; the language vanished entirely not long afterward.In less tragic cases, language shift may proceed so rapidly that no changes can accumulate; one example is the Lenca language of El Salvador, which vanished rapidly after a 1932 massacre in which thousands of Indians were killed and many others – including all the remaining speakers of Lenca – 'simply stopped speaking their native languages as a survival strategy'.

The lack of linguistic changes in these situations is easy to understand, of course. If there is no younger generation in an intact speech community, there will be no semi-speakers; and if parents are afraid to transmit their language to their children, they are likely to transmit the fear itself instead, so that their children will be unlikely to insist on trying to learn the language. The last group of speakers will certainly remember their native language to some extent, but they will also forget much of it if they do not speak it over a period of many years – and, if they also fail to learn the dominant group's language well, they may be left without fluency in any language at all. This may be what happened to White Thunder in Bloomfield's story, but we have too little information to be sure.

Interesting as these individual 'rememberers' are, however, the most significant cases, from the viewpoint of linguistic results of contact, are those in which there is plenty of time for a dying language to undergo

significant changes, but it does not do so. These cases are especially interesting in view of the fairly common belief that they do not exist – as
illustrated in one expert's comment that 'any case of language death
involves . . . language change (at every grammatical level)'. Specialists do
not predict that all dying languages will undergo extensive changes in all
grammatical subsystems; one of the most often quoted observations in the
entire language-death literature is Nancy Dorian's famous reference to East
Sutherland Gaelic dying 'with its morphological boots on'. Still, the general
expectation is that some kinds of changes will occur, and that they will be
extensive.

   Montana Salish is an exception. With fewer than sixty fluent speakers
remaining, the language is seriously endangered, and will die soon if the
current preservation efforts fail to produce a new generation of speakers. But
in spite of a hundred and fifty years of increasingly intense contact with, and
pressure from, English, Montana Salish has borrowed almost nothing from
English – only a handful of words, and no structure at all. The Montana
Salish people have acculturated to English-language culture to a great extent,
but instead of borrowing English words for new objects, they invent new
words out of Salish morphemes; we saw one example in Chapter 1. Nor has
Montana Salish undergone extensive attrition. It has lost some lexical
domains as a result of culture change, as noted above; but these losses
are not obviously more extensive than losses of lexical domains in fully viable
languages such as English. Loss of stylistic resources, for instance rhetorical
devices in storytelling, does look like significant attrition, but the current
elders do not report any gaps in their ability to use their language in most
areas of daily life. They do use it more rarely than they used to, of course,
because many or most of the people they talk to are monolingual English
speakers.

   Like East Sutherland Gaelic, Montana Salish is dying with its morphological boots on, and they are jumbo-sized boots – the morphological systems
of Salishan languages are among the most complex in the world. Its syntax,
semantics, and most areas of the lexicon are also intact. So is its very
elaborate phonology. But what about the tribal elder's complaint, quoted
at the beginning of the chapter, that young people chop their words off, while
elders keep them long? This suggests that the young people in question are
semi-speakers; indeed, other scholars have found that semi-speakers sometimes tend to shorten long words. Here I think the elder was mistaken. The
truncation process he refers to is rather old – it is a phenomenon that is
shared with other dialects of the same language (especially Kalispel) and at
least one other closely related language, and it dates back to a time when
many adult tribal members were monolingual, well before one would have
expected to find incipient processes of language death. (It is an interesting
process: the basic rule is 'truncate all material after the stressed vowel, unless
it's important'; although some truncated forms are now permanently short,

others show up in their original long forms when certain important suffixes are added to the stem.) Some of the oldest current elders truncate more words than fluent (slightly) younger speakers, and yet they are highly respected for their language abilities. So in spite of appearances, the truncation process seems not to be either a symptom or a product of language death; it does illustrate the gap between the complex reality of language structure and change, on the one hand, and speakers' (and linguists'!) perceptions of changes as belonging or not belonging to a process of language death on the other hand.

The Montana Salish situation suggests that there are no semi-speakers in the community – that the reason the language has not changed is that it was not transmitted in any form to the current younger generations. The youngest fluent speakers are now middle-aged, and they were raised by very traditional parents or, in some cases, by traditional grandparents. Some of them seem to worry that their command of the language is imperfect; in fact, however, their occasional insecurity in elicitation sessions does not seem to correlate with any serious deficiencies in their knowledge of the language. Some younger tribal members understand at least some Salish, but they tend not to speak it: when spoken to in Salish, they seem to prefer to answer in English. (But I should add that there may be semi-speakers that I haven't discovered: like most fieldworkers who study extremely endangered and poorly documented languages, my concern has been to find the most fluent speakers to collect data from.) Together with the lack of interference from English, which all current speakers of Montana Salish also speak fluently, the absence of any significant attrition and the apparent absence of a sizable group of semi-speakers make Montana Salish highly unusual among the dying languages that have been described so far in the scholarly literature. It is hardly likely, though, that Montana Salish is a unique case of language death.

Obviously, social differences must explain the different routes to language death followed by (for instance) Montana Salish, Ma'a, and East Sutherland Gaelic. Time certainly cannot be the crucial deciding factor: the time frame for the decline of Montana Salish is longer than that for American Hungarian, for example, and yet the linguistic paths of the two languages have diverged dramatically. Some of the relevant social factors have to do with speakers' attitudes. The nonborrowing of lexicon appears to be an areal feature in languages of the American Northwest – Montana Salish is by no means the only language in the region that has not borrowed words or structure from English, although (like other languages in the area) it has borrowed words and perhaps some structure from other Native languages. And there are numerous other cases in various parts of the world in which a language's speakers do not borrow linguistic material from other languages, even in conditions of extensive bilingualism. We saw in Chapter 4 that contact-induced change is inherently unpredictable; this turns out to be as true in language death as it is in other kinds of language contact. What this means is that we may be able to predict that a language will die in the near future, but we cannot predict with any confidence what will happen to its lexicon and structure as it dies.

Sources and further reading

The systematic study of language death in all its social and linguistic aspects has been pursued only since the 1970s, so it's an even younger field than pidgin/creole studies. Nevertheless, the scholarly literature includes a steadily increasing number of detailed case studies and several important collections of papers on the topic. An especially valuable source for orientation into this topic is Nancy C. Dorian's 1999 survey article 'The study of language obsolescence: stages, surprises, challenges'; Lyle Campbell's 1994 encyclopedia article 'Language death' is also a very good survey, especially of linguistic correlates of language death. One of the most-cited works on the topic, with several very important papers, is Nancy C. Dorian's 1989 edited volume *Investigating Obsolescence: Studies in Language Contraction and Death*. Another important collection is Matthias Brenzinger, ed., *Language Death: Factual and Theoretical Explorations with Special Reference to East Africa* (1992). Book-length case studies of dying languages include Nancy C. Dorian's ground-breaking 1981 study *Language Death: The Life Cycle of a Scottish Gaelic Dialect*, Annette Schmidt's *Young People's Dyirbal: An Example of Language Death from Australia* (1985), Silke Van Ness's *Changes in an Obsolescing Language: Pennsylvania German in West Virginia* (1990), Hans-Jürgen Sasse's 1991 book on the dying Arvanitika variety of Albanian in Greece (*Arvanitika: die albanischen Sprachreste in Griechenland*), Don Kulick's 1992 study of shift from Taiap to Tok Pisin in Papua New Guinea (*Language Shift and Cultural Reproduction: Socialization, Self, and Syncretism in a Papua New Guinean Village*), and Mari C. Jones's *Language Obsolescence and Revitalization: Linguistic Change in Two Contrasting Welsh Communities* (1998).

Hans-Jürgen Sasse's model of language death is presented in his 1992 article 'Theory of language death'; his flow chart is on p. 19. The quotation with multiple question words is the famous title of a 1965 article by Joshua Fishman, 'Who speaks what language to whom and when'.

The example of Nubian plurals is from p. 265 of Aleya Rouchdy's 1989 article 'Urban and non-Urban Egyptian Nubian: is there a reduction in language skill?'. The Dyirbal examples of regularization and simplification are discussed on pp. 229–31 of Annette Schmidt's 1985 book (cited above). The fate of the Pipil rule that devoiced final resonant consonants in Teotepeque Pipil and the overextended glottalization of Jumaytepeque Xinca are described by Lyle Campbell and Martha C. Muntzel in their 1989 article 'The structural consequences of language death' (pp. 189–90). The ongoing Warlpiri merger of exclusive and inclusive pronominal forms is presented by

Edith L. Bavin in her 1989 article 'Some lexical and morphological changes in Warlpiri' (pp. 282–3).

The quotation about Votic becoming Ižora is from Paul Ariste's 1970 article 'Die Wege des Aussterbens zweier finnisch-ugrischer Sprachen' ['The routes to death of two Finno-Ugric languages']; the quoted sentences are my translation of his German sentences ('Ishorische Wörter und grammatische Züge sind ins Wotische fast unmerklich eingedrungen, bis sie das Übergewicht bekamen. Dann war die Sprache dieser Woten nicht mehr Wotisch, sondern schon ishorisch').

The quotation about Lenca (and two other languages of El Salvador) is from p. 1960 of Lyle Campbell's 1994 article 'Language death'. On the same page Campbell cites two other articles, Wolfgang U. Dressler's 'Language shift and language death – a protean challenge for the linguist' (1981) and Jane Hill's 'Language death in Uto-Aztecan' (1983), as sources for discussion of what he calls 'sudden language death' and 'radical language death'.

The quotation about the inevitability of structural change in a (gradually) dying language is from p. 12 of Sasse's 1992 article 'Theory of language death' (cited above). Nancy C. Dorian's comment about East Sutherland Gaelic's morphological boots is from her 1978 article 'The fate of morphological complexity in language death: evidence from East Sutherland Gaelic'; one of the many authors who cite this comment is Lyle Campbell, on p. 1963 of his 'Language death' article, where he also cites several other sources that report lack of morphological reduction in language death. On the same page, Campbell mentions that shortening long words has been reported as a feature of language death.

10 Endangered Languages

'Language is fundamental to cultural identity. This is so for all people everywhere. For Bininj, their unique world is expressed in their language. For this reason, it is important that people keep their own language alive. For Bininj, language and land are linked . . . Each clan has its own name and territory . . . a child's language may not be his or her first language, because a family may spend time in the mother's country and mainly speak her language. In this [Cultural] Centre, Bininj use Balanda [non-Aboriginal] words to talk about their country, but as with the translation of any language, some words cannot convey the original meaning exactly.' (A sign in the Warradjan Aboriginal Cultural Centre, Kakadu National Park, Northern Territory, Australia)

Some 'villages in Myagdi used to speak Chantyal until relatively recently or are now losing it, since their language is not seen as a key feature of their Chantyal identity.' (From 'The fall and rise and fall of the Chantyal language', by Michael Noonan, 1999)

'Now the question no longer is: how shall we learn English so that we may share in the social life of America and partake of her benefits; the great question is, how can we preserve the language of our ancestors here in a strange environment and pass on to our descendants the treasures it contains?' (A comment on Norwegian in America, from *Kort Udsigt over det lutherske Kirkearbeide blandt Normændene i Amerika*, by T. Bothne, 1898, p. 828)

'Sometimes I could just kick myself for not teaching my children the language . . . When I was in school, we were beaten for speaking our language. They wanted to make us ashamed . . . I have 17- and 18-year-old kids coming to me crying because the elders in their tribes will not teach them their own language.' (Comments by Marie Smith Jones, the 80-year-old last speaker of Eyak and chief of the Eyak tribe in Alaska, 1998)

'It is the policy of the United States to preserve, protect, and promote the rights and freedom of Native Americans to use, practice, and develop Native American languages.' (Native American Languages Act, United States Congress, 1990)

'Of supreme significance . . . is the simple truth that language – in the general, multifaceted sense – embodies the intellectual wealth of the people who use it . . . The loss of local languages, and the cultural systems they express, has meant irretrievable loss of diverse and interesting intellectual wealth, the priceless products of human mental industry. The process of language loss is ongoing. Many linguistic field workers have had, and will continue to have, the experience of bearing witness to the loss, for all time, of a language and of the cultural products which the language served to express for the intellectual nourishment of its speakers.' ('Language endangerment and the human value of linguistic diversity', by Ken Hale, 1992, p. 36)

'To what extent are endangered languages a priority in modern linguistics? Are graduate students encouraged to document moribund or endangered languages for their dissertations? How much encouragement is there to compile a dictionary of one? How many academic departments encourage applied linguistics in communities for the support of endangered languages? How many departments provide appropriate training for speakers of these languages who are most ideally suited to do the most needed work? Obviously we must do some serious rethinking of our priorities, lest linguistics go down in history as the only science that presided obliviously over the disappearance of 90% of the very field to which it is dedicated.' ('The world's languages in crisis', by Michael Krauss, 1992, p. 10)

Textbooks usually end with a self-congratulatory summing-up chapter that reviews all the delights encountered in the field under study and in the book itself. The standard closing chapter also points to exciting directions for future research in the field. Because the field of language contact exists only because there are lots of languages in the world, virtually all of them spoken by people who interact regularly with speakers of at least one other language, this final chapter will depart from the norm.

About 6,000 languages are spoken in the world today – roughly 275 in Europe and the Middle East, 900 in the Americas (240 of them in Mexico alone, and 210 in Brazil), 1,900 in Africa (e.g. 410 in Nigeria, 270 in Cameroon, 210 in Zaire), and 3,000 in Asia and the Pacific (e.g. 850 in Papua New Guinea, 670 in Indonesia, and 380 in India). According to one estimate, 90 percent of these languages will be either dead or doomed by 2100; other estimates of languages in serious danger are lower, around 50 percent, but that still predicts 3,000 dead or dying languages by 2100. If we assume that a community language that is no longer learned as a first language by children is moribund – doomed to extinction once the last native speakers have died – we get the following figures for the worst cases: 225 of 250 indigenous languages of Australia are moribund, as are 149 of the 187 languages of the entire United States and Canada (including for example 45 of the 50 languages of Alaska). And many more languages that are not yet moribund are endangered: it isn't likely that children will continue learning them for many more years. A number of endangered languages have been mentioned in this book – Montana Salish, Nez Percé, Michif, Mednyj Aleut, Ma'a, Chinook Jargon, and some others that are designated endangered in the glossary – and some long-dead ancient languages have also been mentioned, among them Sumerian and Akkadian. All these languages, and hundreds of others too, died because of language contact: in the vast majority of cases, and with ever-increasing frequency today, they died because their speakers all shifted to other languages.

If the numbers of moribund and other endangered languages are added up, what is left? Estimating the number of 'safe' languages – languages not in danger of extinction in the near future – is difficult, because although number of speakers is often a good indicator of language health, some languages with many speakers are definitely not safe. Another way of looking for 'safe' languages is to see which ones are official languages of one or more nations, because official state support is also another good indicator of safety. The number of nations and the roster of official languages changes rapidly – for instance, South Africa went from two official languages (Afrikaans and English) to eleven after the end of apartheid – so any figures given will soon be out of date. The following figures, however, will give a good idea of the spread: of the world's 195 nations as of 2000, 51 had English as an, or the, official language, 30 had French, 20 had Spanish, 23 had Arabic, and 8 had Portuguese. These five major languages were thus official in 132 nations, leaving only 63 with none of the big five among their official languages. Other factors that contribute to keeping a language alive are harder to measure. Usefulness in the economic sphere is certainly important; so are social factors such as language and ethnic loyalty and prestige. But some languages that enjoy all these benefits nevertheless die. In any case, an educated guess is that perhaps 600 of the world's languages, 10 percent of the total number, are safe. This figure does not, to put it mildly, compare favorably with the much more widely publicized rate of extinction of biological species: up to 10 percent of mammal species and 5 percent of bird species are endangered or threatened (although one estimate is that half of the world's species will be extinct or nearly so by 2100, an estimate that is much closer to the linguistic situation). This comparison is not meant to downplay the disaster of ongoing biological species extinction; rather, it is meant to highlight the ongoing 'catastrophic destruction of the linguistic world'.

The 1990s saw a sudden onset of serious concern about endangered languages. It was as if linguists suddenly awoke to the realization that they faced a crisis: the languages to which they had devoted their professional lives were vanishing at a horrifyingly rapid rate. The problem was of course perceived much earlier by fieldworkers. Ken Hale, for instance, reported in 1992 that he has conducted fieldwork on eight different languages that are now extinct. But the wider scholarly community of linguists only became concerned in the last years of the twentieth century. Groups of linguists formed organizations to promote the documentation and preservation of endangered languages, among them the Linguistic Society of America's Committee on Endangered Languages and their Preservation, the Endangered Language Fund (New Haven, Connecticut), the Foundation for Endangered Languages (England), and the International Clearing House for Endangered Languages (University of Tokyo); there is also at least one electronic list devoted to endangered languages. As of 1994, the director of the Linguistics Program at the National Science Foundation in the United States reported that 20 percent of his annual research budget was devoted to funding language preservation projects. Articles on the topic have also been appearing rather regularly in newspapers and magazines for some years now, so the issue is receiving attention from the public as well – and from politicians, as the largely symbolic Native American Languages Act, enacted by the United States Congress in 1990, indicates.

Most importantly, speech communities in many regions are taking vigorous action to preserve their languages. Not all communities whose languages are endangered feel the same sense of urgency; in some places, as the quotation about Chantyal at the beginning of this chapter indicates, communities do not see their traditional language as a vital part of their ethnic identity. But more and more communities are reacting to the threatened loss of their language with imaginative and, at least in some instances, effective preservation programs. The dire estimates of language mortality in the next century, ranging from 50 to 90 percent, all assume a lack of successful intervention that could turn things around for a nontrivial number of languages; some of the programs that are being undertaken could possibly lower those estimates significantly, with major sustained worldwide efforts and quite a bit of luck.

One especially valuable effort is the Master-Apprentice Language Learning Program in California, which was founded in 1993. The program brings together teams consisting of two volunteers each – an elder fluent in a native language and a learner (often one of the elder's younger relatives) – who agree to spend ten to twenty hours a week together during the summer, speaking exclusively in the elder's language. Each master–apprentice team spends two days at the beginning of the summer in a training workshop that introduces techniques for learning languages in this kind of context. Not all the teams are successful, but the successful ones have produced several new speakers who can carry on conversations in the language of their ancestors (and even a few new speakers per language, given the precarious state of most Native Californian languages, represent a large proportion of the total speaker population).

Another effective approach to the revitalization of endangered languages is the 'language nest' program used to teach Maori (New Zealand), Hawaiian (Hawaii), and Mohawk (Canada) to children. This is a total immersion program: children hear only the target language during the school day. These programs started with preschool students. In Hawaii, over a period of fifteen years, the program expanded to eleven private Hawaiian language schools and, with the cooperation of the state Department of Education, to sixteen public Hawaiian language schools; the nonprofit foundation Aha Punana Leo ('the language nest') provides a sophisticated computer network for the program and millions of dollars in university scholarships; there is now even a Hawaiian language college at the University of Hawaii at Hilo. And thanks to this program, there are growing numbers of young Hawaiians who have achieved fluency in a language that, a generation ago, was moribund – no longer a home language learned by children.

These are two of the most innovative efforts that are under way. But probably the most common approach by far is the standard language class. In the United States, at least, it isn't always easy to persuade public school officials to incorporate language classes into school curricula on Indian reservations; in one town on the Flathead Reservation of Montana, for instance, white parents protested efforts to introduce Montana Salish and Kutenai language classes (because some white children wanted to take the classes, and their parents objected). Some school boards, however, are more willing to be creative. So, for instance, three Native American languages are currently being taught at public schools in the state of Washington – the Salishan languages Klallam in Port Angeles and Lummi at Ferndale High School, and the Wakashan language Makah at Neah Bay High School – and another Salishan language, Twana, was taught at Shelton High School until the teacher became ill. Thanks to state education legislation passed in 1993, these language classes count just as much as (for instance) French or Spanish for credit toward college-admission language requirements. About half of the students in the Klallam classes are Klallam tribal members; the rest are members of other (non-Klallam) tribes and whites.

Nor is Washington the only state with such classes. Among the others are New York (Mohawk), South Dakota (Lakota), Oklahoma (Kickapoo), Mississippi (Choctaw), Wisconsin (Oneida), and Utah (Ute), and Montana (Montana Salish, in a few Flathead Reservation schools). One especially successful example is the Hualapai Bilingual/Bicultural Program developed in the 1970s by Lucille J. Watahomigie and Akira Y. Yamamoto for the Peach Springs Elementary School in Arizona. The model used for this program is collaborative, involving 'bilingual staff, teachers, school administrators, parents, community leaders, district school officials, government officials, and academic professionals' – an inclusive approach credited by the developers for the success of the program. Elsewhere in the world, too, language preservation efforts are in progress, for instance among the Äyiwo people of the Solomon Islands, the Sámis of Norway, and the Basques of Spain. An eloquent comment on such efforts, and on the grim result of the failure to institute successful preservation efforts, was recently made by Nancy Dorian, one of the most prominent linguists specializing in the study of language death phenomena:

> 'The people who take up the hard, long-term work that goes into restoring an ancestral language to the descendants of its original speakers are testifying to a fundamental truth that everyone already knows deep down: the ancestral language connects a people to its heritage in ways that there is simply no substitute for . . . There is something inexpressibly sad about watching the disappearance of a unique local language that will never again be heard flowing in its full magnificence from the tongue of a verbally gifted speaker. I conversed with a number of speakers of East Sutherland Gaelic who had just such exceptional verbal gifts . . . The sadness lies in the realization that the great-grandchildren of those magnificent speakers will never have the chance to hear the like of what I heard.'

Some say that the current preservation efforts are too little and too late. This is probably true for some of them. But one thing is certain: the study of language contact is possible only because there are so many, and such diverse, language contact situations all over the world. So unless speech communities, together with linguists, school officials, and others who are trying to help them, can manage to save their languages, the whole field of language contact studies might end as abruptly as this book.

Sources and further reading

Perhaps the best place to start reading about endangered languages is the 1992 collection of seven articles edited by Ken Hale in the journal *Language*. Two articles in this set are particularly outstanding: Michael Krauss's 'The world's languages in crisis' and Hale's 'Language endangerment and the human value of linguistic diversity'. Two important book-length collections of papers also appeared in the 1990s: *Endangered Languages: Current Issues and Future Prospects*, edited by Leonore A. Grenoble and Lindsay J. Whaley (1998), and *Endangered Languages*, edited by Robert H. Robins and Eugenius M. Uhlenbeck (1991). On the general topic of preserving endangered languages, see Joshua A. Fishman's 1991 book *Reversing Language Shift: Theoretical and Empirical Foundations of Assistance to Threatened Languages*.

The quotation from T. Bothne's book is cited on p. 238 of Einar Haugen's 1953 Book *The Norwegian Language in America: A Study in Bilingual Behavior*. The quotation from Eyak elder Marie Smith Jones is from 'Say what? Preserving endangered languages', a *Newsweek* article by Joan Raymond, 14 September 1998. The comment about Chantyal is cited in David Bradley's 1999 review of Michael Noonan's book.

Most of the information in the first two paragraphs of the main text in this chapter – the figures on moribund and endangered languages, endangered biological species, and national languages – is taken from Michael Krauss's 1992 article 'The world's languages in crisis'; the phrase 'catastrophic destruction of the linguistic world' is quoted from p. 7 of Krauss's article. The prediction of (near-)extinction of half of the world's biological species by 2100 is cited by Krauss (p. 7) from Jared Diamond's 1991 article 'World of the living dead'. The lower estimate of language mortality in the next century, 40–50 percent, is from Stephen Wurm, as cited in the 1998 article by Joan Raymond (cited above). Ken Hale's report of doing fieldwork on languages that have since died is from the first page of his article 'On endangered languages and the safeguarding of diversity', in the 1992 set of articles cited above. Paul Chapin, then Director of the United States National Science Foundation's Linguistics Program, is cited on the subject of funding language-preservation projects in a 1994 *Washington Post* article by John Schwartz, 'Speaking out and saving sounds to keep native tongues alive'.

Several initiatives dedicated to language preservation are mentioned in Nancy C. Dorian's 1999 article 'Linguistic and ethnographic fieldwork', including those of the Äyiwos, the Sámis, and the Basques. The initiative that Dorian highlights in this article is the Master-Apprentice Language Learning Program of California; a fuller description of this important program can be found in 'Survival of endangered languages: the California Master-Apprentice Program' (1997), by Leanne Hinton, who is one of the prime movers in organizing the program. Dorian's comment quoted at the end of the chapter is from p. 39 of this article. The description of the 'language nest' program that promotes education in Hawaiian is from a *Los Angeles Times* article, 'The struggle to save dying languages', by Robert Lee Hotz, 25 January 2000.

The report of native languages being taught in Washington public schools is from an Associated Press story by Peggy Andersen, 'Living tradition: Northwest schools help keep tribal tongues alive', which appeared in the *Missoulian* on 5 June 2000. The list of other languages taught in United States schools is from Felicity Barringer's *New York Times* article 'Tongues that dance with wolves: saving America's Native languages' (1991). The Hualapai Bilingual/Bicultural Program is discussed by Lucille J. Watahomigie and Akira Y. Yamamoto in their 1992 article 'Local reactions to perceived language decline'.

Appendix 1: A Map of Some Contact Situations Around the World

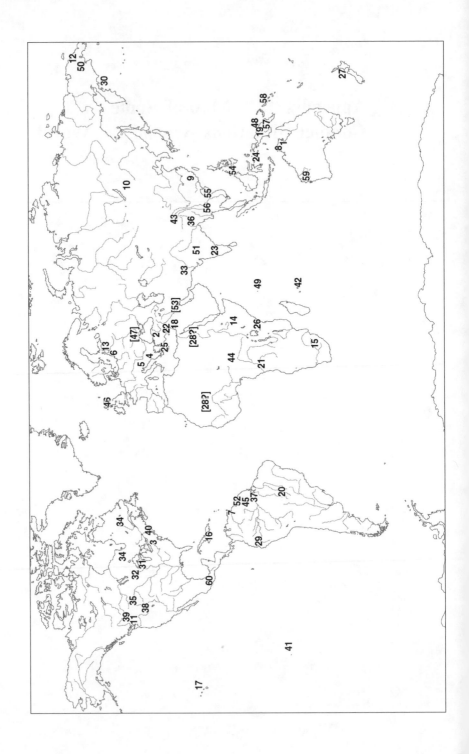

Key to Map

Long-extinct languages are enclosed in square brackets.

1. Arnhem Land
2. Asia Minor Greek
3. American Hungarian
4. Arvanitika (Albanian)
5. Balkan Sprachbund
6. Baltic Sprachbund
7. Berbice Dutch Creole
8. Bininj
9. Chinese Pidgin English
10. Chinese Pidgin Russian
11. Chinook Jargon
12. Chukchi
13. Estonian
14. Ethiopian Highlands Sprachbund
15. Fanagaló
16. Haitian Creole
17. Hawaiian Creole English
18. Hebrew
19. Hiri Motu
20. Kadiwéu
21. Kitúba
22. Kormakiti Arabic
23. Kupwar
24. Laha
25. Lingua Franca
26. Ma'a
27. Maori
28. [Maridi Arabic]
29. Media Lengua
30. Mednyj Aleut
31. Menomini
32. Michif
33. Mõkkī
34. Montagnais
35. Montana Salish
36. Nagamese
37. Ndyuka-Trio Pidgin
38. Nez Percé
39. Pacific Northwest Sprachbund
40. Pidgin Delaware
41. Pitcairnese
42. Réunionese
43. Salar
44. Sango
45. Saramaccan
46. Scottish Gaelic
47. [Scythian]
48. Sepik River Basin Sprachbund
49. Seychellois
50. Siberian Yupik Eskimo
51. South Asia Sprachbund
52. Sranan
53. [Sumerian]
54. Tasaday
55. Tây Bòi
56. Thai
57. Tok Pisin
58. Uisai
59. Yingkarta
60. Zapotec

Appendix 2: Official Languages in the World's Nations

Below is a list of the official languages of all of the world's nations as of 2000. It will not remain up to date, and may not be up to date by the time this book is published, because changes occur frequently as new countries come into existence and old countries change their names or official languages. In addition to official languages, the list includes some major 'national' languages – those spoken by large numbers of people in a country even though they are not widely used in government or education – and languages that are official in particular regions but not in the country as a whole; languages in these two categories are given in parentheses. But sometimes the boundaries among these categories are unclear, so there may be a few discrepancies in the list.

Alternate language names are separated by a slash.

Afghanistan	Pashtu, Dari/Afghan Persian
Albania	Albanian
Algeria	Arabic
Andorra	Catalan
Angola	Portuguese
Antigua and Barbuda	English
Arab Emirates	Arabic
Argentina	Spanish
Armenia	Armenian
Australia	English
Austria	German
Azerbaijan	Azeri/Azerbaijani
Bahamas	English
Bahrain	Arabic
Bangladesh	Bengali
Barbados	English
Belarus	Byelorussian, Russian
Belgium	French, Dutch (German)
Belize	English

Benin	French (Hausa, Fon, Yoruba)
Bhutan	Dzongkha
Bolivia	Spanish, Quechua, Aymara
Bosnia and Herzegovina	Croatian, Serbian, Bosnian
Botswana	English (Setswana)
Brazil	Portuguese
Brunei	Malay
Bulgaria	Bulgarian
Burkina Faso	French
Burundi	French, KiRundi
Cambodia (Kampuchea)	Khmer
Cameroon	French, English
Canada	English, French
Cape Verde	Portuguese (Crioulo)
Central African Republic	French (Sango, Arabic, Hausa, Swahili)
Chad	French, Arabic
Chile	Spanish
China (People's Republic)	Putonghua/Mandarin Chinese
China (Republic)	Mandarin Chinese (Taiwanese/Min, Hakka)
Colombia	Spanish
Comoros	Arabic, French (Comorian Swahili)
Congo	French
Congo, Democratic Republic (former Zaire)	French (Lingala, Swahili)
Cook Islands	English
Costa Rica	Spanish (English)
Croatia	Croatian
Cuba	Spanish
Cyprus, Republic	Greek
Cyprus, Turkish Republic	Turkish
Czech Republic	Czech
Denmark	Danish (Greenlandic, Faroese)
Djibouti	Arabic, French
Dominica	English
Dominican Republic	Spanish
Ecuador	Spanish
Egypt	Arabic
El Salvador	Spanish
Equatorial Guinea	Spanish
Eritrea	Tigrinya, Arabic
Estonia	Estonian
Ethiopia	Amharic (English, Arabic, Italian)

Fiji	Fijian, English
Finland	Finnish, Swedish
France	French
Gabon	French
Gambia	English
Georgia	Georgian
Germany	German
Ghana	English
Greece	Greek
Grenada	English
Guatemala	Spanish
Guinea	French
Guinea-Bissau	Portuguese (Crioulo)
Guyana	English
Haiti	French, Kreyol
Honduras	Spanish
Hungary	Hungarian
Iceland	Icelandic
India	Hindi, English (Assamese, Bengali, Gujarati, Kannaḍa, Kashmiri, Malayalam, Marathi, Oriya, Punjabi, Sanskrit, Sindhi, Tamil, Telugu, Urdu)
Indonesia	Bahasa Indonesia
Iran	Persian/Farsi
Iraq	Arabic
Ireland	Irish Gaelic, English
Israel	Hebrew, Arabic
Italy	Italian (German, French)
Ivory Coast	French
Jamaica	English
Japan	Japanese
Jordan	Arabic
Kazakhstan	Kazakh/Qasaq
Kenya	English, Swahili
Kiribati	English
Korea, North	Korean
Korea, South	Korean
Kuwait	Arabic
Kyrgyzstan	Kyrgyz
Laos	Lao
Latvia	Latvian
Lebanon	Arabic, French
Lesotho	Sesotho, English

Liberia	English
Libya	Arabic
Liechtenstein	German/Alemannic German
Lithuania	Lithuanian
Luxembourg	French, German (Letzebuergesch)
Macao	Portuguese
Macedonia	Macedonian
Madagascar	Malagasy, French
Malawi	Chichewa, English
Malaysia	Bahasa Malaysia
Maldives	Divehi
Mali	French
Malta	Maltese, English
Marshall Islands	English
Mauritania	French, Hasaniya Arabic (Wolof)
Mauritius	English (Mauritian Creole, French)
Mexico	Spanish
Micronesia	English
Moldova	Moldovan/Rumanian
Monaco	French
Mongolia	Khalkha-Mongol
Morocco	Arabic
Mozambique	Portuguese
Myanmar (former Burma)	Burmese
Namibia	English (Herero, Owambo, Afrikaans, German)
Nauru	Nauruan
Nepal	Nepali
Netherlands	Dutch
New Zealand	English, Maori
Nicaragua	Spanish
Niger	French (Hausa)
Nigeria	English (Hausa, Fula, Yoruba, Igbo)
Niue	Niuean, English
Norway	Norwegian
Oman	Arabic
Pakistan	Urdu, English
Palau	Palauan, English
Panama	Spanish
Papua New Guinea	English, Tok Pisin, Hiri Motu
Paraguay	Spanish, Guaraní
Peru	Spanish, Quechua, Aymara
Philippines	Pilipino (English)
Poland	Polish

Portugal	Portuguese
Qatar	Arabic
Rumania	Rumanian
Russia	Russian
Rwanda	French, KiNyarwanda
Saint Kitts and Nevis	English
Saint Lucia	English
Saint Vincent and the Grenadines	English
Samoa	Samoan, English
San Marino	Italian
São Tome and Principe	Portuguese
Saudi Arabia	Arabic
Senegal	French
Seychelles	English, French (Seselwa/French Creole)
Sierra Leone	English
Singapore	Malay, Chinese, Tamil, English
Slovakia	Slovak
Slovenia	Slovenian
Solomon Islands	English (Tok Pisin)
Somalia	Somali (English, Italian, Swahili)
South Africa	English, Afrikaans, Ndebele, Northern Sotho, Southern Sotho, Swazi, Tsonga, Tswana, Venda, Xhosa, Zulu
Spain	Spanish
Sri Lanka	Sinhalese (Tamil)
Sudan	Arabic
Suriname	Dutch (Sranan)
Swaziland	English, SiSwati
Sweden	Swedish
Switzerland	German, French, Italian (Romansh)
Syria	Arabic
Tajikistan	Tajik
Tanzania	Swahili, English
Thailand	Thai
Togo	French (Ewe, Kabye)
Tonga	Tongan
Trinidad and Tobago	English
Tunisia	Arabic
Turkey	Turkish
Turkmenistan	Turkmen
Uganda	English (Swahili)
Ukraine	Ukrainian

United Kingdom	English (Welsh, Gaelic, Manx)
United States	No official language
Uruguay	Spanish
Uzbekistan	Uzbek
Vanuatu	Bislama, French, English
Vatican	Latin, Italian
Venezuela	Spanish
Vietnam	Vietnamese
Yemen	Arabic
Yugoslavia (Serbia and Montenegro)	Serbian (Albanian)
Zambia	English (Bemba, Tonga, Nyanja)
Zimbabwe	English (Shona, Ndebele)

Glossary

AAVE African American Vernacular English.

ACCUSATIVE CASE The case most often used to mark the direct object of a verb, the verb's patient. In the German sentence *Ich sah den Mann* 'I saw the man', the article *den* in the object noun phrase *den Mann* is in the accusative case (compare the nominative, or subject, case form *der Mann*). Similarly, in Russian *čitala knigu* 'I read the book', the object *knigu* 'book' is in the accusative case (compare the nominative case form *kniga*).

AFFRICATE A complex speech sound that begins with a short oral stop component and ends with a short fricative component.

AFRICAN AMERICAN VERNACULAR ENGLISH (AAVE) A dialect of Modern English with partly creole roots (see GULLAH below). AAVE is spoken by some, but not all, African Americans.

AFRO-ASIATIC LANGUAGES A language family named for its range from westernmost Asia (ancient and modern Mesopotamia, the Arabian Peninsula, the eastern Mediterranean coast) to northern Africa. The family consists of five or six branches: Semitic, Egyptian (a one-language branch), Cushitic, Berber, Chadic, and according to some, though not all, specialists a sixth branch, Omotic.

AGGLUTINATIVE MORPHOLOGY A type of morphology, especially inflectional morphology, in which each affix tends to express just one grammatical function such as 'tense' or 'person/number of subject'. See Chapter 4 for an example of a partial change from FLEXIONAL to agglutinative morphology in Asia Minor Greek as a result of interference from Turkish, and see under ANALYTIC MORPHOSYNTAX for another contrasting type.

AGREEMENT Grammatical linkage (feature sharing) between words in a clause (or sentence). The most common type in the world's languages is subject–verb agreement, where the verb is marked (for example) for person and number to agree with its subject, as in Englsh *she walk-s*, where the *-s* indicates, among other things, that the verb has a third-person singular subject. Other common types of agreement are object–verb and adjective–noun, e.g. in Swahili *ni-li-m-penda* 'I liked him' (literally 'I-PAST-him-like') vs. *ni-li-wa-penda* 'I liked them' (literally 'I-PAST-them-like'), where the prefixes *m-* and *wa-* indicate, respectively, members of the singular and plural noun classes that include humans; and Russian *staraja kniga* 'an old book' vs. *staryj dom* 'an old house', where the adjective 'old' agrees in gender, number, and case with its head noun (nominative singular feminine for 'book', nominative singular masculine for 'house').

AINU A language formerly spoken in northern Japan and on several nearby Russian islands, especially Sakhalin; it is no longer used for everyday communication by ethnic Ainu people and is thus moribund or extinct. Ainu is classified as a linguistic ISOLATE.

ALBANIAN A one-language branch of the Indo-European language family, spoken in Albania and, to a lesser extent, in Yugoslavia and Greece. The dying Arvanitika dialect of Albanian is spoken in Greece (see Chapter 9).

ALGONQUIAN LANGUAGES A language family with about twenty members spoken primarily in eastern and midwestern Canada and the United States, but also in some western regions of both countries. Almost all Algonquian languages are gravely endangered; some now have only a handful of fluent speakers. Among the Algonquian languages mentioned in this book are Cree, Delaware (or Lenape), Menomini, and Blackfoot.

ALTAIC LANGUAGES A group of languages spoken from easternmost Europe to East Asia, so called because some specialists believe that they comprise a single language family. The core component branches of Altaic are Turkic (Turkish and its relatives), MONGOLIC (e.g. Mongolian), and Tungusic (e.g. Manchu); Korean is often also included in the proposed family, and a smaller number of scholars include Japanese as well. Japanese is the most controversial member of the proposed family, but some specialists, and many nonspecialist historical linguists, are skeptical about the evidence that has been presented in support of the family grouping even for the core languages.

ALVEOLAR CONSONANT A consonant pronounced with the tip or blade of the tongue approaching or touching the alveolar ridge, which is on the roof of the mouth just behind the upper teeth.

ALVEOPALATAL CONSONANTS Consonants pronounced with the tip or blade of the tongue as the lower articulator and with the part of the hard palate that lies just behind the alveolar ridge as the upper articulator. English has four alveopalatal consonant phonemes: /č/, /ǰ/, /š/, and /ž/. In many languages (but not English), alveopalatal consonants also have the front of the tongue body (the part of the tongue just behind the blade) raised up near the hard palate. In this book PALATAL is distinguished from alveopalatal in that the latter, but not the former, have the tongue tip or blade as the lower articulator; however, since many linguists do not emphasize the phonetic distinction, some cited examples of sounds referred to as 'palatals' may actually be alveopalatals.

AMDO TIBETAN A variety of Tibetan, a member of the TIBETO-BURMAN branch of the SINO-TIBETAN language family; spoken in western China.

AMERICAN INDIAN PIDGIN ENGLISH (AIPE) An English-LEXIFIER pidgin originally spoken in the northeastern United States and probably linked directly or indirectly to later varieties of pidgin English spoken farther west in the United States. This pidgin is the source of 'Indian talk' in (possibly now defunct) children's Cowboys and Indians games, as in *Me like-um horse*: *me* is the regular AIPE first-person singular pronoun and the suffix *-um* indicates that the verb is transitive.

AN WORD ORDER Adjective–Noun word order, i.e. an adjective precedes the noun it modifies, as in English *These are boring books* (not *These are books boring*).

ANALYTIC MORPHOSYNTAX A grammatical system in which derivational and especially inflectional morphology is limited in quantity and scope. Most or all of the grammatical functions which, in morphologically rich languages, are expressed by means of inflection are expressed in analytic languages by syntactic means instead. English is an example. Except for the third-person singular present tense suffix *-s* (for example in *she sits*) and the irregular verb *be*, in which the person and number of the subject is marked, at least in part (in *am, are, is, was, were*), English lacks inflection for a verb's subject; it has tense marking, but no object marking; there are no noun cases, except for the genitive case indicated by *'s* (for example in *John's book*); and so forth. See under AGGLUTINATIVE and FLEXIONAL for other types of morphological systems.

ANGLO-ROMANI A bilingual mixed language spoken by Roms (Gypsies) in England; it consists of some Romani vocabulary combined with the grammar and much of the vocabulary of English.

APICAL CONSONANTS Consonants pronounced with the tip of the tongue as the lower articulator; or, more generally, consonants pronounced with either the tip or the blade of the tongue as the lower articulator (i.e. [+coronal] sounds, in classical distinctive feature terminology). Among the English apical consonants are the phonemes /t/, /d/, /s/, /z/, /l/, and /n/.

ARMENIAN An Indo-European language that comprises a one-language branch of the family; it is spoken primarily in Armenia.

ASPECT Temporal information about processes and events other than their location in time relative to the time of utterance, i.e. other than TENSE. Often, though not always, aspect is grammatically marked on the verb. In English, for instance, the distinction between *I was walking* and *I walked* is aspectual – durative or continuous vs. nondurative action. Perhaps the most common temporal distinction in the world's languages is the aspectual distinction between completed vs. noncompleted action (often called perfective vs. imperfective). Other common aspectual categories are durative (or continuous), iterative (repeated action), and inchoative (the beginning of an action).

ATHABASKAN LANGUAGES The major branch of the Athabaskan-Eyak language family (Eyak is a single language and is now extinct). Subgrouping within the family and boundaries between various pairs of languages are hard to determine, but there are about twenty-four northern Athabaskan languages in Alaska and western Canada, nine languages in Oregon and California, and two southern (Apachean) languages, Navajo and Apache, spoken primarily in New Mexico and Arizona. There are six major dialects of Apache, some of them quite divergent.

ATTESTATION OF A LANGUAGE Documentation – actual recorded data – of a language. For dead languages in particular, the date and nature of the attestation limits our knowledge of the language's lexicon and structure.

ATTRITION IN A DYING LANGUAGE The loss of vocabulary and structure, without any compensating additions in the form of borrowings or new creations. Often, maybe most frequently, the loss is not universal in a dying language, but is confined to the speech of SEMI-SPEAKERS who may well be living among fully fluent speakers who still have the structures that the semi-speakers lack. See Chapter 9.

AUSTRONESIAN LANGUAGES An enormous language family comprising hundreds of languages and covering most of the islands in the Pacific Ocean and large parts of the neighboring Asian mainland. Among the languages in the family are Malagasy (the westernmost Austronesian language, spoken on the island of Madagascar off the coast of Africa), MALAY, Indonesian and other languages of Indonesia, the languages of Polynesia (Hawaiian, Maori, Tahitian, etc.), and the indigenous languages of Formosa.

AYMARA A language spoken by over two million people in Peru, Bolivia, and (to a lesser extent) Argentina and Chile. Some scholars believe that it is related to QUE-CHUA, but others feel that the evidence available so far to support this hypothesis is inconclusive.

BALTIC LANGUAGES A subbranch of the INDO-EUROPEAN language family; together with Slavic languages, the three Baltic languages Lithuanian, Latvian, and the extinct language Prussian form the Balto-Slavic branch of Indo-European.

BANTU LANGUAGES Languages belonging to the Bantu subgroup of the Benue-Congo branch of the NIGER-CONGO language family; one of the most numerous and geographically widespread language groups of Africa. Among the Bantu languages mentioned in this book are Pare, Shambaa, Swahili, and Tumbuka.

BASIC VOCABULARY Vocabulary items that are likely to exist in every language in the world and are therefore less likely to be borrowed than nonbasic vocabulary items. (The term 'core vocabulary' is used sometimes to mean basic vocabulary, though for some authors 'core vocabulary' has a different meaning.) This is a vague concept – there is no solid theoretical basis to support it but it has proved useful as one kind of evidence for establishing GENETIC RELATIONSHIP among languages. As has often been demonstrated, not all items on standard lists of basic vocabulary do in fact occur in every language, and all the items on all the lists can be shown to have been borrowed somewhere, at some time. But in general the expectation that basic vocabulary is less often borrowed than nonbasic vocabulary is valid. Examples of basic vocabulary items are words for *mother, father, dog, water, cloud, sun, walk, run, swim, one, two, white*, and *black*. Typical nonbasic vocabulary items are *airplane, camera, philosophy*, and *church*. Probably the most-used standard lists of basic vocabulary items are the 100- and 200-word lists compiled in the mid-twentieth century by the linguist Morris Swadesh, who used them in his efforts to establish genetic relationships. See Chapter 4 for some discussion of basic and nonbasic vocabulary.

BASQUE An ISOLATE spoken in the Pyrenees Mountains of Spain and France. Most Basque speakers live in Spain; there are several distinctive dialects.

BAZAAR MALAY A MALAY-LEXIFIER pidgin spoken in the markets in Malaysia.

BCE Before the Christian Era; an alternative term for BC ('Before Christ').

BILINGUAL MIXED LANGUAGE A language created by bilinguals, with major components drawn from each of the two languages in a contact situation. It is distinguished from the other category of mixed languages, pidgins and creoles, by the fact that its creators are bilingual. As with pidgins and creoles, the major lexical and structural components of bilingual mixed languages cannot all be traced back primarily to a single source language; in contrast to pidgins and creoles, each major component of a bilingual mixed language can be traced back to a particular source language. The term 'bilingual mixed language' is misleading in that such a language might be composed of subsystems from more than two languages. Examples of bilingual mixed languages are MICHIF, MEDNYJ ALEUT, and MA'A. See Chapter 8.

BORROWING The type of interference that occurs when imperfect learning plays no role in the interference process – that is, when the people who introduce interference features into the receiving language are fluent speakers of the receiving language and know at least the relevant aspects of the source language. See Chapter 4 for explanation and examples.

BORROWING ROUTINE See CORRESPONDENCE RULE.

BORROWING SCALE A scale showing the types of interference features to be expected under conditions of increasing intensity of contact, from casual contact (only nonbasic vocabulary borrowed) to the most intense contact situations (borrowing of nonbasic vocabulary, some basic vocabulary, and structural features of all kinds). The predictions of the borrowing scale can be violated, however, especially when the languages in contact are typologically very similar (less TYPOLOGICAL DISTANCE). See Chapter 4.

BUIN A non-Austronesian language spoken by about 17,000 people in Papua New Guinea. One dialect of Buin is UISAI.

BULGARIAN A South SLAVIC language spoken primarily in Bulgaria, where it is the official language.

BUNDLE OF ISOGLOSSES Dialect features that have the same (or very similar) geographical distributions. (See under ISOGLOSS for further discussion.) An example of bundled isoglosses is the set of lines drawn across most of German-speaking territory, separating High German dialects in the south from Low German dialects in the north; this bundle separates into a fan-like array of isoglosses near the Rhine River in western Germany.

BURUSHASKI A language of India (northwestern Kashmir) and Pakistan; a genetic ISOLATE.

CALQUE A type of interference in which word or sentence structure is transferred without actual morphemes; sometimes called a loan translation. A calque is typically a morpheme-by-morpheme translation of a word from another language, as in German *über-setzen* 'translate' (literally 'across-set') from Latin *trans-* 'across' *-lat-* 'carry'. See Chapter 6, under Mechanism 4, 'Negotiation'.

CAMEROONIAN PIDGIN ENGLISH An English-LEXIFIER pidgin spoken in Cameroon and on the island Fernando Po; also called West African Pidgin English. According to Smith (1995: 342), about two million people speak it as a second language.

CAPE VERDE CREOLE A Portuguese-LEXIFIER creole spoken in the Cape Verde Islands in the Atlantic Ocean off the coast of West Africa; also called Crioulo.

CASE A means of expressing syntactic relations between words in a sentence, especially by morphological marking on noun phrases. Compare, for instance, German *Ich sah den Mann* 'I saw the man' (literally 'I.NOMINATIVE saw the.MASCULINE.sg.ACCUSATIVE man' and *Der Mann sah mich* 'The man saw me' (lit. 'the.MASCULINE.sg.NOMINATIVE saw me.ACCUSATIVE'), where accusative marks the object noun phrase and nominative is used for the subject noun phrase. Other common cases are the genitive, typically the case of a possessor (as in Russian *kniga Ivan-a* 'John's book', lit. 'book.NOMINATIVE.sg John-GENITIVE.sg'), instrumental (as in Serbian *putujem avtobus-om* 'I travel by bus', lit. 'I.travel bus-INSTRUMENTAL.sg'), and various locative cases ('in', 'onto', 'out of', etc.).

CAUCASIAN LANGUAGES Languages spoken in the Caucasus Mountains. This is a geographical designation, not a language family; Caucasian languages belong to at least three different language families. The best-established and most-studied family in the region is Kartvelian, or South Caucasian, whose most prominent member is Georgian.

CAUSATIVE A verb construction that involves x causing y to do something. Typically (though by no means always), a causative construction has an affix added to the verb, adding an extra actor to the verb's set of arguments (actor, patient, etc.). For instance, the English predicate *is thick* in *The soup is thick* is noncausative, but *She thickened the soup (with flour)* has a causative verb *thicken*; compare also noncausative *sit* and causative *set* ('cause to sit'), or *fall* and *fell* as in *He felled the tree* ('caused the tree to fall').

CE Christian Era; an alternative term for AD ('Anno Domini', literally 'year of the Lord').

CELTIC LANGUAGES A branch of the Indo-European language family. Celtic was originally spoken in continental Europe, but after Gaulish became extinct (eliminated by the spread of Latin and its descendent Romance languages) all the remaining Celtic languages were spoken in the British Isles: Irish GAELIC, Scottish Gaelic, Welsh, Cornish (extinct since the late eighteenth century), and Manx (now extinct). The one Celtic language that is now spoken on mainland Europe is Breton (spoken in Brittany, a region of France); the ancestors of Breton speakers migrated to what is now Brittany in the fifth century CE, from the Celtic-speaking region of southern England.

CENTRAL VOWEL In an articulatory analysis of vowel sounds, the front-to-back dimension is divided into three basic categories, front, central, and back, according to the position of the body of the tongue in vowel space. The most common central vowel phoneme by far in the world's languages is /a/, a low central unrounded vowel, as in the English word *father*. The second most common central vowel is the mid-central vowel called schwa; it is the first vowel in the English word *about* and the last vowel in *sofa*.

CHIMAKUAN LANGUAGES A two-language Native American language family whose member languages are, or were, spoken in the state of Washington in the United States. Quileute has been extinct for some decades; Chimakum is probably also dead by now.

CHINESE A group of closely related languages which, though mutually unintelligible, are usually called 'dialects'; they comprise the Sinitic branch of the SINO-TIBETAN language family.

CHINESE PIDGIN ENGLISH An English-LEXIFIER pidgin, now extinct, that developed in Canton as a trade pidgin and was used between speakers of English and different Chinese languages along the China coast; according to some accounts, the pidgin was also used among the Chinese themselves, and the Chinese-to-Chinese version was said not to have been understood (much less spoken) by English speakers.

CHINESE PIDGIN RUSSIAN A Russian-LEXIFIER trade pidgin used in the Russian–Chinese trade, especially in the border town of Kyakhta, south of Lake Baikal. Speakers of this pidgin may have included speakers of Mongolic, Turkic, and/or Uralic languages as well as Russian and Chinese speakers; it is also said to have been used among Chinese speakers alone, that is, between speakers of different Chinese languages.

CHINOOK JARGON A Lower Chinook-LEXIFIER trade pidgin that was spoken in the Pacific Northwest of North America, primarily in what is now Oregon, Washington, and British Columbia, though it spread as far south as northern California and north into Alaska during the late nineteenth century; the language also takes some lexicon, including several basic vocabulary items, from the NOOTKA JARGON, and by the late nineteenth century it had acquired numerous words from French and English. The pidgin probably arose among the powerful Lower Chinook speakers and their slaves and trading partners before white contact, but it was spread far beyond its early region after whites arrived. It is now seriously endangered, but vigorous revitalization efforts are under way. See Chapter 7.

CHIPAYA (or URU-CHIPAYA) A language spoken in Bolivia. Its speakers were formerly bilingual mainly in Aymara, and the language has many Aymara loanwords and possibly (though not demonstrably) some structural interference from Aymara; currently they are mainly bilingual in Spanish. Various genetic links to other languages have been proposed for Chipaya (e.g. Arawakan and less plausibly Mayan), but none is generally accepted.

CHUKCHI A member of the Chukotko-Kamchatkan language family, all of whose members are spoken in northeastern Siberia in Russia. The other members of the family are Alutor, Kerek, Koryak, and Itelmen. All of them are endangered.

CLICKS Speech sounds formed in the mouth with a closure at the back of the mouth and a second closure farther forward; the forward closure is released with a loud popping sound (a click) on an ingoing airstream. Clicks are found as regular speech sounds primarily in southern Africa, in KHOISAN languages and as interference features in Zulu and a few other southern Bantu languages. Although they hardly occur as regular phonemes elsewhere, clicks are very common as 'para-linguistic' sounds, vocal but not regular speech sounds. Examples in English are the kissing sound (made by suction from a bilabial stop closure), the tongue-tip sound often spelled *tsk-tsk*, and the clucking sound that is sometimes used to urge a horse to start moving.

CODE ALTERNATION A mechanism of interference in which bilinguals use one of their languages in one set of environments and the other language in a largely different set of environments (so that CODE-SWITCHING is minimized or absent). See Chapter 6, Mechanism 2.

CODE-MIXING A term sometimes used for switching from one language to another within a single sentence (intrasentential switching). See CODE-SWITCHING.

CODE-SWITCHING The use of material from two (or more) languages by a single speaker with the same people in the same conversation. As used in this book, the term includes both switches from one language to another at sentence boundaries (intersentential switching) and switches within a single sentence (intrasentential switching); the latter is sometimes called CODE-MIXING. See especially Chapter 6, Mechanism 1.

COGNATES Forms that are descended from the same proto-language form in related (sister) languages. Examples are easy to find in (for instance) English and German, both descendants of Proto-Germanic: *to* and *zu*, *ten* and *zehn*, *house* and *Haus*, *hound* and *Hund*, *eight* and *acht*, *night* and *Nacht*, and so forth.

COMPARATIVE METHOD The most valuable method in the field of historical linguistics; the main methodology by means of which genetic linguistic relationships are established and unattested parent languages (PROTO-LANGUAGES) of language families are reconstructed. The Comparative Method dates from the 1870s in essentially its modern form. It provides us with a window on prehistory by enabling us to reconstruct sizable portions of proto-language lexicon, phonology, and morphology, and to a lesser extent syntax as well; in this way it greatly expands our ability to examine language changes over considerable time depths.

CONTACT-INDUCED LANGUAGE CHANGE Any linguistic change that would have been less likely to occur outside a particular contact situation. See the beginning of Chapter 4 for a discussion of this definition.

CONTACT LANGUAGE Any new language that arises in a contact situation. Linguistically, a contact language is identifiable by the fact that its lexicon and grammatical structures cannot all be traced back primarily to the same source language; they are therefore MIXED LANGUAGES. See Chapters 7 and 8.

CONVERGENCE A process through which two or more languages in contact change to become more like each other – especially when both or all of the languages change. The term is not usually used to designate unidirectional changes, except (sometimes) when one language changes very extensively to become more like another. The term is not normally used for ordinary borrowing in which a language takes on a scattering of structural features from another language. But it is often used to refer to changes in (or changes that create) LINGUISTIC AREAS, especially where the sources of particular areal features cannot be discovered. See Chapter 4 for discussion of convergence, and Chapter 5 for discussion of problems with establishing sources for areal features.

COOK, CAPTAIN JAMES A famous English navigator and explorer (1728–79).

CORRESPONDENCE RULE A phonological generalization drawn by people who are bilingual in two languages that are closely related and thus share much of their vocabularies. The generalization is of the form 'Your language has *x* where my language has *y*', and the rule is applied to nativize the phonology of loanwords. The notion may also be applicable to certain cases of nonphonological correspondence. See Chapter 6. This notion is similar to what has been called a 'borrowing routine' (Heath 1989).

CREOLE LANGUAGE A mixed language that is the native language of a speech community. Like PIDGINS, creoles develop in contact situations that typically involve more than two languages; also like pidgins, they typically draw their lexicon, but not their grammar, primarily from a single language, the LEXIFIER language. Some creoles arise as nativized pidgins, some arise abruptly with no pidgin stage, and others arise gradually, with or without a pidgin stage. Crucially, the creators of a creole (unless it is a nativized pidgin) are not bilingual in their interlocutors' languages.

CRYSTALLIZATION OF CONTACT LANGUAGES A stage of development at which an emerging contact language has a grammar stable enough to have to be learned as such. Before crystallization, the creators of a contact-language-to-be produce highly variable ad-hoc utterances, without community-wide grammatical norms that have to be learned by would-be speakers. Calling the speech form a 'language' is justified only after crystallization.

CUNEIFORM WRITING An ancient Near Eastern writing system comprised of groupings of wedge-shaped marks pressed by a stylus into clay tablets. Cuneiform writing was developed by the Sumerians and passed on to successor ancient cultures, such as the Akkadians and the Hittites.

CUSHITIC LANGUAGES A branch of the AFRO-ASIATIC language family. Cushitic languages are spoken in Ethiopia and other African countries.

DAUGHTER LANGUAGE Any of the descendants of a single parent language. For example, the Romance languages are all daughters of Latin.

DELAWARE A two-language group belonging to the Eastern branch of the Algonquian language family, spoken aboriginally in the northeastern United States. Its member languages are Unami, also called Lenape (a few speakers in Oklahoma, United States), and Munsee (a few speakers in Ontario, Canada). The language is very seriously endangered.

DENTAL CONSONANT A consonant pronounced with the tip or blade of the tongue approaching or touching the teeth, usually the upper teeth.

DERIVATIONAL MORPHOLOGY Affixation or other morphological processes that form new words. Unlike INFLECTIONAL MORPHOLOGY, derivational morphology may (but need not) change the part of speech of the stem it is added to. Derivation is often less productive than inflection, and it usually occurs closer to the word's root than inflection does. Examples of derivational affixes in English are -*ness* in *goodness*, *un*- in *unhappy*, and -*en* in *thicken*. An example of a derivational process in Montana Salish is the diminutive formation consisting of a prefix ɫ and reduplication of the first consonant of the root, as in *ɫkkapí* 'a little coffee' (the root is *kapí*, borrowed from French).

DIACHRONIC ANALYSIS The analysis of (part of) a language as it changes over time; historical analysis. The other possibility is SYNCHRONIC ANALYSIS. Latin, for instance, can be studied either synchronically (e.g. a structural analysis of Classical Latin) or diachronically (e.g. the history of Latin as it changed from Proto-Indo-European to the earliest Latin inscriptions to the Vulgar Latin that ultimately diverged into the modern Romance languages).

DRAVIDIAN LANGUAGES A language family of South Asia. Most Dravidian languages are spoken in India, especially in the south (which is solidly Dravidian-speaking); one Dravidian language, Brahui, is spoken in Pakistan.

DUAL NUMBER A morphological and syntactic category that refers to two entities. Most languages that have a dual have three number categories in all, singular, dual, and plural; singular means one of anything, dual means two things, and plural means more than two things. The dual is not an exceedingly rare category, but it is not especially common in the world's languages. Most languages distinguish only singular and plural, and some languages do not even distinguish those very prominently in their morphology and syntax. A few of the world's languages, mainly languages belonging to the AUSTRONESIAN family, have more complicated systems of number categories, adding a TRIAL ('three things') or a paucal ('a few things') category. For instance, Tok Pisin, an English-vocabulary pidgin created in large part by speakers of Austronesian (specifically Melanesian) languages, has the following second-person pronouns: *yu* 'you' (singular), *yutupela* 'you (dual)', *yutripela* 'you (trial)', and *yupela* 'you (plural, i.e. more than three of you)'. The

English sources of the morphemes in these pronouns are, respectively, *you*, *two*, *fella* (*fellow*), and *three*.

EJECTIVES Glottalized oral consonants – specifically stops and affricates – that are pronounced on an outgoing airstream, i.e. with air that is first trapped in the space between an oral (e.g. a bilabial stop) closure and the closed glottis and then compressed by the raising of the larynx. The oral closure is released first, then the glottal closure.

ESTONIAN A language of eastern Europe belonging to the Finnic subbranch of the URALIC language family. Estonian is the official language of Estonia.

EWE A KWA language spoken in Ghana; very closely related to FON (in fact they may be dialects of the same language).

EXCLUSIVE 'WE' A first-person plural form – pronoun, verb, or any other form that includes the speaker (as all first-person forms do) and one or more others, but excludes the hearer. See INCLUSIVE 'WE' for further discussion and examples of languages in which this distinction is part of the grammar.

EXOGAMY Out-marriage, marrying someone from outside your own ethnic group.

FA D'AMBU A Portuguese-LEXIFIER creole spoken on the island of Annobón in Equatorial Guinea, West Africa; one of four Gulf of Guinea creoles.

FANAGALÓ A Zulu-LEXIFIER pidgin that arose (like several other Bantu-lexifier mining pidgins) in Europeans' African mines – specifically, in this case, in South Africa.

FINITE VERB A verb that can (but need not) be the main verb of a sentence and that typically (but not always) has INFLECTIONAL MORPHOLOGY marking the person and number of the verb's subject and also tense and/or aspect. As the hedges in this definition indicate, defining finiteness precisely is difficult, and in some languages there seems to be no distinction between finite and nonfinite verbs. But in other languages the distinction is important because nonfinite verbal forms, such as participles, gerunds, and infinitives, appear in SUBORDINATE constructions. See Chapter 8 for discussion of the formation of MEDNYJ ALEUT, in which the finite verb morphology comes from Russian but the nonfinite verb morphology, together with most of the rest of the language's structure, is Aleut in origin.

FINNISH A language of eastern Europe belonging to the Finnic subbranch of the URALIC language family. Finnish is one of the two official languages of Finland (Swedish is the other official language).

FLEXIONAL MORPHOLOGY A type of morphology, especially inflectional morphology, in which a single affix performs several different functions. An example is Latin noun inflection, in which a single suffix expresses case, number, and (in some instances) gender. See Chapter 4 for discussion of a partial change from flexional to AGGLUTINATIVE MORPHOLOGY in Asia Minor Greek as a result of interference from Turkish.

FON A KWA language spoken mainly in Benin; very closely related to EWE (in fact they may be dialects of the same language).

FOREIGNER TALK Speech addressed to foreigners who (in the opinion of the speaker) have limited skills in the speaker's language. Foreigner talk results from speakers' efforts to simplify their language in order to make it more intelligible to foreigners. Some of its typical features are a slow rate of speech, greater use of simple sentence structures than one finds in other stylistic registers of the language, and use of fewer and simpler words (as perceived by the speaker). Foreigner talk is one component of the development of at least some pidgins and creoles; see Chapter 7.

FRICATIVE A speech sound in which two articulators are brought close enough together for the airstream to be thrown into turbulence on its way out from the lungs; the turbulence in turn results in audible friction as the air passes through the narrowed passage. Examples of fricatives in English are the phonemes /f/, /z/, /š/, and /ð/.

FUNCTION WORDS Words that have grammatical rather than lexical meanings. If (as is very often the case) they are monomorphemic, they are GRAMMATICAL MORPHEMES. Typical categories of function words are prepositions and POSTPOSITIONS, negative particles, and tense/aspect/mood particles (in languages in which these functions are not expressed morphologically, e.g. by affixation).

GAELIC Scottish Gaelic is an endangered Celtic language spoken primarily in the Scottish highlands. It is very closely related to Irish Gaelic.

GENDER A system of noun classification that has grammatical relevance, usually in the morphology and/or the syntax. In most Indo-European languages, gender is biologically based – hence the term 'gender'. In French, for instance, masculine creatures have masculine gender and feminine creatures have feminine gender; but since all nouns belong to one of these two gender categories, each category also includes a great many inanimates as well as gendered animates. The most common type of grammatical relevance is AGREEMENT. Here are a few French examples in which the definite article 'the' agrees in gender with the following noun: *le chien* 'the male dog', *la chienne* 'the female dog', *le livre* 'the book', *la table* 'the table'. Some noun-classification systems have different semantic bases. In Swahili and other BANTU languages, for instance, the numerous noun classes include such categories as 'humans and animals', 'trees and plants', and 'abstract concepts'.

GENETIC RELATEDNESS Genetic relationship in languages refers to language families that arise through descent with modification from a parent language. Genetically related languages, or sister languages, are changed later forms of a single common parent language, which is called a PROTO-LANGUAGE if (as is almost invariably the case) it is not ATTESTED. Genetic relationship is established by means of the COMPARATIVE METHOD. (The term 'genetic' is metaphorical in this context: it does not imply a claim about inheritance of languages through biological genes.)

GERMANIC LANGUAGES A branch of the Indo-European language family. Before the Age of Exploration, Germanic languages were spoken in northwestern Europe; they are still spoken there, but English, Dutch, and German were carried through-out the world by explorers and colonizers. The Germanic languages of Scandinavia, primarily Swedish, Norwegian, and Danish, were also spread from their homeland by explorers, but not quite so far.

GLOTTALIZED STOPS (AND AFFRICATES) Oral stopped consonants pronounced on a glottalic airstream, i.e. with a closure of the glottis that is maintained until the release of an oral closure. There are two types of glottalized stops, EJECTIVES (pronounced on outgoing air) and IMPLOSIVES (pronounced on ingoing air).

GN WORD ORDER An ordering in which a genitive precedes its head noun, as in English *John's book* or Montana Salish *Mali sic'ms* 'Mary's blanket' (literally 'Mary her.blanket').

GRAMMATICAL MORPHEMES Morphemes with grammatical rather than lexical func-tions; they belong to closed classes (i.e. classes in which the member items can easily be listed, usually in rather short lists) and refer to such grammatical categories as case, person, number, tense, aspect, mood, possession, and locations (e.g. English third singular present tense *-s* in *walks*, plural *-s* in *horses*, genitive case *'s* in *children's*, and the locative prepositions *in* and *under*). Derivational morphemes that perform such functions as deriving nouns from verbs (e.g. English *-ment* in *adornment*) or from adjectives (e.g. *-ness* in *happiness*) and vice versa (*-ize* in *customize*, *-ish* in *childish*) are also grammatical morphemes.

GUARANÍ An indigenous language spoken by 95 percent of the population of Paraguay and in neighboring regions of Argentina and Brazil, about 4 million speakers in all as of 1991 (according to the 12th edition of the *Ethnologue* – Grimes 1992). It is a member of the Tupi-Guaraní language family.

GULLAH An English-LEXIFIER creole spoken in the southeastern United States, especially South Carolina and Georgia, on the coast and off-shore islands; also called Sea Island Creole English and Geechee; about 250,000 speakers, according to Smith (1995: 339). Gullah is spoken primarily in what was once England's Carolina colony (founded in 1670). Direct links between Gullah and African American Vernacular English have often been hypothesized but are still considered controversial, although the claim that AAVE has partly creole roots is now widely accepted.

HAMER (or HAMER-BANNA) A language of the (proposed) Omotic branch of the Afro-Asiatic language family, spoken in Ethiopia.

HAWAIIAN CREOLE ENGLISH An English-LEXIFIER creole spoken in Hawaii by (according to Smith 1995: 344) about 500,000 speakers, or roughly half of the islands' population. The language developed among plantation workers about a hundred years ago.

HAWAIIAN PIDGIN ENGLISH An English-LEXIFIER pidgin, now extinct or nearly so, spoken in Hawaii. There is historical evidence for the presence of an English-lexifier pidgin in Hawaii during the nineteenth century – Hawaii lay along Pacific trade routes taken by English whalers and other traders – but the few remaining elderly speakers (if any) came to Hawaii in the early twentieth century as part of the plantation work force.

HIRI MOTU A MOTU-LEXIFIER pidgin spoken primarily in and around Port Moresby, Papua New Guinea; also (formerly) called Police Motu because it was used by police officers whose work took them beyond Port Moresby to the interior of New Guinea. Hiri Motu is now one of the country's three official languages (with English and Tok Pisin), and according to Smith (1995: 360) it has 200,000 speakers. It arose through trade between the Motus and neighboring groups.

HUNGARIAN A language belonging to the Ugric branch of the Uralic language family; spoken primarily in Hungary.

HURRIAN An ancient Near Eastern language, now long extinct, that is not known to have been related to any other language.

IMPERSONAL CONSTRUCTIONS A construction with no notional subject, as in English sentences like *It's raining* and *There's dancing here on Saturday nights.*

IMPLOSIVES Glottalized oral stop consonants that are pronounced on an ingoing airstream – specifically, air that is trapped between an oral closure (e.g. a bilabial stop) and the closed glottis and then reduced in pressure by the lowering of the larynx. Either the oral closure is released first or the oral and glottal closures are released virtually simultaneously; in the second instance, the vocal cords generally begin vibrating at once, so that the implosive stop sounds voiced.

INCLUSIVE 'WE' A nonsingular (usually plural) first-person pronoun, verb, or any other form that includes the hearer as well as the speaker. All first-person forms include the speaker, of course; but only some include the hearer. If I say *We're going to the movies tonight, better get your coat*, obviously the hearer is included (inclusive 'we'). If I say *We're not taking you along to the movies tonight*, obviously the hearer is excluded (EXCLUSIVE 'WE'). English has only one set of first-person plural forms, and the hearer has to infer from the context (with the possibility of misunderstanding!) whether the speaker intends an inclusive or an exclusive 'we'; but some languages, like the Wakashan language Kwakwala and the Dravidian language KANNADA, make the distinction explicitly, typically in 'we' pronouns and in verb forms.

INDIC LANGUAGES (also called Indo-Aryan languages) A subbranch of the Indo-European language family; together with IRANIAN, Indic forms the Indo-Iranian branch of Indo-European. Indic languages are spoken primarily in India, but they are also widely spoken by immigrants in other parts of Asia and in Africa, the Pacific, the Caribbean, and elsewhere. Among the Indic languages mentioned in this book are Hindi (one of the two official languages of India), Urdu (the official language of Pakistan), Marathi, Bengali, Shina, Assamese, and Romani.

INDO-EUROPEAN The name of a very large and widespread language family that includes (among other languages) English and the other Germanic languages, Latin and its daughters the Romance languages, Greek, Russian and the other Slavic languages, Gaelic and the other Celtic languages, Albanian, Armenian, Hindi and other Indic languages together with Persian and other Iranian languages, and the long-extinct ancient languages Hittite and Tocharian.

INFLECTIONAL MORPHOLOGY Affixation or other morphological processes that alter words, typically to express syntactic relations between words in a sentence. Inflection never changes the part of speech of the stem it is added to, it is highly productive and in fact usually obligatory in the appropriate contexts, and it usually occurs farther from the stem than DERIVATIONAL MORPHOLOGY does. Among the most common inflectional categories are CASE and number on nouns and TENSE, ASPECT, MOOD, and person and number of subjects and/or objects on verbs. AGREEMENT morphology is inflectional. Examples of inflection in English (there are not many) are the past tense suffix *-ed* in *walked*, the comparative and superlative suffixes *-er* and *-est* in the adjectives *safer* and *safest*, and the third-person singular subject, present tense suffix *-s* in *walks*. An example of a more complex inflectional process is the Ancient Greek first-person singular perfect aspect form *le-loip-a* 'I have left' from the verb *leip-* 'leave', with a reduplicative prefix *le-* that repeats the first root consonant and a vowel change in the root from *e* to *o*, both marking the perfect aspect, plus the special perfect aspect first-person singular subject suffix *-a*.

INTERFERENCE Contact-induced change that involves the importation of material and/or structures from one language into another language, whether by borrowing or by shift-induced interference. All interference is contact-induced change, but not all contact-induced change is interference: see the beginning of Chapter 4 for discussion of contact-induced changes that do not involve interference.

INTONATION Pitch variation at the clause or sentence level. Meaningful intonation patterns, such as yes/no question intonation in an English sentence like *You're going home?* vs. declarative nonquestion intonation in *You're going home* contrasts with distinctive pitch variation at the word or syllable level, as in a TONE language like Chinese or Thai. Different tones distinguish word meanings; different intonations distinguish sentence meanings. Probably all languages have distinctive intonation patterns. At least some languages also have characteristic nondistinctive intonation patterns, such as the falling pitch that is typical of Finnish sentences (as spoken by native speakers). See Chapter 6 (under Mechanism 2, code alternation) for an example of a contact-induced change in intonation.

INUIT An Eskimo language spoken in Alaska, Canada, and Greenland, sometimes called Inuit-Inupiaq (Inuit, the speakers' own name, means 'people'; Inupiaq means 'real, genuine person': Campbell 1997: 394, citing Goddard 1984: 7), and often called Inuktitut in eastern Canada (Campbell 1997: 394). Inuit is a one-language subbranch of the Eskimo branch of the Eskimo-Aleut language family. The other subbranch of Eskimo comprises the three YUPIK languages. See Chapter 7 for mention of two Inuit-LEXIFIER pidgins.

IRANIAN LANGUAGES A subbranch of the Indo-European language family; together with INDIC, Iranian forms the Indo-Iranian branch of Indo-European. Iranian languages are spoken primarily in Pakistan, Iran, Afghanistan, and parts of the former Soviet Union. The most important Iranian language politically is Farsi, or Standard Persian, the official language of Iran. Other Iranian languages mentioned in this book are Baluchi, Ossetic, and Tajik.

ISOGLOSS A line on a map, typically a dialect map, that surrounds the area in which a particular feature is found. The notion is sometimes extended to a map of a linguistic area, so that the term can also be used for a line that surrounds the languages that share a particular feature due to contact-induced change. When two or more dialect features have nearly the same distribution in space, their isoglosses are said to bundle (i.e. they form a BUNDLE OF ISOGLOSSES).

ISOLATE A language that has no known relatives; thus, a one-language family.

JAMAICAN CREOLE ENGLISH An English-LEXIFIER creole spoken in Jamaica in the Caribbean; also called Patwa; about 2,250,000 speakers, according to Smith (1995: 341).

KANNADA A DRAVIDIAN language spoken in Karnataka and other states of southern India; according to the *Ethnologue* (13th edition), it had about 33.6 million speakers (44 million if second-language speakers are included) as of 1994.

KARELIAN A member of the Finnic branch of the Uralic language family, spoken primarily in the Republic of Karelia in northern Russia. The language is endangered; most or all of its speakers are bilingual in Russian.

KHOISAN LANGUAGES A group of languages which were for some time believed to constitute a single language family, but which are now considered to form two or more different language families. They share the phonological property of CLICK phonemes and are therefore sometimes called 'click languages'. Most languages in the family are spoken in southern Africa, but two of them, Sandawe and Hadza, are spoken farther north, in Tanzania.

KITÚBA A Kikongo-LEXIFIER creole spoken in Zaire and the Republic of the Congo in western Africa. See Chapter 7.

KRIYOL An English-LEXIFIER creole spoken in the Australian states of Queensland, Western Australia, and especially the Northern Territory. According to Smith (1995: 345), it arose as a nativized pidgin, from Northern Territory Pidgin English, around 1908, and currently has about 10,000 native speakers.

KUTENAI A Native American language spoken in northwestern Montana, Idaho, and southern British Columbia; it is not known to be related to any other language. It is gravely endangered.

KWA LANGUAGES A subbranch of the Atlantic-Congo branch of the Niger-Congo language family, comprising languages spoken in West Africa, primarily in Ghana, Benin, Togo, and Ivory Coast. Among the Kwa languages are EWE and FON.

LAHA A BILINGUAL MIXED LANGUAGE spoken in the central Moluccas, Indonesia; its lexicon is native, but its grammar is borrowed from Ambonese MALAY. Both Laha (before its grammar was replaced) and Malay are AUSTRONESIAN languages, but they are not especially closely related.

LANGUAGE FAMILY One or more languages that are descended from – that is, changed later forms of – a single parent language. The notion of descent with modification, as applied to languages, does not mean that the entire lexicon and structure of a language must come from a single parent language; rather, it means that at least most of the basic vocabulary and most of the structure of the language come from a single parent language. (Since 'most of' is vague, it isn't surprising that there are some borderline cases: see Chapters 7 and 8 for discussion of fuzzy boundaries between languages that belong to language families and languages that do not.)

One large and well-known language family is INDO-EUROPEAN; a much smaller example is the one-language family BASQUE (a linguistic ISOLATE). Among the numerous other language families that are mentioned in this book are AFRO-ASIATIC, ALGONQUIAN, AUSTRONESIAN, DRAVIDIAN, SAHAPTIAN (just two languages), SALISHAN, SINO-TIBETAN, URALIC, WAKASHAN, and the isolates BURUSHASKI, HURRIAN, KUTENAI, and SUMERIAN.

LANGUAGE SHIFT The shift, by a person or a group, from the native language to a second language. Bilingualism is not language shift, though shifts usually involve a period in which individuals or whole groups are bilingual; a shift occurs when people give up their native language and start speaking another group's language instead.

LATERAL CONSONANT A consonant pronounced with the tongue blocking passage through the center of the mouth, but not at both sides, so that the air passes out along the side(s) of the tongue. The most common lateral consonant by far in the world's languages is an /l/ like the English sound in *like*, but there are others as well. Most of the languages of the Pacific Northwest linguistic area, for instance, also have two or more lateral OBSTRUENTS, a lateral AFFRICATE and a voiceless lateral FRICATIVE.

LEXICAL MORPHEMES Morphemes belonging to the basic word classes nouns, verbs, and (if they exist in the language as separate word classes) adjectives and adverbs. By contrast, GRAMMATICAL MORPHEMES refer to such grammatical categories as case, number, gender, tense, aspect, mood, possession, and location (as with prepositions).

LEXIFIER LANGUAGE The language that provides most or all of the vocabulary of a pidgin or creole language. See Chapter 7.

LINGUA FRANCA A language of wider communication – that is, a language that is used for communication between groups who do not speak each other's languages, as well as between native speakers (if any) of the lingua franca and other groups (see Chapters 2 and 7). A lingua franca is by definition learned as a second language by at least some of its speakers. Some lingua francas are also learned as a first language by some speakers; the most obvious example is English, a (or the) worldwide modern lingua franca. Others are spoken solely as second languages; these are PIDGIN languages (see Chapter 7). The term 'lingua franca' literally means 'Frankish language', that is, the language of the Franks, a German-speaking people who also gave their name to France after invading and conquering it in the early Middle Ages. The original Lingua Franca was spoken in the eastern Mediterranean at the time of the Crusades.

LINGUA FRANCA An Italian-LEXIFIER pidgin (also called Sabir), with some French and many Spanish words in its western varieties. It arose sometime during the Crusades, which were carried out from 1095 CE until the mid-fifteenth century, and was used for intergroup communication in the lands bordering the Mediterranean Sea. Some scholars believe that it underlies at least some later pidgins and creoles elsewhere as well. See Chapter 7 (especially under the MONOGENESIS HYPOTHESIS of pidgin/creole genesis).

LINGUISTIC AREA (also called a Sprachbund) A geographical region containing a group of three or more languages that share some structural features as a result of contact rather than as a result of accident or inheritance from a common ancestor. See Chapter 5.

LIT. Literally – a notation that precedes a literal translation of a word or sentence.

LIVONIAN A gravely endangered Uralic language closely related to Finnish and Estonian, spoken in Latvia.

LOANWORD A word borrowed from another language.

Luo A language belonging to the Nilotic branch of the proposed Nilo-Saharan language family; spoken primarily in Kenya (*ca.* 3.2 million speakers as of 1994, according to the *Ethnologue*).

Maʾa A BILINGUAL MIXED LANGUAGE spoken in the Usambara Mountains of northeastern Tanzania. Ma'a lexicon is about half Bantu and half Cushitic, though it also has a sizable number of Masai words; its grammar is almost entirely Bantu. See Chapter 6 (under Mechanism 7) and Chapter 8.

MACANESE CREOLE PORTUGUESE A Portuguese-LEXIFIER creole spoken in Macao and Hong Kong.

MALAY An Austronesian language spoken primarily in Malaysia (*ca.* 10 million speakers, including second-language speakers) and Indonesia (*ca.* 10 million), but also in Brunei, Singapore, Thailand, and elsewhere.

MAORI A language belonging to the Polynesian branch of Oceanic, which is in turn a branch of the AUSTRONESIAN language family. Maori is spoken in New Zealand, where the Maori people settled sometime before 1000 CE.

MARATHI A language spoken in Maharashtra and neighboring states in India, with nearly 65 million speakers as of 1994; it belongs to the INDIC subbranch of the Indo-European language family.

MARIDI ARABIC An Arabic-LEXIFIER pidgin (or possibly a prepidgin rather than a fully CRYSTALLIZED pidgin language) attested briefly in a report by the medieval Arab geographer Abu 'Ubayd al-Bakrī (*ca.* 1028–94 CE), in his book *Roads and Kingdoms* (in Arabic, *al-Masālik wa 'l-Mamālik*). See Chapter 7.

MARKEDNESS A distinction between linguistic features that derives from universal tendencies of occurrence. The basic claim of markedness theory is that UNMARKED features are easier to learn than marked features (or even, in some versions of the theory, innate). According to the theory, this difference in learnability is reflected primarily in typological distribution (unmarked features are more common than marked features in languages of the world) and age of learning in first-language acquisition (children learn unmarked features before marked features); other ways of determining markedness have also been explored. So, for instance, the presence of nasal consonants in a phonological system is considered unmarked and the absence of nasals is considered marked, because almost all languages have at least one nasal stop; a sibilant fricative phoneme /s/ is considered unmarked by comparison to an interdental fricative phoneme /θ/ because /s/ is much more common crosslinguistically than /θ/ and is usually learned earlier in those languages that have both (e.g. English).

MEDNYJ ALEUT A BILINGUAL MIXED LANGUAGE that arose on Mednyj ('Copper') Island off the east coast of Russia. Its lexicon and structure are primarily Aleut, with some lexical and structural borrowing from Russian, but the entire FINITE VERB morphology is from Russian.

METATHESIS A process by which the order of two or more elements in a word is reversed. A familiar example that does not involve language contact is English *aks*, which arose by metathesis from *ask* about a thousand years ago, in Old English times. See Chapter 6 (under Mechanism 7) for an example involving language contact, from Lambayeque Quechua (Peru).

MICHIF A BILINGUAL MIXED LANGUAGE spoken by some Métis (mixed-blood) people on the Turtle Mountain reservation in North Dakota and in scattered locations in the western United States and Canada. It is comprised of French noun phrases combined with Cree verb phrases and sentence structure, but most of its current speakers know neither French nor Cree. See Chapter 8.

MID VOWEL A vowel pronounced with the tongue body in the middle of the vertical dimension in vowel space. An example is English /e/ in *bet* (lower than the vowel of *bit* and higher than the vowel of *bat*) or /o/ in *boat* (lower than the vowel of *boot* and *book*, higher than the vowel of *bark*). See VOWEL HEIGHT.

MISKITO COAST CREOLE ENGLISH An English-LEXIFIER creole spoken on Nicaragua's Atlantic coast. According to Smith (1995: 341), the language arose after plantations were established, bringing in African slaves, in the early eighteenth century; it has about 40,000 native speakers.

MIXED LANGUAGE A language that did not arise primarily through descent with modification from a single earlier language. There are two types of mixed languages (or CONTACT LANGUAGES). On the one hand there are PIDGINS and CREOLES, which typically (though not always) derive their lexicon from one language but their grammar from no single language; on the other hand there are BILINGUAL MIXED LANGUAGES, which derive one or more grammatical subsystems (including their lexicon) from one language and the other grammatical subsystem(s) from another language. By definition, mixed languages are not members of any language family and thus belong in no family tree except perhaps as the ancestor of a language family: a contact language has no single parent language in the historical linguist's usual sense, but it may have descendants. This of course does not mean that mixed languages have no historical links to their source languages; the definition derives from the technical historical linguistic analysis of language history, as developed over the past century and a half and elaborated on the basis of a rich body of data from language families all over the world (but most importantly Indo-European, the focus of most of the research). See Chapters 7 and 8.

MONGOLIC LANGUAGES A family of languages spoken in Mongolia, China, Russia, and several countries (besides Russia) that formerly comprised the Soviet Union. Mongolic is one of the three main branches of the proposed (but controversial) ALTAIC language family.

MONOGENESIS HYPOTHESIS OF PIDGIN/CREOLE GENESIS The hypothesis that some or (in the strong version) all known PIDGINS and CREOLES are descendants of the medieval LINGUA FRANCA via RELEXIFICATION.

MONTANA SALISH (also called Flathead, mainly by whites) A Native American language belonging to the Southern Interior branch of the SALISHAN language family, of which it is the westernmost member. The language is gravely endangered, with at most sixty fluent native speakers remaining as of 2000.

MOOD A verbal category that expresses the speaker's attitude toward an event or action. The neutral mood is the indicative, as in English *John went home*; this is opposed in English to the imperative mood, as in *Go home!*, and to the conditional or subjunctive mood, as in English *If John would go home . . .* or *If John were to go home . . . .* Some analysts prefer to restrict the category of mood to morphological verbal distinctions, as in Finnish *hän tulee* 'he is coming' (indicative mood) vs. *hän tullee* 'he may be coming' (potential mood).

MORPHEME The smallest unit of grammatical analysis. Some morphemes are LEXICAL, with independent semantic content, e.g. *dog* or *run*. Others are GRAMMATICAL, with little or no independent semantic content; examples are the *-s* of *dogs*, the *un-* of *unhappy*, and the English infinitive marker *to* in *to run*.

MORPHOLOGY Word-structure – roots and affixes (prefixes before the root, suffixes after the root, and sometimes infixes within the root), shape-altering morphological processes such as reduplication (repeating part of a root or stem), and also compounds (combinations of two or more roots).

MORPHOSYNTAX The combined morphology and syntax (sentence structure) of a language. In contact-induced change, one language's syntax may influence another language's morphology, or vice versa, so it is often useful to consider these two grammatical subsystems as a unified set of structures.

MOTU An Austronesian language spoken in Port Moresby, Papua New Guinea. It is the LEXIFIER language of the pidgin HIRI MOTU.

MUNDA LANGUAGES A subbranch of the Austro-Asiatic language family. Munda languages are spoken in India and are related to Austro-Asiatic languages of Southeast Asia, for instance Vietnamese and Khmer (Cambodian).

NA WORD ORDER Noun–Adjective word order, i.e. an adjective follows the noun it modifies, as if English had *books green* instead of *green books*.

NAGAMESE A pidgin spoken in Nagaland in India, in the states of Assam, Maharashtra, and perhaps also in Myanmar (former Burma). The LEXIFIER language is Assamese, an INDIC language closely related to Bengali. The pidgin is also called Naga Pidgin; and, because it has some native speakers (in ethnically mixed marriages), it is sometimes called Naga Creole Assamese. Most speakers of Nagamese are native speakers of Naga languages, a group of about twenty-nine languages of the TIBETO-BURMAN branch of the SINO-TIBETAN language family.

NATIVIZATION The phonological adaptation of a borrowed word to fit receiving-language structure. For instance, the name of the famous German composer *Bach* is often nativized by English speakers, with a velar stop /k/ replacing the German velar fricative /x/; other English speakers, often (but not always) those who know some German retain the German fricative. See Chapter 6 (under Mechanism 1) for the use of nativization as a criterion – unfortunately an unreliable one – for distinguishing code-switching from borrowing.

NDYUKA An English-LEXIFIER creole spoken by descendants of African slaves who escaped from coastal plantations into the interior of Suriname in northern South America; Ndyuka is one of the so-called 'Bushnegro' languages (and societies). The language probably dates from the eighteenth century. According to Huttar and Velantie (1997: 101), there are currently about 16,000 Ndyukas. Ndyuka is one of the two components of the NDYUKA-TRIO PIDGIN. See Chapter 7.

NDYUKA-TRIO PIDGIN A two-language trade pidgin spoken by native speakers of the English-LEXIFIER creole NDYUKA and the Cariban language TRIO in east-central Suriname in northern South America. See Chapter 7.

'NEGOTIATION' IN CONTACT-INDUCED CHANGE A mechanism of change whereby speakers change their language to approximate what they believe to be the patterns of another language or dialect. See Chapter 6, Mechanism 4.

NEZ PERCÉ A Sahaptian language spoken in northern Idaho, United States. It is gravely endangered.

NEZ PERCÉ JARGON A Nez Percé-LEXIFIER pidgin (possibly not fully crystallized as a language) that was used for communication between the Nez Percé people and their slaves in northern Idaho.

NG WORD ORDER A genitive (possessor) follows its head noun, as if English had *book John's* instead of *John's book* (and compare the postnoun phrasal English genitive *of John* in *the book of John*).

NGBANDI A member of the UBANGIAN (or Eastern) branch of the NIGER-CONGO language family, spoken in the Central African Republic.

NIGER-CONGO LANGUAGE FAMILY The most widespread African language family, with hundreds of member languages distributed throughout most of sub-Saharan Africa. Among the branches of Niger-Congo are Benue-Congo, which includes the BANTU languages, and UBANGIAN (or Eastern).

NOOTKA (NUUCHAN'ULH) A WAKASHAN language spoken on Vancouver Island in southwestern British Columbia.

NOOTKA JARGON A Nootka-LEXIFIER trade pidgin that was used in the late eighteenth and the early nineteenth centuries for communication between European explorers and traders and NOOTKA speakers on Vancouver Island in what is now southwestern British Columbia. Some vocabulary of this pidgin was transmitted to the more widespread pidgin CHINOOK JARGON by white intermediaries.

NORSE Any of the older languages and dialects of the North Germanic subgroup of the Germanic branch of the Indo-European language family. The two best-known dialects of Norse during the Viking period were Norwegian (western Norse) and Danish–Swedish (eastern Norse).

OBSTRUENT A consonant sound pronounced with major obstruction in the vocal tract; the three categories of obstruents are oral (nonnasal) stops, AFFRICATES, and FRICATIVES. The airstream is completely blocked for a short time in an oral stop or affricate, and forced through a narrow passage in a fricative. Obstruents form a natural class of sounds for many phonological processes.

OBVIATIVE The less prominent third person in an ALGONQUIAN sentence containing two third-person forms. Sometimes called the 'fourth person', the obviative is used to refer to a third person (he, she, it, they) that is less important in the particular context than another third person. So, for instance, imagine a story about someone named Mildred. In an Algonquian translation of the sentence *Mildred saw Bill on the street, and she greeted him*, *Bill* and *him* would be marked as obviative, because the main character is Mildred, not Bill.

PALATAL CONSONANTS Consonants pronounced with the front of the tongue body (not the tip or blade of the tongue, but the part of the tongue behind the blade) raised up to or near the hard palate. The only English consonant in this articulation category is the phoneme /y/, as in the word *yes*, but some languages have palatal stops, fricatives, and other consonant types. In this book palatal is distinguished from ALVEOPALATAL in that the latter, but not the former, has the tongue tip or blade as the lower articulator; in addition alveopalatal sounds are generally pronounced just behind the alveolar ridge, while palatals may be pronounced farther back along the roof of the mouth. However, since many linguists do not emphasize this phonetic distinction, some cited examples of sounds referred to in the literature (and therefore in this book) as 'palatals' may actually be alveopalatals.

PASSIVE FAMILIARITY AS A MECHANISM OF CONTACT-INDUCED LANGUAGE CHANGE A process of contact-induced change in which a speaker acquires a feature from a language that s/he understands (at least to some extent) but does not speak. See Chapter 6, Mechanism 3.

PENNSYLVANIAN GERMAN A dialect of German spoken by Amish, Mennonite, and other religious and also secular groups, descendants of nineteenth-century immigrants from Germany. The language is sometimes called Pennsylvania Dutch, but it is German, not Dutch. It is now an endangered language.

PIDGIN DELAWARE A seventeenth-century Delaware-lexicon trade pidgin that was spoken on and near the Middle Atlantic coast of the United States by DELAWARE Indians (a two-language group whose member languages are Munsee and Unami) and speakers of Dutch, Swedish, and English. See Chapter 7.

PIDGIN GERMAN A German-LEXIFIER pidgin once spoken in parts of what is now Papua New Guinea (then owned in part by Germany) in the late nineteenth and early twentieth centuries. (Other varieties of pidginized German were once spoken in Africa.)

PIDGIN INUIT (PIDGIN ESKIMO) A trade pidgin formerly used along the coasts of Alaska and northern Canada between European whalers and Inuits.

PIDGIN LANGUAGE A mixed language that arises in a contact situation involving (typically) more than two linguistic groups; the groups have no shared language – that is, no single language is widely known among the groups in contact – and they need to communicate regularly, but for limited purposes, such as trade; they do not learn each other's languages. The new pidgin's vocabulary typically (but not always) comes from one of the languages in contact; the grammar does not come from that language or from any other single language. New pidgins have less linguistic material than nonpidgin languages: fewer words, fewer stylistic resources, less morphology than the source languages, and so forth. See Chapter 7.

PITCAIRNESE An English-LEXIFIER creole spoken on the island of Pitcairn in the southern Pacific Ocean. The language developed among the nine *Bounty* mutineers and their nineteen mostly TAHITIAN-speaking companions, who settled on Pitcairn Island after the mutiny in 1790, and then among their children. See Chapter 7.

POLYNESIAN LANGUAGES A subbranch of the huge Austronesian language family. All the Polynesian languages are spoken on islands in the Pacific Ocean, ranging from New Zealand in the south to Hawaii in the north (but not very far north). Among the many languages in this group are Maori (New Zealand), Hawaiian, Tahitian, and Samoan.

POSTPOSITION A particle that has the same function as a preposition (like English *of*, *with*, *from*, or *in*) but occurs after the noun instead of before it, as if English *in this book* were ordered *this book in*. Prepositions are typical of languages with SVO word order (like English), while postpositions are typical of languages with SOV word order.

PROTO-LANGUAGE The parent language of a language family, that is, the language from which all the other languages in the family are descended. By definition, proto-languages are not ATTESTED – they are not documented at all, but were rather prehistoric in the literal sense: before recorded history. The descendants of a proto-language are GENETICALLY RELATED; genetically related languages, or sister languages, are changed later forms of their single common parent language (see also the COMPARATIVE METHOD).

QUECHUA The most widely spoken indigenous language in the Americas, with up to 8 million speakers in all, in Peru (2.5 million), Bolivia (3 million), Argentina (1 million), Ecuador (1.5 million), and Chile. There are numerous different Quechua dialects, some of them different enough to be considered separate languages, though the designation 'Quechua' is retained for the entire set. Quechua was the language of the Inca empire that was destroyed by the Spanish invaders. It is sometimes thought to be related to AYMARA, the second most widely spoken indigenous language in the Americas, but this genetic grouping remains controversial.

RECEIVING LANGUAGE The language that receives an interference feature. See SOURCE LANGUAGE.

RELATIVE CLAUSE A clause that modifies a noun. In some languages (typically, for instance, in Indo-European languages), relative clauses contain a relative pronoun, e.g. English *who* in *I met the man who married Dorothy*.

RELEXIFICATION The replacement of most or all of one language's lexicon by the vocabulary of another language. Certain theories of pidgin and creole genesis posit relexification as a, or the, main process involved; see Chapter 7. Sometimes a process of relexification produces a bilingual mixed language; see Chapter 8.

RETROFLEX CONSONANTS Consonants pronounced with the tip of the tongue approaching or touching the hard palate behind the ALVEOLAR ridge; or, in a narrower sense, consonants pronounced with the tongue tip curled under so that the underside of the tip approaches or touches the roof of the mouth on or behind the alveolar ridge. Retroflex consonants occur in numerous languages as distinct phonemes; they are especially common in the languages of South Asia (see Chapter 5).

ROMANCE LANGUAGES The languages descended from ('daughter languages' of) Latin, among them Catalan, French, Galician, Italian, Portuguese, Provençal, Romansh, Rumanian, and Spanish.

ROMANI An INDIC language whose speakers – the Roms, commonly known as Gypsies – left India around 1000 CE and spread northward and westward into Asia Minor, North Africa, and Europe. European varieties of Romani have undergone a great deal of contact-induced change, sometimes to the point where almost nothing is left of the original Indic structure; and in a few cases, such as ANGLO-ROMANI, the Roms have shifted entirely to a European language but retained some of their original Romani vocabulary to form a mixed secret language.

ROMANSH A ROMANCE language, one of the four national languages of Switzerland. It is now an endangered language.

RUMANIAN A ROMANCE language; the official language of Rumania. Some varieties of Rumanian are spoken in other Balkan countries – Bulgaria, Macedonia, Greece, and Croatia. Rumanian is one of the core languages of the Balkan Sprachbund.

RUSSENORSK A trade pidgin of far northern Europe; its lexicon is (or was) drawn from both Russian and Norwegian, with some words also from Sámi (Lapp), Low German, and Swedish.

SAHAPTIAN LANGUAGES A family of two languages, Nez Percé and Sahaptin, spoken in Oregon, Idaho, and Washington in the northwestern United States. The languages have several dialects each, some of them with alternative names (e.g. Yakima instead of Northwest Sahaptin). Both languages are endangered.

SALISHAN LANGUAGES A family of about twenty-one Native American languages spoken in Washington, British Columbia, Oregon, Idaho, and Montana.

SANGO A NGBANDI-LEXIFIER creole (nativized from a former pidgin) spoken by nearly the entire population, at least as a second language, in the Central African Republic: it has about three million speakers and is the country's second official language (after French). See Chapter 7.

SÃO TOMENSE CREOLE A Portuguese-LEXIFIER creole spoken on the island of São Tomé, off the coast of West Africa in the Gulf of Guinea.

SARAMACCAN A mixed-lexicon creole, with (according to one estimate) about 50 percent English words and about 35 percent Portuguese words (the rest of the vocabulary comes from African languages, in particular the Bantu language Kikongo and the Kwa languages Ewe, Fon, and Twi). It is spoken in Suriname in northern South America; it emerged in the late seventeenth century and currently has about 25,000 speakers. See Chapter 7.

SCANDINAVIAN LANGUAGES Languages spoken in Scandinavia. Most are North Germanic languages (Swedish, Norwegian, Danish, Faroese, and the outlier language Icelandic), but Finnish and Sámi (Lapp), both members of the Finnic branch of the Uralic language family, are also spoken in Scandinavia – Finnish in Finland and Sámi in northern Finland, Sweden, and Norway.

SEMI-SPEAKER Someone who does not speak a particular language with full fluency because he or she never learned it correctly. Typically, semi-speakers are the last speakers of a language that is undergoing attrition as it gradually dies – the children of some of the last fully fluent speakers. (By fluency, in this context, I mean full control of the language's traditional structure, rather than the ability to speak the language quickly and confidently: some semi-speakers are able to carry on conversations with ease and confidence.)

SEMITIC LANGUAGES A branch of the AFRO-ASIATIC language family. Semitic languages are spoken on the Arabian Peninsula, in North Africa, and in parts of sub-Saharan Africa, and they were prominent among ancient Near Eastern languages. The best-known Semitic languages are Arabic and Hebrew, but there are numerous other modern and ancient Semitic languages. Akkadian, for example, was one of the earliest known written languages (but it has been extinct for several thousand years, and it left no direct descendants).

SERBO-CROATIAN A South Slavic language spoken primarily in Serbia, Croatia, Montenegro, and Bosnia. With the recent split of the former Yugoslavia into several different countries, Serbian and Croatian are now considered by their speakers to be different languages rather than dialects of the same language; immediately before the political split, however, the varieties of the standard language spoken in Serbia and Croatia were fully mutually intelligible. The language has numerous quite divergent nonstandard dialects, not all of which are mutually intelligible with each other or with the standard varieties. Some Serbian dialects belong to the Balkan linguistic area; see Chapter 5.

SHIFT-INDUCED INTERFERENCE The type of interference that occurs when imperfect learning plays a role in the interference process. See Chapter 4 for explanation and examples.

SINGULATIVE NUMBER A number category specifying one of a group of things; the singulative is used to designate one individual for things that are usually thought of in groups. So, for instance, a language with a singulative category might use it to refer to one fish out of a school of fish, or to one leaf in a tree's foliage. A specific context for the use of a singulative form 'leaf' might be this: *I was raking leaves, and there was a particularly beautiful red leaf that caught my attention.* The singulative is a very rare category in the world's languages.

SINO-TIBETAN LANGUAGE FAMILY A very large language family of Asia, consisting of two branches, Sinitic (CHINESE languages) and TIBETO-BURMAN.

SLAVIC LANGUAGES One of the two subbranches of the Balto-Slavic branch of the INDO-EUROPEAN language family. Slavic languages, spoken primarily in eastern Europe, are further subdivided into East Slavic (Russian and its closest relatives), South Slavic (Serbian, Croatian, Macedonian, Bulgarian, and Slovenian), and West Slavic (Czech, Slovak, Polish, and their closest relatives).

SOURCE LANGUAGE FOR AN INTERFERENCE FEATURE The language from which the interference feature comes, or (if the source-language feature is not identical to the receiving-language innovation) the language that provided the feature from which the interference feature was derived. Compare RECEIVING LANGUAGE.

SOV WORD ORDER A sentential word order pattern in which the subject precedes the object and the object precedes the verb.

SPLIT INFINITIVE An infinitive construction in which the infinitive marker *to* and the verb are separated by another word or phrase, usually an adverb. Compare the prescribed standard sentence *He intends never to go there* with the proscribed nonstandard sentence *He intends to never go there*, in which the two words of the infinitive construction *to go* are split by the adverb *never*. See Chapter 6 (under Mechanism 7).

SPRACHBUND See LINGUISTIC AREA.

SRANAN An English-LEXIFIER creole spoken in Suriname in northern South America. See Chapter 7.

SRI LANKA CREOLE PORTUGUESE A Portuguese-LEXIFIER creole spoken in Sri Lanka.

SUBA A Bantu language spoken in Kenya. It is an endangered language.

SUBORDINATE CLAUSE A clause that is part of a sentence and is an adjunct to some part of speech elsewhere in the sentence. English examples of subordinate clauses are *when we were Elvis fans* and *because you didn't go to that movie* in the sentences *We used to go to Graceland when we were Elvis fans* and *You missed seeing Alice because you didn't go to that movie.* These two clauses are marked as subordinate by their subordinate conjunctions (*when, because*); comparable sentences with coordination rather than subordination would be *We were Elvis fans and we used to go to Graceland* and *You didn't go to that movie and so you missed seeing Alice.* Many languages, like English, have subordinate clauses with FINITE VERBS and subordinate conjunctions; but in many other languages subordination is expressed by nonfinite verb forms (e.g. participles). This distinction is a major typological split among languages, and a common locus of contact-induced change.

SUBSTRATUM INTERFERENCE The most common term in the literature for what is called SHIFT-INDUCED INTERFERENCE in this book. The term 'substratum' refers to the fact that a shifting population is often socially, economically, and/or politically subordinate to the people whose language they are shifting to. But substratum interference is flawed as a general label for interference in which imperfect learning plays a role, both because not all shifting groups are subordinate and because imperfect learning has similar effects regardless of the sociopolitical relations of the speaker groups.

SUMERIAN The language of the ancient Near Eastern kingdom of Sumer; it is now long extinct and is not known to have been related to any other language.

SVO WORD ORDER A sentential word order pattern in which the subject precedes the verb and the verb precedes the object.

SYNCHRONIC ANALYSIS The analysis of (part of) a language at a particular time, either the present or some past period; the opposite of DIACHRONIC ANALYSIS, which is the study of a language as it changes over time. Latin, for instance, can be studied either synchronically (e.g. a structural analysis of Classical Latin) or diachronically (e.g. the history of Latin as it changed from the earliest inscriptions to the Vulgar Latin that ultimately diverged into the modern Romance languages).

SYNTAX The structure of sentences. The syntactic features that are most commonly affected by contact-induced change (to judge by the examples in the literature) are sentential word order and other word-order features, the syntax of SUBORDINA-TION, and RELATIVE CLAUSE formation.

TABOO In linguistics, a prohibition on using certain words or expressions because of particular social factors. Verbal taboo is a widespread phenomenon throughout the world. In American culture, for instance, the strongest taboos are against the classic 'four-letter Anglo-Saxon words', terms for excretory functions, and derogatory terms for racial and ethnic minority groups. In some cultures the name of a person who has died is taboo, so that the name, and also other words that sound like or contain meaningful parts of the name, are taboo; in other cultures a son-in-law is not permitted to utter his mother-in-law's name; and so forth. Sometimes phonological distortion can make a tabooed word 'respectable'; see the example of click phonemes acquired by Zulu and some other southern Bantu languages from Khoisan languages in Chapter 4, under effects of contact-induced change on the system.

TAHITIAN A Polynesian language, of the Oceanic branch of the AUSTRONESIAN language family, spoken in Tahiti in the South Pacific. Tahitian speakers were (with English) one of the two groups who created the English-LEXIFIER creole PITCAIRNESE.

TAMIL A DRAVIDIAN language spoken in Tamil Nadu and other states of southern India, as well as in Sri Lanka, Singapore, Fiji, South Africa and elsewhere; according to the *Ethnologue* (12th edition), it had at least 48 million speakers (66 million if second-language speakers are included) as of 1991.

TARGET LANGUAGE (TL) The language that is being learned as a second (or third, or fourth, or . . .) language – that is, the language that is 'targeted' by learners. The notion is especially important for shift-induced interference (see Chapters 4, 5, and 6) and for some theories of pidgin/creole genesis (Chapter 7).

TELUGU A DRAVIDIAN language spoken primarily in southern India in Andhra Pradesh and neighboring states (*ca.* 66.3 million speakers as of 1994).

TENSE Temporal information about processes and events that locates them in time relative to the time of utterance – present (occurring right now), past, and future. In English, for instance, *I'm walking* is present tense (continuous aspect), *I walked* is past, and *I will walk* is future. See ASPECT for the other major type of time indication.

THAI A member of the Tai-Kadai language family of southeast Asia. There are several Tai languages in addition to Thai itself. Wider genetic affiliations have been proposed for Tai-Kadai, perhaps most prominently Austronesian; but none of the hypotheses is generally accepted, at least not on the basis of the currently available evidence.

TIBETO-BURMAN LANGUAGES The larger branch in terms of number of languages, but not number of speakers, of the SINO-TIBETAN language family. Tibeto-Burman languages are spoken in Tibet, western China, Nepal, Bhutan, northern India, Pakistan, Burma, and, to a lesser extent, Bangladesh, Thailand, Laos, and Vietnam. (The other branch of the family, Sinitic, comprises CHINESE languages.)

TL_2 The version of a target language (TL) spoken by members of a group that is shifting to that language but not learning it perfectly. The linguistic features of the TL_2 that distinguish it from the original TL are a combination of features carried over from the shifting group's original native language and features that replace TL features that they have not learned. See Chapter 4 (under imperfect learning), and Chapter 6 (under Mechanism 3, passive familiarity, and Mechanism 4, 'negotiation').

TL_3 The version of a target language (TL) spoken by an integrated community consisting of a group that shifted to the TL and also (the descendants of) the original TL speakers. The linguistic features of the TL_3 will be a subset of TL_2 features that distinguish the TL_2 from the original TL. See Chapter 4 (under imperfect learning) and Chapter 6 (under Mechanisms 3 and 4).

TOK PISIN A English-LEXIFIER creole language spoken in Papua New Guinea. Tok Pisin is one of the country's three official languages; the other two are English and a Motu-LEXIFIER pidgin called HIRI MOTU. The substrate languages that contributed to the emerging grammar of Tok Pisin were members of the Melanesian group of the AUSTRONESIAN language family, e.g. Tolai. See Chapter 7.

TONE Distinctive pitch variation at the word or syllable level – that is, pitch differences that distinguish word meanings. Many, possibly most, of the world's languages are tone languages; examples are CHINESE, ZULU and most other BANTU languages, THAI, and Vietnamese. Tone contrasts with INTONATION, which usually refers to meaningful patterns of pitch variation that distinguish clause or sentence meanings.

TONGAN The language of the Tonga Islands in the Pacific. Tongan is a member of the Polynesian branch of Oceanic, which is in turn a branch of the AUSTRONESIAN language family.

TRIAL NUMBER A number category referring to three of anything. Languages with trial number also have singular, dual, and plural categories; in such languages, plural means 'more than three things'. Some AUSTRONESIAN languages have a TRIAL ('three things') number. Also, Tok Pisin, an English-vocabulary pidgin created in large part by speakers of Austronesian (specifically Melanesian) languages, has a trial category, as in the following set of second-person pronouns: *yu* 'you' (singular), *yutupela* 'you (dual)', *yutripela* 'you (trial)', and *yupela* 'you (plural, i.e. more than three of you)'. The English sources of the morphemes in these pronouns are, respectively, *you, two, fella* (*fellow*), and *three*. (See also under DUAL.)

TRIO A language of the Cariban family, spoken on and near the Tapanahoni River and the Curuni River in southern Suriname in northern South America; one component of the NDYUKA-TRIO PIDGIN. Huttar and Velantie report their current population as about 1,200 in two villages (1997: 101). See Chapter 7.

TURKIC LANGUAGES A family of languages spoken primarily in western and northern Asia. Turkic may be a member of a larger family known as ALTAIC, though the validity of the larger family is still in doubt. The best-known Turkic language is Turkish, the official language of Turkey. Other Turkic languages mentioned in this book are Azeri and Uzbek.

TYPOLOGICAL DISTANCE The degree of diversity between two languages in their structural categories and in their ways of expressing those categories. Typological distance is not something that can be precisely measured, in part because categories may match in some aspects but not in others. But it is nevertheless a useful linguistic predictor of kinds of interference. See Chapter 4.

TYPOLOGY A subfield of linguistics that focuses on the distribution of structural linguistic features in languages of the world. It is typological investigation that provides evidence for such statements as these: only a very few languages of the world lack nasal consonants; suffixes are more numerous than prefixes cross-linguistically; and SOV word order is more common crosslinguistically than VSO word order.

UBANGIAN LANGUAGES A branch of the NIGER-CONGO language family; the branch is also called Eastern. The languages are spoken in the Central African Republic and neighboring countries. One Ubangian language is NGBANDI, the LEXIFIER language of the pidgin-turned-creole SANGO.

UISAI A dialect of the non-Austronesian language Buin, spoken in southern Bougainville, an island in Papua New Guinea. Uisai has about 1,500 speakers. It is noteworthy especially for its reversal of gender AGREEMENT markers; see Chapter 6 (under Mechanism 7).

UNMARKED LINGUISTIC FEATURES Features that are more easily learned by speakers of any language, according to theories of universal MARKEDNESS. Because they are easier to learn, universally unmarked features are predicted to occur more commonly in languages of the world and to be learned earlier than marked features by children acquiring their first language.

URALIC LANGUAGES A family of languages spoken around the Baltic Sea, in the interior of Russia, and in Hungary; the family is named for the Ural Mountains of Russia, the region that is thought to have been the original homeland of the parent language of this family. Three Uralic languages are official national languages: Finnish in Finland, Estonian in Estonia, and Hungarian in Hungary.

URDU An Indic language spoken by Muslims in Pakistan and India. Urdu is either extremely closely related to, or a dialect of the same language as, Hindi, one of the official languages of India; but whereas Urdu speakers have borrowed many words from Classical Arabic, the language of the sacred text of Islam, Hindi speakers have borrowed instead from Sanskrit, the sacred language of the Hindu religion.

VOCOID A speech sound pronounced with no significant obstruction, either partial or total, in the vocal tract. Probably all vowel phonemes in the world's languages are vocoids; the most common vocoid consonants are [w], [y], and [h]. There are other vocoid consonants too; for instance, the English phoneme /r/ is phonetically a vocoid.

VOWEL HARMONY A phonological process in which the vowel(s) of one or more syllables assimilate phonetically to some other vowel(s) in the same word. The assimilation need not be, and usually is not, complete; more often, vowels assimilate (become more similar) in just one or two features, such as front/back or rounded/unrounded or tense/lax or high/nonhigh.

VOWEL HEIGHT In an articulatory analysis of vowel sounds, the vertical dimension is divided into three basic categories, high, mid, and low, according to the position of the body of the tongue in vowel space in the mouth. High vowel phonemes are exemplified, roughly, by English /i/ in *seat* and /u/ in *suit*, mid vowel phonemes by English /e/ in *set* and /o/ in *horse*, and low vowel phonemes by English /a/ in *father*.

VSO WORD ORDER A sentential word order pattern in which the verb precedes the subject and the subject precedes the object.

WAKASHAN LANGUAGES A family of six languages of the Pacific Northwest. Kwak-wala (sometimes called Kwakiutl), Heiltsuk (sometimes called Bella Bella), and Haisla are spoken on mainland British Columbia; NOOTKA and Nitinaht are spoken on Vancouver Island, British Columbia; and Makah is spoken in Washington. All the languages in the family are seriously endangered.

WEST AFRICAN PIDGIN ENGLISH See CAMEROONIAN PIDGIN ENGLISH.

WEST AFRICAN PIDGIN PORTUGUESE A poorly attested early Portuguese-LEXIFIER pidgin spoken in West Africa. This language, which was spoken roughly from the fifteenth to the eighteenth centuries, is presumed to be at least in part the ancestor of later Portuguese-based pidgins and creoles, such as CAPE VERDE CREOLE (Crioulo) and SÃO TOMENSE CREOLE.

YIDDISH An offshoot of medieval German which probably had its origins between 1000 and 1200 CE. Yiddish has mostly Germanic vocabulary and grammar, but it also has many loanwords from Hebrew and considerable grammatical interference from Slavic languages, especially Polish and Russian. It is an endangered language, but in the late twentieth century it was still spoken by about two million people in Israel, the United States, and elsewhere.

YUPIK One of the two major subbranches of the Eskimo branch of the Eskimo-Aleut language family. Yupik comprises at least three different languages: Siberian Yupik (St. Lawrence Island, Alaska, and far eastern Russia), Central Alaskan Yupik (southwestern Alaska), and Alutiiq or Pacific Yupik (several other areas of Alaska) (see Kaplan 1992). The other subbranch of Eskimo has just one member language, INUIT.

ZULU A BANTU language spoken in South Africa. Zulu has acquired CLICK phonemes from KHOISAN languages, and it is the LEXIFIER language for the mining pidgin FANAGALÓ.

References

Adamson, Lilian, and Norval Smith, 'Sranan' (in Arends, Muysken, and Smith 1995: 219–32).

Allen, Robert B., Jr., 'The present situation of local languages in an Indonesian region' (paper presented at the Workshop on Language Maintenance and Death: Reports from the Field and Strategies for the Millennium, University of Illinois, July, 1999).

Alleyne, Mervyn C., *Comparative Afro-American: An Historical-Comparative Study of English-Based Afro-American Dialects of the New World* (Ann Arbor: Karoma, 1980).

Andersen, Peggy, 'Living tradition: Northwest schools help keep tribal tongues alive' (an Associated Press story in the *Missoulian*, Missoula, MT, 5 June 2000).

Andersen, Roger, ed., *Pidginization and Creolization as Language Acquisition* (Rowley, MA: Newbury House, 1983).

Ansaldo, Umberto, and Stephen Matthews, 'The Minnan substrate and creolization in Baba Malay' (Stockholm University and University of Hong Kong, MS., *ca.* 1999).

Aoki, Haruo, 'The East Plateau linguistic diffusion area' (in *International Journal of American Linguistics* 41 (1975): 183–99).

Apte, Mahadev, 'Multilingualism in India and its socio-political implications: an overview' (in O'Barr and O'Barr 1976).

Arends, Jacques, and Adrienne Bruyn, 'Gradualist and developmental hypotheses' (in Arends, Muysken, and Smith 1995: 111–20).

Arends, Jacques, Silvia Kouwenberg, and Norval Smith, 'Theories focusing on the non-European input' (in Arends, Muysken, and Smith 1995: 99–109).

Arends, Jacques, Pieter Muysken, and Norval Smith, eds., *Pidgins and Creoles: An Introduction* (Amsterdam: John Benjamins, 1995).

Ariste, Paul, 'Die Wege des Aussterbens zweier finnisch-ugrischer Sprachen' [The routes to death of two Finno-Ugric languages] (in *Monda Lingvo-Problemo* 2 (1970): 77–82).

Asher, R. E., ed., *The Encyclopedia of Language and Linguistics* (Oxford: Pergamon Press, 1994).

Backus, Albert Marie, *Two in One: Bilingual Speech of Turkish Immigrants in the Netherlands* (Tilburg: Tilburg University Press, 1996).

Bailey, Charles-James N., 'Linguistic change, naturalness, mixture, and structural principles' (in *Papiere zur Linguistik* 16 (1977): 6–73).

Baker, Philip, 'Pidginization, creolization and *français approximatif*: review article on *Des îles, des hommes, des langues*, by Robert Chaudenson' (in *Journal of Pidgin and Creole Languages* 11 (1996): 95–121).

Baker, Philip, and Chris Corne, *Isle de France Creole: Affinities and Origins* (Ann Arbor: Karoma, 1982).

Bakker, Peter, *'A language of our own': The Genesis of Michif, the Mixed Cree-French Language of the Canadian Métis* (Oxford: Oxford University Press, 1997).

Bakker, Peter, and Maarten Mous, eds., *Mixed Languages: 15 Case Studies in Language Intertwining* (Amsterdam: Institute for Functional Research into Language and Language Use (IFOTT), 1994).

Bakker, Peter, and Pieter Muysken, 'Mixed languages and language intertwining' (in Arends, Muysken, and Smith 1995: 41–52).

Bakker, Peter, and Robert A. Papen, 'Michif: a mixed language based on Cree and French' (in Thomason 1997: 295–363).

Bakker, Peter, Marike Post, and Hein van der Voort, 'TMA particles and auxiliaries' (in Arends, Muysken, and Smith 1995: 247–58).

Bakker, Peter, Norval Smith, and Tonjes Veenstra, 'Saramaccan' (in Arends, Muysken, and Smith 1995: 165–78).

al-Bakrī, Abu 'Ubayd, *al-Masālik wa 'l-Mamālik* [Roads and kingdoms] (1068; the work exists in several manuscripts).

Barringer, Felicity, 'Tongues that dance with wolves: saving America's Native languages' (in the *New York Times*, 8 January 1991).

Baugh, Albert C., *A History of the English Language* (2nd edn., New York: Appleton-Century-Crofts, 1957).

Bavin, Edith L., 'Some lexical and morphological changes in Warlpiri' (in Dorian 1989: 267–86).

Bereznak, Catherine, *The Pueblo region as a linguistic area* (Baton Rouge: Louisiana State University dissertation, 1996).

Bergsland, Knut, *Aleut Dictionary / Unangam tunudgusii: An Unabridged Lexicon of the Aleutian, Pribilof, and Commander Islands Aleut Language* (Fairbanks: Alaska Native Language Center, University of Alaska, 1994).

den Besten, Hans, Pieter Muysken, and Norval Smith, 'Theories focusing on the European input' (in Arends, Muysken, and Smith 1995: 87–98).

Bickerton, Derek, *Roots of Language* (Ann Arbor: Karoma, 1981).

Bickerton, Derek, 'The language bioprogram hypothesis' (in *Behavioral and Brain Sciences* 7 (1984): 173–221).

Bickerton, Derek, 'On the supposed "gradualness" of creole development' (in *Journal of Pidgin and Creole Languages* 6: 25–58, 1991).

Bickerton, Derek, 'How to acquire language without positive evidence: what acquisitionists can learn from creoles' (in Michel DeGraff, ed., *Language Creation and Language Change: Creolization, Diachrony, and Development*, Cambridge, MA: MIT Press, 1999: 49–74).

Bloomfield, Leonard, 'Literate and illiterate speech' (in *American Speech* 2/10 (1927): 432–9; reprinted in Charles F. Hockett, ed., *A Leonard Bloomfield Anthology*, Bloomington: Indiana University Press, 1970: 147–56).

Boas, Franz, 'Introduction' (in Franz Boas, ed., *The Handbook of American Indian Languages*, pt. 1, Washington, DC: Government Printing Office, 1911: 5–83).

Boretzky, Norbert, *Kreolsprachen, Substrate und Sprachwandel* (Wiesbaden: Otto Harrassowitz, 1983).

Boretzky, Norbert, 'Sind Ziegeunersprachen Kreols?' [Are Gypsy languages creoles?] (in Norbert Boretzky, Werner Enninger, and Thomas Stolz, eds., *Akten des 1. Essener Kolloquiums über 'Kreolsprachen und Sprachkontakte' vom 26.1.1985 an der Universität Essen*, Bochum: Studienverlag Dr. N. Brockmeyer, 1985: 43–70).

Boretzky, Norbert, and Birgit Igla, 'Romani mixed dialects' (in Bakker and Mous 1994: 35–68).

Borg, Alexander, *Cypriot Arabic: A Historical and Comparative Investigation into the Phonology and Morphology of the Arabic Vernacular Spoken by the Maronites of Kormakiti Village in the Kyrenia District of North-Western Cyprus* (Stuttgart: F. Steiner Wiesbaden, 1985).

Bothne, T., *Kort Udsigt over det lutherske Kirkearbeide blandt Normændene i Amerika* [A short look at the Lutheran church work among the Norwegians in America] (Chicago; publisher unknown, 1898).

Bradley, David, review of Michael Noonan, with Ram Prasad Bhulanja, Jag Man Chhantyal, and William Pagliuca, *Chantyal Dictionary and Texts* (Berlin: Mouton de Gruyter, 1999) (in *Anthropological Linguistics* 41 (1999): 388–9).

Bray, Denys de S., *Census of India, 1911*, vol. 4: *Baluchistan* (Calcutta: Superintendent Government Printing, India, 1913).

Brendemoen, Bernt, 'Pronominalsyntax in den türkischen Schwarzmeerdialekten – syntaktische Innovation oder Archaismus?' [Pronominal syntax in the Turkish Black Sea dialects – syntactic innovation or archaism?] (in Jens Peter Laut and Klaus Rohrborn, eds., *Sprach- und Kulturkontakte der türkischen Völker*, Wiesbaden: Harrassowitz, 1993: 51–73).

Brendemoen, Bernt, 'Turkish-Greek language contact on the eastern Black Sea coast: code-copying with or without a language shift?' (paper presented at the First International Symposium on Bilingualism, Vigo, Spain, 1997).

Brenzinger, Matthias, *Die sprachliche und kulturelle Stellung der Mbugu (Ma'a)* [The linguistic and cultural position of Mbugu (Ma'a)] (Cologne: University of Cologne M.A. thesis, 1987).

Brenzinger, Matthias, ed., *Language Death: Factual and Theoretical Explorations with Special Reference to East Africa* (Berlin: Mouton de Gruyter, 1992).

Bright, William, ed., *International Encyclopedia of Linguistics* (Oxford: Oxford University Press, 1992).

Broderick, George, *Language Death in the Isle of Man* (Tübingen: Niemeyer, 1999).

Calvet, Louis-Jean, *Language Wars and Linguistic Politics* (Oxford: Oxford University Press, 1998).

Camden, W. G., 'Parallels in structure of lexicon and syntax between New Hebrides Bislama and the South Santo language spoken at Tangoa' (paper presented at the International Conference on Pidgins and Creoles, Honolulu, 1975).

Campbell, Lyle, 'Areal linguistics and its implications for historical linguistic theory' (in Jacek Fisiak, ed., *Proceedings of the Sixth International Conference on Historical Linguistics*, Amsterdam: John Benjamins, 1985: 25–56).

Campbell, Lyle, 'Language death' (in Asher 1994, vol. 4: 1960–8).

Campbell, Lyle, 'Phonetics and phonology' (in Goebl *et al.* 1997: 98–104).

Campbell, Lyle, *American Indian Languages: The Historical Linguistics of Native America* (Oxford: Oxford University Press, 1997).

Campbell, Lyle, Terrence Kaufman, and Thomas C. Smith-Stark, 'Meso-America as a linguistic area' (*Language* 62 (1986): 530–70).

Campbell, Lyle, and Martha C. Muntzel, 'The structural consequences of language death' (in Dorian 1989: 181–96).

Chatterton, Percy, 'The origin and development of Police Motu' (in *Kivung* 3 (1970): 95–8).

Chaudenson, Robert, *Des îles, des hommes, des langues* [Islands, people, languages] (Paris: L'Harmattan, 1992).

Cifoletti, Guido, *La Lingua Franca Mediterranea* (Padua: Unipress, 1989).

Cluver, August, untitled comment (on the LINGUIST list 1068-4875, 5 March 1995).

Clyne, Michael, 'Multilingualism in Australia' (in *Annual Review of Applied Linguistics* 17 (1997): 191–203 (special issue on multilingualism, ed. William Grabe)).

van Coetsem, Frans, *Loan Phonology and the Two Transfer Types in Language Contact* (Dordrecht: Foris, 1988).

Collins, James T., 'Laha, a language of the Central Moluccas' (in *Indonesia Circle* 23 (1980): 3–19).

Comrie, Bernard, *The Languages of the Soviet Union* (Cambridge: Cambridge University Press, 1981).

Cooper, Robert L., ed., *Language Spread: Studies in Diffusion and Social Change* (Bloomington, IN, & Washington, DC: Indiana University Press and Center for Applied Linguistics, 1982).

Copland, B. D., 'A note on the origin of the Mbugu with a text' (in *Zeitschrift für Eingeborenen-Sprachen* 24 (1933–4): 241–5).

Coulmas, Florian, ed., *Perspectives on Language Contact and Language Policy* (*International Journal of the Sociology of Language* 86, 1990).

Court, Christopher, untitled posting (on the SEALTEACH list, 30 April 1998).

Crystal, David, *The Cambridge Encyclopedia of Language* (Cambridge: Cambridge University Press, 1987).

Csató, Éva Ágnes, 'Some typological properties of North-Western Karaim in areal perspectives' (in Norbert Boretzky, Werner Enninger, and Thomas Stolz, eds., *Areale, Kontakte, Dialekte: Sprache und ihre Dynamik in mehrsprachigen Situationen*, Bochum: Brockmeyer, 1996: 68–83).

Dahl, Östen, and Maria Koptjevskaja-Tamm, *Language Typology around the Baltic Sea: A Problem Inventory* (Papers from the Institute of Linguistics, University of Stockholm, 61, 1992).

Davis, Susannah, 'Legal regulation of language contact in Nebraska' (Pittsburgh: University of Pittsburgh, MS., 1998).

Dawkins, R. M., *Modern Greek in Asia Minor* (Cambridge University Press, 1916).

Dench, Alan, *Yingkarta* (Munich: LINCOM Europa, 1998).

Diamond, Jared, 'World of the living dead' (in *Natural History* 9/91 (1991): 30, 32–7).

Dorian, Nancy C., 'The fate of morphological complexity in language death: evidence from East Sutherland Gaelic' (in *Language* 54 (1978): 590–609).

Dorian, Nancy C., *Language Death: The Life Cycle of a Scottish Gaelic Dialect* (Philadelphia: University of Pennsylvania Press, 1981).

Dorian, Nancy C., ed., *Investigating Obsolescence: Studies in Language Contraction and Death* (Cambridge: Cambridge University Press, 1989).

Dorian, Nancy C., 'The study of language obsolescence: stages, surprises, challenges' (in *Langues et Linguistique/Languages and Linguistics: Revue Internationale de Linguistique* 3 (1999): 99–122).

Dorian, Nancy C., 'Linguistic and ethnographic fieldwork' (in Joshua A. Fishman, ed., *Handbook of Language and Ethnic Identity*, Oxford: Oxford University Press, 1999: 25–41).

Drapeau, Lynn, 'Michif replicated: the emergence of a mixed language in northern Quebec' (paper presented at the 10th International Conference on Historical Linguistics, Amsterdam).

Dressler, Wolfgang U., 'Language shift and language death – a protean challenge for the linguist' (in *Folia Linguistica* 15 (1981): 5–27).

Dressler, Wolfgang U., and Ruth Wodak-Leodolter, eds., *Language Death* (*International Journal of the Sociology of Language* 12, 1977).

Durie, Mark, and Malcolm Ross, eds., *The Comparative Method Reviewed: Regularity and Irregularity in Language Change* (Oxford: Oxford University Press, 1996).

Dutton, Tom, *Police Motu: iena sivarai* (Port Moresby: University of Papua New Guinea Press, 1985).

Dutton, Tom, 'Hiri Motu' (in Thomason 1997: 9–41).

Dutton, Tom, and H. A. Brown, 'Hiri Motu: the language itself' (in Stephan A. Wurm, ed., *New Guinea Area Languages and Language Study*, Canberra: Australian National University, 1977, vol. 3: 759–93).

Dutton, Tom, and Darrell T. Tryon, eds., *Language Contact and Change in the Austronesian World* (Berlin: Mouton de Gruyter, 1994).

Dwyer, Arienne, 'Dominant-language influence on serial verb constructions in Salar' (paper presented at the 1995 Linguistic Society of America Annual Meeting, New Orleans).

Edwards, John, *Multilingualism* (London and New York: Routledge, 1994; reprinted by Penguin Books, 1995).

Eliasson, Stig, 'English–Maori language contact: code-switching and the free-morpheme constraint' (in Rudolf Filipović and Maja Bratanić, eds., *Languages in Contact: Proceedings of the Symposium 16. 1 of the 12th International Congress of Anthropological and Ethnological Sciences, Zagreb, July 25–7, 1988*, Zagreb: Institute of Linguistics, Faculty of Philosophy, 1990: 33–49).

Eliasson, Stig, 'Grammatical and lexical switching in Maori-English "grasshopper speech"' (in *Papers from the Summer School on Code-Switching and Language Contact, 14–17 September, 1994, Ljouwert/Leeuwarden*, Friesland: Fryske Akademy, 1995: 45–57).

Eliasson, Stig, and Ernst Håkon Jahr, eds., *Language and its Ecology: Essays in Memory of Einar Haugen* (Berlin: Mouton de Gruyter, 1997).

Emeneau, Murray B., 'India as a linguistic area' (in *Language* 32 (1956): 3–16).

Emeneau, Murray B., *Brahui and Dravidian Comparative Grammar* (Berkeley: University of California Press, 1962).

Emeneau, Murray B., 'Bilingualism and structural borrowing' (in *Proceedings of the American Philosophical Society* 106 (1962): 430–42; reprinted in Emeneau 1980: 38–65).

Emeneau, Murray B., 'Dravidian and Indo-Aryan: the Indian linguistic area' (in André F. Sjoberg, ed., *Symposium on Dravidian Civilization*, Austin, TX, and New York: Jenkins Publishing Co. and Pemberton Press, 1971: 33–68; reprinted in Emeneau 1980: 167–96).

Emeneau, Murray B., *Language and Linguistic Area* (ed. Anwar Dil, Stanford: Stanford University Press, 1980).

Fenyvesi, Anna, 'Language contact and language death in an immigrant language: the case of Hungarian' (*University of Pittsburgh Working Papers in Linguistics* 3 (1995): 1–117).

Ferguson, Charles A., 'The Ethiopian language area' (in M. Lionel Bender, J. Donald Bowen, R. L. Cooper, and C. A. Ferguson, eds., *Language in Ethiopia*, London: Oxford University Press, 1976: 63–76).

Fishman, Joshua A., 'Who speaks what language to whom and when' (in *La Linguistique* 2 (1965): 67–88).

Fishman, Joshua A., *Reversing Language Shift: Theoretical and Empirical Foundations of Assistance to Threatened Languages* (Clevedon: Multilingual Matters, 1991).

Foley, William A., *The Papuan Languages of New Guinea* (Cambridge: Cambridge University Press, 1986).

Foley, William A., 'Language birth: the processes of pidginization and creolization' (in Frederick Newmeyer, ed., *Linguistics: The Cambridge Survey*, Cambridge: Cambridge University Press, 1988, vol. 4: 162–83).

Foster, Michael K., review of Silver and Miller 1997 (in *Anthropological Linguistics* 41 (1999): 396–400).

Friedrich, Paul, 'Language and politics in India' (in *Daedalus* 91 (1962): 543–59).

Gal, Susan, *Language Shift: Social Determinants of Linguistic Change in Bilingual Austria* (New York: Academic Press, 1979).

Gensler, Orin David, *A typological evaluation of Celtic/Hamito-Semitic syntactic parallels* (Berkeley: University of California dissertation, 1993).

Giles, Howard, *The Dynamics of Speech Accommodation* (*International Journal of the Sociology of Language* 46, 1984).

Givón, Talmy, 'Prolegomena to any sane creology' (in Hancock 1979: 3–35).

Goddard, Ives, 'Synonymy' (in David Damas, ed., *Arctic*, vol. 5 of *The Handbook of North American Indians*, ed. William C. Sturtevant, Washington, DC: Smithsonian Institution, 1984: 5–7.

Goddard, Ives, 'Pidgin Delaware' (in Thomason 1997: 43–98).

Godenzzi, Juan Carlos, 'Lengua y variacion sociolectal: el castellano en Puno' [Language and sociolectal variation: Castillian in Puno] (in Luis Enrique Lopez, ed., *Pesquisas en linguistica andina*, Lima: Consejo Nacional de Ciencia y Tecnologia-Universidad Nacional del Antiplano-GTZ, 1988).

Goebl, Hans, Peter H. Nelde, Zdeněk Starý, and Wolfgang Wölck, eds., *Kontaktlinguistik / Contact Linguistics / Linguistique de contact: ein internationales Handbuch zeitgenössischer Forschung / An International Handbook of Contemporary Research / Manuel international des recherches contemporaines* (Berlin: Walter de Gruyter, 1997).

de Goeje, C. H., *Verslag der Toemoekhoemak-expeditie* [Report on the Toemoekhoemak expedition] (Leiden: E. J. Brill, 1908).

Golovko, Evgenij V., and Nikolai B. Vakhtin, 'Aleut in contact: the CIA enigma' (in *Acta Linguistica Hafniensia* 72 (1990): 97–125).

Grabe, William, ed., *Annual Review of Applied Linguistics 17: Multilingualism* (Cambridge: Cambridge University Press, 1997).

Grenoble, Lenore A., and Lindsay J. Whaley, eds., *Endangered Languages: Current Issues and Future Prospects* (Cambridge: Cambridge University Press, 1998).

Grimes, Barbara Dix, 'Cloves and Nutmeg, Traders and War: Language Contact in the Spice Islands' (in Dutton and Tryon 1994: 251–74).

Grimes, Barbara F., 'Language attitudes: identity, distinctiveness, survival in the Vaupes' (*Journal of Multilingual and Multicultural Development* 6(5) (1985): 389–401).

Grimes, Barbara F., *Ethnologue: Languages of the World* (12th edn., Dallas, TX: Summer Institute of Linguistics, 1992).

Grosjean, François, *Life with Two Languages: An Introduction to Bilingualism* (Cambridge, MA: Harvard University Press, 1982).

Grosjean, François, and Carlos Soares, 'Processing mixed language: some preliminary findings' (in Jyotsna Vaid, ed., *Language Processing in Bilinguals: Psycholinguistic and Neuropsychological Perspectives*, Hillsdale, NJ: Erlbaum, 1986: 145–79).

Gumperz, John J., and Robert Wilson, 'Convergence and creolization: a case from the Indo-Aryan/Dravidian border' (in Hymes 1971: 151–67).

Haas, Mary R., *The Prehistory of Languages* (The Hague: Mouton, 1969).

Hakuta, Kenji, *Mirror of Language: The Debate on Bilingualism* (New York: Basic Books, 1986).

Hale, Ken, 'On endangered languages and the safeguarding of diversity' (in Hale *et al.* 1992: 1–3).

Hale, Ken, 'Language endangerment and the human value of linguistic diversity' (in Hale *et al.* 1992: 35–41).

Hale, Ken, *et al.*, 'Endangered languages' (in *Language* 68 (1992): 1–42).

Hall, Robert A., Jr., *Pidgin and Creole Languages* (Ithaca, NY: Cornell University Press, 1966).

Hancock, Ian F., ed., *Readings in Creole Studies* (Ghent: Story-Scientia, 1979).
Haugen, Einar, *The Norwegian Language in America: A Study in Bilingual Behavior* (Philadelphia: University of Pennsylvania Press, 1953).
Haugen, Einar, 'Language contact' (in *Proceedings of the International Congress of Linguists* 8 (1958): 771–85).
Headland, Thomas N., ed., *The Tasaday Controversy* (American Anthropological Association Special Publications, Scholarly Series, 1991).
Heath, Jeffrey, *Linguistic Diffusion in Arnhem Land* (Canberra: Australian Institute of Aboriginal Studies, 1978).
Heath, Jeffrey, *From Code-Switching to Borrowing: A Case Study of Moroccan Arabic* (London: Kegan Paul International, 1989).
Heath, Shirley Brice, *Telling Tongues: Language Policy in Mexico, Colony to Nation* (New York: Teachers College Press, 1972).
Heine, Bernd, 'African languages' (in Bright 1992, vol. 1: 31–6).
Herbert, Robert K., ed., *Language and Society in Africa: The Theory and Practice of Sociolinguistics* (Johannesburg: Witwatersrand University Press, 1992).
Hermans, Daan, Theo Bongaerts, Kees de Bot, and Robert Schreuder, 'Producing words in a foreign language: can speakers prevent interference from their first language?' (in *Bilingualism: Language and Cognition* 1: 213–29, 1998).
Herodotus, *The Persian Wars* (5th century BCE; the Sauromatae are mentioned in book IV, chapter 117).
Hetzron, Robert, 'Genetic classification and Ethiopic Semitic' (in James Bynon and Thodora Bynon, eds., *Hamito-Semitica*, The Hague: Mouton, 1975: 103–27).
Hill, Jane H., 'Language death in Uto-Aztecan' (in *International Journal of American Linguistics* 49 (1983): 258–76).
Hill, Jane H., and Kenneth C. Hill, *Speaking Mexicano: Dynamics of Syncretic Language in Central Mexico* (Tucson, AZ: University of Arizona Press, 1986).
Hinton, Leanne, 'Survival of endangered languages: the California Master-Apprentice Program' (in *International Journal of the Sociology of Language* 123 (1997): 177–91).
Hiranburana, Samang, untitled posting (on the SEALTEACH list, 22 April 1998).
Hock, Hans Henrich, 'Substratum influence on (Rig-Vedic) Sanskrit?' (*Studies in the Linguistic Sciences* 5/2 (1975): 76–125).
Hock, Hans Henrich, '(Pre-)Rig-Vedic convergence of Indo-Aryan with Dravidian? Another look at the evidence' (*Studies in the Linguistic Sciences* 14/1 (1984), 89–107).
Holm, John, *Pidgins and Creoles*, vol. 1: *Theory and Structure*, vol. 2: *Reference Survey* (Cambridge: Cambridge University Press, 1988 and 1989).
Hoonchamlong, Yuphaphann, 'Some observations on phom and dichan: Male and female first person pronouns in Thai' (in Carol J. Compton and John F. Hartmann, eds., *Papers on Tai Languages, Linguistics and Literature: In Honor of William J. Gedney on his 77th Birthday*, Dekalb: Center for Southeast Asian Studies, Northern Illinois University, 1992: 186–204).
Hotz, Robert Lee, 'The struggle to save dying languages' (in the *Los Angeles Times*, 25 January 2000).
De Houwer, Annick, 'The separate development hypothesis: method and implications' (in G. Extra and L. Verhoeven, eds., *The Cross-Linguistic Study of Bilingualism*, Amsterdam: North-Holland, 1994: 39–50).
De Houwer, Annick, 'By way of introduction: methods in studies of bilingual first language acquisition' (in *International Journal of Bilingualism* 2 (1998): 249–63).
De Houwer, Annick, and Jürgen M. Meisel, 'Analyzing the relationship between two developing languages in bilingual first language acquisition: methodology, data

and findings' (paper presented at the Workshop on Language Contact Linking Different Levels of Analysis, NIAS, Wassenaar, The Netherlands, June, 1996).

Hovdhaugen, Even, 'Some aspects of language contact in Anatolia' (in *University of Oslo Working Papers in Linguistics* 7 (1976): 142–60).

Huttar, George L., and Mary L. Huttar, *Ndyuka* (London: Routledge, 1994).

Huttar, George L., and Frank J. Velantie, 'Ndyuka-Trio Pidgin' (in Thomason 1997: 99–124).

Hvenekilde, Anne, 'Kinship systems, language choice and the construction of identity among academics in Shillong, North East India' (paper presented at the First International Symposium on Bilingualism, Vigo, Spain, October, 1997).

Huffines, Marion Lois, 'Case usage among the Pennsylvania German sectarians and nonsectarians' (in Dorian 1989: 211–26).

Hymes, Dell, ed., *Pidginization and Creolization of Languages* (Cambridge: Cambridge University Press, 1971).

Ibn Khaldun, *Histoire des Berbères et des dynasties musulmanes de l'Afrique septentrionale* [History of the Berbers and the muslim dynasties of northern Africa] (translated from Arabic by Baron de Slane Mac Guckin (1852–6); new edition published under the direction of Paul Casanova, Paris: Librairie orientaliste, Paul Geuthner S.A., 1968).

Ishwaran, K., 'Multilingualism in India' (in Nels Anderson, ed., *Studies in Multilingualism*, Leiden: E. J. Brill, 1969: 122–50).

Ivić, Pavle, 'Balkan Linguistics', a lecture course taught at the Linguistic Institute of the Linguistic Society of American, Indiana University, June–August 1964.

Jackson, Jean, 'Language identity of the Colombian Vaupes Indians' (in Richard Bauman and Joel Sherzer, eds., *Explorations in the Ethnography of Speaking*, Cambridge: Cambridge University Press, 1974: 50–64).

Jackson, Jean, *The Fish People: Linguistic Exogamy and Tukanoan Identity in Northwest Amazonia* (Cambridge: Cambridge University Press, 1983).

Jackson, Kenneth H. *Language and History in Early Britain* (Edinburgh: Edinburgh University Press, 1953).

Jacobs, Melville, 'The areal spread of sound features in the languages north of California' (in Murray B. Emeneau, ed., *Papers from the Symposium on American Indian Linguistics*, Berkeley: University of California Press, 1954: 46–56).

Jakobson, Roman, 'Über die phonologischen Sprachbünde' [On phonological Sprachbünde] (*Travaux du Cercle Linguistique de Prague* 4 (1931): 234–40).

Jakobson, Roman, *K xarakteristike evrazijskogo jazykovogo sojuza* [On the nature of the Eurasian Sprachbund] (Paris: Imprimerie de Navarre, 1931).

Jakobson, Roman, 'Sur la théorie des affinités phonologiques entre des langues' [On the theory of phonological affinities between languages] (in his *Selected Writings*, The Hague: Mouton, 1962, vol. 1: 234–46; reprinted from *Actes du Quatrième Congrès International de Linguistes*, Copenhagen: Munksgaard, 1938: 48–59).

Jameson, J. F., ed., *Narratives of New Netherland 1609–1664* (New York: Charles Scribner's Sons, 1909; reprinted New York: Barnes and Noble, 1967).

Johanson, Lars, *Strukturelle Faktoren in türkischen Sprachkontakten* [Structural factors in Turkish language contacts] (Stuttgart: Franz Steiner, 1992).

Johanson, Lars, 'The dynamics of code-copying in language encounters' (in Bernt Brendemoen, Elizabeth Lanza, and Else Ryen, eds., *Language Encounters across Time and Space*, Oslo: Novus, 1998: 37–62).

Jones, Mari C., *Language Obsolescence and Revitalization: Linguistic Change in Two Contrasting Welsh Communities* (Oxford: Oxford University Press, 1998).

Joseph, Brian D., *The Synchrony and Diachrony of the Balkan Infinitive: A Study in*

Areal, General, and Historical Linguistics (Cambridge: Cambridge University Press, 1983).

Joseph, John Earl, *Eloquence and Power: The Rise of Language Standards and Standard Languages* (New York: Basil Blackwell, 1987).

Joshi, Aravind, 'Processing of sentences with intrasentential code switching' (in David R. Dowty, Lauri Karttunen, and Arnold Zwicky, eds., *Natural Language Parsing*, Cambridge: Cambridge University Press, 1985: 190–205).

Justeson, John S., and George A. Broadwell, 'Language and languages in Mesoamerica' (in Robert M. Carmack, Janine Gasco, and Gary H. Gossen, eds., *The Legacy of Mesoamerica: History and Culture of a Native American Civilization*, Upper Saddle River, NJ: Prentice Hall, 1996: 379–406).

Kaplan, Lawrence D., 'Eskimo-Aleut languages' (in Bright 1992, vol. 1: 415–19).

Kaufman, Stephen A., *The Akkadian Influences on Aramaic* (Chicago: University of Chicago Press, 1974).

Kinkade, M. Dale, 'More on nasal loss on the Northwest coast' (*International Journal of American Linguistics* 51 (1985): 478–80).

Kinkade, M. Dale, 'Transmontane lexical borrowing in Salish' (in *Papers for the 30th International Conference on Salish and Neighbouring Languages*, 1995: 28–46).

Kinkade, M. Dale, 'The emergence of shared features in languages of the Pacific Northwest' (paper presented at the symposium 'The Pacific Northwest as a Linguistic and Cultural Area', American Association for the Advancement of Science annual meeting, Seattle, 1997).

Klaiman, M. H., 'Bengali syntax: possible Dravidian influences' (in *International Journal of Dravidian Linguistics* 6 (1977): 303–17).

Kontra, Miklós, 'Hungary' (in Goebl *et al.* 1997, vol. 2: 1708–23).

Kopitar, Bartholomäus, 'Recension: *Abbildung und Beschreibung der südwest- und östlichen Wenden, Illyrier und Slaven*, von B. Hacquet' (in his *Kleinere Schriften*, ed. Franz von Miklosich, Vienna: Beck, 1857, vol. 1: 120–34).

Koptjevskaja-Tamm, Maria, and Bernhard Wälchli, 'An areal typological perspective on the circum-Baltic/North-East European languages: Sprachbund vs. contact superposition area' (paper presented at the Annual meeting of the Deutsche Gesellschaft für Sprachwissenschaft, Halle, 1998).

Kouwenberg, Silvia, 'From OV to VO: linguistic negotiation in the development of Berbice Dutch Creole' (in *Lingua* 88 (1992): 263–99).

Kouwenberg, Silvia, *A Grammar of Berbice Dutch Creole* (Berlin: Mouton de Gruyter, 1994).

Kouwenberg, Silvia, 'Berbice Dutch' (in Arends, Muysken, and Smith 1995: 233–43).

Kramer, Samuel Noah, *History Begins at Sumer: Thirty-Nine Firsts in Man's Recorded History* (Philadelphia: University of Pennsylvania Press, 1981).

Krauss, Michael, 'The world's languages in crisis' (in Hale *et al.* 1992: 4–10).

Kreindler, Isabelle, ed., *The Changing Status of Russian in the Soviet Union* (*International Journal of the Sociology of Language* 33, The Hague: Mouton, 1982).

Kremnitz, Georg, ed., *Sprachen im Konflikt* [Languages in conflict] (Tübingen: G. Narr, 1979).

Krishna, Sumi, *India's Living Languages: The Critical Issues* (New Delhi: Allied Publishers, 1991).

Kulick, Don, *Language Shift and Cultural Reproduction: Socialization, Self, and Syncretism in a Papua New Guinean Village* (Cambridge: Cambridge University Press, 1992).

Kunene, E. C. L., and J. G. Mulder, 'Linguistic considerations of some cultural attitudes in Siswati' (in Herbert 1992: 335–44).

290   *Language Contact*

Lanham, L. W., 'An outline history of the languages of South Africa' (in L. W. Lanham and K. P. Prinsloo, eds., *Language and Communication Studies in South Africa*, Cape Town: Oxford University Press, 1978: 13–52).

Lanza, Elizabeth, *Language Mixing in Infant Bilingualism: A Sociolinguistic Perspective* (Oxford: Oxford University Press, 1997).

Laycock, Donald C., 'Melanesian linguistic diversity: a Melanesian choice?' (in R. J. May and Hank Nelson, eds., *Melanesia: Beyond Diversity*, Canberra: Australian National University Press, 1982: 33–8).

Lefebvre, Claire, 'The role of relexification and syntactic analysis in Haitian Creole: methodological aspects of a research program' (in Salikoko S. Mufwene, ed., *Africanisms in Afro-American Language Varieties*, Athens, GA: University of Georgia Press, 1993: 254–79).

Lefebvre, Claire, *Creole Genesis and the Acquisition of Grammar: The Case of Haitian Creole* (Cambridge: Cambridge University Press, 1999).

Legère, Karsten, ed., *African Languages in Basic Education: Proceedings of the First Workshop on African Languages in Basic Education* (Windhoek, Namibia: Gamsberg Macmillan Publishers, 1997).

Lehiste, Ilse, 'Cross-linguistic comparison of prosodic patterns in Finnish, Finland Swedish, and Stockholm Swedish' (in Eliasson and Jahr 1997: 367–77).

Leopold, Werner F., *Speech Development of a Bilingual Child: A Linguist's Record*, vol. 1: *Vocabulary Growth in the First Two Years*; vol. 2: *Sound-Learning in the First Two Years*; vol. 3: *Grammar and General Problems*; vol. 4: *Diary from Age 2* (Evanston, IL: Northwestern University Press, 1939; 1947; 1949a; 1949b).

Leopold, Werner F., 'A child's learning of two languages' (in H. J. Mueller, ed., *Report on the 5th Round Table Conference on Linguistics and Language Teaching*, Washington, DC: Georgetown University Press, 1954).

Le Page, Robert B., *The National Language Question: Linguistic Problems of Newly Independent States* (Oxford: Oxford University Press, 1964).

Le Page, Robert B., and Andrée Tabouret-Keller, *Acts of Identity* (Cambridge: Cambridge University Press, 1985).

Leslau, Wolf, 'The influence of Cushitic on the Semitic languages of Ethiopia: a problem of substratum' (in *Word* 1 (1945): 59–82).

Leslau, Wolf, 'The influence of Sidamo on the Ethiopic languages of the Gurage' (in *Language* 28 (1952): 63–81).

Lewis, E. Glyn, *Multilingualism in the Soviet Union: Aspects of Language Policy and its Implementation* (The Hague: Mouton, 1972).

Li, Charles N., 'The rise and fall of tones through diffusion' (*Berkeley Linguistics Society* 12 (1986): 173–85).

Lickey, Sara, *Khoisan influence in southern Bantu: an investigation* (Pittsburgh: University of Pittsburgh M.A. thesis, 1985).

Lieberson, Stanley G., G. Dalto, and M. E. Johnson, 'The course of mother tongue diversity in nations' (in *American Journal of Sociology* 81 (1975): 34–61).

Lindeström, Peter, *Geographia Americae with an Account of the Delaware Indians: Based on Surveys and Notes Made in 1654–1656*, transl. Amandus Johnson (1925 [1691]).

Lindstedt, Jouko, 'Linguistic Balkanization: contact-induced change by mutual reinforcement' (in Dicky Gilbers, John Nerbonne, and Jos Schaeken, eds., *Proceedings of the Groningen Conference on Languages in Contact*, Amsterdam: Rodopi, 2000: 231–46).

Little, Greta D., 'Syntactic evidence of language contact: Cushitic influence in Amharic' (in Roger W. Shuy and Charles-James N. Bailey, eds., *Towards Tomorrow's Linguistics*, Washington, DC: Georgetown University Press, 1974: 267–75).

Lorimer, D. L. R., 'Burushaski and its alien neighbors: problems in linguistic contagion' (in *Transactions of the Philological Society* 1937: 63–98).

Lydall, Jean, 'Hamer' (in M. Lionel Bender, ed., *The Non-Semitic Languages of Ethiopia*, East Lansing, MI: African Studies Center, 1976: 393–438).

Mackey, William Francis, *Bilingualism as a World Problem | Le bilinguisme, phénomène mondial* (Montreal: Harvest House, 1967).

McWhorter, John H., 'Identifying the creole prototype: vindicating a typological class' (in *Language* 74 (1998): 788–818).

Masica, Colin P., *Defining a Linguistic Area: South Asia* (Chicago: University of Chicago Press, 1976).

Meillet, Antoine, *Linguistique historique et linguistique générale* [Historical linguistics and general linguistics] (Paris: Champion, 1921).

Meisel, Jürgen M., ed., *Bilingual First Language Acquisition: French and German Grammatical Development* (Amsterdam: John Benjamins, 1994).

Mellinkoff, David, *The Language of the Law* (Boston: Little, Brown, 1963).

Mencken, H. L., *The American Language* (New York: Alfred A. Knopf, 1936).

Menges, Karl H., 'Indo-European influences on Ural-Altaic languages' (in *Word* 1: 188–93, 1945).

Menovščikov, G. A., 'O nekotoryx social'nyx aspektax èvoljucii jazyka' [On some social aspects of the evolution of language] (in *Voprosy social'noj lingvistiki*, Leningrad: Nauka, 1969: 110–34).

Mertz, Elizabeth, 'Sociolinguistic creativity: Cape Breton Gaelic's linguistic "tip" ' (in Dorian 1989: 103–16).

von Miklosich, Franz, 'Die slavischen Elemente in Rumanischen' [The Slavic elements in Rumanian] (in *Denkschriften der philosophisch-historische Classe, Kaiserliche Akademie der Wissenschaften, Wien*, Commission 20: 1-88, Vienna: K. Gerolds Sohn, 1861).

Milroy, James, and Lesley Milroy, 'Linguistic change, social network and speaker innovation' (in *Journal of Linguistics* 21 (1985): 339–84).

Milroy, James, and Lesley Milroy, 'Exploring the social constraints on language change' (in Eliasson and Jahr 1997: 75–101).

Milroy, Lesley, and Pieter Muysken, eds., *One Speaker, Two Languages: Cross-Disciplinary Perspectives on Code-Switching* (Cambridge: Cambridge University Press, 1995).

de Mishaegen, Anne, *In de canadeesche wouden* [In the Canadian forests] (Naarden: Rutgers, 1947).

Moffatt, Suzanne, and Lesley Milroy, 'Panjabi/English language alternation in the early school years' (in *Multilingua* 11 (1992): 355–85).

Möhlig, Wilhelm J. G., 'Mbugu' (in Hermann Jungraithmayr and Wilhelm J. G. Möhlig, eds., *Lexikon der Afrikanistik*, Berlin: Dietrich Reimer, 1983: 158–9).

Molony, Carol, 'The Truth about the Tasaday' (in *The Sciences*, Sept.–Oct. 1988).

Moravcsik, Edith, 'Language contact' (in Joseph H. Greenberg, ed., *Universals of Human Language*, vol. 1: *Method and Theory*, 1978: 93–122).

Moreno, Martino Mario, 'L'azione del cuscito sul sistema morfologico delle lingue semitiche dell'Ethiopia' [The influence of Cushitic on the morphological system of the Semitic languages of Ethiopia] (in *Rassegna di Studi Etiopici* 7 (1948): 121–30).

Mous, Maarten, 'Ma'a or Mbugu' (in Bakker and Mous 1994: 175–200).

Mufwene, Salikoko, 'The founder principle in creole genesis' (in *Diachronica* 13 (1996): 83–134).

Mufwene, Salikoko, 'Kitúba' (in Thomason 1997: 173–208).

Müller, Max, *Lectures on the Science of Language* (2nd revised edn., New York: Scribner, 1890; 1st edn. 1871–2).

Müller, Natascha, 'Transfer in bilingual first language acquisition' (in *Bilingualism: Language and Cognition* 1 (1998): 151–71, followed by seven peer commentaries and the author's response: 173–92).

Muysken, Pieter, 'Media Lengua' (in Thomason 1997: 365–426).

Muysken, Pieter, and Tonjes Veenstra, 'Universalist approaches' (in Arends, Muysken, and Smith 1995: 121–34).

Myers-Scotton, Carol, *Duelling Languages: Grammatical Structure in Codeswitching* (Oxford: Oxford University Press, 1993).

Myers-Scotton, Carol, 'A way to dusty death: the Matrix Language turnover hypothesis' (in Lenore A. Grenoble and Lindsay J. Whaley, eds., *Endangered Languages*, Cambridge: Cambridge University Press, 1998: 289–316).

Nelde, Peter H., *Languages in Contact and in Conflict* (Wiesbaden: Steiner, 1980).

Nelde, Peter H., 'Sprachkontakt als Kulturkonflikt' [Language contact as culture conflict] (in H. Kühlwein, ed., *Sprache, Kultur, Gesellschaft*, Tübingen: Narr, 1984: 31–40).

Nelde, Peter H., 'Multilingualism and contact linguistics' (in Martin Putz, ed., *Thirty Years in Linguistic Evolution*, Amsterdam: John Benjamins, 1992: 379–97).

Nelde, Peter H., 'Identity among bilinguals: an ecolinguistic approach' (in *Estudios de Sociolingüística* 1/1 (2000): 41–46).

Van Ness, Silke, *Changes in an Obsolescing Language: Pennsylvania German in West Virginia* (Tübingen: Gunter Narr, 1990).

Neumann, Gunter, 'Zur chinesisch-russischen Behelfssprache von Kjachta' [On the Chinese–Russian makeshift language of Kyakhta] (in *Die Sprache* 12 (1966): 237–51).

Newton, Brian, 'An Arabic-Greek dialect' (in Robert Austerlitz, ed., *Papers in Memory of George C. Pappageotes* (supplement to *Word* 20), 1964: 43–52).

Nichols, Johanna, 'Pidginization and foreigner talk: Chinese Pidgin Russian' (in Elizabeth C. Traugott et al., eds., *Papers from the Fourth International Conference on Historical Linguistics*, Amsterdam: John Benjamins, 1980: 397–407).

Noonan, Michael, 'The fall and rise and fall of the Chantyal language' (*Milwaukee Studies on Language* 9 (1999): 248–60).

Noonan, Michael, with Ram Prasad Bhulanja, Jag Man Chhantyal, and William Pagliuca, *Chantyal Dictionary and Texts* (Berlin: Mouton de Gruyter), 1999.

O'Barr, William M., and Jean O'Barr, eds., *Language and Politics* (The Hague: Mouton, 1976).

Odlin, Terence, *Language Transfer: Cross-Linguistic Influence in Language Learning* (Cambridge: Cambridge University Press, 1989).

Oksaar, Els, 'Bilingualism' (in Thomas A. Sebeok, ed., *Current Trends in Linguistics*, vol. 9: *Linguistics in Western Europe*, The Hague: Mouton, 1972: 476–511).

Oksaar, Els, ed., *Spracherwerb, Sprachkontakt, Sprachkonflikt* [Language acquisition, language contact, language conflict] (Berlin: de Gruyter, 1984).

Olmstead, A. T., *History of the Persian Empire* (Chicago:University of Chicago Press, 1948).

Oswalt, Robert, 'Russian loanwords in southwestern Pomo' (in *International Journal of American Linguistics* 24 (1958): 245–7).

Owens, Jonathan, 'Arabic-based pidgins and creoles' (in Thomason 1997: 125–72).

Pasch, Helma, 'Sango' (in Thomason 1997: 209–70).

Paulston, Christina Bratt, *Linguistic Minorities in Multilingual Settings: Implications for Language Policies* (Amsterdam: John Benjamins, 1994).

Paulston, Christina Bratt, 'Multilingualism' (in Asher 1994: 2630–2).

Peirce, Bonny Norton, and Stanley G. M. Ridge, 'Multilingualism in southern Africa' (in *Annual Review of Applied Linguistics* 17 (1997): 170–90 (special issue on multilingualism, ed. William Grabe)).

Pfaff, Carol W., 'Constraints on language mixing: intrasentential code-switching and borrowing in Spanish/English' (in *Language* 55 (1979): 291–318).

Pfaff, Carol W., 'Sociolinguistic aspects of language contact' (paper presented at the Weekend on Language Contact, Berlin, 1998).

Polomé, Edgar, 'Creolization processes and diachronic linguistics' (in Albert Valdman and Arnold Highfield, eds., *Theoretical Orientations in Creole Studies*, New York: Academic Press, 1980: 185–202).

Poplack, Shana, 'Sometimes I'll start a sentence in Spanish Y TERMINO EN ESPAÑOL: toward a typology of code-switching' (in *Linguistics* 18 (1980): 581–618).

Poplack, Shana, and Marjory Meechan, 'Patterns of language mixture: nominal structure in Wolof-French and Fongbe-French bilingual discourse' (in Milroy and Muysken 1995: 199–232).

Poser, William, 'Areal phonological features in languages of the Pacific Northwest' (paper presented at the symposium The Pacific Northwest as a Linguistic and Cultural Area, American Association for the Advancement of Science annual meeting, Seattle, 1997).

Post, Marike, 'Fa d'Ambu' (in Arends, Muysken, and Smith 1995: 191–204).

Queen, Robin Michelle, *Intonation in contact: a study of Turkish–German bilingual intonation patterns* (Austin, TX: University of Texas dissertation, 1996).

Rayfield, J. R., *The Languages of a Bilingual Community* (The Hague: Mouton, 1970).

Raymond, Joan, 'Say what? Preserving endangered languages' (in *Newsweek*, 14 September 1998: 14).

Reichard, Gladys A., 'Coeur d'Alene' (in Franz Boas, ed., *Handbook of American Indian Languages*, pt. 3, Locus Valley, NY: Augustin, 1938: 517–707).

Reichard, Gladys A., *An Analysis of Coeur d'Alene Indian Mythology* (*Memoir of the American Folklore Society* 41, 1947).

Reid, Lawrence A., untitled essay on the Tasaday controversy (on web site http://www2.hawaii.edu/ling/fac_pages/reid.html, 1997).

Reinecke, John E., 'Tây Bôi: notes on the Pidgin French spoken in Vietnam' (in Hymes 1971: 47–56).

van Rheeden, Hadewych, 'The role of functional categories in language contact and change' (paper presented at the annual meeting of the Deutsche Gesellschaft für Sprachwissenschaft, Halle, March, 1998).

Rickford, John R., *African American Vernacular English: Features, Evolution, Educational Implications* (Oxford: Oxford University Press, 1999).

Rischel, Jørgen, *Minor Mlabri: A Hunger-Gatherer Language of Northern Indochina* (Copenhagen: Museum Tusculanum Press, University of Copenhagen, 1995).

Robertson, Stuart, and Frederic G. Cassidy, *The Development of Modern English* (2nd edn., Englewood Cliffs, NJ: Prentice-Hall, 1934).

Robins, R. H., and E. M. Uhlenbeck, eds., *Endangered Languages* (Oxford and New York: Berg, 1991).

Romaine, Suzanne, *Pidgin and Creole Languages* (London: Longman, 1988).

Romaine, Suzanne, *Bilingualism* (2nd edn., Oxford: Basil Blackwell, 1995).

Ross, Alan S. C., and A. W. Moverley, *The Pitcairnese Language* (New York: Oxford University Press, 1964).

Rottland, Franz, and Duncan Okoth Okombo, 'Language shift among the Suba of Kenya' (in Brenzinger 1992: 273–83).

Rouchdy, Aleya, 'Urban and non-Urban Egyptian Nubian: is there a reduction in language skill?' (in Dorian 1989: 259–66).

Rubin, Joan, *National Bilingualism in Paraguay* (The Hague: Mouton, 1968).

Saagpakk, Paul F., *Estonian–English Dictionary* (New Haven: Yale University Press, 1982).

Sala, Marius, *Lenguas en contacto* (Madrid: Gredos, 1998).

Samarin, William J., *A Grammar of Sango* (The Hague: Mouton, 1967).

Sandalo, Filomena, *A Grammar of Kadiwéu* (Pittsburgh: University of Pittsburgh dissertation, 1995).

Sandfeld, Kristian, *Linguistique balkanique: problèmes et résultats* (Paris: Librairie C. Klincksieck, 1930).

Sankoff, David, Shana Poplack, and Swathi Vanniarajan, 'The case of the nonce loan in Tamil' (in *Language Variation and Change* 2 (1990): 71–101).

Sankoff, Gillian, 'The genesis of a language' (in Kenneth C. Hill, ed., *The Genesis of Language*, Ann Arbor: Karoma, 1979: 23–47).

Sankoff, Gillian, *The Social Life of Language* (Philadelphia: University of Pennsylvania Press, 1980).

Sankoff, Gillian, and Suzanne Laberge, 'On the acquisition of native speakers by a language' (in David DeCamp and Ian Hancock, eds., *Pidgins and Creoles: Current Trends and Prospects*, Washington, DC: Georgetown University Press, 1974: 73–84).

Sapir, Edward, *Language: An Introduction to the Study of Speech* (New York: Harcourt, Brace and World, 1921).

Sarhimaa, Anneli, *Syntactic Transfer, Contact-Induced Change, and the Evolution of Mixed Codes: Focus on Karelian–Russian Language Alternation* (Helsinki: Finnish Literature Society, 1999).

Sasse, Hans-Jürgen, *Arvanitika: die albanischen Sprachreste in Griechenland* [Arvanitika: the remnants of Albanian language in Greece] (pt. 1, Wiesbaden: Harrassowitz, 1991).

Sasse, Hans-Jürgen, 'Theory of language death' (in Brenzinger 1992: 7–30).

Sasse, Hans-Jürgen, 'Language decay and contact-induced change: similarities and differences' (in Brenzinger 1992: 59–80).

Sawchuk, Joe, *The Métis of Manitoba: Reformulation of an Ethnic Identity* (Toronto: Peter Martin Associates Ltd., 1978).

Schach, Paul, ed., *Languages in Conflict: Linguistic Acculturation on the Great Plains* (Lincoln, NE: University of Nebraska Press, 1980).

Schiffman, Harold F., *Linguistic Culture and Language Policy* (London: Routledge, 1996).

Schmidt, Annette, *Young People's Dyirbal: An Example of Language Death from Australia* (Cambridge: Cambridge University Press, 1985).

Schwartz, John, 'Speaking out and saving sounds to keep native tongues alive' (in the *Washington Post*, 14 March 1994).

Sekerina, Irina A., 'Copper Island (Mednyj) Aleut (CIA): a mixed language' (in *Languages of the World* 8 (1994): 14–31).

Sicoli, Mark, 'Overview of the history of language issues and policy in Mexico' (Pittsburgh: University of Pittsburgh, MS., 1998).

Silva-Corvalán, Carmen, *Language Contact and Change: Spanish in Los Angeles* (Oxford: Oxford University Press, 1994).

Silver, Shirley, and Wick R. Miller, *American Indian Languages: Cultural and Social Contexts* (Tucson, AZ: University of Arizona Press, 1997).

Singler, John V., 'Theories of creole genesis, sociohistorical considerations, and the evaluation of evidence: the case of Haitian Creole and the Relexification Hypothesis' (in *Journal of Pidgin and Creole Languages* 11 (1996): 185–230).

Slater, Keith W., 'Language mixing and creolization in areal convergence: the case of China's Qinghai-Gansu Sprachbund' (in Peter Bakker, ed., *University of Århus Working Papers Volume on Language Mixing*, in press, 2000).

Smalley, William, *Linguistic Diversity and National Unity: Language Ecology in Thailand* (Chicago: University of Chicago Press, 1994).

Smith, Norval, 'An annotated list of creoles, pidgins, and mixed languages' (in Arends, Muysken, and Smith 1995: 331–74).

Smith, Norval, Ian Robertson, and Kay Williamson, 'The Ịjọ element in Berbice Dutch' (in *Language in Society* 16 (1987): 49–90).

Solé, Yolanda Russinovich, 'Language, affect and nationalism in Paraguay' (in Ana Roca and John B. Jensen, eds., *Spanish in Contact: Issues in Bilingualism*, Somerville, MA: Cascadilla Press, 1996: 93–111).

Sommerfelt, Alf, 'External versus internal factors in the development of language' (*Norsk tidsskrift for sprogvidenskap* 19 (1960): 296–315).

Sorensen, Arthur P., 'Multilingualism in the Northwest Amazon' (*American Anthropologist* 69 (1967): 670–83).

Sorensen, Arthur P., 'An emerging Tukanoan linguistic regionality: policy pressures' (in Harriet Manelis Klein and Louisa R. Stark, eds., *South American Indian Languages: Retrospect and Prospect*, Austin, TX: University of Texas Press, 1985: 140–56).

Spicer, Edward, *Perspectives in American Indian Culture Change* (Chicago: University of Chicago Press, 1961).

Splawn, A. J., *Ka-Mi-Akin: Last Hero of the Yakimas* (2nd edn., Yakima, WA, & Caldwell, ID: The Caxton Printers, 1944; 1st edn. 1917).

Sridhar, S. N., 'Linguistic convergence: Indo-Aryanization of Dravidian languages' (in *Studies in the Linguistic Sciences* 8/1 (1978): 197–215).

Taylor, Allan R., ed., *Language obsolescence, shift, and death in several Native American communities* (*International Journal of the Sociology of Language* 93, 1992).

Teit, James A., *The Salishan Tribes of the Western Plateaus* (Bureau of American Ethnology Annual Report 44, Washington, DC: Smithsonian Institution, 1930).

Teo, Kok Seong, 'The language of Malaysia's Kelantan Peranakan Chinese: the issue of the classification of a mixed code' (paper presented at the Ninth Annual Meeting of the Southeast Asian Linguistic Society (SEALS), Berkeley, CA, 1999.).

Thomason, Sarah Grey, 'Chinook Jargon in areal and historical context' (in *Language* 59 (1983): 820–70).

Thomason, Sarah Grey, 'Genetic relationship and the case of Ma'a (Mbugu)' (in *Studies in African Linguistics* 14 (1983): 195–231).

Thomason, Sarah Grey, 'Languages of the world' (in Christina Bratt Paulston, ed., *International Handbook of Bilingualism and Bilingual Education*, Westport, CT: Greenwood Press, 1988: 17–45).

Thomason, Sarah Grey, 'On mechanisms of interference' (in Eliasson and Jahr 1997: 181–207).

Thomason, Sarah Grey, 'A typology of contact languages' (in Arthur K. Spears and Donald Winford, eds., *Pidgins and Creoles: Structure and Status*, Amsterdam: John Benjamins, 1997: 71–88).

Thomason, Sarah Grey, ed., *Contact Languages: A Wider Perspective* (Amsterdam: John Benjamins, 1997).

Thomason, Sarah Grey, 'Ma'a (Mbugu)' (in Thomason 1997: 469–87).

Thomason, Sarah Grey, 'Mednyj Aleut' (in Thomason, 1997: 449–68).

Thomason, Sarah Grey, 'Linguistic areas and language history' (in Dicky Gilbers, John Nerbonne, and Jos Schaeken, eds., *Proceedings of the Groningen Conference on Languages in Contact*, Amsterdam: Rodopi, 2000: 311–27).

Thomason, Sarah Grey, and Alaa Elgibali, 'Before the Lingua Franca: pidginized Arabic in the eleventh century A.D.' (*Lingua* 68 (1986): 317–49).

Thomason, Sarah Grey, and Terrence Kaufman, *Language Contact, Creolization, and Genetic Linguistics* (Berkeley: University of California Press, 1988).
Thompson, Laurence C., 'Salishan and the Northwest' (in Lyle Campbell and Marianne Mithun, eds., *The Languages of Native America: Historical and Comparative Assessment*, Austin, TX: University of Texas Press, 1979: 692–765).
Thompson, R. W., 'A note on some possible affinities between the creole dialects of the Old World and those of the New' (in Robert B. Le Page, ed., *Proceedings of the Conference on Creole Language Studies*, London: Macmillan, 1961: 107–13).
Todd, Loreto, *Pidgins and Creoles* (London: Routledge and Kegan Paul, 1974).
Trubetzkoy, Nikolai S., Proposition 16 (in *Acts of the 1st International Congress of Linguists*, Leiden, 1928: 17–18).
Trudgill, Peter, *Dialects in Contact* (Oxford: Basil Blackwell, 1986).
Tsitsipis, Lukas D., 'Skewed performance and full performance in language obsolescence: the case of an Albanian variety' (in Dorian 1989: 117–37).
Tucker, G. Richard, 'Multilingualism and language contact: an introduction' (in *Annual Review of Applied Linguistics* 17 (1997): 3–10).
Turner, Nancy, 'Patterns in Pacific Northwest ethnobotany' (paper presented at the symposium The Pacific Northwest as a Linguistic and Cultural Area, American Association for the Advancement of Science annual meeting, Seattle, 1997).
Valkhoff, Marius F., *Studies in Portuguese and Creole* (Johannesburg: Witwatersrand University Press, 1966).
Vildomec, Věroboj, *Multilingualism* (Leiden: A. W. Sijthoff, 1971).
Voorhoeve, Jan, 'Historical and linguistic evidence in favor of the relexification theory in the formation of creoles' (in *Language in Society* 2 (1973): 113–45).
van der Voort, Hein, 'Eskimo pidgin in West Greenland' (in Ernst Håkon Jahr and Ingvild Broch, eds., *Language Contact in the Arctic: Northern Pidgins and Contact Languages*, Berlin: Mouton de Gruyter, 1996: 157–258).
Watahomigie, Lucille J., and Akira Y. Yamamoto, 'Local reactions to perceived language decline' (in Hale *et al.*, 1992: 10–17).
Weinreich, Uriel, *Languages in Contact* (The Hague: Mouton, 1953; reprinted in 1968).
Whinnom, Keith, *Spanish Contact Vernaculars in the Philippine Islands* (Hong Kong: Hong Kong University Press, 1956).
Whinnom, Keith, 'Lingua Franca: historical problems' (in Albert Valdman, ed., *Pidgin and Creole Linguistics*, Bloomington: Indiana University Press, 1977: 295–310).
Whiteley, Wilfred Howell, 'Linguistic hybrids' (in *African Studies* 19/2 (1960): 95–7).
Wurm, Stefan A., 'Comment on question: "Are there areas of *affinité grammaticale* as well as of *affinité phonologique* cutting across genetic boundaries?" ' (in F. Norman, ed., *Proceedings of the 7th International Congress of Linguists*, London: Permanent International Committee of Linguists, Section B, 1956: 450–2).
Wurm, Stephen A., Peter Mühlhäusler, and Darrell T. Tryon, *Atlas of Languages of Intercultural Communication* (Berlin: Walter de Gruyter, 1996).
Young, Douglas, 'Bilingualism and bilingual education in a divided South African society' (in Christina Bratt Paulston, ed., *International Handbook of Bilingualism and Bilingual Education*, Westport, CT: Greenwood Press, 1988: 405–28).
Zentella, Ana Celia, *Growing Up Bilingual: Puerto Rican Children in New York* (Oxford: Basil Blackwell, 1997).

Language index

African American Vernacular English, 141, 142,
  189, 195, 256, 266
Afrikaans, 40, 47, 49, 189, 195, 242, 253, 254
Afro-Asiatic languages, 111, 113, 123, 256, 263,
  266, 269, 275
Ainu, 9, 256
Akkadian, 6, 88, 89, 98, 242, 263, 275
Alamblak, 63, 119–20
Alaskan Russian Pidgin, 167
Alaskan Yupik, Central, 97, 280
Albanian, 29, 47, 105, 106, 108, 109, 250, 255,
  257, 267
  Arvanitika Albanian, 222, 225, 226, 238, 249,
  257
Aleut, 1, 11, 151, 202–3, 212, 217, 264, 270; see
  also Mednyj Aleut
Algonquian languages, 91, 149, 212, 216, 257, 269,
  273
Altaic languages, 105, 257, 271, 279
Alutiiq (Pacific Yupik), 280
Alutor, 261
Amazonia (Amazon linguistic area), 120
Ambonese Malay see Malay
American Indian Pidgin English, 164–5, 166, 257
Amharic, 36, 112, 251
Andean linguistic area, 120
Anglo-Romani, 200, 202, 204, 207, 208, 209, 210,
  211, 212, 214, 215, 218, 234, 258, 275
Apache, 258
Arabic, 2, 3, 7, 13, 19, 21, 36, 41, 44, 49, 73, 91,
  92, 133, 163, 164, 173, 191–2, 200–1, 204, 212,
  242, 250, 251, 252, 253, 254, 255, 270, 275;
  see also Cypriot Arabic, Kormakiti Arabic,
  Maridi Arabic
  Hasaniya Arabic, 253
  Moroccan Arabic, 216, 221
Arafundi, 173
Arawakan languages, 261
Armenian, 250, 258, 267
Arnhem Land Sprachbund, 13, 117, 118, 127, 249
Arumanian, 107, 109
Aryan see Indic
Asia Minor Greek, 11, 14, 59, 63–4, 65, 66–7, 74,
  86, 87, 95–6, 98, 206, 249, 256, 264
Assamese, 25, 44, 56, 173, 252, 267, 272
Athabaskan languages, 11, 14, 33, 120, 124, 166,
  258
Athabaskan-Eyak languages, 258
Australian Sprachbund, 117
Austro-Asiatic languages, 114, 115, 272
Austronesian languages, 18, 117, 118, 161, 171–2,

182, 214, 233, 258, 263, 268, 269, 270, 272,
  274, 277, 278
Äyiwo, 245, 246
Aymara, 94–5, 251, 258, 261, 274
Azerbaidzhani see Azeri
Azeri, 62, 95, 250, 279

Babine, 33
Babylonian, 6
Bahasa Indonesia, 252
Bahasa Malaysia see Malay
Balkan Sprachbund, 77, 105–9, 113, 126–7, 153,
  249, 276
Baltic languages, 87, 110, 111, 258
Baltic Sprachbund, 110–11, 113, 127, 249
Balto-Slavic languages, 110, 258, 276
Baluchi, 62, 87, 95, 98, 268
Bantu languages, 15, 18, 37, 64, 65, 82, 87, 133,
  150, 166, 172, 175, 199–200, 208, 209–10, 234,
  235, 258, 261, 264, 265, 272, 275, 276, 277,
  278
Basque, 31, 165, 245, 246, 259, 269; see also
  Pidgin Basque
Bella Bella see Heiltsuk
Bella Coola, 124
Bemba, 255
Bengali, 44, 87, 98, 116, 250, 252, 267, 272
Benue-Congo languages, 272
Berber languages, 256
Berbice Dutch Creole, 160, 172, 173, 181–2, 188,
  190–1, 194, 249
Bininj, 240, 249
Bislama, 182, 194, 255
Blackfoot, 257
Bosnian, 251
Brahui, 62, 87, 95, 98, 263
Breton, 31, 260
Buin, 150, 217, 259, 279
Bulgarian, 77, 105, 106, 108, 109, 153, 251, 259,
  276
Burmese, 253
Burushaski, 16, 44, 87, 98, 114, 260, 269
Byelorussian, 250

Callahuaya, 219
Cambodian see Khmer
Cameroonian Pidgin English, 165, 260
Cape Breton Gaelic see Gaelic, Scottish
Cape Verde Creole (Crioulo), 164, 251, 252, 260
Cariban languages, 278
Caribbean creoles, 169, 172–3, 177, 179, 181, 183,

186; *see also* Berbice Dutch Creole, Haitian
    Creole, Jamaican Creole, Papiamentu
Carrier, 33, 35
Catalan, 32, 250, 274
Caucasian languages, 73, 87, 98, 123, 260
Cayuse, 123
Celtic languages, 18, 260, 265, 267
Chadic languages, 256
Chantyal, 36, 56, 240, 243, 246
Chasta Costa, 124
Chichewa, 37, 253
Chilliwack, 144, 155
Chimakuan languages, 16, 120–4, 261
Chimakum, 124, 261
Chinese languages, 1, 8, 16, 19, 21, 23, 29, 31, 32,
    36, 76, 84, 86, 98, 161, 218, 254, 261, 267,
    276, 278
    Hokkien Chinese, 161,
    Kelantan Peranakan Chinese, 218
    Mandarin Chinese, 21, 216, 251
    see also Putonghua
Chinese Pidgin English, 161, 165, 173, 191, 249, 261
Chinese Pidgin Russian, 165, 172, 173, 193, 249,
    261
Chinookan languages, 28, 31, 53, 120, 121–2, 123,
    124; *see also* Chinook Jargon, Lower
    Chinook, Wasco, Wishram
Chinook Jargon, 24, 28, 55, 87, 121, 122, 145,
    166, 169–70, 172, 173, 174, 175, 182, 183, 188,
    192, 205, 242, 249, 261, 273
Chipaya, 94–5, 261
Choctaw, 244
Chukchi, 62, 95, 153, 249, 261
Chukotko-Kamchatkan languages, 261
Church Slavic, 49
Classical Latin, 263, 277
Clear Lake (California) linguistic area, 120
Coast Salishan languages, 124
Coeur d'Alene, 31, 54
Colombian–Central American linguistic area, 120
Comox, 86, 98, 124
Coos, 124
Coptic, 21, 49; *see also* Egyptian
Cornish, 18, 260
Cree, 48, 151, 196, 199, 201–2, 212, 215, 216, 257,
    270
Crioulo *see* Cape Verde Creole
Croatian, 27, 33, 47, 109, 251, 276
Cushitic languages, 65, 82, 86, 88, 98, 111–13, 125,
    147, 150, 200, 209–10, 211, 256, 263
Cypriot Arabic, 220
Czech, 251, 276

Danish, 54, 139–40, 251, 265, 273, 275
Dari (Afghan Persian), 250
Delaware languages, 28, 84, 97, 157, 257, 263, 273;
    see also Pidgin Delaware
Dhuwal, 4, 10, 13, 23, 36, 46
Divehi, 253
Dravidian languages, 16, 43, 44, 45, 62, 64, 65, 73,
    87, 88, 93, 97, 98, 114–16, 125, 127, 173, 263,
    266, 268, 269, 277; *see also* Proto-Dravidian
Dutch, 18, 21, 31, 136, 137, 138, 155, 165, 181–2,
    213, 215, 221, 250, 253, 254, 265, 273
Dyirbal, 228, 238
Dzongkha, 251

Eastern Sudanic languages, 228
East Slavic languages, 276
East Sutherland Gaelic *see* Gaelic, Scottish

Ecuadoran–Colombian subarea, 120
Egyptian, 6, 19, 21, 256; *see also* Coptic
Elamite, 6
Enga, 63, 119–20; *see also* Proto-Engan
English, 1, 2, 3, 4, 5, 8, 9, 10, 11, 14, 18, 21, 24,
    25, 28, 29, 30, 31, 32, 33, 34, 36, 37, 38, 39,
    40, 41, 42–3, 44, 47, 49, 50, 54, 55, 57, 62,
    67, 68, 70, 72, 73, 74, 75, 76, 77, 79, 80–2,
    83, 84, 86, 87, 88–9, 90, 91, 92, 96, 97, 100,
    109, 114, 132, 134, 135, 136, 137, 138, 139–
    40, 141, 147, 149, 151, 154, 155, 161, 164–5,
    170, 171, 175, 177, 178, 181, 182, 183, 189,
    194, 200, 212, 215, 216, 221, 222, 225, 227,
    228, 231, 236, 240, 242, 250, 251, 252, 253,
    254, 255, 257, 258, 260, 261, 262, 263, 264,
    265, 266, 267, 268, 269, 270, 271, 272, 273,
    274, 275, 276, 277, 278, 279, 280; *see also*
    Indian English, Irish English, Middle
    English, Old English
Eskimo languages, 267; *see also* Alaskan Yupik,
    Greenlandic Eskimo, Inuit, Pidgin Inuit,
    Siberian Yupik
Eskimo-Aleut languages, 267, 280
Estonian, 110, 111, 138, 149, 155, 156, 249, 251,
    264, 269
Ethiopian highlands Sprachbund, 76, 111–13, 127,
    206, 249
Ethiopic Semitic languages, 65, 86, 88, 98, 111–13,
    125, 147
Ewe, 175, 254, 264, 268, 275
Eyak, 240, 246, 258

Fa d'Ambu, 172, 173–4, 193, 264
Fanagaló, 166, 173, 249, 264, 280
Faroese, 251, 275
Farsi, 36, 252, 268
Fijian, 252
Finnic languages, 110, 234, 264, 268, 275
Finnish, 11, 19, 40, 88, 110, 138, 149, 155, 252,
    264, 269, 271, 275
Flathead *see* Montana Salish
Fon (Fongbe), 154, 175, 179–80, 186, 251, 264,
    268, 275
French, 3, 10, 11, 13, 18, 20, 23, 24, 32, 34, 35–6,
    37, 38, 40, 41, 46, 47, 48, 51, 53, 54, 55, 57,
    72, 79, 80, 90, 91, 97, 137, 147, 148, 151, 154,
    155, 165, 171, 175, 179–80, 181, 184–5, 189,
    194, 196, 199, 201–2, 212, 215, 216, 224, 242,
    244, 250, 251, 252, 253, 254, 255, 265, 269,
    270, 274, 275
    Canadian French (Métis French), 201
    Norman French, 18, 23, 75, 79
    see also Old French
French Guiana Creole, 173
Fula, 253

Gaelic, Irish, 4, 9, 18, 32, 79, 252, 260, 265, 267
Gaelic, Scottish, 18, 222, 225, 238, 249, 255, 260,
    265, 267
    East Sutherland Gaelic, 225, 236, 237, 239, 245
Galician, 274
Gaulish, 260
Gbe, 186; *see also* Ewe, Fon(gbe), Twi
Georgian, 73–4, 87, 252, 260
German, 3, 13, 19, 21, 31, 32, 35–6, 39, 46, 48, 51,
    53, 57, 68, 87, 90, 98, 99, 100, 110, 111, 134,
    148, 155, 165, 250, 252, 256, 260, 262, 265,
    269, 272, 273
    High German dialects, 259
    Low German dialects, 165, 259, 275

Alemannic German, 253
  Swiss German, 3, 21, 53, 57
Germanic languages, 8, 87, 88, 90, 91, 111, 265, 267, 273; *see also* Proto-Germanic
Gondi, 88, 98, 116
Great Basin linguistic area, 120
Greek, 2, 6, 16, 22, 24, 26, 36, 63–4, 79, 89, 91, 105, 106, 107, 109, 251, 252, 267; *see also* Asia Minor Greek
  Ancient Greek, 2, 267
  Cypriot Greek, 200–1, 203, 212
Greenlandic Eskimo, 251
Guaraní, 5, 9, 13, 253, 265–6
Gujarati, 42, 44, 252
Gullah, 31, 165, 266

Hadza, 268
Haida, 123, 124
Haisla, 280
Haitian Creole (Kreyol), 31, 179–80, 181, 188, 189, 193–4, 249, 252
Hakka, 251
Halkomelem, 124
Hamer (Hamer-Banna), 162, 266; *see also* Pidgin Hamer
Hausa, 24, 32, 37, 251, 253
Hawaiian, 244, 246, 258, 274
Hawaiian Creole English, 165, 167, 178, 179, 181, 182, 192, 249, 266
Hawaiian Pidgin English, 165, 166, 167, 192, 266
Hebrew, 41, 46, 49, 224–5, 249, 252, 275
Heiltsuk (Bella Bella), 124, 280
Herero, 253
Hindi, 25, 42–4, 45, 46, 88, 98, 116, 252, 267
Hiri Motu (Police Motu), 166, 167, 172, 173, 187, 188, 191, 194, 249, 253, 266, 272
Hittite, 6, 263, 267
Hmong, 19, 27
Hualapai, 244, 246
Hungarian, 19, 21, 36, 50, 143, 155, 230–1, 252, 266
  American Hungarian, 12, 14, 230–1, 237, 249
Hurrian, 6, 266, 269

Icelandic, 8–9, 36, 252, 275
Igbo, 37, 253
Ijọ, Eastern, 160, 172, 181–2, 191
Illyrian, 106, 127
Indian English, 74, 75
Indic languages, 1, 6, 16, 18, 25, 44, 64, 87, 88, 93, 98, 106, 114–16, 125, 127, 173, 200, 267, 268, 272, 275
Indo-Aryan languages *see* Indic languages
Indo-European languages, 25, 44, 74, 88, 91, 92, 96, 105, 106, 110, 111, 114, 173, 258, 265, 267, 268, 269, 271, 273, 274, 276; *see also* Proto-Indo-European
Indo-Iranian languages, 114, 267, 268; *see also* Proto-Indo-Iranian
Indonesian, 83, 258; *see also* Bahasa Indonesia
Ingrian *see* Ižora
Inuit (Inuit-Inupiaq), 267
Inuit-Russian Pidgin, 167
Inuktitut *see* Inuit
Inupiaq *see* Inuit
Iranian languages, 62, 73–4, 86, 87, 95, 114, 267, 268
Irish English, 79
Irish Gaelic *see* Gaelic, Irish
Istro-Rumanian, 105, 107

Italian, 3, 19, 20, 22, 26, 36, 46, 137–8, 155, 162, 176, 191, 224, 251, 252, 254, 255, 269, 274
Itelmen, 261
Ižora (Ingrian), 234, 239

Jamaican Creole English, 31, 165, 227, 268
Japanese, 9, 19, 68, 252, 257

Kabye, 254
Kadiwéu, 89, 143, 155, 249
Kalapuya, 124
Kalispel, 236
Kannaḍa, 1, 4, 44, 45, 116, 252, 266, 268
Karaim, 110, 127
Karelian, 110, 151, 156, 268
Kartvelian languages, 260
Kashaya (Southwestern Pomo), 72–3, 97
Kashmiri, 44, 252
Kazakh (Kasakh, Qasaq), 252
Kelantan Peranakan Chinese, 218, 221
Kerek, 261
Khalkha-Mongol *see* Mongolian
Khesa, 25
Khmer (Cambodian), 19, 36, 84, 251, 272; *see also* Northern Khmer
Khoisan languages, 15, 17, 64, 87, 261, 268, 277, 280
Kickapoo, 244
Kikongo, 171, 172, 175, 268, 275
KiNyarwanda, 254
KiRundi, 251
Kitúba, 32, 37, 171, 172, 182, 192, 249, 268
Klallam, 124, 244
Korean, 19, 252, 257
Koriki Hiri, 167
Kormakiti Arabic, 200–1, 202, 203, 204, 207, 208, 210, 211, 219–20, 249
Koryak, 261
Kreyol *see* Haitian Creole
Krio, 37
Kriyol, 32, 165, 268
Kupwar languages, 1, 4, 5, 10, 13, 45–6, 56, 152, 156, 249
Kurdish, 30
Kuṟukh, 116
Kutenai, 4, 16, 31, 120, 122, 244, 268, 269
Kuy, 27
Kwa languages, 175, 181, 264, 268, 275
Kwakiutl *see* Kwakwala
Kwakwala (Kwakiutl), 124, 266, 280
Kyrgyz, 252

Laha, 82, 97, 125, 196, 208, 209, 210, 211, 214, 233, 234, 249, 268
Lakota, 244
Lao, 27, 252
Lapp *see* Sámi
Latin, 2, 7, 10, 20–1, 40, 41, 42, 46, 49, 87, 88, 89, 90, 91, 106, 108, 109, 149, 189, 223–4, 225, 255, 260, 263, 264, 267, 274, 277
  Neo-Latin, 7
  see also Classical Latin, Vulgar Latin
Latvian, 9, 11, 14, 46, 87, 98, 110, 148, 155, 252, 258
Lenape *see* Unami
Lenca, 235, 239
Letzebuergesch, 253
Lingala, 251
Lingua Franca, 162–3, 176, 191, 193, 249, 269, 271

Lithuanian, 87, 110, 253, 258
Livonian, 9, 11, 14, 87, 98, 110, 148, 269
Lower Chinook, 166, 175, 235, 261
Lowland South American linguistic area, 120
Lummi, 244
Luo, 9, 14, 270
Lushootseed, 123

Ma'a, 65, 82, 125, 133, 150, 156, 199–200, 202,
    204, 205, 207, 208, 209–11, 212, 218, 219, 220,
    233, 234, 235, 237, 242, 249, 259, 270
Macanese Creole Portuguese, 164, 270
Macedonian, 105, 106, 108, 109, 253, 276
Makah, 123, 124, 244, 280
Malagasy, 253, 258
Malay, 1, 2, 32, 82, 161, 213–14, 218, 233, 251,
    254, 258, 259, 270
  Ambonese Malay, 196, 233, 268
  Baba Malay, 160–1, 191
  Bahasa Malaysia, 253
  Bazaar Malay, 166, 259
Malayalam, 44, 116, 252
Malayo-Polynesian languages, 233
Maltese, 253
Malto, 115
Manchu, 16, 23, 257
Manipuri, 25
Manx, 18, 26, 255, 260
Maori, 18, 135, 136, 154, 244, 249, 253, 258, 270,
    274
Marathi, 1, 4, 44, 45, 87, 116, 252, 267, 270
Maridi Arabic, 7, 163–4, 176, 191, 249, 270
Masai, 200, 210, 270
Mauritian Creole, 185, 253
Mayan languages, 261
Mbugu, 199; *see also* Ma'a
Media Lengua, 180, 202, 203, 204, 205, 206, 212,
    213, 214, 215, 219, 249
Mednyj Aleut, 11, 14, 65, 151, 202–3, 205, 206, 212,
    213, 216–17, 219, 220, 242, 249, 259, 264, 270
Megleno-Rumanian, 77, 107, 108, 109, 153
Melanesian languages, 97, 166, 263, 278
Menomini, 222, 249, 257
MesoAmerican linguistic area, 120, 126, 128
Michif, 11, 14, 48, 151, 199, 201–2, 203, 204, 205,
    206, 212, 213, 215, 216, 219, 220, 242, 249,
    259, 270
Middle English, 224
Min Chinese *see* Taiwanese
Minnan, 191
Miskito Coast Creole English, 165, 271
Mizo, 25
Mlabri, 27, 31
Mohawk, 244
Mōkkī, 196, 214–15, 249
Moldovan (Rumanian), 253
Mongolian, 172, 257
  Khalkha-Mongol, 253
Mongolic languages, 86, 257, 261, 271
Monguor, 86
Montagnais, 216, 221, 249
Montana Salish, 1, 4, 5, 9, 10, 11, 12, 31, 80–2,
    97, 122, 124, 126, 143–4, 166, 223, 228, 236–7,
    242, 244, 249, 263, 265, 271
Motu, 162, 166, 173, 187, 188, 266, 272
Munda languages, 44, 114–15, 116, 272
  South Munda, 116
Munsee, 263, 273

Naga Creole Assamese, 272

Naga languages, 272
Nagamese (Naga Pidgin), 25, 173, 193, 249, 272
Nahuatl, 42
Nauruan, 253
Navajo, 23, 258
Ndebele, 37, 254, 255
Ndyuka, 31, 157, 160, 165, 170, 172, 173, 190, 272
Ndyuka-Trio Pidgin, 31, 157, 160, 173, 190, 249,
    272, 279
Nepali, 253
Nez Percé, 4, 11, 28, 54, 80, 122, 123, 157, 191,
    242, 249, 272, 275
Nez Percé Jargon, 157, 161, 166, 272
Ngbandi, 165, 171, 272, 275
Niuean, 253
Niger-Congo languages, 272
Nigerian Pidgin English, 37
Nilo-Saharan languages, 228, 270
Nilotic languages, 270
Nitinaht, 123, 280
non-Austronesian languages of New Guinea and
    Indonesia, 18, 63, 83, 97, 118, 127, 167, 214,
    259
Nootka (Nuuchan'ulh), 123, 124, 175, 272
Nootka Jargon, 166, 261, 272
Norse languages/dialects, 18, 83, 87, 92, 273; *see
    also* Danish, Norwegian, Swedish
Northeast (North America) linguistic area, 120
Northern California linguistic area, 120
Northern Eurasian Sprachbund, 110, 114, 115
Northern Khmer, 27
Northern Northwest Coast linguistic area, 120
Northern Territory Pidgin English, 268
North Germanic languages, 273
Northwest Coast Sprachbund *see* Pacific
    Northwest Sprachbund
Norwegian, 19, 50, 165, 240, 246, 253, 265, 273,
    275
Nubi, 173
Nubian, 228, 238
Nuuchan'ulh *see* Nootka
Nyanja, 255

Oceanic languages, 270, 277, 278
Old English, 79, 224, 270
Old French, 79, 224
Omotic languages, 111, 113, 256, 266
Oneida, 244
Orinoco–Amazon linguistic area, 120
Oriya, 44, 116, 252
Ossetic, 73–4, 87, 98, 268
Owambo, 253

Pacific Northwest Sprachbund, 16, 94, 120–5, 126,
    128, 170, 174, 249, 269
Palauan, 253
Pāli, 2
Papiamentu, 173
Papuan languages *see* non-Austronesian languages
    of New Guinea
Pare, 199, 258
Pashtu, 250
Patwa *see* Jamaican Creole English
Pengo, 116
Pennsylvania Dutch *see* Pennsylvanian German
Pennsylvania German, 19, 151, 238, 273
Penutian languages, 124
Persian, 2, 6, 41, 87, 252, 267, 268; *see also* Dari
    (Afghan Persian), Farsi
Philippine languages, 8; *see also* Pilipino, Tasaday

Pidgin Basque, 165
Pidgin Chukchi, 167
Pidgin Delaware, 157, 162, 165, 166, 173, 174, 182, 183, 191, 249, 273
Pidgin Eskimo *see* Pidgin Inuit
Pidgin Fiji, 167
Pidgin German, 165, 273
Pidgin Hamer, 162, 191
Pidgin Hawaiian, 166
Pidgin Hindustani, 167
Pidgin Inuit (Pidgin Eskimo), 165, 166, 192, 273
Pidgin Russian, 167
Pidgin Yimas(-Arafundi), 173, 193
Pig Latin, 150, 215
Pilipino, 253
Pipil (Teotepeque Pipil), 228, 238
Pirahã, 78
Pitcairnese, 165, 172, 178, 182–3, 188, 192, 249, 274, 277
Plains Indian Sign Language, 121, 166
Plains linguistic area, 120
Plateau linguistic area, 120
Police Motu *see* Hiri Motu
Polish, 19, 21, 32, 36, 253, 276
Polynesian languages, 165, 258, 270, 274, 277
Pomo, Southwestern *see* Kashaya
Portuguese, 20, 31, 36, 37, 68, 89, 143, 164, 170, 172, 175, 176, 180, 242, 250, 251, 252, 253, 254, 264, 270, 274, 275, 276, 280
Proto-Austronesian, 117
Proto-Dravidian, 93, 114, 115
Proto-Engan, 119
Proto-Germanic, 262
Proto-Indo-European, 77, 108, 111, 114, 115
Proto-Indo-Iranian, 114
Proto-Salishan, 144
Proto-Semitic, 88, 111
Proto-Slavic, 147
Provençal, 191, 274
Prussian, Old, 258
Pueblo linguistic area, 120, 126
Punjabi, 44, 154, 252
Putonghua (Mandarin Chinese), 21, 24, 32, 251

Quechua languages/dialects, 16, 76, 178, 203, 212, 215, 251, 253, 258, 274
    Lambayeque Quechua, 150, 156, 270
Quileute, 123, 124, 261

Réunionese, 185, 249
Romance languages, 7, 20, 77, 90, 105, 106, 108, 223–4, 263, 267, 274, 275, 277
Romani, 105–6, 108, 200, 204, 208, 209, 211, 212, 215, 219, 234, 258, 267, 275; *see also* Anglo-Romani
Romansh, 3, 5, 254, 274, 275
Rumanian, 20, 77, 105, 106, 107, 108, 109, 127, 153, 224, 253, 254, 274, 275; *see also* Arumanian, Istro-Rumanian, Megleno-Rumanian, Moldovan
Russenorsk, 165, 173, 267, 275
Russian, 1, 11, 20, 24, 32, 36, 39–40, 46, 49, 50, 56, 65, 73, 97, 110, 135, 145–6, 147–8, 151, 156, 165, 172, 202–3, 217, 250, 254, 256, 260, 261, 264, 268, 270, 275, 276; *see also* Alaskan Russian Pidgin, Chinese Pidgin Russian, Inuit-Russian Pidgin, Russenorsk

Sabir *see* the Lingua Franca
Sahaptian, 80, 120, 123, 269, 272, 275

Sahaptin, 28, 123, 275
Salar, 76, 249
Salishan languages, 16, 54, 120–4, 144, 175, 236, 244, 269, 271, 275; *see also* Proto-Salishan, Coast Salishan, Bella Coola, Chilliwack, Coeur d'Alene, Comox, Halkomelem, Lushootseed, Montana Salish, Shuswap, Spokane, Squamish, Thompson River Salish, Twana, Upper Chehalis
Sámi (Lapp), 40, 165, 245, 246, 275
Samoan, 32, 254, 274
Sandawe, 268
Sango, 37, 38, 165, 170, 171, 182, 192, 249, 251, 275
Sanskrit, 8, 44, 73, 97, 252
São Tomense Creole, 164, 275
Saramaccan, 170, 171, 174, 175, 182, 192, 249, 275
Scottish Gaelic *see* Gaelic, Scottish
Scythian, 6, 59, 67, 249
Semitic languages, 88, 123, 147, 256, 275; *see also* Ethiopic Semitic languages, Proto-Semitic
Sepik River basin Sprachbund, 62–3, 117–20, 127, 173, 249
Serbian, 47, 105, 108, 109, 251, 255, 276
Serbo-Croatian, 47, 105, 106, 107, 108, 109, 143, 145–6, 155, 276; *see also* Torlak
Seselwa (Seychellois, French Creole), 189, 249, 254
Sesotho *see* Sotho
Setswana, 37, 38, 251
Seychellois *see* Seselwa
Shambaa (Shambala), 199, 233, 258
Shina, 87, 98, 267
Shona, 37, 255
Shuswap, 124
Siberian Yupik Eskimo, 62, 73, 95, 97, 135, 146, 153, 155, 249, 280
Sindhi, 43, 44, 252
Sinhalese, 29, 47, 116, 254
Sinitic languages, 261, 276
Sino-Tibetan languages, 25, 44, 114, 115, 257, 261, 269, 272, 276
Siouan languages, 123
SiSwati, 26, 254
Siuslawan languages, 124
Slavic languages, 77, 105, 106, 109, 110, 111, 143, 145, 258, 267, 276; *see also* Church Slavic
Slovak, 254, 276
Slovenian, 254, 276
Somali, 254
Sotho (Sesotho), 252
    Northern Sotho, 254
    Southern Sotho, 254
South Asia Sprachbund, 76, 98, 114–17, 127, 249, 274
South Caucasian languages *see* Kartvelian
South Coast Range (California) linguistic area, 120
Southeast Asia Sprachbund, 83–4, 114, 115
Southeast (North America) linguistic area, 120
Southern California–western Arizona linguistic area, 120
Southern Cone (South America) linguistic area, 120
South Slavic languages, 106, 276
Spanglish, 28, 31
Spanish, 4, 5, 8, 9, 10, 13, 14, 17, 18, 19, 20, 24, 28, 31, 32, 34, 39, 42, 54, 68, 76, 83, 163, 165, 180, 181, 191, 203, 206, 212, 215, 224, 230, 242, 244, 250, 251, 252, 253, 254, 255, 261, 269, 274

Spokane, 4, 54
Squamish, 124
Sranan, 165, 169, 172, 185, 193, 249, 254, 276
Sri Lanka Creole Portuguese, 164, 173, 276
Standard Average European (SAE) linguistic area, 110, 169, 170, 181
Steurtjestaal, 213, 220
Stoney, 123
Suba, 9, 14, 276
Sudanic, Eastern *see* Eastern Sudanic languages
Sumerian, 6, 13, 88, 89, 98, 242, 249, 263, 269, 277
Swahili, 24, 32, 36, 37, 78, 92, 98, 251, 252, 254, 256, 258, 265
  Comorian Swahili, 251
Swati *see* SiSwati
Swazi, 254
Swedish, 19, 40, 53, 54, 149, 165, 252, 254, 265, 273, 275

Tadzhik *see* Tajik
Tagalog, 178
Tahitian, 32, 165, 183, 258, 274, 277
Tai languages, 278
Taiap, 238
Tai-Kadai languages, 278
Taiwanese (Min Chinese), 251
Tajik, 86, 87, 98, 254, 268
Takelma, 124
Tamil, 1, 19, 29, 32, 43, 44, 47, 252, 254, 277
Tangkul, 25
Tasaday, 8, 13, 249
Tây Bôi, 171, 192, 249
Telugu, 4, 44, 45, 116, 252, 277
Teotepeque Pipil *see* Pipil
Ternatean, 213–14, 220–1
Thai, 19, 27, 31, 46, 48, 83–4, 87, 97, 218, 249, 254, 267, 278
Thompson River Salish, 144, 155
Thonga (alternate name for Tsonga), 23
Thracian, 127
Tibetan, Amdo, 86, 257
Tibeto-Burman languages, 36, 257, 272, 276, 278
Tigrinya, 251
Tin Mal, 27
Tlingit, 124
Toaripi Hiri Trading Pidgin, 167
Tocharian, 267
Tok Pisin, 49, 161, 165, 167, 171–2, 173, 178, 182, 183, 188, 191, 227, 238, 249, 253, 254, 263, 266, 278
Tolai, 278
Tolowa, 124
Tonga, 255
Tongan, 72, 141, 254, 278
Torlak (Serbo-Croatian dialects), 105, 109
Trio, 31, 157, 160, 173, 272, 278
Tsimshian, 120, 121–2, 124
Tsonga, 254; *see also* Thonga
Tswana, 254
Tumbuka, 92, 98, 258

Tungusic languages, 16, 257
Turkic languages, 86, 110, 257, 261, 279
Turkish, 2, 11, 14, 36, 41, 56, 59, 63–4, 65, 66–7, 73, 74, 86, 87, 90, 96, 98, 106, 108, 136, 148, 155, 251, 254, 256, 257, 279
Turkmen, 254
Tupi-Guaraní languages, 266
Twana, 123, 124, 244
Twi, 175, 275

Ubangian (Eastern) languages, 165, 272, 279
Ugric languages, 266
Uisai, 84–5, 150, 217, 249, 259, 279
Ukrainian, 36, 255
Unami (Lenape), 263, 273
Upper Chehalis, 145, 146
Uralic languages, 9, 11, 87, 88, 104, 110, 111, 147–8, 155, 234, 261, 264, 266, 268, 269, 275, 279
Urdu, 1, 4, 44, 45, 252, 253, 267, 279
Uru-Chipaya, 261
Ute, 244
Uto-Aztecan languages, 228
Uzbek, 86, 87, 98, 255, 279

Vaupes River languages, 36, 56
Venda, 254
Venezuelan–Antillean linguistic area, 120
Vietnamese, 19, 20, 30, 32, 39, 171, 255, 272, 278
Votic, 234, 239
Vulgar Latin, 263, 277

Waikurúan languages, 143
Wakashan languages, 16, 86, 120–4, 244, 266, 269, 272, 280
Warlpiri, 229, 238, 239
Wasco (Chinookan), 28
Welsh, 18, 32, 238, 255, 260
West African Pidgin English *see* Cameroonian Pidgin English
West African Pidgin Portuguese, 164, 176, 280
West Slavic languages, 276
Wishram (Chinookan), 28
Wolof, 38, 154, 253
Wutun, 86, 97–8

Xhosa, 254
Xinca, Jumaytepeque, 230, 238
Xincan languages, 230

Yakima *see* Sahaptin
Yiddish, 46, 67, 76, 96, 132, 154, 225, 280
Yimas, 63, 119–20, 173
Yingkarta, 222, 225, 228, 249
Yoruba, 37, 251, 253
Yupik languages, 267, 280; *see also* Alaskan Yupik, Siberian Yupik

Zapotec, 83, 97, 249
Zulu, 15, 23, 64, 87, 166, 254, 261, 264, 277, 278, 280

Names index

Aavik, Johannes, 149, 156
Adamson, Lilian, 193
al-Bakrī, Abu 'Ubayd, 7, 13, 163–4, 192, 270
Alexander the Great, 16
Allen, Robert B., Jr., 220
Andersen, Peggy, 246
Ansaldo, Umberto, 191
Aoki, Haruo, 58
Apple, Marcel A., 28
Apte, Mahadev, 56
Arends, Jacques, 14, 26, 189, 190, 191, 193, 194
Ariste, Paul, 239
Artaxerxes I, King of Persia, 7
Artaxerxes II, King of Persia, 7

Bach, Johann Sebastian, 134, 272
Backus, Albert Marie, 137, 155
Bailey, Charles-James N., 96
Baker, Philip, 194
Bakker, Peter, 14, 192, 193, 219, 220
Barringer, Felicity, 246
Baugh, Albert C., 155
Bavin, Edith L., 239
Bereznak, Catherine, 126
Bergsland, Knut, 220
den Besten, Hans, 193
Bickerton, Derek, 178–9, 180, 182, 192, 193, 194
Bligh, Captain William, 165
Bloomfield, Leonard, 223, 229, 235
Boas, Franz, 128
Boretzky, Norbert, 194, 219, 220
Borg, Alexander, 219–20
Bothne, T., 240, 246
Bradley, David, 56, 246
Bray, Denys de S., 196
Brendemoen, Bernt, 96
Brenzinger, Matthias, 14, 220, 238
Broadwell, George Aaron, 56
Broderick, George, 26
Brown, H. A., 191
Bruyn, Adrienne, 193, 194
Burling, Robbins, 193

Calvet, Louis-Jean, 34
Camden, W. G., 194
Campbell, Lyle, 98, 120, 126, 128, 238, 239, 267
Capell, Arthur, 17, 25, 118, 127
Cassidy, Frederic G., 156
Chapin, Paul, 246
Charles V, King of Spain, 41–2
Chatterton, Percy, 191

Chaudenson, Robert, 184–5, 186, 187, 190, 194
Cifoletti, Guido, 191
Cluver, August, 56
Clyne, Michael, 26
van Coetsem, Frans, 95
Collins, James T., 97, 196, 233
Comrie, Bernard, 14, 98, 155
Cook, Captain James, 16, 72, 141, 262
Copland, B. D., 219
Court, Christopher, 83–4, 97
Crystal, David, 13
Csató, Éva Ágnes, 127

Dahl, Östen, 127
Dalto, G., 26
Darius the Great, 6, 13
Davis, Susannah, 56
Dawkins, R. M., 14, 59, 95, 98
De Michele, Greg, 155
Dench, Alan, 222, 228
Diamond, Jared, 246
Dorian, Nancy C., 14, 26, 155, 225, 236, 238, 239, 245, 246
Drapeau, Lynn, 221
Dressler, Wolfgang U., 239
Durie, Mark, 155
Dutton, Tom, 191, 194

Edwards, John, 13
Elgibali, Alaa, 13, 191
Eliasson, Stig, 154
Elizabeth I, Queen of England, 7
Emeneau, Murray B., 95, 98, 127
Ezra, 7

Fenyvesi, Anna, 14, 57, 230–2
Ferguson, Charles A., 127
Fishman, Joshua A., 225, 238, 245
Foley, William A., 83, 97, 118–20, 126, 127, 193
Foster, Michael K., 56
Friedrich, Paul, 56

Gal, Susan, 26
Galan, Nely, 28
Gandhi, Mohandas Karamchand (Mahatma), 42, 56
Giles, Howard, 155
Givón, T., 96
Goddard, Ives, 191, 267
Goebl, Hans, 13
de Goeje, C. H., 157, 190

Golovko, Evgenij V., 202, 220
Grenoble, Leonore A., 245
Grimes, Barbara F., 56, 266
Grosjean, François, 3, 13, 31, 53, 55, 57, 138, 153
Gumperz, John J., 13, 45, 56, 156

Haas, Mary R., 128
Hakuta, Kenji, 55
Hale, Ken, 241, 243, 245, 246
Hall, Robert A., Jr., 177, 190, 191
Haugen, Einar, 154, 246
Headland, Thomas N., 13
Heath, Jeffrey, 13, 127, 132, 155, 221, 262
Heath, Shirley Brice, 56
Heine, Bernd, 127
Henry the Navigator, Prince of Portugal, 4, 164
Herbert, Robert K., 26
Hermans, Daan, 57
Herodotus, 6–7, 59, 67
Hetzron, Robert, 127
Hill, Jane H., 26, 239
Hill, Kenneth C., 26
Hinton, Leanne, 246
Hiranburana, Samang, 97
Hock, Hans Henrich, 96, 127
Holm, John, 14, 189, 190, 194
Hoonchamlong, Yuphaphann, 97
Hotz, Robert Lee, 246
De Houwer, Annick, 33, 51, 55, 57, 155
Hovdhaugen, Even, 95
Huffines, Marion Lois, 156
Huttar, George, 190, 272, 279
Huttar, Mary, 190
Hvenekilde, Anne, 26
Hymes, Dell H., 14

Ibn Khaldun, 7, 13
Igla, Birgit, 219
Ishwaran, K., 56
Ivić, Pavle, 155

Jackson, Jean, 56
Jackson, Kenneth, 26
Jacobs, Melville, 128
Jakobson, Roman, 63–4, 96
Jameson, J. Franklin, 157
Jensen, Karen Anne, 139, 155
John, King of England, 79
Johanson, Lars, 96
Johnson, M. E., 26
Jones, Mari C., 238
Jones, Marie Smith, 240, 246
Joseph II, Emperor of Austro-Hungarian empire, 21
Joseph, Brian D., 127
Joshi, Aravind, 154
Justeson, John S., 56

Kaplan, Lawrence D., 280
Kaufman, Stephen A., 98
Kaufman, Terrence, 13, 95, 96, 97, 126, 128, 155, 190, 194, 219, 220, 221
Kemke, Andreas, 54
Kennedy, John F., 2
Khrushchev, Nikita Sergeyevich, 40
Kilpatrick, Paul, 83, 97
Kinkade, M. Dale, 123, 128, 155
Kinzer, Stephen, 56
Klaiman, M. H., 98
Kontra, Miklós, 26
Kopitar, Bartholomäus, 105

Koptjevskaja-Tamm, Maria, 110, 127
Kouwenberg, Silvia, 181, 190, 193, 194
Kramer, Samuel Noah, 13
Krauss, Michael, 241, 245, 246
Kreindler, Isabelle, 56
Kremnitz, G., 55
Krishna, Sumi, 56
Kulick, Don, 84, 97, 238
Kunene, E. C. L., 26

Laberge, Suzanne, 191
Lanham, L. W., 25
Lanza, Elizabeth, 50, 51, 57
Lawes, Frank, 162
Lawes, W. G., 162
Laycock, Donald C., 84, 97, 156, 221
Lefebvre, Claire, 179–80, 193, 194
Legère, Karsten, 56
Lehiste, Ilse, 149, 155, 156
Lenin (Vladimir Ilyich Ulyanov), 39–40
Leopold, Werner, 50, 57
Le Page, Robert B., 55, 219
Leslau, Wolf, 111, 127
Lewis, E. Glyn, 56
Li, Charles N., 97
Lickey, Sara, 98
Lieberson, Stanley, 23, 26
Lindeström, Peter, 97
Lindstedt, Jouko, 126
Little, Greta D., 127
Liu, Eric, 221
Lorente, Beatriz, 14
Lorimer, D. L. R., 98
Lumsden, John S., 194
Lydall, Jean, 191

Mackey, William F., 34, 55
McWhorter, John, 190
Masica, Colin P., 115, 127
Matthews, Stephen, 191
Meechan, Marjory, 134, 154
Meillet, Antoine, 63, 96
Meisel, Jürgen, 51, 57, 155
Mellinkoff, David, 97
Mencken, H. L., 56
Mengarini, Gregory, S. J., 4
Menges, Karl H., 98
Menovščikov, G. A., 95, 97, 155, 202, 219, 220
Mertz, Elizabeth, 222
Michaëlius, Jonas, 157
von Miklosich, Franz, 105, 127
Mikone, Eve, 155
Miller, Wick R., 56
Milroy, James, 154
Milroy, Lesley, 57, 154
de Mishaegen, Anne, 196, 219
Moffatt, Suzanne, 57, 154
Möhlig, Wilhelm J. G., 220
Molony, Carol, 8
Moraru-de Ruijter, Saskia, 127
Moravcsik, Edith, 96
Moreno, Martino Mario, 127
Mous, Maarten, 97, 156, 219, 220
Moverley, A. W., 192
Mufwene, Salikoko, 190, 192, 194
Mühlhäusler, Peter, 192
Mulder, J. G., 26
Müller, Max, 198, 219
Müller, Natascha, 57
Muntzel, Martha C., 238

Mutorwa, John, 40
Muysken, Pieter, 14, 154, 189, 193, 219, 220
Myers-Scotton, Carol, 35, 55, 154

Nehemiah, 7
Nehru, Jawaharlal, 44
Nelde, Peter H., 13, 34–5, 55
Van Ness, Silke, 238
Neumann, Gunter, 193
Newton, Brian, 218, 219
Nichols, Johanna, 193
Noonan, Michael, 56, 240, 246

O'Barr, Jean, 55
O'Barr, William M., 55
Odlin, Terence, 57
Okombo, Duncan Okoth, 14
Oksaar, Els, 55, 156
Oswalt, Robert, 97
Owens, Jonathan, 13, 191–2

Papen, Robert A., 14, 219, 220
Pasch, Helma, 192
Paul, John Peter, 97
Paulston, Christina Bratt, 26
Peirce, Bonny Norton, 26
Pfaff, Carol W., 56, 154
Philip II, King of Spain, 42
Philip IV, King of Spain, 42
Pizarro, Francisco, 16
Polomé, Edgar, 98
Poplack, Shana, 134, 154
Poser, William, 33, 55, 128
Post, Marike, 193
Presley, Elvis, 62

Queen, Robin Michelle, 98, 155

Rayfield, J. R., 67, 96, 154
Raymond, Joan, 246
Reichard, Gladys A., 58
Reid, Lawrence A., 13
Reinecke, John, 192
van Rheeden, Hadewych, 220
Rickford, John R., 195
Ridge, Stanley G. M., 26
Rischel, Jørgen, 27
Robertson, David, 55
Robertson, Ian, 191
Robertson, Stuart, 156
Robins, Robert H., 245
Romaine, Suzanne, 13, 57, 96
Ross, Malcolm, 155, 192
Rottland, Franz, 14
Rouchdy, Aleya, 238
Rubin, Joan, 14

Saagpakk, Paul F., 156
Saksena, Baburam, 43
Samarin, William J., 192
Sandalo, Filomena, 89, 155
Sandfeld, Kristian, 108, 127
Sankoff, David, 154
Sankoff, Gillian, 191
Sapir, Edward, 11, 14, 63–4, 96
Sarhimaa, Anneli, 156
Sasse, Hans-Jürgen, 95, 220, 225–6, 227, 228, 229, 232, 233, 238, 239
Schaengold, Charlotte, 13
Schiffman, Harold F., 56

Schmidt, Annette, 238
Schuchardt, Hugo, 177
Schwartz, John, 246
Sekerina, Irina A., 220
Shaver, Dwight, 156
Shigley-Giusti, Michela, 155
Sicoli, Mark, 56
Silver, Shirley, 56
Singler, John V., 186, 193–4
Slater, Keith W., 98
Smalley, William, 27, 56
Smith, Norval, 14, 189, 191, 192, 193, 199, 219, 260, 266, 268, 271
Smith-Stark, Thomas C., 126, 128
Soares, Carlos, 53, 57, 138
Solé, Yolanda Russinovich, 14
Sorensen, Arthur P., 56
Spicer, Edward, 28, 55
Splawn, A. J., 157
Sridhar, S. N., 97, 98
Stalin, Joseph, 40
Starý, Zdeněk, 13
de Steur, 213
Swadesh, Morris, 72, 259

Tabouret-Keller, Andrée, 219
Teit, James A., 58
Teo, Kok Seong, 221
Thomason, Sarah, 13, 14, 55, 95, 96, 97, 126, 153, 155, 190, 191, 194, 219, 220, 221
Thompson, Laurence C., 98
Thompson, R. M. W., 193
Torres, Liz, 28
Trubetzkoy, Nikolai S., 99, 126
Trudeau, Pierre, 47
Trudgill, Peter, 13
Tryon, Darrell T., 192
Tsitsipis, Lukas D., 222
Turner, Nancy, 128

Uhlenbeck, Eugenius M., 245

Vaid, Jyotsna, 153
Vakhtin, Nikolai B., 202, 220
Valkhoff, Marius F., 25
Veenstra, Tonjes, 192, 193
Velantie, Frank, 190, 272, 279
Verspoor, Marjolyn, 221
Vildomec, Věroboj, 57
Voorhoeve, Jan, 193
van der Voort, Hein, 192, 193

Wälchli, Bernhard, 110, 127
Watahomigie, Lucille J., 244, 246
Weber, David, 156
Weinreich, Uriel, 13, 53, 57, 97
Whaley, Lindsay J., 245
Whinnom, Keith, 193
Whiteley, Wilfred Howell, 218, 220
White Thunder, 222, 229, 235
Williamson, Kay, 191
Wilson, Robert, 13, 45, 56, 156
Wölck, Wolfgang, 13
Wurm, Stefan, 25, 128, 192, 246

Yamamoto, Akira, 244, 246
Yasar, Suleyman, 29
Young, Douglas, 25

Zentella, Ana Celia, 54, 57

Subject index

abrupt genesis of bilingual mixed languages, 205–7, 210–11, 212–17, 218, 234
abrupt pidgin/creole genesis theories, 177–83, 185, 186, 227
absolutive constructions, 115
Académie française, 41
academies *see* language academies
accent change, 11
accident as a source of shared structural features, 99, 100–1
accommodation, 75, 155
activation of two languages in the brain, 53, 138–9
addition of features, 60, 74, 85, 87
affixes, 110, 112, 116, 119, 121, 122, 147, 200, 201, 202, 209
    in pidgins and creoles, 172
agglutinative morphology, 71, 105, 115
agreement, 84–5, 150, 193, 203, 217, 279, *see also* inflection, transferred
ancient language contacts, 6–8, 16
apartheid, 5, 26, 49
aphasia in bilinguals, 53
areal features, 99, 101–5, 119, 126, 127; *see also* linguistic areas
    area-wide features, 102, 116, 121–2
    features not restricted to the area, 103
    restricted distribution of, 101–2, 109, 110, 111, 114, 116, 122–4
    sources of, 99
aspect *see* tense/aspect
aspirated stops, 116, 138, 147
attitudes in language contact, 12, 22, 32–6, 60, 77–85, 94, 97, 189, 191, 213, 225, 233, 237
attrition in dying languages, 12, 60, 62, 222, 227–32, 233, 234, 235, 236
    lack of attrition, 12, 235–7

Bantuization of Ma'a, 199–200, 220, 234
basic vs. nonbasic vocabulary in borrowing, 69, 70–3, 80, 90, 91, 108, 175, 200, 203, 204, 209, 232, 259
bilingual education, 29, 34
bilingual first-language acquisition, 49–51, 129, 146, 148–9, 152
    effects, in contact-induced change, 60
bilingualism, 1, 31, 78, 82, 125, 133, 143, 151, 158, 197, 201, 213, 225, 232, 269
    asymmetrical, 3, 4, 9
    beliefs about, 33–4
    contact without, 2
    definition of, 1–3, 13

encouragement of, 28, 47, 48
in individuals, 48–54
mutual, 4, 107
prevalence of, 31
stable, 4
transitional, 4
see also multilingualism
bilingual mixed languages, 10, 48, 60, 85, 151, 157, 158, 180, 189, 192, 196–221, 259, 270
    abrupt genesis in new ethnic groups, 205–7, 210–11, 212–17, 218
    genesis in persistent ethnic groups, 204–5, 207–12, 217, 218, 233, 234
boarding schools and language policy, 5, 39
body part terms, 112
borrowing, 8, 12, 66–74, 76, 78, 93, 96, 106, 116, 125, 136, 146, 151, 153, 212, 226, 229, 230
    vs. shift-induced interference, 66–76, 77, 93, 95, 97, 125, 129, 130, 136, 139, 146, 158, 180, 197, 207, 212, 230, 259
borrowing routine, 155; *see also* correspondence rules
borrowing scale, 70–1, 93, 96, 259
break in transmission, 226, 227, 233; *see also* abrupt pidgin/creole genesis theories
British Isles, 18

calquing, 81, 143, 260
case systems, 74, 109, 110, 115, 121, 140, 147, 228, 231, 260
causative constructions, 112, 115, 119, 120, 147, 172, 260
central vowels, 108, 119
clicks, borrowed, 15, 64, 87, 98, 261, 277
code alternation, 60, 129, 136–9, 146, 152, 155, 261
code-copying, 96
code-mixing, 132, 154, 262
code-switching, 53–4, 60, 129, 130, 131–6, 152, 154, 215–17, 219, 262, 272
colonialism, 6, 9–10, 24, 32, 42, 44, 164, 176–7, 204
Comparative Method, 102–3, 117, 198, 262
competition between old and new features, 88–9, 135–6
complication of grammar, 65, 96, 230, 231
conflict claimed as inevitable in contacts, 34–5, 55
conjunctions, borrowing of, 62, 73, 74, 153, 202
    subsequent syntactic changes as a result of, 62
conquest and language contact, 25
consonant clusters, 73, 86, 124, 167, 169–70

constraints, possible, on contact phenomena, 61, 63–5, 78–81, 85, 131, 151, 209, 216
contact as a source of shared structural features, 99, 103; *see also* linguistic areas
contact-induced change, defined, 62, 262
contact-induced change, proving existence of *see* proof of contact-induced change
contact language, 12, 157–221
   defined, 158, 262
content words, borrowed, 70–4
convergence, 89–90, 125, 152, 214, 233, 262
   lack of total convergence, 118, 125
copula, 110
correspondence rules, 144–6, 155, 262
creativity, speakers', 11
creole continuum, 189
creoles, 4, 10, 12, 31, 32, 60, 157–95
   claims about similarities among, 159, 167–8, 172–4, 177
   crosslanguage compromise in structure, 159, 160, 181–3, 197
   defined, 159–60, 262
   sources of vocabulary, 12, 174–5
   sources of grammar, 12, 174–5
   structural diversity in, 169, 172–4, 177, 182
   see also pidgin/creole genesis theories
critical period hypothesis, 51
Crusades, 162, 176, 269
crystallization of mixed languages, 169, 173, 178, 183, 186, 187, 188, 192, 199, 201, 215, 216, 263, 270, 272
cuneiform writing, 6, 263
Cyrillic alphabet, 40

dates of first contact, 15–16
defensive alliances and language contact, 20
deliberate change, 9, 68, 77, 81–2, 84–5, 129, 133, 142, 143–4, 146, 149–52, 161–2, 196, 204, 214–15, 217, 229, 230
demographics in creole genesis, 178, 179, 183–5, 186, 188
demonstrative systems, 124, 201
deterministic predictions, lack of, 80
devanāgarī, 42–3, 44
dialect vs. language, 2
dialect contact vs. language contact, 2, 13, 77
dialect variation, 2, 102, 104, 107, 201
diplomacy, languages used in, 7, 20–1, 223
discrimination against minority languages, 5
double-articulated stops, 170, 182
double marking in morphosyntactic change, 152–3
dying languages, break in transmission of, 226, 227, 233, 235

echo-word formations, 115
education and language contact, 24–5, 45, 200, 244; *see also* bilingual education
email and language contact *see* internet
endangered languages, 9, 201, 223, 240–6, 257, 268, 269, 271, 273, 275, 276, 280
English as a non-creole, 189, 194
errors in speech *see* speech errors
ethnic identity, language as symbol of, 11, 22, 48, 198, 203, 205–6, 213, 214, 217, 218, 219, 226, 240, 243
ethnobotany, 121
exaggeration of differentness *see* deliberate change
exogamy, 3, 20, 23, 104, 117, 121, 201
expanded pidgins, 160, 161, 183

exploration and language contact, 15, 16, 18, 19, 20, 163, 164, 176–7

first-language acquisition, bilingual *see* bilingual first-language acquisition
flexional morphology, 63–4, 71, 74
foreigner talk, 187, 264
fossilized code-switching, 215–16
Free Morpheme Constraint on code-switching, 135
frequency, change in, 81, 89, 148
frequency in code-switching, 134–5
frequentative constructions, 112
friendly contacts, 3
function words, borrowed, 70–4
future constructions, 106, 112, 119
fuzzy boundaries
   between code-switch and borrowing, 133, 154, 272
   between creole and noncreole, 189, 190
   between dialect and language, 2, 276
   between language and ephemeral speech form, 186, 215
   between mixed languages and 'unmixed' languages, 268
   of linguistic areas, 101, 104

Gastarbeiter, 19
gender, 11, 84–5, 87, 113, 116, 124, 147, 148, 150, 171, 172, 182, 217, 265
generalization of one variant in language death, 228–9, 230
genesis theories for pidgins and creoles *see* pidgin/creole genesis theories
genetic relationship, 100, 176, 177, 198–9, 218, 258, 259, 261, 268, 274, 278
Gilgamesh Cycle, 6
glottalized consonants, 65, 73, 81, 87, 111, 121, 124, 170, 230, 264, 265, 266
gradual genesis of bilingual mixed languages, 204–5, 206, 207, 208–12, 217
gradual pidgin/creole genesis theories, 174, 183–8
grammatical interference *see* structural interference
grammatical replacement, total, 60, 82–3, 196, 208–12, 214, 227, 232–5

'have', 110, 115
hostile contacts, 3, 5, 17–18, 29, 46–8, 205

immigration and language contact, 12, 18–19, 25, 31–2, 34, 53, 189, 231–2
   three-generation shift pattern, 9
imperfect second-language learning, 6–7, 60, 74–6, 95, 106, 111, 113, 114, 116, 129, 147, 151, 158, 161, 176, 180, 184–5, 197, 207, 214, 226, 229, 230
   as a predictor in contact-induced change, 66–76, 78, 130, 136, 142, 146
impersonal constructions, 110, 116
implicational constraints, 64, 80
imported labor force, 19–20, 165, 266
inclusive vs. exclusive 'we', 65, 87, 92, 124, 171, 229, 231, 264, 266
India, 30, 42–6, 252
infinitives, 109, 116, 126, 149, 276
inflection, transferred, 65, 70, 77, 116, 151, 153, 202–3, 206, 209, 212, 217, 267
in-group language *see* ethnic identity, language as symbol of

inheritance as a source of shared structural features, 99, 100
innovation, first instance of, 130, 135
institutional support for minority languages, 4–5, 22, 240
integration of features into a linguistic system, 60, 69, 76–7, 96
intensity of contact, 9, 60, 66, 69, 70–4, 77, 78, 92–3, 95, 100, 101, 116, 118, 121, 125, 151, 204, 223, 233
interdental fricatives, 86, 124
interference *see* structural interference
interference, unwanted, 137–8, 140–1
internally-motivated change, 62–3, 86, 88–9, 91, 92, 94, 117, 127, 130, 173, 229, 230
internal reconstruction, 102
internet and language contact, 2
intonation change, 67, 90, 138, 148, 267
isogloss, 104, 107, 116, 259–60, 268
isolates, genetic, 16, 87, 95, 120, 256, 259, 260, 268, 269, 277, 268, 277
isomorphism *see* convergence

kinship terms, 112, 228
Kupwar, 45–6, 152

labialized consonants, 112, 121
labials, paucity of, 124
language academies, 41, 42
language as a symbol of ethnic identity *see* ethnic identity, language as a symbol of
Language Bioprogram Hypothesis, 178–9
language death, 10, 12, 14, 60, 61, 137, 177, 222–39, 242, 243
  lack of linguistic change in, 12, 60, 227, 235–7
  precipitated by negative attitudes, 53, 225–6
  theoretical framework for study of, 225–6, 228, 229, 233, 234
language maintenance *see* maintenance
language nest program, 244
language planning, 38–42, 149–50
language policies, 38–46, 47
language shift *see* shift
lateral obstruents, 81, 94, 121, 124, 150, 170, 200, 269
learnèd contacts, 20–1
length distinctions, 110, 149
length of contact period as a predictive factor, 66
lexical borrowing, 8, 10–11, 64, 67, 69, 70–4, 76, 78, 79, 80, 81, 87, 88, 90–1, 92, 93, 96, 97, 108, 112, 116, 122–3, 124, 133, 135, 136, 138, 141, 149, 151, 202–3, 210, 212, 217, 220, 232, 280
lexical creation, 84
lexical non-borrowing, 80–2
lexical replacement *see* relexification
lexical suffixes, 122
lexifier languages, 159, 161, 164–6, 169, 170, 171, 174, 176, 179, 180, 181, 182, 187, 189, 198, 227, 269
lingua francas, 21, 24, 32, 37, 38, 43, 44, 49, 158, 167, 192, 269
linguistic areas, 76, 90, 94, 98, 99–128, 262; *see also* areal features
  definition of, 99–104, 269
  Australia, 117, 126
  Balkans, 105–9, 126, 248–9
  Baltic, 110–11, 248–9
  Ethiopian highlands, 76, 111–13, 248–9
  list of, in the Americas, 120

New Guinea, 17, 63, 248–9
number of features required for, 101
Pacific Northwest, 16, 94, 120–5, 126, 128, 170, 237, 248–9
Sepik River basin, 63, 117–20, 248–9
South Asia, 76, 98, 114–17, 248–9
Standard Average European, 110, 169, 170, 181
'strong' vs. 'weak' areas, 101
vs. culture areas, 120
linguistic constraints on interference *see* constraints, possible, on contact phenomena
loanwords as evidence of language contact, 11; *see also* lexical borrowing
long consonants *see* length distinctions
loss of features, 60, 70, 74, 85, 86–7, 200, 207–12, 226, 227, 230–2, 236

maintenance of languages, 9, 22–3, 26, 31
markedness, 52, 60, 65, 75, 76, 77, 94, 142–3, 148, 168, 169, 181, 182, 184, 230, 270, 279
Master-Apprentice Language Learning Program, 243–4
mechanisms of contact-induced change, 61, 129–56
  multiple mechanisms for one change, 152
metathesis, 150, 270
Mexico, 41–2
minority languages, 4–5, 22, 32, 36, 53, 225
mixed languages, 10, 11, 12, 48, 60, 61, 85, 157–221, 271
monogenesis hypothesis of pidgin/creole genesis, 176–7, 179, 269, 271
monolingualism, 4, 9, 22, 31, 34, 48, 133, 137, 226
  infrequency worldwide, 31–2
mood, 87, 167, 174, 181, 271
moribund languages, 242, 244, 256
morphological interference *see* affixes, morphosyntactic interference
morphology in pidgins and creoles, 168, 172, 193, 257
morphophonemic interference, 74
morphosyntactic interference, 65, 70, 74, 76, 77, 78, 79, 81–2, 86–7, 88, 93, 96, 108, 109, 110, 112–13, 115, 121–2, 124, 143–4, 145–6, 147–8, 149, 150, 201, 202–3, 209, 217; *see also* double marking in morphosyntactic change
multilingualism, 1, 24, 25, 27, 30–6, 45, 46, 107, 118, 121, 125, 133, 158, 197, 201, 215, 222, 225, 229
  in individuals, 48–54
  in nations, 27–32, 34–5, 36–46, 48; *see also* bilingualism
multiple causation in language change, 62–3, 94, 119, 230–2
munch-present, 86
mutual intelligibility, 2, 276
mutual interference, 76, 89–90, 98, 117, 142, 214

Namibia, 40–1
'nasalless' languages, 123–4, 145
nasal vowels, 116
nativization of pidgins, 160, 161, 167, 175, 177, 183, 186, 268
nativization of transferred features, 72, 73, 134, 135, 144–5, 203, 272
'naturalness' and change, 65, 77; *see also* markedness
necessary vs. sufficient conditions for change, 85
negation, 112, 116, 121, 172, 173–4, 201, 213
negative borrowing, 231

'negotiation', 60, 75, 129, 142–6, 147, 148, 152, 155, 160, 168, 180–3, 187, 272
New Guinea, 17, 49, 62–3
No-Man's Land, contact in, 20
nonce borrowing, 134, 154
non-identity of source- and receiving-language features, 89–90, 93, 112
Norman Conquest, 10, 23, 75, 79, 97
noun classes *see* gender
noun vs. verb distinction, 94, 100, 121
number categories, 86, 87, 113, 171, 263, 276, 278
numbers in speaker groups as a predictive factor, 66, 78–9, 242
numeral classifiers, 115, 122
numerals, 112, 145–6

obviation, 201, 273
'Official English', 39
official languages, 5, 9, 29, 32, 36–8, 42–6, 47, 48, 112, 242, 250–5, 266, 275, 278, 279
Old Testament, 7
other-directed world view *see* self-directed vs. other-directed world view

palatal consonants, 119
paradigms, transferred, 65
particles, borrowed, 70
passive familiarity, 60, 129, 139–42, 152, 273
pharyngeal consonants, 81, 123, 126
phoneme borrowing, 70, 112
phoneme loss, 70, 74, 86, 200
phonological interference, 65, 69, 76, 79, 86, 87–8, 93, 108, 112, 115, 121, 123, 146, 148, 150, 201, 209
phonological nativization *see* nativization, phonological, of loanwords
pidgin/creole genesis, 174–88
    different routes to, 175, 187–8
pidgins, 10, 12, 27–8, 37, 60, 121, 142, 157–95
    claims about maximum simplicity in, 159, 167–72
    claims about similarities among, 159, 167–8, 169, 172, 177
    crosslanguage compromise in structure, 159, 160, 170, 181–3, 197
    defined, 159, 273–4
    earliest known pidgin, 163
    overlapping distribution of, 166–7
    sources of vocabulary, 12, 174–5
    sources of grammar, 12, 142–3, 174–5
    structural diversity in, 169, 172–4, 177, 182
    trade pidgins, 12, 27–8, 157, 161, 165, 166, 167, 168, 169, 176, 183, 197, 273
    see also pidgin/creole genesis theories
plantation creoles, 75, 178, 181, 183–7, 194, 266
plural formations, 89, 94, 109, 112, 113, 115, 116, 119, 122, 210, 228
possessive constructions, 119, 121
possibilities of contact-induced change, 61, 63, 68, 71, 78, 96, 130–1, 198
postposed articles, 109
postpositions, 74, 113, 115, 274
predicting contact-induced change *see* borrowing scale, imperfect second-language learning, intensity of contact, length of contact, numbers in speaker groups, possibilities of contact-induced change, probabilities of contact-induced change, unpredictability of contact-induced change
prefixes *see* affixes

prepidgins, 178–9
preservation of endangered languages, 18, 26, 243–5
probabilities of contact-induced change, 61, 68–71, 72, 80, 131
pronoun borrowing, 83–4, 87, 92, 97, 116, 119
pronoun systems, 'closed' vs. 'open', 84
proof of contact-induced change, 61, 91–5, 102–3
prototypical pidgins and creoles, 160, 190, 197

Qing dynasty, 23
question markers, 116, 121
quotative constructions, 115

rate of language change, 185–6, 229
reduction of variants in language death, 228–9
reduplication, 112, 115, 122
relative clauses, 88, 116, 274
relexification, 84, 87, 88–9, 90–1, 176, 203, 211, 212, 217, 234, 274
Relexification Hypothesis, 179–80
replacement of features, 60, 85, 87–8, 90
resistance to borrowing, 11, 14, 82, 126, 237
resistance to cultural assimilation, 12, 82–3, 126, 204–5, 208, 210–12, 218, 233
retroflex consonants, 93, 115, 274
revitalization of dying languages, 18, 26, 243–5
revival of a dead language, 224
riots over language, 29, 47
Rosetta Stone, 6

sacred languages in language contact, 2, 21, 44, 49, 73, 224–5, 226, 279
second-language acquisition, 48–9, 51–2, 143, 180–3, 187
    strategies, in contact-induced change, 60, 129, 130, 146–8, 180–3
secret languages, 150, 157, 161–2, 196, 198, 200, 203, 210, 211, 214–15, 217, 219, 226, 275
self-directed vs. other-directed world view, 118, 126, 150
semantic borrowing, 80–1, 138, 209
semicreole, 189, 195
semi-speakers, 211, 222, 226, 227, 229, 230, 234, 235, 236, 237, 275
shift, 9, 12, 14, 22–3, 26, 74–5, 75–6, 104, 108, 114, 116, 141, 199, 210–12, 225, 233, 234–5, 242, 269
    pressures toward, 9, 23, 82–3, 225, 235
    resistance to pressures toward, 12, 23, 82–3, 199, 208, 233
shift-induced interference, 6–7, 74–6, 77, 78–9, 80, 87, 92, 93, 106, 107, 111–13, 125, 129, 136, 141–2, 146–8, 151, 158, 180–3, 184–5, 230, 276
simplification of structure, 12, 64–5, 96, 226, 229, 231
slang, 84, 86, 141
slavery, 4, 12, 19–20, 157, 161, 169, 176, 178–9, 183–7, 188, 189, 205, 261
South Africa, 5, 15, 25–6, 40, 47, 49, 254
Soviet Union, 24, 39–40
speech errors, 130
Sprachbünde *see* linguistic areas
stable contact situations, 4, 9, 21, 23
standard languages, 9, 24, 38, 47, 149–50
stress change, 11, 69, 143, 231
structural interference, 11, 61, 62, 63–5, 69, 70–4, 80, 81, 91, 91–5, 100, 151
    delayed effects, 62

subordinate constructions, 113, 276
subordinate groups and shift, 23, 75–6, 227
subordinate status and contact-induced change,
    66, 67, 77
substratum interference, 75, 111, 127, 184–5, 277
suffixes *see* affixes
superordinate groups and shift, 23, 75, 79
switch-reference constructions, 120
syllable structure, 73, 86, 91, 169–70
symbiotic mixed languages, 219
symbolic function of language *see* ethnic identity,
    language as a symbol of

taboo, 72, 87, 98, 141, 277
target language, 74, 75, 76–7, 78–9, 136, 141–2,
    143, 147, 148, 161, 180, 184, 185, 187, 277,
    278
Tasaday, 8
tense/aspect systems, 112, 119, 167, 172, 174, 178,
    181, 203, 258, 278; *see also* future
    constructions
tone systems, 86, 92, 98, 110, 124, 170–1, 278
trade and language contact, 15, 20, 27–8, 37, 104,
    121, 123, 142, 157, 160, 161, 164, 165, 166,
    167, 169, 176, 197, 201, 202, 261
transfer in second-language acquisition, 52, 57, 75
transitive morphology in pidgins, 172
transmission, break in *see* abrupt pidgin/creole
    genesis theories

trilingual mixed language, 218
truncation, 223, 236–7
two-language pidgins and creoles, 160–1
typological distance between languages, 60, 63–4,
    71, 77, 94–5, 96, 97, 169, 181, 219, 279
typologically significant contact-induced change,
    70–4
typologies of language contact, 10, 60, 85–6, 157,
    226–7

unborrowable features *see* constraints, proposed,
    for contact-induced change
Universal Grammar and language acquisition, 51,
    52
universal structural tendencies *see* markedness
unpredictability of contact-induced change, 21, 22,
    59, 61, 77–85, 182, 204, 206, 226, 236, 237–8
unstable contact situations, 4–5, 9, 21–3
uvular consonants, 81, 121, 123, 124, 170

vowel harmony, 74, 86, 87, 105, 108, 279
vowel length *see* length distinctions

women and language contact, 22–3
word order, 11, 69, 70, 82, 88, 89, 94, 110, 113,
    115, 118, 121, 138, 139–40, 143, 147, 167,
    172–4, 181–2, 231
written evidence of language contact, 7–8